s to h

BUSINESS LAW

BUSINESS LAW

Helen J Bond

Principal Lecturer in Law, University of Central Lancashire

and

Peter Kay

Principal Lecturer in Law, University of Central Lancashire

BLACKSTONE
PRESS LIMITED

*This book has been printed digitally and produced in a standard specification
in order to ensure its continuing availability*

OXFORD
UNIVERSITY PRESS

Great Clarendon Street, Oxford OX2 6DP

Oxford University Press is a department of the University of Oxford.
It furthers the University's objective of excellence in research, scholarship,
and education by publishing world-wide in

Oxford New York

Auckland Bangkok Buenos Aires Cape Town Chennai
Dar es Salaam Delhi Hong Kong Istanbul Karachi Kolkata
Kuala Lumpur Madrid Melbourne Mexico City Mumbai Nairobi
São Paulo Shanghai Taipei Tokyo Toronto

Oxford is a registered trade mark of Oxford University Press
in the UK and in certain other countries

Published in the United States
by Oxford University Press Inc., New York

ISBN 1-85431-437-8

Printed in Great Britain by

Antony Rowe Ltd., Eastbourne

CONTENTS

PART II   THE LAW OF CONTRACT

ACKNOWLEDGMENTS

The authors and publishers wish to thank the following for permission to reprint material from the books and periodicals indicated:

Butterworth Law Publishers Ltd: *All England Law Reports*; *The Discipline of Law*, Lord Denning (1979).

Eclipse Group Limited: *Industrial Relations Law Reports*.

Incorporated Council of Law Reporting for England and Wales: *The Weekly Law Reports and Industrial Cases*.

Lloyd's of London Press Ltd: *Lloyd's Law Reports*.

Sweet and Maxwell Ltd: *Common Market Law Reports*; *Property and Compensation Reports*.

The Law Book Company Ltd: *Commonwealth Law Reports*.

Times Newspapers Ltd: *The Times Law Reports*.

PREFACE

Developments in the law and feedback from readers have contributed to the changes contained in this new edition. New chapters on sale of goods law including the changes introduced by the Sale and Supply of Goods Act 1994 are incorporated. In addition, the chapters on torts have been completely re-written with a heavy emphasis on negligent misstatement to make them more appropriate to students studying business, accountancy and management.

The style of the second edition remains unchanged and continues to contain self-check and examination style question and answers.

We would like to thank James Kirkbride of Manchester Metropolitan University for his contribution and Barbara Sutcliffe for her good humour and patience when word processing the revisions to the manuscript. Once again the professionalism of all the staff at Blackstone Press, especially Paula Doolan, was second to none — many thanks.

And finally congratulations to Landa and Dean on the birth of their daughter, Sofia. A brother or sister in time for the next edition?

Helen Bond
Peter Kay
September 1995

PREFACE TO THE FIRST EDITION

A great many students are required to study a one-year course in law as part of a degree or diploma course in another discipline. We realise that many of these students do not acquire the necessary legal skills to allow them to gain a good level of understanding of the material in the short time available. Consequently, we have tried to produce a book which provides a realistic treatment of business law. We have not covered every possible topic but have concentrated on the important ones; we have provided extracts from important cases to save students wading through the whole law report; we have provided simple self check questions and answers to help students measure their progress, and examination-type questions and answers to help them prepare for the examination.

All authors have people to thank. We would like to thank Madeleine Walsh for giving up part of her holiday to get the manuscript typed, and all at Blackstone Press for their help in producing this book.

Most of all, thanks go to the business studies students who acted as guinea-pigs and made very helpful suggestions as to how the book could be improved.

And finally, congratulations to Landa and Dean.

Helen Bond
Peter Kay

TABLE OF CASES

1 CLASSIFICATION OF LAW I

1 Criminal and civil law

It is possible to classify law from two standpoints. Chapter 1 classifies law into criminal and civil law. Each of these can be further sub-divided:

(a) *Criminal law* can be divided into categories such as murder, manslaughter, theft and assault.
(b) *Civil law* can be divided into categories such as contract, tort, company, and partnership.

There are a number of ways to distinguish between criminal and civil law.

Criminal cases are called prosecutions and they are initiated by the State on behalf of the nation to protect individuals. If the prosecution is successful the accused is found guilty and liable to punishment which may be a community sentence, a fine and/or imprisonment. If the prosecution is unsuccessful the accused is acquitted.

In criminal cases no attempt is made to compensate victims although it is possible for the criminal courts to order the criminal to make reparation directly to his victim under the Powers of Criminal Courts Act 1973.

Civil cases are brought by private individuals who are known as plaintiffs. A plaintiff will be either seeking compensation for a loss he has suffered or to establish his legal rights. If the plaintiff is successful against the defendant he will win damages to compensate him for any loss he has suffered or may win a court order which establishes his legal rights.

Activity
Many wrongful acts may give rise to both criminal and civil proceedings. Consider the following example and try to think of one of your own involving a car accident in which a person is injured.

If Alan Jones punches Bob Smith in the face, Alan Jones will be prosecuted for assault and Bob Smith may sue him in the tort of trespass to the person.

In the two cases described in the example above, the criminal case would be described as *R v Jones*. R stands for Regina which is a Latin term for Queen and signifies that the Crown prosecutes on behalf of the nation. Jones is the accused. The civil case would be described as *Smith v Jones* which indicates that this is a dispute between two individuals. Bob Smith would be the plaintiff and Alan Jones the defendant.

Self check questions
1. When a criminal offence is committed whom is the offence against?
2. Who initiates action in a criminal case?
3. In the cases involving Alan Jones:
    (a) in whose name would the prosecution be brought?
    (b) in whose name would the civil case be brought?
4. Who initiates an action in a civil case?
5. What is the remedy provided by the court in:
    (a) a criminal case?
    (b) a civil case?

Answers
1. A criminal offence is regarded as being committed against society.
2. The State takes action in the name of the Queen.
3. (a) The prosecution would be brought in the Queen's name: *R v Jones*.
    (b) The civil action would be brought in the name of the plaintiff, Bob Smith: *Smith v Jones*.
4. A wronged individual known as the plaintiff.
5. (a) A person found guilty in a criminal case is punished by a community sentence, a fine and/or imprisonment.
    (b) In a civil case the winner will receive compensation usually by way of damages.

Activity
Compare the main differences between criminal and civil law summed up in table 1.1.

Table 1.1 — Civil and criminal law compared

Criminal law	**Civil law**
1. *Whom the offence is against* An offence is regarded as being committed against society.	1. *Whom the wrong is against/ dispute is between* The wrong or dispute only concerns individuals against or between other individuals.

2. *Who takes action*
The State takes action in
the name of the Queen —
R v *Snigger.*

2. *Who takes action*
An individual takes action
against another individual
— *Bounder* v *Snigger.*

3. *The purpose of the action*
To protect society and punish the
offender.

3. *The purpose of the action*
To remedy the wrong often by
compensation.

4. *Where the action is taken*
The criminal courts e.g.,
Magistrates' Court, Crown Court.

4. *Where the action is taken*
The civil courts e.g.,
County Court, High Court.

5. *Terminology*
The prosecution prosecute the
accused who is found guilty or not
guilty.

5. *Terminology*
The plaintiff sues the defendant
who is found liable or not liable.

6. *Who must prove what*
The prosecution must prove
beyond all reasonable doubt that
the accused is guilty, so that the
jury feel sure or satisfied of his
guilt.

6. *Who must prove what*
The plaintiff must prove his case
on a balance of probabilities.

NB   Some events or wrongful acts may give rise to both criminal and civil
proceedings. For example, if A punches B in the face, A will be prosecuted for
assault and B may sue him in the tort of trespass to the person. If A is driving
badly and runs down B, then A may be prosecuted for a driving offence and
sued by B in the tort of negligence.

One can also classify law in other ways such as public and private law.

Problems
In the following examples state whether the situation involves criminal or civil
law and give a reason for your decision.
1.   John has purchased a table from a furniture shop for £100 and has failed
to pay for it.
2.   Chris has been arrested in possession of a stolen video and has been
charged with handling stolen property.
3.   Bill has been stopped by the police for speeding in his car.
4.   Paul has run Alice over. The accident occurred when Paul turned to wave
to a friend while driving his car. Alice has suffered a broken leg.

Suggested answers
1.   It is a civil law dispute. This is because the dispute is between private
individuals.

2. It is a criminal offence. Although it is a wrong against a particular individual handling stolen goods it is classed as a wrong against society and therefore a crime.

3. This is clearly a crime. The police are enforcing the law. It is also a wrong against society.

4. This particular event will give rise to an action in civil law in the tort of negligence for negligent driving and allow Alice to sue for damages for the injury she has suffered. A criminal offence will also have been committed and the police may prosecute Paul for driving without due care and attention.

2 CLASSIFICATION OF LAW II

1 Introduction

The other way of classifying law is by reference to the source of the legal rule. (Sources are explained in detail in ch. 3.) In this classification the categories will consist of common law, equity and legislation.

Within each of these three categories will be rules relating to criminal and civil law. Thus the overall picture can be looked at from two different standpoints. The relationships are explained in figures 2.1 and 2.2.

Activity
Spend about 15 minutes looking at these diagrams to try to understand the relationship between the classifications.

Figure 2.1

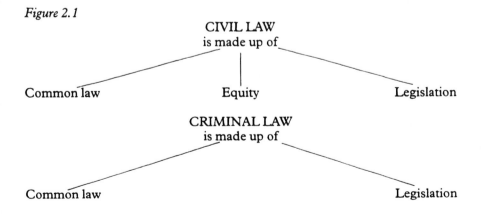

Figure 2.2

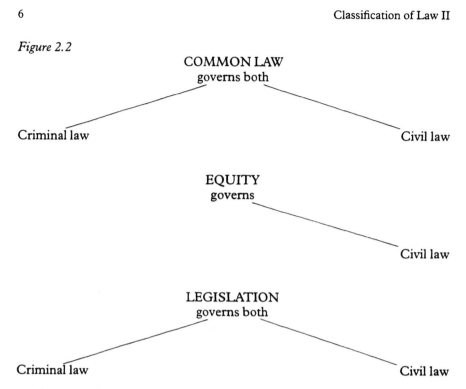

COMMON LAW
governs both

Criminal law

Civil law

EQUITY
governs

Civil law

LEGISLATION
governs both

Criminal law

Civil law

2 Common law

Common law is the law made by judges. It is contained in the decisions of judges over the centuries and forms a vast body of legal rules which have nothing to do with any laws created and passed by Parliament.

The decisions of judges are recorded in law reports which form a large library of legal rules which lawyers and judges can refer to in the preparation and conduct of court cases.

Courts are arranged in a hierarchical system. A decision of a judge of a court at the top of the hierarchy will bind judges lower down the hierarchy. This is known as the system of judicial precedent which is discussed fully in ch. 5.

3 Equity

Equity is a body of law independant of the common law. The two types of law are related in as much as they bear certain similarities. Equity like common law is law created by judges and is found in the law reports. However, there are a number of differences between them.

Before the passing of the Judicature Acts of 1873-1875 two separate court systems existed, common law courts administering common law and the Courts of Chancery administering equitable rules. The Judicature Acts fused these two court systems but they did not fuse the two bodies of rules. Consequently, a case involving both common law and equitable principles can now be heard in one court which can, where necessary, apply both sets of rules.

Equity is therefore a body of rules developed by the Courts of Chancery. The main reason that the Courts of Chancery and equity developed was that the common law had become very rigid and could not adapt to cope with the rapidly changing social and economic conditions between 1500 and 1900. During this time the body of law known as equity developed very rapidly to supplement and lessen the harshness of the common law.

Perhaps the best definition of the nature of equity is that of Lord Cowper in *Dudley* v *Dudley* (1705):

> Now equity is no part of the law, but a moral virtue, which qualifies, moderates, and reforms the rigour, hardness, and edge of the law, and is a universal truth; it does also assist the law where it is defective and weak in the constitution (which is the life of the law) and defends the law from crafty evasions, delusions, and new subtleties, invented and contrived to evade and delude the common law, whereby such as have undoubted right are made remediless; and this the office of equity, to support and protect the common law from shifts and crafty contrivances against the justice of the law. Equity therefore does not destroy the law, nor create it, but assists it.

The rules of equity developed by the Court of Chancery were either entirely new rights totally unknown to the common law, or remedies designed to counter the inefficiency or injustice of the common law. Equity provided remedies on a 'one off' basis in its early years. However, the amount of uncertainty that was created by this method soon became counter-productive. Thus equitable remedies and rules began to take on a more permanent form.

3.1   Content of equity

The rules of equity although based on conscience soon became uniform and certain in extent. They were nearly all created between 1529 and 1827. Equity no longer 'varies as the length of the Chancellor's foot'. Specifically, two new categories of rights have been created:

(a)   *The rights of a beneficiary under a use or trust* — A trust is a relationship in which one person has property vested in him (legal ownership) subject to an obligation to permit another person to have the beneficial enjoyment of the property (equitable ownership).

(b)   *The equity of redemption* — 'equity looks to the intent and not the form'. Hence under the old common law mortgage a party was entitled to a reconveyance of the property after the due date for redemption had passed. This right was termed the 'equity of redemption' and was an equitable interest in land which the mortgagor could deal with in the same way as a beneficiary under a trust could deal with his beneficial interest.

Furthermore, the following new remedies now exist:

(a)   *Injunction* — This is an order of the court compelling or restraining the performance of some act. An injunction which orders the defendant to perform some act is termed 'mandatory' as opposed to a 'prohibitory' injunction which restrains the defendant from committing some wrong, usually a tort.

(b) *Specific performance* — This is a decree of the court constituting an order compelling a person to perform an obligation existing under either a contract or a trust.

(c) *Rectification* — Where an instrument under seal did not reflect the true intention of the parties through a mistake in transcribing, the Court of Chancery claimed jurisdiction to rectify the document. (NB only documents, not 'contracts', can be rectified.) This mistake must be mutual.

(d) *Rescission* — This remedy, like rectification, grew out of the inability of the common law to prevent a party from suing on a contract or covenant where it was obviously unjust for him to do so because of some collateral matter. In certain circumstances the Court of Chancery would rescind a contract where it was possible to restore the status quo between the parties. The most important grounds for applying rescission are fraud and innocent misrepresentation.

It must be remembered that whereas common law remedies are as of right, equitable remedies are discretionary. The court may exercise its discretion in each case as to whether it will grant an equitable remedy.

Self check questions
1. Why does equity not govern the criminal law?
2. Where can a lawyer find decisions of judges recorded?
3. When a decision of a higher court binds a judge in a lower court, what is this known as?
4. Why did equity develop as a branch of the common law?
5. Name two new remedies created by equity.

Answers
1. Equity has developed on the basis of fairness and good conscience, therefore it is not appropriate that it should apply to the criminal law.
2. A lawyer can find the decisions of judges recorded in the law reports.
3. This is known as judicial precedent.
4. To supplement the common law in areas where it had failed to develop and to lessen the harshness of its application where it had failed to adapt to the changing social and economic conditions.
5. Any two of the following four are correct: injunction; specific performance; rectification; rescission.

Problem
Explain why equity developed and describe the essential nature of equity.

Suggested answer
Equity developed because the common law had become defective in a number of ways. First, the early common law in respect of breaches of contract was grossly inadequate. Secondly, the only remedy available at common law was damages and this was often not an effective remedy for the parties. Finally, the

court system became very rigid. It was often the case that a litigant could not sue because he could not find a writ appropriate to his cause. As a consequence many litigants petitioned the King, as the fountain of justice, to hear their case and grant them an appropriate remedy. As the number of cases increased the King delegated this task to his principal Minister, the Chancellor. Because he was acting on behalf of the King, the Chancellor was not bound by the rules of common law. Consequently, the Chancellors slowly began to evolve a set of rules which remedied the defects of the common law and to grant new forms of remedies different from and more effective than the common law remedies.

A Court of Chancery was established which sat on a regular basis to hear petitions and grant remedies. The rules administered by the Court of Chancery became known as rules of equity.

A knowledge of the history and development of equity is essential to an understanding of the nature of this body of law. Equity is not a rival system to the common law. It is intended that equity should supplement the common law not supersede it. Equity 'acts *in personam*' upon the conscience of a defendant. A person who 'seeks equity must do equity'; consequently equitable remedies are not something a plaintiff is entitled to but something awarded at the discretion of the court. In addition there is the maxim (rule) 'he who comes to equity must come with clean hands' or no remedy will be awarded.

Equity's essential function is to ensure that a person who has suffered a wrong and is entitled to a remedy will be awarded an appropriate one and that neither the defendant nor inadequate rules of common law stand in his way.

4 Legislation

This is a collection of rules passed by Parliament. Legislation in the form of an Act of Parliament may govern either civil law or criminal law. A particular Act of Parliament usually concentrates on one area of law. The function of legislation is discussed in the next chapter.

3   SOURCES OF LAW

1   Introduction

The methods by which law is created make up the legal sources. The three major sources of law are legislation, common law and equity. The only other source of law, which is not very important today, is custom.

2   Legislation

Legislation is a collection of rules passed by Parliament and embodied in an *Act of Parliament* — sometimes referred to as a *statute*.

The rules which form a particular Act of Parliament normally relate to the same subject, for example: the Theft Act 1968 lays down the law against crimes of theft.

Activity
Try to think of three areas of our everyday lives which are governed by legislation e.g., the assessment of income tax is governed by the Income and Corporation Taxes Act 1988.

Legislation is passed by Parliament for three main purposes which are outlined below.

2.1   *Revision of substantive rules of law*
All legislation that is passed revises law in the broadest sense; however, some statutes set out to revise the substantive rules which form a certain area of law and completely change the law. One example is the Torts (Interference with Goods) Act 1977, which completely revises the law relating to goods, trespass to, detaining and conversion of goods. This law had previously been a complex and unsatisfactory web of rules.

Statutes like the Torts (Interference with Goods) Act 1977 are usually passed when the existing common law (see below) has become stale, restrictive, complex and incapable of adapting to meet the needs of society. The task of reforming such law has been given to a Government created body — the Law Commission. The Law Commission is charged with reviewing and developing areas of law which have become outdated and with drafting suggested reforming legislation.

2.2 Consolidation
Where an area of law has evolved piecemeal, a consolidating statute may be passed to clarify the law. The consolidating Act will put all the existing statute law into one Act of Parliament. This makes the law on a particular subject easier to find as it will be all in one place and therefore easier to administer. Examples of consolidating Acts are the Companies Act 1985 and the Sale of Goods Act 1979.

2.3 Codification
Codification differs from consolidation in that an Act may only be said to consolidate existing statute law, whereas codification consists of the gathering of existing case law and statute law and codifying it in one act. Codification performs a similar function to consolidation in that it simplifies and clarifies existing law rather than changing it. An example of codification is the Offences against the Person Act 1861.

3 Delegated legislation

Some Acts of Parliament give or delegate powers to institutions such as the Crown, Ministers, public corporations and local authorities to make legislation. This type of legislation is referred to variously as delegated legislation, subordinate legislation or secondary legislation. The Act of Parliament giving or delegating the power to legislate is known as the parent Act.

A vast amount of legislation will be created or brought into being by delegated legislation. Such legislation is made under the authority of an Act of Parliament by some person or body other than Parliament and known as 'Statutory Instrument', 'Order', 'Regulation' or 'By-law' depending on who makes it. For example, the Local Government Act 1972, s. 235(1) empowers local authorities to make by-laws for the good rule and government of the whole or any part of the district or borough, as the case may be, and for the prevention and suppression of nuisances therein.

By-laws which are made under the parent Act mentioned above affect all of us in our daily lives. Local councils use by-laws to regulate conduct on council-run buses, at council-run swimming-baths and at council parks.

Activity
Next time you are in a building which is council run or owned see if you can find examples of any by-laws made by the council.

3.1   Advantages of delegated legislation

There are a number of clear advantages associated with the use of delegated legislation. Some of them are listed below.

(a)   Parliamentary time is valuable. Delegated legislation allows broad and general laws to be passed by Parliament and the more detailed provisions to be supplied by the relevant government minister in the form of regulations and orders.

(b)   Where a very technical matter needs the attention of Parliament it is often the case that MPs lack the necessary expertise. Delegated legislation allows such matters to be tackled and legislated for by experts within the relevant government department.

(c)   Where powers are delegated to a government minister it will enable him to act quickly in times of crisis e.g., a strike within an essential industry.

(d)   Delegated legislation can be quickly and easily updated to cope with changing economic and social conditions.

3.2   Disadvantages of delegated legislation

The main disadvantage is the fact that delegated legislation is now so popular and widely used that Parliament cannot effectively supervise its use despite the controls that exist. These controls are discussed below.

3.3   Parliamentary controls

'Parliament has no real control over the executive, it is a pure fiction' (Lloyd George). In a sense Parliament has complete control over delegated legislation since the power to take it can only be granted by statute. Thus it is possible for Parliament to debate whether such power should be delegated at all, and if so, on what terms, during the passage of any Bill in which it is proposed. Matters concerning delegated legislation may also be raised at Question Time or in debates on the adjournment.

However, the same pressure on Parliamentary time which makes delegated legislation necessary, inevitably limits the effectiveness of these safeguards and such control which Parliament has is mainly exercised through what are termed 'laying requirements' and the work of scrutiny committees.

3.3.1   Laying requirements   Many enabling Acts contain provisions requiring delegated legislation made under them to be laid before Parliament. There are two main forms:

(a)   Negative procedure — statutory instrument is laid before either House and if not annulled by resolution within 40 days it becomes law.

(b)   Affirmative procedure — requires each house to pass a resolution approving the instrument either to bring it into operation or to allow it to continue.

Not all forms of delegated legislation have to be laid before Parliament e.g., local by-laws.

3.3.2 Scrutiny committees   Both Houses of Parliament have a select committee whose task is to scrutinise certain forms of delegated legislation. The House of Lords has a Special Orders Committee, but its consideration is confined to statutory instruments which require an affirmative resolution and these are not very numerous. Parliament has a Joint Committee on Statutory Instruments laid or laid in draft before the two Houses to determine whether the special attention of the House should be drawn to it on the following grounds:

(a)   it imposes charges on public funds or requires payments to public bodies;

(b)   it is not open to challenge in the courts;

(c)   it appears to make unusual or unexpected use of the powers conferred;

(d)   it purports to have unauthorised retrospective effect;

(e)   it has been subject to unjustifiable delay in publication or laying before Parliament;

(f)   its form calls for elucidation.

The committee cannot inquire into the merits of an instrument nor can the committee annul it, but it can demand an explanation from the Government department concerned.

3.3.3 Special Parliamentary procedure   Where important public issues are involved some statutory instruments are subject to 'special Parliamentary procedure'. This gives people the opportunity to object to the order at a local inquiry and also by petition to Parliament thereby ensuring maximum publicity and Parliamentary control. The relevant Acts governing such procedure are the Statutory Orders (Special Procedure) Acts of 1945 and 1965.

3.3.4 Defence of lack of publication   By the Statutory Instruments Act 1946, s. 3 it is a defence, when charged with contravening a statutory instrument, to prove that it had not been issued by HMSO at the date of the alleged offence provided that the prosecution cannot prove that at that date reasonable steps had been taken to bring the purport of the instrument to the notice of the public, those likely to be affected by it or the person charged.

3.4 Judicial controls

Any scrutiny by the courts is *ex post facto* (after the event). Problems encountered include the initiative and funds to go to court to question the disputed piece of delegated legislation, although if the delegated legislation in question contains a power of prosecution for failure to comply with its provisions, then the validity of the delegated legislation can be questioned and raised as a defence if a prosecution ensues.

Scrutiny of delegated legislation by the courts is an important aspect of the judicial control of the executive and is implemented by using the *ultra vires* (beyond the powers) doctrine; if the delegated legislation does not conform with the parent statute that conferred the power to make the delegated legislation then it is *ultra vires* and void; it never was lawful. Delegated legislation can be procedurally *ultra vires* in that it does not conform with the procedure laid down in the parent Act (which might include some form of consultation, see *post*), or it can be substantively *ultra vires* in that it does not comply with judicially created norms that are implied into the parent Act unless expressly excluded. Such norms of substantive compliance can be categorised:

3.4.1 *Fundamental rights* — The courts assume that Parliament in delegating its power does not intend that fundamental rights can be taken away. This can be seen from the following case.

Attorney-General v *Wilts United Dairies Ltd*
(1921) 38 TLR 781, HL

The Food Controller was given power to make Regulations for controlling the sale, purchase and consumption of food and to control prices. To this end the Controller levied a 2d. per gallon tax on a dairy company to which he had given a licence to deal in milk, the tax going towards a scheme for regulating prices. The dairy company later refused to pay.

ATKIN LJ: The circumstances would be remarkable indeed which would induce the court to believe that the legislature had sacrificed all the well-known checks and precautions, and not in express terms, but merely by implication had entrusted a minister with undefined and unlimited powers of imposing charges upon the subject for purposes connected with his department.

3.4.2 *Repugnance to the general law*

White v *Morley*
[1899] 2 QB 34

CHANNELL J: A by-law is a local law, and may be supplementary to the general law; it is not bad because it deals with something that is not dealt with by the general law. But it must not alter the general law by making that lawful which the general law makes unlawful; or that unlawful which the general law makes lawful.

3.4.3 *Uncertainty* Jaconelli (*Enacting a Bill of Rights*, Oxford, Clarendon Press, 1980, pp. 132-3) sees this test as a '... particularly useful one in the protection of civil liberties, since loose drafting and uncertainty of application seem to be the hallmark of laws which invade fundamental rights'.

3.4.4 *Unreasonableness* The test of unreasonableness derived from *Kruse* v *Johnson* (1898) where it was unsuccessfully applied to a by-law prohibiting the playing of music or singing in a public place within 50 yards of a dwelling-house.

Kruse v *Johnson*
[1898] 2 QB 91

LORD RUSSELL: I think the courts ought to be slow to condemn as invalid any by-law . . . on the ground of unreasonableness.

This rather negative acceptance that by-laws can be condemned as unreasonable has also been applied to statutory instruments. There is judicial reluctance to apply the same principle to delegated powers given to ministers and expressed on subjective terms, especially if the delegated legislation is made at a time of emergency. For example, the case of *McEldowney* v *Forde* (1969).

McEldowney v *Forde*
[1969] 2 All ER 1053

Under the Civil Authorities (Special Powers) Acts (Northern Ireland) 1922-43, the Minister had the power, 'to make regulations . . . for the preservation of peace and maintenance of order'. The Minister made a Regulation making it an offence to belong to a proscribed organisation, and in 1967 a Regulation added to the list of proscribed organisations, any organisation, 'describing themselves as "Republican Clubs" or any like organisation howsoever described'.

LORD HODSON (for the majority): . . . Is the whole Regulation too vague and so arbitrary as to be wholly unreasonable? . . .

[Is the Regulation] capable of being related to . . . the preservation of the peace and the maintenance of order. The authorities show that where, as here, there is no question of bad faith the courts will be slow to interfere with the exercise of wide powers to make regulations.

Powerful dissenting judgments were delivered:

LORD PEARCE: Even where such wide words are used as 'may make such regulations as he may think fit', the subjective power is limited to such things as the general context of the statute shows to be its objectives. It cannot be suggested that he can make any regulations that he likes, regardless of the intentions to be derived from the statute conferring the power. *A fortiori* is this so when no subjective licence is given; for it certainly should not be implied. . . .

The convention by which our courts construe statutes in order to find the so-called 'intention of Parliament' compels one to disregard the fact that this was an Act passed by members of Parliament. It subjects the words of a statute to critical analysis and construction with all the expertise of legal professional experience. Our courts also (unlike the courts of some other countries) disregard the debate which preceded the passing of the Act and any assurances that may have been given to the members by their law officers.

This somewhat artificial convention makes it all the more important to avoid refinements of construction which may be attractive to the expertise of the skilled lawyer but could never conceivably have occurred to a member of Parliament when he read an apparently comprehensible statute. In my opinion the normal ordinary meaning which this statute would bear is that the Minister, whether making orders or regulations or enforcing the statute, must confine himself to that which any crisis made necessary, and which caused the minimum disruption of the citizen's rights. It is within that limited area that his discretion was confined.

Does the regulation of 1967 come within the power thus given? In my opinion it does not. . . .

It is argued that it is for the Minister alone to decide how he should use his power and that the court should not interfere, however wrong it thinks that decision, unless there is some element of bad faith. But in my opinion the duty of surveillance entrusted to the courts for the protection of the citizen goes deeper than that. It cannot take the easy course of 'passing by on the other side' when it seems clear to it that the Minister is using a power in a way which Parliament, who gave him that power, did not intend. When there is doubt, of course the courts will not interfere. But if it seems clear on grounds of rationality and common sense that he was exceeding the power with which Parliament was intending to clothe him to further the purposes of the Act, the courts have a duty to interfere. The fact that this is not an easy line to draw is no reason why the courts should give up the task and abandon their duty to protect the citizen. . . .

Further, the regulation of 1967 is too vague and ambiguous. A man must not be put in peril on an ambiguity under the criminal law. When the regulation of 1967 was issued the citizen ought to have been able to know whether he could or could not remain a member of his club without being subject to a criminal prosecution. Yet I doubt if one could have said with certainty that any man or woman was safe in remaining a member of any club in Northern Ireland, however named or whatever its activities or objects.

Had the final phrase 'or any like organisation howsoever described' been absent, the regulation would have simply been an attack on the description 'Republican Club', however innocent the club's activities. Presumably the justification for it would have to be that the mere existence of the word republican in the name of a club was so inflammatory that its suppression was 'necessary for preserving the peace and maintaining order' and that the 'exigencies' of the need for its suppression did not permit the citizen's right in that respect to prevail. . . . I do not accept that such a justification could suffice. But be that as it may, the final phrase shows that this is more than an attack on nomenclature, since the club is deemed equally unlawful if it is a like organisation whatever be the name under which it goes.

And what is the 'likeness' to a republican club which makes an organisation unlawful 'howsoever described'? Since a republican club is banned whatever may be its activities, the likeness cannot consist in its activities. And since the organisation is unlawful, howsoever described, the 'likeness' cannot consist in a likeness of nomenclature. The only possibility left seems to be that the 'likeness' may consist in the mere fact of being a club. In which case all clubs, however named, are unlawful — which is absurd.

One cannot disregard the final phrase, since that would wholly alter the meaning of the regulation. Without the final phrase it is simply an attack on nomenclature. But with the final phrase it cannot simply be an attack on nomenclature. One cannot sever the bad from the good by omitting a phrase when the omission must alter the meaning of the rest. One must take the whole sentence as it stands. And as it stands it is too vague and ambiguous to be valid.

3.5   Consultation

Delegated legislation is often technical and expert advice is often required. Also, it is perhaps only fair to consult those who may be affected, although this is not a legal requirement of the rules of natural justice. Consultation is an important aspect of obtaining general approval and acceptance of the delegated legislation, and may be required by the enabling Act.

For example, The Industrial Training Act 1964 established Industrial Training Boards which were supported by levies on employers in the industry concerned. These levies are made by delegated legislation, this time called 'Orders':

Industrial Training Act, 1964, s. 1(4)

Before making an Order, the Minister shall consult any organisation or association appearing to him to be representative of a substantial number of employers.

Similarly the Act applied to agriculture, horticulture etc. This gave rise to the following case:

Agricultural, Horticultural and Forestry Industry Training Board v Aylesbury Mushrooms Ltd
[1972] 1 WLR 190

The Mushroom Growers Association had not been consulted prior to an Order levying a tax on the employers in the industry. They were held to be an organisation as defined by s. 1(4).

DONALDSON J: [I]t was an organisation which had to be consulted, although its small membership and the specialised nature of their activities could well have led the Minister to take a different view.

Activity
Does Donaldson J's argument correspond to the actual provisions of the statute in s. 1(4) above?

Consultation may also take place voluntarily. 'Consultation with interests and organisations likely to be affected by rules and regulations is one of the firmest and most carefully observed conventions'.

4   Autonomic legislation

This is 'legislation' made by the Crown or by autonomous associations within the State under powers not necessarily delegated by Parliament. However, the courts will recognise them. Examples of autonomous association are professional bodies like the Law Society and trade unions. Their legislation is binding on their members. The doctrine of *ultra vires* does apply. Other types of autonomous legislative bodies are public undertakings such as transport authorities whose by-laws affect the public at large.

The Crown makes autonomic legislation by use of the royal prerogative. The prerogative does not give the Crown power to alter the general law of the land; it is limited to legislating for the armed forces, colonies and the civil service. The prerogative is not subject to the doctrine of *ultra vires*. However, as stated above, *ultra vires* will apply to most other forms of autonomic legislation.

5   The relevance of subordinate legislation to the world of business

Subordinate legislation is of great importance to the world of business. Numerous regulations whether concerning health and safety at work, food and drugs, the technical regulation of vehicles for transport of goods and people, in particular road haulage, must all be complied with. Consumer credit is one area where many important rules are made by statutory instrument. Entire industries must carefully comply with subordinate legislation; the construction industry and the building regulations being one example. Autonomic legislation whether relating to public undertakings such as the transport authorities or the internal regulation of a profession or trade union is also important. Both forms of subordinate legislation, especially delegated legislation, play an important role in every aspect of business activity.

6   Procedure for passing an Act of Parliament

Most legislation is initiated by the government of the day. A proposed piece of legislation starts life as a Bill of Parliament which must be approved by both the House of Commons and the House of Lords before it can become law. Both Houses have the opportunity to discuss and debate the Bill before voting on it. Once both Houses pass the Bill it is sent for the Royal Assent. Only after it has received the Royal Assent does the Bill become an Act and become law.

7   EC legislation

In addition to Acts of Parliament and delegated legislation, we also have to consider legislation passed by the EC. Since the UK joined the EC, we have been subject to rules and regulations made by the European Commission and the Council of Ministers. Indeed EC law automatically overrides subsequent inconsistent national legislation.

Thus by joining the EC, the UK has given up certain sovereign rights and transferred them to the law-making bodies of the EC. By the signing of the

Treaty of Rome when the UK joined the EC, English law became subject to legislation made by the European bodies under the Treaty of Rome. (See figure 3.1 showing the constitutional bodies of the EC.) There are additional treaties that produce legislation that is effective in the UK e.g., the treaty forming Euratom and the Single European Act. The latter greatly increases the powers and importance of the European Parliament which in its supervisory role now exercises direct political control over the Commission (the main legislating body of the EC).

The supremacy of the UK Parliament and the difficulties presented by membership of the EC in this respect have already been discussed above. However, it is now proposed to deal with EC legislation in such a way as to elucidate its nature and discuss its relationship with UK legislation.

7.1   Legislation of the European Communities
The primary legislation of the EC consists of the treaties themselves. For example the Treaty of Rome, the treaty forming Euratom.

Under these treaties the Council and Commission of the Communities have the duty to make regulations, issue directives, make decisions and recommendations and deliver opinions. These are the instruments by which the policy of the treaties is implemented. Regulations, directives and decisions only may be classified as legislation.

7.1.1   Regulations   These have general application, are binding in their entirety and directly applicable to all Member States. Hence they confer individual rights and duties which the national courts of the Member States must protect. Therefore, in the UK there is no need for further legislation to implement community regulations.

NB   The European Communities Act 1972, s. 2(4) provides that any like enactment has effect subject to existing 'enforceable community rights'. Parliament ought not, therefore, to pass legislation which conflicts with that of the EC.

7.1.2   Directives   These do not necessarily have immediate binding force. It is left to the individual Member States to implement them. In the UK this may be done by Order in Council or by regulations made by way of statutory instrument or occasionally by statute as in the case of the European Communities Act, 1972.

Article 189 of the Rome Treaty distinguishes between regulations, which are of direct effect within Member States, and directives which, though binding on Member States, are not of direct effect. But a few directives may be directly applicable in the sense of having direct effect. Two cases give good examples of this. First *Van Duyn* v *Home Office* (1974). Here the European Court held a directive to be of immediate binding effect so as to confer rights upon the plaintiff even though the UK had not implemented that directive. Hence it had direct effect in the UK. Secondly, *Franz Grad* v *Finanzamt Traunstein* (1971). This case held that whether or not a directive is of direct effect depends on an examination of the nature, general scheme and wording of its provisions to see whether they are capable of producing direct effect on the Member States to whom they are directed.

An example of the difficulty of deciding whether a directive produces a direct effect is the case of:

Pubblico Ministero v *Ratti*
[1979] ECR 1629

On June 4, 1973, the Council issued a directive on the classification, packaging and labelling of dangerous preparations (solvents) which was due to be implemented by Member States before December 8, 1974. After that date, an Italian producer had decided to package and label its products according to the Council Directive which so far had not been implemented by the Italian authorities. Signor Ratti, the responsible representative of the firm, was therefore prosecuted for having infringed certain provisions of an Italian law of 1963 relating to the labelling of certain dangerous products, which had not yet been adapted to the Community directive. It was under these circumstances that the Pretura Penale of Milan, finding that 'there was a manifest contradiction between the Community rules and internal Italian law' and wondering 'which of the two sets of rules should take precedence', referred to the Community Court a question asking whether the said Council Directive constitutes 'directly applicable legislation conferring upon individuals personal rights which the national courts must protect.'

In its judgment of April 5, 1979, the Court recalled the standard formula stemming from Grad *and* Van Duyn, *adding that 'consequently a Member State which has not adopted the implementing measures required by the directive in the prescribed periods may not rely, as against individuals, on its own failure to perform the obligations which the directive entails.' The answer to the question was therefore that 'after the expiration of the period fixed for the implementation of a directive, a Member State may not apply its internal law — even if it is provided with penal sanctions — which has not yet been adapted in compliance with the directive, to a person who has complied with the requirements of the directive'.*

There were some adverse reactions from some national courts, for example in *Ministre de l'Intérieur* v *Cohn-Bendit* where the French Conseil d'Etat stated that national authorities remained exclusively competent to decide on the method of implementing directives.

The European Court clarified the positon in the case of *Becker* v *Finanzamt Münster Innenstadt* (1982) upholding the case law from *Franz Grad* and *Van Duyn*. After recalling the wording of Article 189 and underscoring the fact that States to which a directive is addressed are under an obligation to achieve the result aimed at by the directive in the period prescribed, the Court continues: 'It follows that wherever a directive is correctly implemented, its effects extend to individuals through the medium of the implementing measures adopted by the Member State concerned.'

However, special problems arise where a Member State has failed to implement a directive correctly and, more particularly, where the provisions of the directive have not been implemented by the end of the period prescribed for that purpose.

It follows from well-established case-law of the Court and, most recently, from the judgment of April 5, 1979, in Case 148/78 *Pubblico Ministero v Ratti* (1979) that whilst under Article 189 regulations are directly applicable and, consequently, by their nature capable of producing direct effects, that does not mean that other categories of measures covered by that article can never produce similar effects. It would be incompatible with the binding effect which Article 189 ascribes to directives to exclude in principle the possibility of the obligations imposed by them being relied on by persons concerned.

Particularly in cases in which the Community authorities have, by means of a directive, placed Member States under a duty to adopt a certain course of action, the effectiveness of such measures would be diminished if persons were prevented from relying upon it in proceedings before a court and national courts were prevented from taking it into consideration as an element of Community law.

Consequently, a Member State which has not adopted the implementing measures required by the directive within the prescribed period may not plead, as against individuals, its own failure to perform the obligations which the directive entails.

Thus, wherever the provisions of a directive appear, as far as their subject matter is concerned, to be unconditional and sufficiently precise, those provisions may, in the absence of implementing measures adopted within the prescribed period, be relied upon as against any national provision which is incompatible with the directive or in so far as the provisions define rights which individuals are able to assert against the State.

7.1.3 Decisions These may be made by the Council and Commission as a formal method of enunciating policies or initiating actions. They are binding but like directives may in certain cases be directly applicable.

Self check questions
1.   What are the three main sources of English law?
2.   What main purposes does legislation serve?
3.   What is delegated legislation?
4.   List any two advantages of delegated legislation.
5.   What are the three main processes through which a Bill must pass to become an Act of Parliament?
6.   What is autonomic legislation?
7.   What effect has joining the EC had on the British Parliament's ability to legislate?

Answers
1.   The three main sources are legislation, common law and equity.
2.   There are three main purposes — revision, consolidation, codification.
3.   It is legislation passed by government bodies rather than Parliament. The body must be properly authorised by the parent Act to legislate in this way.

4. Time saving; allows technical matters to be dealt with more effectively; provides greater flexibility for a minister to respond quickly in an emergency; it can be easily and quickly updated.

5. House of Commons; House of Lords; Royal Assent.

6. Autonomic legislation is 'legislation' made by the Crown or by other autonomous bodies within the State under powers not necessarily delegated by Parliament.

7. It has meant that any legislation passed by Parliament must be consistent with that passed by the EC.

8 Common law

This source of law is equally as important as legislation. It consists of the decisions of the courts which are made as a result of litigation. The decisions are recorded in law reports and make up the body of law known as common law which was discussed in chapter 2. Common law is governed by the system of judicial precedent. The way in which judicial precedent operates will be discussed in chapter 5 and reference should be made to that chapter for further information.

9 Equity

Equity is an important source of law in as much as it supplements the common law. Equitable principles are still being developed by the courts today, although the growth of equity is much slower now than it was between 1500 and 1900. See chapter 2 for a fuller discussion of the nature of equity.

10 Custom

Most of the customs that made up the law in the Middle Ages have become so established that they are now recognised as rules of common law. Consequently custom is no longer very important as a source of English law. However, something needs to be said about custom as a source of law.

Binding custom may be subdivided into particular or local custom; and general customs.

Both types are limited in their application by the rules which must be satisfied before they are recognised by the courts.

10.1 Local customs

A local custom is a usage which has obtained the force of law and is binding within a particular area or place upon the persons and things which it concerns. In practice a plaintiff or defendant relying on a custom must plead it and give particulars of it. At the trial the evidence of the custom is provided like any other fact.

A modern example is *New Windsor Corporation* v *Mellor* (1975). Here an 81-year-old lady successfully established the customary right of local inhabitants to indulge in lawful sport and pastimes on an area of land in the middle of New Windsor. It was alleged that the right went back to at least AD 900.

To be accepted as legally binding the custom must satisfy the following tests:

(a)   Custom must have existed from time immemorial — which is fixed at 1189, the end of Henry II's reign. In *Simpson v Wells* (1872), S was convicted for obstructing a public footpath. He pleaded as his defence that he had put his stall on the footpath in exercise of a custom — a fair for the exchange of servants. It was shown by the prosecution that these fairs arose from the Statutes of Labour in the 14th century. The defence therefore failed.

(b)   Continuance test — the custom must have been continuously in operation without lawful interruption. It need not have been continuously exercised but it must have been possible to exercise it lawfully. An example is the case of *Wyld v Silver* (1963). In 1799 it was a recognised custom that fairs could be held on a piece of land during Whit week. But in 1963 no fair had been held in living memory. S acquired part of the land intending to build on it. W applied for an injunction to prevent him from doing so on grounds of the custom. The court held that the fact that no fair had been held within living memory made no difference. The custom still existed and an injunction was granted.

(c)   Peaceable enjoyment — the custom must have been exercised peaceably, openly and as of right. Hence a custom must be exercised by consensus. In *Mills v Colchester Corporation* (1867) M owned an oyster fishery. M was refused a licence to operate it. He argued that there was a local custom giving him the right as owner to operate the fishery. The court held that since he needed a licence he could not fish as of right and there was therefore no custom.

(d)   Reasonableness — a custom must not be unreasonable. The party denying the custom must show that at the time of its origin it was unreasonable. In *Bryant v Foot* (1868) a rector claimed 13 shillings per marriage he performed as a custom. He established that it existed in 1820. It was up to the other party to disprove it before that date. The court however held such a custom unreasonable because 13 shillings would have been a huge sum for an ordinary person in 1189. Hence there was no custom.

(e)   Certainty — a custom must be certain because a custom cannot exist from time immemorial when it is not certain what it is. In *Wilson v Willes* (1806) an alleged custom that the tenants of a manor might take from the manorial common as much turf as they required for their lawns was held to be unreasonable and uncertain. There was no limit to how much they could take — hence an uncertainty of quantity.

(f)   The custom must be compulsory — the people involved must regard it as binding.

(g)   The custom must be consistent with other customs — otherwise they cannot all be good.

(h)   A custom must not be contrary to any statute.

(i)   It must apply to a definite locality. Local customs apply only to the things or inhabitants of a particular area such as a shire, a borough, a parish or a manor.

The decisions however, are not always clear cut. In *Mercer v Denne* (1905) D owned part of a beach and wanted to erect a house on it. The local fishermen sought to stop him on the grounds that they had a customary right to dry their nets on the land. Witnesses proved the custom back for 70 years and by reputation earlier. The presumption of antiquity thus arose and D was not allowed to build on his own land. (But note the element of uncertainty as to the techniques of drying; the fluctuations in the sea level since 1189 and as to which piece of land the custom related.)

In *Alfred F. Beckett Ltd* v *Lyons* (1967) local inhabitants claimed a customary right to a nine-mile stretch of sea-washed coal. The court held that there was no custom because the area of operations was too small; there was no evidence that people thought they collected coal as of right and it was not right to say that the custom extended to everyone in the County Palatine of Durham because it would have been too far to travel in 1189.

10.2   General custom

A general custom relates to a trade or commercial practice not restricted to a particular locality. In *Goodwin* v *Roberts* (1875) a court of appeal held that immemoriality is not necessary for a general custom. In *Edlestein* v *Schuler & Co.* (1902) the court recognised a new type of negotiable instrument — a negotiable debenture — and said, 'the Law Merchant is not fixed or stereotyped'. (Negotiable instruments are however the only case in which a general custom arising after the year 1189 has been recognised as supplanting the common law.)

When the courts are considering the validity of an alleged general custom they do not require that the custom should have existed since 1189, nor do they require it to be confined to a particular locality. However, the other tests, set out above, must be satisfied. (*Alfred F. Beckett Ltd* v *Lyons* (1967).)

10.3   Conventional usage

To be distinguished from custom in the strict sense of binding rules of law is that body of rules sometimes known as custom which binds only by agreement, express or implied, of the parties concerned. Because such usage is not binding of itself it can be excluded by agreement but as a general rule usages of a trade or a particular area are impliedly included in contracts within the trade or area.

Before the usage will be implied it must have existed for so long and become so well established that it is reasonable to incorporate it by implication in an agreement where there is no express term to the contrary. In *Smith* v *Wilson* (1832) a usage of the fur trade that 'a thousand rabbits' meant one thousand two hundred rabbits was implied in a contract. In *Dashwood* v *Magniac* (1891) a custom of Buckinghamshire that 'timber' included beech (as well as the usual oak, ash and elm) was recognised.

Self check questions
1.   How important is custom as a source of English law today?
2.   What is the difference between local and general custom?
3.   What is the difference between custom and conventional usage?
4.   What is the difference between common law and custom?

Answers

1.   Custom is no longer very important as a source of law as most customs have established themselves as common law rules.

2.   Local custom is a usage which has obtained the force of law and is binding within a particular area. General custom relates to a trade or commercial practice and is not restricted to a particular locality.

3.   Conventional usage unlike custom has not attained the binding effect of a rule of law but is binding by agreement of both parties unless expressly excluded.

4.   Common law is law created by judges as a result of litigation. Custom is law which arises as a result of long practice and which satisfies the tests that establish custom.

Figure 3.1 — The structure of the EC

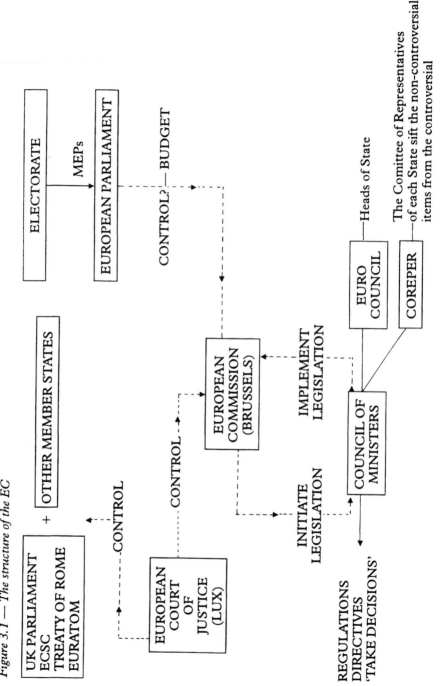

4 STATUTORY INTERPRETATION AND CONSTRUCTION

1 Introduction

The English courts are often faced with the task of determining the exact meaning of a piece of legislation and whether a particular activity or person's conduct falls within the scope of that piece of legislation. The task of the courts in these circumstances is to place a particular 'interpretation' or 'construction' on a piece of legislation. Interpretation is simply the process whereby a meaning is assigned to the words in a statute. Construction is the process whereby uncertainties or ambiguities in the words of a statute are resolved. Draftsmen cannot visualise all future developments and may forget to make provision for a current situation hence the need for statutory interpretation and construction.

There are two major types of problem. First, there is ambiguity. Ambiguity arises through an error in drafting whereby words used in a statute are found to be capable of bearing two or more literal meanings (see *Pharmaceutical Society of Great Britain* v *Boots Cash Chemists (Southern) Ltd* (1953), discussed in chapter 7, concerning the words 'offer for sale').

Secondly, there is uncertainty. Uncertainty occurs where the words of a statute are intended to apply to various factual situations and the courts are called upon to decide whether or not the set of facts before them amounts to a factual situation envisaged by the Act. For example what is 'an accident arising out of and in the course of his employment'?

There are three so-called rules of interpretation which the judges follow or which they say they follow (although sometimes the courts are inconsistent with the rules even amongst themselves):

(a) literal rule;
(b) golden rule;
(c) mischief rule.

There is also a fourth approach called the purposive approach.

There are also aids to interpretation:

(a)   The Interpretation Act 1978 e.g., the masculine gender includes female, singular includes plural (see in particular s. 5 of and sch. 1 to that Act).

(b)   The interpretation section in the Act itself. This applies to all parts unless a contrary intention appears in the statute.

(c)   'Precedent' — earlier decisions on interpretation of particular words in a statute.

2   The rules of interpretation

2.1   The literal rule

The basic rule of statutory interpretation is the literal rule which states that Parliament's intention must be found by interpreting the words used in their ordinary literal or grammatical sense in context.

If the words of the statute can be interpreted as suggested above, then a judge must give effect to that interpretation even though that interpretation produces an absurd or unjust result. In *IRC* v *Hinchey* (1960) the House of Lords was faced with the interpretation of the Income Tax Act 1952. A person not filling in his tax form properly lost £20 and treble the tax he ought to pay under the Act. This ought to mean treble the difference and not treble the whole tax. The House of Lords held the latter to be the case (this was later rectified by statute). The House of Lords made the following points:

(a)   give a word its common or ordinary meaning if it applies generally to people;

(b)   if the word applies to business then interpret it as business people understand it;

(c)   apply the meaning as understood at the time of its enactment.

The court's first task was to apply the literal rule to see if a decision could be reached. However, since the decision in that case, judges have become more flexible in their approach to statutory interpretation with a resulting shift away from a rigid application of the literal rule. Today the judges are prepared to ignore the literal rule altogether and have taken a 'purposive' approach to interpretation. For example, in some recent tax cases where the literal rule has normally been adhered to the change in attitude is quite evident. In the case of *W. T. Ramsay Ltd* v *IRC* (1981) (involving tax avoidance/evasion), Lord Wilberforce said that when a taxing Act has to be construed the courts are not confined to literal interpretations. They may, indeed should, be considered within the context and scheme of the relevant Act as a whole and its purpose should be regarded.

2.2   The golden rule

In the circumstances where the interpretation of the statute according to the literal meaning of the words produces absurdity, repugnancy or inconsistency with the rest of the statute, the golden rule may be used. The operation of the golden rule is explained by Parke B in *Gray* v *Pearson* (1857):

> I have been long and deeply impressed with the wisdom of the rule now, I believe, universally adopted, at least in the courts of law in Westminster Hall, that in construing wills and indeed, statutes, and all written instruments, the grammatical and ordinary sense of the words is to be adhered to, unless that would lead to some absurdity, or some repugnance or inconsistency with the rest of the instrument, in which case the grammatical and ordinary sense of the words may be modified, so as to avoid the absurdity and inconsistency, but no farther.

Also note *R* v *Callan* (1872). The Offences against the Person Act 1861, s. 57 stated 'Whosoever, being married, shall *marry* any other person during the life of the former husband or wife' shall be guilty of an offence. The word marry permits alternative meanings i.e., to contract a valid marriage or go through a ceremony of marriage. Since the former would produce an absurd result, the latter must be applied.

Where a literal interpretation is rejected in favour of a more rational one then the golden rule is being applied in preference to the literal rule. In *Re Sigsworth* (1935) the golden rule was applied to prevent a murderer from taking on the intestacy of his victim, although he was, as her son, the sole 'issue' on a literal interpretation of the Administration of Estates Act 1925.

A criticism of the golden rule is that it is very subjective. The court reaches the conclusion that something is absurd by referring to things outside the statute. Judges may have different opinions as to what is absurd. Such subjectivity arguably takes judges beyond their judicial function.

2.3 The mischief rule

When the wording of the statute is ambiguous the literal and golden rules cannot be used to good effect. In such a case the judge may apply the mischief rule — this is sometimes referred to as the rule in *Heydon's case* (1584) as the rules for its application were formulated in that case. The rules are:

1. What was the law before the Act?
2. What was the defect in the law for which there was no provision?
3. What remedy did Parliament implement?
4. What was the purpose behind the Parliamentary remedy?

This gives the courts a considerable amount of licence.

Activity

Refer to the cases of *Corkery* v *Carpenter* (1951) and *Gorris* v *Scott* (1874) below, to see how the mischief rule has been used by the courts.

In *Corkery* v *Carpenter* (1951), Corkery was charged with being drunk in charge of a bicycle on a highway (and probably as a result with causing malicious damage to a police cell). He was wheeling and not riding the bicycle.

The relevant Act said 'drunk on any highway in charge of a carriage, horse, cow
...'. Was a bicycle a carriage? The Court held yes — a carriage can include any
vehicle for carrying persons or even goods.

In *Gorris* v *Scott* (1874) an Act of Parliament provided that when certain
livestock were carried by ship they should be carried in pens. The plaintiff's
sheep were swept overboard because there were no pens. The plaintiff sued the
shipowner on this basis. It was held that he had no cause of action because by
applying the mischief rule pens were to prevent the spread of disease not to
prevent animals being washed overboard. Therefore the mischief rule requires
the judges 'to make such construction as shall, suppress the mischief and
advance the remedy'.

2.4   Choosing the right rule of interpretation

There is no hard and fast rule telling the judges which rule of interpretation
they should use in a particular case. Traditionally judges have used the rule they
prefer. However, towards the middle of the nineteenth century as statutes
became more detailed the literal rule became popular. Its popularity waned in
the 1960s because of some of the absurd results its use produced. Around this
time signs appeared that a completely new method of interpreting statutes was
gaining favour in the courts, this has become known as the purposive approach
(see para. 2.5). It should also be remembered that the aim of the golden rule
and mischief rule is to discover Parliament's intention from what Parliament
has said, not what it meant to say or would have said if confronted with the
present situation. In the final analysis the rules are limited to giving effect to the
words of the statute. A judge cannot attribute to Parliament an intention which
Parliament never had as this would amount to a usurpation of Parliament's
function.

Self check questions

1.   What is the difference between interpreting a statute and construing a
statute?
2.   Give a brief description of the literal, golden and mischief rules.
3.   How does a judge know which rule of interpretation to use?
4.   What is the main limit placed upon the use of the golden and mischief rules?

Answers

1.   *Interpretation* is simply the process whereby a meaning is assigned to the
words in the statute. *Construction* is the process whereby uncertainties or
ambiguities in a statute are resolved.
2.   *Literal rule* — words of the statute are given their ordinary and literal
meaning.

Golden rule — words of the statute are given their ordinary and literal
meaning but if this results in absurdity the ordinary and literal meaning is
modified to avoid the absurdity.

Mischief rule — interprets the statute by looking at the law before the Act,
looking at the mischief which the Act was designed to deal with and
interpreting the Act to remedy the mischief.

3. The judge is free to choose whichever rule he thinks best in the circumstances.

4. The golden and mischief rules are limited to discovering Parliament's intention from what Parliament has said, not what it meant to say or would have said if confronted with the present case.

2.5   *The purposive approach*

The purposive approach is in its infancy in England and advocates the inclusion of statements of purpose in statutes. This statement of purpose is to be included in the Bill rather than the preamble. This approach is favoured by English judges and by some Commonwealth parliaments e.g., both New Zealand and Australia have included statements of purpose in some of their recent legislation. However, attempts to introduce such an approach have met with opposition in the English Parliament. Attempts in 1980 and 1981 to introduce an Interpretation of Legislation Bill by Lord Scarman ended in defeat. The judges want a more liberal purposive approach, the parliamentary draftsmen and the civil servants want to retain the literal approach. Thus we have the 'literalists' drafting in parliament and the 'liberalists' interpreting in the courts.

The conclusions reached by Lord Renton writing on the subject in 1982 were as follows:

(a)   The words used should always be considered in their broadest statutory context.

(b)   Fiscal statutes are a special case. They are construed strictly and taxpayers are given the benefit of the doubt. Detailed provisions are necessary but they should be made easier to understand by broad statements of intention.

(c)   The intention of Parliament should be clearly expressed in legislation and should not have to be gleaned from other sources, such as Hansard or Law Commission and other Reports.

(d)   That intention should, where necessary, be expressed in purpose clauses.

(e)   The Purpose rule should prevail over other rules.

(f)   It should become statutory so as to resolve the conflict between the judiciary and the draftsmen. Ministerial directions are unsuitable; they could be changed too easily and this would lead to uncertainty.

Lord Denning describes his approach to statutory interpretation in his book *The Discipline of Law* (Butterworths, 1979) pp. 9-10. The relevant extract is set out below.

In almost every case on which you have to advise you will have to interpret a statute. There are stacks and stacks of them. Far worse for you than for me. When I was called in 1923 there was one volume of 500 pages. Now in 1978 there are three volumes of more than 3,000 pages. Not a single page but it can give rise to argument. Not a single page but the client will turn to you and say: 'What does it mean?' The trouble lies with our methods of drafting. The principal object of the draftsman is to achieve certainty — a laudable object in itself. But in pursuit of it, he loses sight of the equally important object — clarity. The draftsman — or draftswoman — has conceived certainty: but has brought forth obscurity; sometimes even absurdity.

Books and books have been written upon the interpretation of statutes. All for the old hand. Not one for the beginner. Maxims are given to help. They are called 'Rules of Construction'. Have recourse to them when they suit your case, but do it with discretion. You will sometimes discover that if you find a maxim or rule on your side, your opponent will find one on his side to counteract it.

Beyond doubt the task of the lawyer — and of the judge — is to find out the intention of Parliament. In doing this, you must, of course, start with the words used in the statute: but not end with them — as some people seem to think. You must discover the meaning of the words. I have known statutes where there is no discernible meaning. Then we can say with the King in Alice in Wonderland: 'If there's no meaning in it, that saves a world of trouble, you know, as we needn't try to find any'. But in most cases there is some meaning: so we have to go on as the King did: 'And yet I don't know', he went on, 'I seem to see some meaning in it after all'.

3   Other aids to interpretation and construction

In addition to the rules discussed above the following rules are also available to the courts to aid them in their interpretation and construction of statutes.

3.1   Canons of construction

3.1.1   Noscitur a sociis — each word is looked at in relation to its section and each section in relation to the other section. In *Beswick* v *Beswick* (1967) the House of Lords held that s. 56(1) and s. 205(1) of the Law of Property Act 1925 could not be read together to enable a third party to sue on a contract to which they were not a party. Section 205(1) applied 'unless the context otherwise requires'; s. 56(1) was in a part of the Act relating to real property only and not to 'anything in action'.

3.1.2   Ejusdem generis rule   A few words are used to create a genus followed by a general expression such as 'or other place' — this extends the application of the Act to all circumstances within the genus created. An example of this is the case of *Powell* v *Kempton Park Racecourse* (1899). An Act prohibited the keeping of a house, office, room or other place for betting. There was a open air betting ring at Kempton. The House of Lords held that the genus created did not include open air places and betting in such circumstances was therefore legal.

3.1.3   Expressio unius est exclusio alterius   The mention of one thing emphasises the exclusion of other things. Also a list of things emphasises the absence of a thing, hence inclusion emphasises exclusion.

These rules of construction are often used by judges as it suits them since they are often difficult to reconcile with each other.

3.2   Presumptions

A presumption is something which is presumed to be the case unless there is clear evidence to the contrary or where reasons of policy override the application of the presumption. The following are relevant to statutory interpretation:

(a)   An Act applies only to the UK.

(b)   The Crown is not bound by an Act of Parliament unless specifically stated.

(c)   There is a presumption against alteration of the common law — certain fundamental principles are not to be changed unless statute specifically states so.

(d)   A presumption against the restriction of the liberty of an individual and the deprivation of property without compensation.

(e)   A requirement of *mens rea* (guilty mind) for criminal liability unless clear words of the statute provide otherwise. The case of *Sweet* v *Parsley* (1970) concerned an appeal by a schoolteacher convicted of being concerned with the management of premises being used for smoking cannabis. She had simply let property to students and occasionally called to collect the rent. The appeal was allowed because she had no *mens rea* and there was a presumption that it was required. Contrast the case of *Hobbes* v *Winchester Corporation* (1910) in which it was held that the accused could be convicted if unfit meat was sold in his butcher's shop whether he had *mens rea* or not. Here considerations of policy and the public well-being overrode the application of the presumption and liabiity was strict, i.e., a person can be guilty *with* or *without* a guilty mind.

(f)   A presumption against the retrospective effect of an Act, i.e., an Act is presumed not to affect events which happened prior to its coming into force.

(g)   There is a presumption against the infringement of international law.

3.3   Intrinsic aids

These are used for guidance only if the words of the Act are unclear or ambiguous. For example, the long title is part of the Act and can be referred to for guidance as can the short title (e.g., 'this Act may be cited as the Ancient Monuments and Archaeological Areas Act 1979') which may help us to establish Parliament's intention.

3.4   Casus omissus

This basically means that courts cannot legislate and fill in gaps in an Act. This is however a controversial issue and it has been argued that the courts do this. It has been described as 'naked usurpation of the legislative function under the thin disguise of interpretation'. It is Parliament's function to legislate: that of the courts to interpret.

3.5   Extrinsic aids

These would include such things as international conventions, Parliamentary debates and statements, Royal Commission and Parliamentary Committee reports. Opinions vary as to their relevance; they are often called *travaux préparatoires* and the rules as to their use are much more restrictive. In *Letang* v *Cooper* (1965) Lord Denning said that it is legitimate to look at reports of committees to find out the mischief to be remedied but that the judge must not be influenced by its recommendations. In the recent House of Lords decision of *Pepper* v *Hart* (1993) the court referred to the official reports of Parliamentary debates (Hansard) to assist it in the interpretation of a tax statute. However, in this case Lord Mackay of Clashfern LC warned about the use of such assistance indicating that he felt it would lead to an increase in litigation inasmuch as it created more scope for argument.

Self check questions
1.   Describe the three canons of construction.
2.   List three presumptions which may apply when construing a statute.
3.   Explain the difference between the application of intrinsic and extrinsic aids to construction and interpretation.

Answers
1.   (a)   *Noscitur a sociis* — each word is looked at in relation to its section and each section in relation to the other section.
       (b)   *Ejusdem generis rule* — a few words are used to create a genus followed by a general expression such as 'or other place' — this extends the application of the Act to all circumstances within the genus created.
       (c)   *Expressio unius est exclusio alterius* — The mention of one thing emphasises the exclusion of other things.
2.   (a)   An Act applies only to the UK.
       (b)   The Crown is not bound by an Act of Parliament unless specifically stated.
       (c)   There is a presumption against alteration of the common law — certain fundamental principles are not to be changed unless statute specifically states so.
       (d)   A presumption against the restriction of the liberty of an individual and the deprivation of property without compensation.
       (e)   A presumption that *mens rea* (guilty mind) is required for criminal liability unless the clear words of the statute provide otherwise.
3.   Intrinsic aids are used for guidance if the words of the Act are unclear. They are contained in the Act itself e.g., the long title to the Act can be used to explain Parliament's intention. Extrinsic aids include such things as a record of the Parliamentary debate during the passing of the Act. The use of extrinsic aids is very restricted as they do not form part of the lesiglation.

4   The interpretation of EC legislation

Community legislation is drafted in terms of broad principle, leaving the courts to supply the detail by giving effect, in particular cases, to the general intention of the institution that has enacted the instrument in question.

An example of the different methods of drafting is shown in a comparison of two similar clauses, one from the UK, the other from the French Civil Code:

Sale of Goods Act 1979, s. 41

(1)   Subject to this Act, the unpaid seller of goods who is in possession of them is entitled to retain possession of them until payment or tender of the price in the following cases—

(a)   where the goods have been sold without any stipulation as to credit;
(b)   where the goods have been sold on credit, but the term of credit has expired;
(c)   where the buyer becomes insolvent.

(2)   The seller may exercise his right of lien notwithstanding that he is in possession of the goods as agent or bailee or custodier for the buyer.

Civil Code

1612   The seller is not bound to deliver the property if the buyer does not pay the price for it, unless the seller has granted him time for payment.
1613   He shall also have no duty of time for payment, if after the sale the buyer has become bankrupt or insolvent so that the seller is in imminent danger of losing the price, unless the buyer gives him security for payment on the due date.

The difference in drafting is clear and EC legislation is drafted in a similar way to the Civil Code on Sale of Goods. Hence, within the EC the golden, mischief and purposive approaches are very important. It is clear that an application of the literal rule would be inappropriate here because it would not give effect to the spirit of the code.

Clearly there is a fundamental difference in the approach to drafting and interpretation of legislation as between the UK and the EC. In the EC, preambles stating the purpose of legislation are extremely important unlike the attitude displayed toward them by the English Parliament.

Activity
Read the decision in *H. P. Bulmer Ltd* v *J. Bollinger SA* (1974) for an illustration of the principles of interpretation used when construing EC legislation.

5 JUDICIAL PRECEDENT

1 Judicial precedent and the courts

All decisions by judges on questions of law are precedents, but the value and weight of a precedent depends on a variety of factors. The most important of these factors is the seniority of the court which decided the case. The hierarchy of courts (see figures 5.1 and 5.2) and the rules of the doctrine of precedent are central to the English legal system; for the system proceeds on the basis that decisions made on questions of law by higher courts are binding on judges of lower courts.

The decisions of the House of Lords are therefore binding on all other courts, though since a 1966 Practice Direction they are no longer binding on the House itself. This means that once the House of Lords has pronounced on a question of law the matter is settled either until they change their minds or until both Houses of Parliament change the law. The decisions of the Court of Appeal are binding on all lower courts *and* are generally also binding on the Court of Appeal itself. But other courts do not bind themselves.

Being bound by a decision means that a future court must follow the decision of the earlier court if the material facts are substantially similar. Judges will also normally follow precedents that are not technically binding (e.g., decisions of courts lower in the hierarchy or decisions of American or Commonwealth courts). The precedent is then said to be persuasive. Frequently there are not one but many precedents that the court has to consider — often pointing in contradictory directions. The judge then arrives at the applicable rule of law by analysing the factual situations in the earlier cases and considering the reasoning of the earlier judges.

Under the English system, the principles of the law are normally worked out slowly through individual decisions from which general principles gradually emerge. Often the build-up takes decades before a creative judge sees that the narrow rules of several individual cases can be restated in a form to give expression to a general rule.

Figure 5.1   Hierarchy of the civil courts

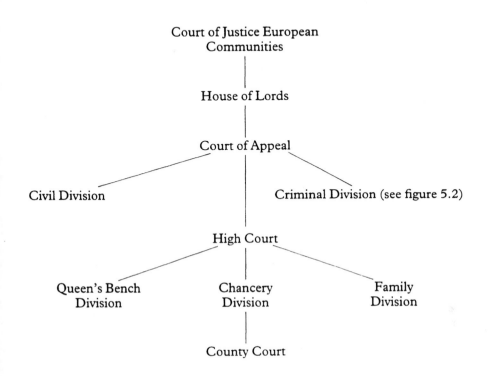

Court of Justice European
Communities

House of Lords

Court of Appeal

Civil Division   Criminal Division (see figure 5.2)

High Court

Queen's Bench   Chancery   Family
Division   Division   Division

County Court

Figure 5.2   Hierarchy of the criminal courts

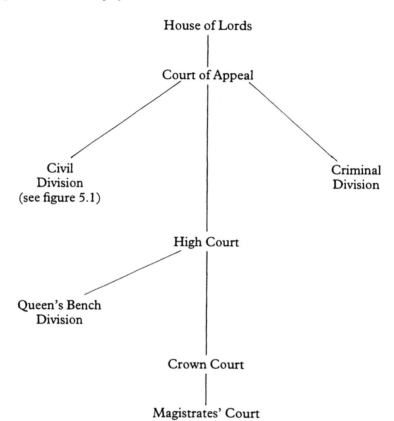

2   *Stare decisis:* The nature of judicial precedent

This is basically the doctrine that judges are bound to follow a previous decision if the facts before them are the same or similar to those in the earlier case. The name of this doctrine is *stare decisis* which means 'let the decision stand'.

2.1   *Ratio decidendi*

The *ratio decidendi* is the rule of law contained in the decision of the court in a case. The 'ratio' comprises the material facts and the rule of law applied to those facts. It is the *ratio decidendi* that is the binding element in the case.

Consequently it is misleading to talk about a 'decision' in a case being binding just as it is not correct to regard a 'decision' as being overruled. It is not the decision that binds anymore than it is the decision that is overruled. The really important element in the case is the *ratio decidendi* which is the rule of law which has to be distilled from the decision. For this reason it is important to be able to analyse a decision and isolate from it the *ratio decidendi*. Every decision has the following basic ingredients:

(a)   The finding of material facts. These facts may be direct and inferential. An inferential finding of fact is the inference which the judge (or jury if there is one) draws from the direct or obvious facts. For example, in a case involving an allegation of negligent driving the direct facts are the speed of a vehicle, the length of skid marks and the state of the road. From these direct facts the jury may infer negligence;

(b)   a statement of the principles of law applicable to the legal problems raised by the facts; and

(c)   the judgment based on the combined effect of (a) and (b).

For the purposes of the parties to the case (c) is the important element in the decision. This is the material element as it determines their rights and liabilities in relation to the subject matter of the action. However, for the purposes of judicial precedent (b) is the vital element in the decision. This is the *ratio decidendi*. Thus the *ratio decidendi* may be defined as the statement of law applied to the legal problems raised by the facts as found, upon which the decision is based.

The other two elements in the case are not of a binding nature. The judgment (c) is not binding on later courts; it is only binding on the parties themselves in the present case. The findings of fact (a) are not binding on later courts. This means that even where the direct facts of an earlier case appear to be identical to those of the case before the court, the judge or jury is not bound to draw the same inference as that drawn in the earlier case.

Not every single statement of law uttered by the judge in a case is binding. To be binding and amount to a *ratio decidendi* the statement of law must be based on the facts as found in the case. Other statements of law are superfluous and are called *obiter dictum* which means something said by the way.

2.2   Obiter dictum

A statement of legal principle is *obiter* if it relates to facts which were not found to exist in the case or, if found were not material to the *ratio decidendi*. Dissenting judgments are *obiter*. These arise where a number of judges hear a case and one of them disagrees with the others. He delivers a dissenting judgment. The majority judgment becomes the *ratio decidendi* and the dissenting judgment becomes *obiter dicta*.

All *obiter dicta* are not binding but only persuasive. Examples of *obiter dicta* are found in two famous cases. In *Central London Property Trust Ltd* v *High Trees House Ltd* (1947), Denning J's statement of promissory estoppel was *obiter* since it applied to a set of facts which were not found to exist in the case. (This case is discussed fully in ch. 7.) An example of the second type of *obiter* (dissenting judgments) is the notable instance of Denning LJ's dissenting judgment in *Candler* v *Crane Christmas & Co.* (1951), where he stated that there was liability for a negligent misstatement resulting in pure economic loss. Interestingly enough this proposition was later accepted by the House of Lords in *Hedley Byrne & Co. Ltd* v *Heller and Partners Ltd* (1964).

There are sometimes problems in determining what is *obiter* and what is *ratio*. In some cases all the judges may reach the same decision but give different reasons. Sometimes a judge may dissent from the majority decision but the majority each give differing reasons for their decision. These difficulties arise where a case is argued on more than one ground. Sometimes the court decides the issue on one ground only, leaving the other grounds undecided.

Activity
The Times newspaper has a section on court cases. Try to look at these regularly and see if you can isolate the *ratio decidendi* of any of the cases reported there.

Self check questions
1.   How important is the hierarchy of the courts to the doctrine of judicial precedent?
2.   Explain the meaning of '*ratio decidendi*' and '*obiter dicta*'.
3.   How is the *ratio decidendi* arrived at in a case?

Answers
1.   The hierarchy of the courts is fundamental of precedent, without it the doctrine could not operate.
2.   The *ratio decidendi* is the statement of law applied to the legal problems raised by the facts as found, upon which the decision is based.
    The *obiter dicta* is a statement of legal principle which relates to facts which were not found to exist in the case, or if found were found not to be material.
3.   The *ratio decidendi* is arrived at by applying the relevant principle of law to the facts raised by the case.

3   Literary sources of judicial precedent

The reporting of cases is fundamental to the doctrine of judicial precedent, obviously because they record decisions. Early reports were sporadic and sometimes inaccurate. In the late nineteenth century the 'semi-official' law reports were begun. The close nexus between law reporting and the doctrine of judicial precedent is evidenced by the fact that the modern doctrine of binding precedent was formulated only when an integrated system of law reporting evolved. Other reliable and quickly reported series of law reports are published like the All England Law Reports and the Weekly Law Reports, both of which appear weekly. Lloyds of London also report important decisions relating to insurance, shipping and the international sale, finance and carriage of goods. There are specialist reports such as Simon's Tax Cases and Butterworths' Company Law Cases.

Only important decisions are reported so that no more than ten per cent of all cases in the Supreme Court are reported. However, a copy of the transcript of every case is kept in an official library. Recently many unreported cases have been included in legal databases on computerised systems of legal information retrieval such as Eurolex and Lexis. However the courts have recently expressed disapproval of barristers quoting these cases too often in court. Too many precedents obscure basic principles of law. On the other hand the choice of which cases to report is still somewhat haphazard.

4 Judicial precedent and legislation

As already discussed above most new law is created by Parliament or subordinate or autonomous bodies in the form of legislation. Parliament is supreme but the disadvantages of legislation as a source of law is that statutes require interpretation by judges and these interpretations are in themselves judicial precedents. As a result it is an over-simplification to regard legislation as superior to precedent as a source of law. On the other hand many statutory changes to the law come about because of unpopular court decisions, particularly unpopular House of Lords decisions. Unpopular can also mean unpopular with the Government. For example, a recent House of Lords decision held that scholarships awarded to children of employees were not taxable as emoluments of employment. The Finance Act 1983 makes them chargeable to income tax.

5 The hierarchy of the courts and judicial precedent

In this discussion the word 'decision' will be used to indicate *ratio decidendi*.

5.1 Court of Justice of the European Communities
This is the ultimate court on the law of the EC e.g., the interpretation of the EC Treaty and EC Directives, Decisions and Regulations. However, this court does not observe a doctrine of binding precedent and does not regard itself as bound by its previous decisions — although it does lean in favour of consistency with its previous decisions.

5.2 The House of Lords
A decision of the House of Lords binds all courts inferior to it. But it can depart from a previous decision of its own where it appears right to do so. See *Murphy v Brentwood District Council* (1990) where the House of Lords overruled a recent decision of its own.

5.3 The Court of Appeal
The Court of Appeal is bound by the decision of the House of Lords. It is also bound by previous Court of Appeal decisions except:

(a) Where two of its previous decisions conflict, the decision not followed will be deemed to be overruled.

(b) The court must refuse to follow a previous decision of its own which though not expressly overruled, is inconsistent with a later House of Lords decision.

(c) The court need not follow a previous decision of its own if that decision was reached *per incuriam* i.e., a relevant statute or precedent was overlooked or misunderstood in that previous decision.

This rule and the three exceptions to it was settled by the Court of Appeal in *Young* v *Bristol Aeroplane Co. Ltd* (1944). Note also that the Criminal Division of the Court of Appeal may also depart from its own previous decision if it thinks that the law has been 'misapplied or misunderstood'.

5.4   Divisional courts
These are bound by decisions of the House of Lords and of the Court of Appeal except where a Court of Appeal decision is *per incuriam*. The divisional court is also bound by its own previous decisions but the same exceptions apply as in the Court of Appeal.

5.5   High Court judges
A High Court judge sitting at first instance is bound by the decisions of the courts mentioned above, but he is not bound by decisions of another High Court judge sitting at first instance, although he will treat such a decision as strong persuasive authority and will only refuse to follow it if he is convinced that it is wrong, and with a clear statement of the reasons for doing so.

5.6   Other courts
County courts, circuit judges and Recorders in the Crown Court, magistrates' courts and other inferior tribunals are bound by the decisions of all the courts mentioned above and by High Court judges sitting alone. The decisions of one of these courts are not binding on another mainly because they are not reported.

6   The application of judicial precedent: its advantages and disadvantages

Judicial precedent is important; it makes judge-made law certain but at the same time it puts a brake on its development (hence the need for legislation to revise substantive rules of law).

The advantages of the precedent system are said to be certainty, precision and flexibility. Legal certainty is achieved, in theory at least, in that, if the legal problem raised has been solved before, the judge is bound to adopt that solution. Precision is achieved by the sheer volume of reported cases containing solutions to innumerable factual situations arising in any particular branch of the law. No code of statute, no matter how carefully drafted, could anticipate the legal problems which these variations of fact may promote. Consequently, the judge in a continental legal system must generally decide cases on the basis of broad principles. Finally, flexibility is achieved by the possibility of decisions being overruled and by the possibility of distinguishing and confining the operation of decisions which appear unsound, the latter process being of particular importance.

7   Distinguishing precedents

As stated above the courts can get around precedent by distinguishing a case on its facts. In a House of Lords case, facts A and B exist and principle X applies.

A High Court judge in a case where facts A, B and E exist may distinguish the case before him because of fact E which he finds material or from which he infers a finding of fact material and apply principle Y.

The obvious disadvantages of the system are its inherent rigidity, which may occasionally cause hardship, and the vast and ever-increasing bulk of reported cases to which the court must refer to determine what is the law, since, as already emphasised, an excess of case law can obscure basic principles. There is also the problem of the 'accidents of litigation'.

As opposed to overruling by statute, judicial overruling operates retrospectively, which may have the effect of disturbing financial interests and vested rights generally. For this reason the courts are reluctant to overrule a previous decision unless they consider it is clearly wrong. In this sense the doctrine is a brake on the law. However, where commercial and business practice has developed ahead of the law the courts are often unwilling to allow precedent to act as an archaic restraint. Indeed it is often in the field of commercial development that the courts are most willing to alter doctrine and depart from precedent expounding new or wider principles of law as they do so:

Miliangos v *George Frank (Textiles) Ltd*
[1976] AC 443

LORD WILBERFORCE: If I am faced with the alternative of forcing commercial circles to fall in with a legal doctrine which has nothing but precedent to commend it or altering the doctrines so as to conform with what commercial experience has worked out, I know where my choice lies. The law should be responsive as well as, at times, enunciatory, and good doctrines can seldom be divorced from sound practice.

Therefore business or commercial efficacy is often used as a reason for departing from precedent as well as for implying terms into business contracts.

8 New law

Essentially, judicial decisions are declaratory of the common law, merely applying existing law to new situations. However, if there is no relevant statement of judicial precedent on a particular point, as still happens occasionally, a judge decides the case in accordance with general principles and his decision becomes the original source of a new rule since he is making law rather than applying it. Such cases are called cases of first impression. (See *Donoghue* v *Stevenson* (1932) discussed in chapter 15.)

9 Law reform

Every legal system faces the problem of the proper balance between the need for certainty and the need for flexibility. On the other hand, the law must be constant, so that people can arrange their affairs in reliance on it. This is of particular importance in commercial law where the effect on contracts and of business relationships needs to be settled to create a suitable trading climate. A system of law that is constantly changing creates confusion and bewilderment. On the other hand, there must be some way in which the law can change to keep pace with commercial practice.

Self check questions
1.   How important was a reliable organised system of law reporting to the development of the doctrine of precedent?
2.   The House of Lords decisions bind all courts inferior to it. Does it bind itself?
3.   Generally speaking the Court of Appeal is bound by its own decisions. What are the exceptions to this general rule?
4.   What are the main advantages of the doctrine of precedent?
5.   Explain what is meant by 'distinguishing precedents'.

Answers
1.   Reliable and organised law reporting was crucial to the development of the doctrine. The modern doctrine of precedent was only really formulated once a reliable system of law reporting had been established.
2.   No, the House of Lords can depart from a previous decision where it appears right to do so.
3.   (a)   Where two of its previous decisions conflict the decision not followed is deemed to be overruled.
        (b)   The Court must refuse to follow a previous decision of its own which though not expressly overruled is inconsistent with a later House of Lords decision.
        (c)   The court need not follow a previous decision of its own if the decision was reached *per incuriam* i.e., a relevant statute or precedent was overlooked or misunderstood in the previous decision.
4.   The main advantages of the doctrine are certainty, precision and flexibility.
5.   Distinguishing is the process of avoiding the binding nature of decisions which appear unsound.

Problem
Explain the importance of judicial precedent. Discuss its advantages and disadvantages.

Suggested answer
Judicial precedent stands on a par with legislation as far as its importance as a source of law is concerned. A large amount of English law is 'common law' created by judges. The doctrine of judicial precedent is one of the major distinctive characteristics of the English legal system and has built the body of English common law bit by bit.

There are two important reasons why the system of precedent operates as it does. The first is psychological, the other practical. The psychological reason is that anyone who is called upon to decide a dispute will prefer to justify his decision if he can by reference to what has been done in the past rather than to take the whole responsibility of decision on his own shoulders. The practical reason is that it is clearly desirable that decisions shall be uniform, for it is often asserted that it is more important that the law shall be certain than that it shall always promote justice in an individual case.

The creation of certainty in the law is always a great advantage, however at the same time it can be a disadvantage in that it can put a brake on the development of the law. This is the main disadvantage of the system. The other two main advantages are precision and flexibility. Precision is achieved by the sheer volume of reported cases containing solutions to innumerable factual situations arising in any particular branch of law. No code or statute, no matter how carefully drafted would anticipate the legal problems which these variations of fact may promote. Flexibility lies in decisions being overruled or distinguished and confirming the operation of decisions which appear unsound.

6 ALTERNATIVE METHODS OF RESOLVING LEGAL DISPUTES

1 Introduction

Not all legal disputes will be settled by bringing an action in a court of law. Many cases are instead dealt with by *tribunals* or resolved through the process of *arbitration*.

Tribunals and arbitration are used increasingly by businesses because they tend to be quicker and cheaper than the formal courts. Tribunals and arbitration are quite different processes and need to be considered separately.

2 Tribunals

A variety of tribunals exist to hear different disputes ranging from a mental health review tribunal which will sit to determine whether a patient should be released from a mental hospital to an industrial tribunal which will sit to determine statutory employment law disputes such as unfair dismissal or redundancy.

Industrial tribunals are important to businesses as they now handle the majority of employment law disputes between employers and employees. Consequently we will examine the operation of tribunals in detail using the industrial tribunal as our example.

2.1 Industrial tribunals

Industrial tribunals are regulated by the Employment Protection (Consolidation) Act 1978 and regulations that have been made under this Act by the Secretary of State for Employment.

The Act regulates the three main areas of the tribunals' business:

(a)   Composition of the tribunal.
(b)   Jurisdiction.
(c)   Procedure.

2.2   Composition
Industrial tribunals are composed of three members, a legally qualified chairperson and two lay members. The lay members are usually drawn from an employers' organisation and a trade union.

2.3   Jurisdiction
Industrial tribunals have a wide jurisdiction over statutory employment law disputes. They may hear disputes relating to, e.g., unfair dismissal, redundancy, sexual discrimination, maternity rights, racial discrimination and questions relating to written particulars of employment.

2.4   Procedure
An industrial tribunal sits in public unless it can be shown that it is in the interests of national security or confidentiality that it sits in private (Employment Protection (Consolidation) Act 1978, sch. 9, para. 1(5)). The hearing will not be conducted with the same degree of formality as a trial in a court and the tribunal will take into account whether or not the parties are legally represented in deciding whether, e.g., strict rules of evidence will be applied.

The decision of the tribunal may be unanimous or by a majority of members. The tribunal may award a variety of remedies depending on the exact nature of the claim but these include reinstatement of the employee, and compensation.

If either party is unhappy at the outcome of the proceedings at the tribunal they may appeal. Appeals are made to the Employment Appeal Tribunal (EAT). However, an appeal may only be made on questions of *law* not *fact*, i.e., where the appellant feels that the original industrial tribunal made an error in its interpretation or application of the law. The appellant may not challenge the original tribunal's findings of fact. Appeals from decisions of the EAT can be made to the Court of Appeal and from there to the House of Lords.

3   Arbitration

The principle underpinning arbitration is to effect a *binding resolution* of a dispute by an arbitrator.

The arbitrator's jurisdiction usually arises as a result of a clause in a contract between the parties. The parties agree that in the event of a dispute between them arising they will submit the matter to an arbitrator rather than a court of law.

Care is needed in the drafting of such a clause as the parties must not be attempting to oust the jurisdiction of the courts: any such clause would be declared void on the ground of public policy. Instead the arbitration clause should be a condition precedent to litigation in the courts, i.e., the parties are forced by the clause to submit the dispute to arbitration and only after an award has been made by the arbitrator may they commence proceedings in the court.

Such clauses are known as *Scott* v *Avery* clauses. If one party to an arbitration agreement breaches it by commencing court proceedings then the other party may plead the rule in *Scott* v *Avery* (1856) so as to have the proceedings struck out.

3.1   Procedure
The process of arbitration is governed by the Arbitration Acts 1950 and 1979. The Acts do not lay down procedures for the conduct of arbitration hearings but allow the arbitrator and the parties to agree the nature of the proceedings. This provides a flexible method of resolving the dispute.

3.2   Advantages of arbitration
The main advantages of arbitration over court proceedings are:

(a)   Proceedings are private.
(b)   In disputes of a specialised or technical nature an appropriately qualified expert can be appointed as arbitrator.
(c)   Proceedings are speedy, informal and flexible.
(d)   Proceedings are usually cheaper than court proceedings.

3.3   Disadvantage
Arbitration awards must be enforced by the courts as arbitrators have no powers to enforce the awards they make.

3.4   Appeals
The Arbitration Act 1979 allows a party to appeal to the High Court on a question of law, from there appeals lie to the Court of Appeal and the House of Lords.

Self check questions
1.   Why do many business people prefer to use tribunals or arbitration rather than the formal courts of law?
2.   What is the composition of an industrial tribunal?
3.   Over what employment matters does the tribunal enjoy jurisdiction?
4.   What is the effect of a *Scott* v *Avery* clause in a contract?
5.   List three advantages that arbitration is said to have over formal court proceedings.

Answers
1.   Tribunals and arbitration are preferred because they are usually both cheaper and quicker than proceedings in a court of law.
2.   It is composed of three members, a legally qualified chairperson and two lay members, one drawn from an employers' organisation and one from a trade union.
3.   It will enjoy jurisdiction over employment disputes e.g., unfair dismissal, redundancy.

4. The effect of such a clause is to force the parties to submit to arbitration as a condition precedent to litigation in the courts.

5. Any three of the following are correct:

   (a) Proceedings are private.

   (b) In disputes of a specialised or technical nature an appropriately qualified expert can be appointed as arbitrator.

   (c) Proceedings are speedy, informal and flexible.

   (d) Proceedings are usually cheaper than court proceedings.

7 FORMATION OF CONTRACT

1 Introduction

In English law in order for a contract to be binding four factors must be present: offer, acceptance, consideration and intention to create legal relations. Initially, we shall concentrate on the first two.

The devices of offer and acceptance have been used since the nineteenth century in order to decide whether there is agreement between the parties. However, the advent of standard forms and the way in which these forms were used by the potential contracting parties (the so called 'battle of forms' — see below) led to an alternative approach to agreement being suggested. In *Butler Machine Tool Co. Ltd* v *Ex-Cell-O Corporation (England) Ltd* (1979) it was suggested that the courts should look at the 'correspondence as a whole' in order to decide whether or not a contract has been formed. The House of Lords, however, in *Gibson* v *Manchester City Council* (1979) stated that this new approach should only be used in exceptional circumstances and that offer and acceptance are still appropriate.

2 Offer

2.1 Basic definitions

(a) *Offer:* An offer is an expression of willingness to contract made with the intention that it shall become binding on the person making it as soon as it is accepted by the person to whom it is addressed.

(b) *Offeror:* the person who makes the offer.

(c) *Offeree:* the person to whom the offer is made.

2.2 Distinction between offer and invitation to treat

The key factor in an offer is that of an 'intention to be bound' and this is usually shown by the wording: for example, 'I shall sell you this package for £20.00'.

However, sometimes the intention may not be present in which case the statement/correspondence (or whatever) may only be an 'invitation to treat'.

An invitation to treat has been defined as '... offers to negotiate ... receive offers ...'. The crucial distinction between an offer and an invitation to treat is that an offer once accepted creates a valid contract, whereas purporting to accept an invitation to treat does not create legal relations.

Self check questions
1.   What is the crucial factor in deciding whether something amounts to an offer?
2.   Why is it important to distinguish between an offer and an invitation to treat?

Answers
1.   The intention to be bound.
2.   An offer once accepted creates a legally binding contract. The same does not apply to the purported acceptance of an invitation to treat.

This distinction can be further explored by looking at four separate situations:

2.2.1   Auction sales   Section 57(2), Sale of Goods Act 1979 states: 'A sale by auction is complete when the auctioneer announces its completion by the fall of the hammer, or in other customary manner; and until the announcement is made any bidder may retract his bid'. Using our analysis the holding of an auction amounts merely to an invitation to treat and it is the bidder who makes the offer and the auctioneer who accepts it. The logic of this argument is shown by the decision in *Harris* v *Nickerson* (1873) which states that an advertisement indicating that an auction is to be held on a particular day merely amounts to an invitation to treat. Therefore, anybody who travels to it only to find that it has been cancelled cannot sue for breach of contract. It should be emphasised that the key to this principle concerns the proposed sale of an item at an auction, rather than the holding of the auction itself.

2.2.2   Display of goods for sale   What in law does the display of goods in a shop amount to? Two theories have been put forward: first, the display amounts to an offer which is accepted either when the shopper places the goods in his basket or when he indicates the desire to buy the goods. Or, secondly, the display merely amounts to an invitation to treat; therefore it is the shopper who makes the offer and it is for the shopkeeper to decide whether or not to accept the offer. The leading case on this question is:

Pharmaceutical Society of Great Britain v *Boots Cash Chemists (Southern) Ltd*
[1953] 1 QB 401

The defendants' branch shop, consisting of a single room, was adapted to the 'self-service' system. The room contained a chemist's department, under the control of a registered pharmacist, in which various drugs and proprietary medicines included, or containing substances included in Part I of the Poisons List compiled under section 17(1) of the Pharmacy and Poisons Act 1933, were displayed on shelves in packages or other containers, with the price marked on each. A customer, on entering the shop, was provided with a wire basket, and having selected from the shelves the articles which he wished to buy, put them in the basket and took them to the cashier's desk at one or other of the two exits, where the cashier stated the total price and received payment. The latter stage of every transaction involving the sale of a drug was supervised by the pharmacist in control of the department, who was authorised to prevent the removal of any drug from the premises.

In an action brought by the plaintiffs alleging an infringement by the defendants of section 18(1)(a)(iii) of the Pharmacy and Poisons Act, 1933, which requires the sale of poisons included in Part I of the Poisons List to be effected by or under the supervision of a registered pharmacist:

SOMERVELL LJ: The point taken by the plaintiffs is this: it is said that the purchase is complete if and when a customer going round the shelves takes an article and puts it in the receptacle which he or she is carrying, and that therefore, if that is right, when the customer comes to the pay desk, having completed the tour of the premises, the registered pharmacist, if so minded, has no power to say: 'This drug ought not to be sold to this customer.' Whether and in what circumstances he would have that power we need not inquire, but one can, of course, see that there is a difference if supervision can only be exercised at a time when the contract is completed. . . .

Whether the view contended for by the plaintiffs is a right view depends on what are the legal implications of this layout — the invitation to the customer. Is a contract to be regarded as being completed when the article is put into the receptacle, or is this to be regarded as a more organised way of doing what is done already in many types of shops — and a bookseller is perhaps the best example — namely, enabling customers to have free access to what is in the shop, to look at the different articles, and then, ultimately, having got the ones which they wish to buy, to come up to the assistant saying 'I want this'? The assistant in 999 times out of 1,000 says: 'That is all right', and the money passes and the transaction is completed . . . in the case of an ordinary shop, although goods are displayed and it is intended that customers should go and choose what they want, the contract is not completed until, the customer having indicated the articles which he needs, the shop-keeper, or someone on his behalf, accepts that offer. Then the contract is completed. I can see no reason at all, that being clearly the normal position, for drawing any different implication as a result of this layout.

The Lord Chief Justice, I think, expressed one of the most formidable difficulties in the way of the plaintiffs' contention when he pointed out that, if the plaintiffs are right, once an article has been placed in the receptacle the customer himself is bound and would have no right, without paying for the first article, to substitute an article which he saw later of a similar kind and which he perhaps preferred. I can see no reason for implying from this self-service arrangement any implication other than that which the Lord

Chief Justice found in it, namely, that it is a convenient method of enabling customers to see what there is and choose, and possibly put back and substitute, articles which they wish to have and then to go up to the cashier and offer to buy what they have so far chosen. On that conclusion the case fails, because it is admitted that there was supervision in the sense required by the Act and at the appropriate moment of time. For these reasons, in my opinion, the appeal should be dismissed.

The court in the above case clearly came down on the side of the second theory, that is the display of goods merely amounts to an invitation to treat. The court in making this decision was obviously taking into account the practicality of the situation and made a common sense decision.

Activity
When shopping in your local supermarket ask yourself whether all aspects of the shop fit into the decision in *Pharmaceutical Society* v *Boots*, for example, the cold meats/delicatessen counter.

2.2.3 Advertisements Advertisements pose some difficulty as to their nature and should be considered under two separate headings:

(a) *Bilateral contracts* — The essence of a bilateral contract is one of mutual exchange and negotiation. For example, suppose the following advertisement is placed in a newspaper: 'For sale: Volkswagen Polo (1993) model. Bargain at £4,500 o.n.o. Contact A. Seller'. The essence of such an advertisement is the start of a negotiating process between the seller and whoever responds to the advertisement. Therefore the law will treat it as an invitation to treat which is illustrated by:

Partridge v *Crittenden*
[1968] 1 WLR 1204

The appellant inserted an advertisement in a periodical, Cage and Aviary Birds *for April 13, 1967, containing the words 'Quality British ABCR . . . bramblefinch cocks, bramblefinch hens . . . 25s. each' which appeared under the general heading 'classified advertisements'. In no place was there any direct use of the words 'offers for sale'. In answer to the advertisement, T. wrote, enclosing a cheque for 25s., and asked that a hen be sent to him. The hen arrived wearing a closed ring which could be removed without injury to the bird.*

The appellant was charged with unlawfully offering for sale a bramblefinch hen contrary to section 6(1) of the Protection of Birds Act, 1954. The justices convicted him.

On appeal, the appellant contended that his advertisement was merely an invitation to treat and not an offer for sale. Held, allowing the appeal, that the advertisement inserted by the appellant under the title 'classified advertisements' was not an offer for sale but merely an invitation to treat; and that, accordingly, the appellant was not guilty of the offence charged.

LORD PARKER CJ: I think when one is dealing with advertisements and circulars unless they indeed come from manufacturers, there is business sense in their being construed as invitations to treat and not offers for sale. In a very different context in *Grainger & Son* v *Gough* Lord Herschell said dealing with a price-list:

> The transmission of such a price-list does not amount to an offer to supply an unlimited quantity of the wine described at the price named, so that as soon as an order is given there is a binding contract to supply that quantity. If it were so, the merchant might find himself involved in any number of contractual obligations to supply wine of a particular description which he would be quite unable to carry out, his stock of wine of that description being necessarily limited.

It seems to me accordingly that not only is it the law but common sense supports it.

Again in this case, as in the *Pharmaceutical Society* case above, the court is emphasising the 'business sense' of the situation. Added to this are the factors of supply and demand. It is clear from the judgment that the fact that demand might well exceed supply is a factor in holding the advertisement to be an invitation to treat rather than an offer.

(b) *Unilateral contracts* — The emphasis in such contracts moves away from exchange of promises to one of performance; therefore, if only performance is required for acceptance then the advertisement may well be construed as an offer. However, the essence of the definition of an offer should always be kept in mind — i.e., an intention to be bound — and consequently the wording of the advertisement is critical. The leading case on this concept is *Carlill* v *Carbolic Smoke Ball Co.* (1893). (NB. The case is also authority for the way in which an offer is accepted in a unilateral contract situation (see 4.4, below).)

Carlill v *Carbolic Smoke Ball Co.*
[1893] 1 QB 256

D issued an advert in which they offered to pay £100 to any person who contracted influenza after having used one of their smoke balls in a specified manner and for a specified period. P bought a smoke ball, on faith of the advert, and contracted influenza. Held: A contract was established and D were bound to pay £100.

BOWEN LJ: . . . Was it intended that the £100 should, if the conditions were fulfilled, be paid? The advertisement says that £100 is lodged at the bank for the purpose. Therefore, it cannot be said that the statement that £100 would be paid was intended to be a mere puff. I think it was intended to be understood by the public as an offer which was to be acted upon.

But it was said that was no check on the part of the persons who issued the advertisement, and that it would be an insensate thing to promise £100 to a person who used the smoke ball unless you could check or superintend his manner of using it. The answer to that argument seems to me to be that if a person chooses to make extravagant promises of this kind he probably does so because it pays him to make them, and, if he has made them, the extravagance of the promises is no reason in law why he should not be bound by them.

It was also said that the contract is made with all the world — that is, with everybody; and that you cannot contract with everybody. It is not a contract made with all the world. There is a fallacy of the argument. It is an offer made to all the world; and why should not an offer be made to all the world which is to ripen into a contract with anybody who comes forward and performs the condition? It is an offer to become liable to anyone who, before it is retracted, performs the conditions and, although the offer is made to the world, the contract is made with that limited portion of the public who come forward and perform the condition on the faith of the advertisement. It is not like cases in which you offer to negotiate, or you issue advertisements that you have got a stock of books to sell, or houses to let, in which case there is no offer to be bound by any contract. Such advertisements are offers to negotiate — offers to receive offers — offers to chaffer, as, I think, some learned judge in one of the cases has said. If this is an offer to be bound, then it is a contract the moment the person fulfils the condition . . .

The case is an important one as it clearly states that where there is an intention to be bound an advertisement can amount to an offer. The offer is made to the world at large and is only accepted by the people performing the conditions required.

2.2.4 Tenders The general principle is that where a person invites another to tender for a piece of work, that tender is an invitation to treat. Therefore the offer is made by the person who tenders for the work and it is for the person inviting the tenders to accept, or not, one of the tenders made. The cases, below, do show interesting divergence from this general principle.

Harvela Investments Ltd v Royal Trust Co. of Canada (CI) Ltd
[1985] 2 All ER 966

The plaintiff and the second defendant were rival offerors for a parcel of shares which would give effective control of a company to the plaintiff or to the second defendant, whichever was the successful offeror. The parcel of shares was held by the first defendants, the vendors, who invited both parties to submit by sealed offer or confidential telex a 'single offer' for the whole parcel by a stipulated date. The vendors stated in the invitation to bid that 'we bind ourselves to accept [the highest] offer' received by them which complied with the terms of the invitation. The invitation to bid further stated that interest was payable by the successful purchaser in the event of delay in completing the purchase, unless completion was unable to take place 'by reason of any delay on our [the vendors'] part'. The plaintiff tendered a bid of $2,175,000. The second defendant tendered a bid for '$2,100,000 or . . . $101,000 in excess of any other offer . . . expressed as a fixed monetary amount, whichever is the higher'. The vendors accepted the second defendant's bid, as being *a bid of $2,276,000, and entered into a contract with the second defendant for the sale of the parcel of shares. The vendors also informed the plaintiff of the terms of the second defendant's bid, whereupon the plaintiff commenced proceedings against the vendors and the second defendant, contending that the second defendant's bid was invalid.*

Held:

(a)   If a vendor of property chose to sell his property by calling for fixed bids from prospective purchasers then a referential bid, i.e., a bid framed by reference to the other bids and which depended on the other bids for its price to be ascertained, was invalid, since a referential bid was inconsistent with the purpose of a sale by fixed bidding, which was to provoke the best price which the prospective purchasers were prepared to pay regardless of what rival bidders were prepared to pay.

(b)   Whether an invitation from a vendor to prospective purchasers was to be construed as an invitation to participate in a fixed bidding sale or in an auction sale depended on the presumed intention of the vendor as deduced from the express provision of the invitation bid. The facts that the vendors had undertaken to accept the highest offer, that they had extended the same invitation to both parties and that they had insisted that offers were to be confidential were only consistent with a presumed intention to create an auction sale by means of referential bids, since those facts showed that the vendors had been anxious to ensure that a sale resulted from their invitation, that they had been desirous that no one else should have the opportunity of purchasing the shares and that they had been desirous that each prospective purchaser should put forward, in ignorance of the other bid, the best price he was prepared to pay. Accordingly, the second defendant had not been entitled to submit and the vendors had not been entitled to accept a referential bid.

It would seem that referential bids will be allowed only when the wording of the invitation to tender clearly states this to be the case; that is, a person who bids must be aware of this fact. The case also suggests that the person inviting tenders in this case was bound to accept the highest bid.

Blackpool and Fylde Aero Club Ltd v Blackpool Borough Council
[1990] 3 All ER 25

The council owned and managed an airport and raised revenue by granting a concession to an air operator to operate flights from the airport. The plaintiff club was granted the concession in 1975, 1978 and 1980. Shortly before the last concession was due to expire in 1983 the council sent invitations to tender to the club and six other parties, all of whom were connected with the airport. The invitations to tender stated that tenders were to be submitted in the envelope provided and were not to bear any name or mark which would identify the sender, and that tenders received after the date and time specified, namely 12 noon on 17 March 1983, would not be considered. Only the club and two other tenderers responded to the council's invitation. The club's tender was recorded as being received late and was not considered. The club brought an action against the council claiming damages for breach of contract contending that the council had warranted that if a tender was received by the deadline it would be considered and that the council had acted in breach of that warranty. The judge held tht the council had acted in breach of contract and negligently. The council appealed.

Held: In certain circumstances an invitation to tender could give rise to binding contractual obligations on the part of the inviter to consider tenders which conformed with the conditions of tender. Since tenders had been solicited by the council from selected parties, all of whom were known to the council, and since the council's invitation to tender prescribed a clear, orderly and familiar procedure, which included draft contract conditions available for inspection but not open to negotiation, a prescribed common form of tender, the supply of envelopes designed to preserve the absolute anonymity of tenderers and an absolute deadline, it was to be implied that if an invitee submitted a conforming tender before the deadline he would be entitled as a matter of contractual right to have his tender opened and considered along with any other tenders that were considered. It followed that the appeal would be dismissed.

The Court of Appeal in this case is not saying that the original tender amounted to an offer but that there was a second unilateral offer, running parallel to the original tender. This second obligation is a duty to consider the tender made due to the fact that the invitee followed the prescribed procedures in making its offer.

Self check questions
What is the status of the following advertisements?
1.   '£100 will be given to anybody walking from Preston to Lancaster on April 1st'.
2.   'For sale — a number of second-hand golf clubs. Contact J. Smith on Happytown 123'.

Answers
1.   The advertisement would be seen as offer. The words 'will be' indicate an intention to be bound and thus fit into the definition of an offer.
2.   The second advertisement would be construed as an invitation to treat. The words 'for sale' are not sufficient for an offer and added to this the supply and demand position are unclear.

Activity
Look through the classified advertisement section of your local paper and decide upon the legal status of the advertisements. Check the wording of any invitations to tender to see whether the principles from either of the two cases discussed apply.

3   Acceptance

Once an offer has been established the next question to be asked is whether the offer has been accepted. The following definition of acceptance shall be used: 'An acceptance is a final and unqualified expression of assent to the terms of an offer'. Two main problems arise in relation to acceptance: first, the question of 'unqualified expression of assent' and secondly, communication of acceptance.

3.1   Unqualified expression of assent

Here the position of counter-offers must be resolved. An illustration of this principle may be given: suppose A offers to sell B his car for £1,500. In reply B says 'I shall only give you £1,400'. What is the effect of B's counter-offer on A's original offer? In *Hyde* v *Wrench* (1840) the effect of the counter-offer was to destroy the original offer. Therefore any attempt to accept the original offer after this was not possible.

Hyde v *Wrench*
(1840) 49 ER 132

D, on the 6th June, offered in writing to sell his farm for £1,000; but P offered £950 which D on 27th June refused to accept. On 29th June P decided in fact to offer £1,000 but D refused to accept this. Held: There was no binding contract.

LORD LANGDALE MR: ... the plaintiff made an offer of his own, to purchase the property for £950, and he thereby rejected the offer previously made by the defendant. I think that it was not afterwards competent for him to revive the proposal of the defendant.

Therefore an acceptance must correspond exactly to the terms of the offer. If the acceptance contains varied or new terms it constitutes a counter-offer which has the effect of destroying the previous offer to which it relates. A counter-offer must be distinguished from a mere inquiry or request for information — such an inquiry does not effect the offer. In *Stevenson* v *McLean* (1880) the effect of the telegram requesting time to pay was held to be a mere inquiry and therefore did not affect the original offer. The distinction between a counter-offer/mere inquiry depends very much on the wording and therefore the two cases merely provide illustrations of the principles rather than a definitive answer.

Stevenson, Jacques and Co. v *McLean*
(1880) 5 QBD 346

The defendant, being possessed of warrants for iron, wrote from London to the plaintiffs at Middlesbrough asking whether they could get him an offer for the warrants. Further correspondence ensued, and ultimately the defendant wrote to the plaintiffs fixing 40s. per ton, net cash, as the lowest price at which he could sell, and stating that he would hold the offer open till the following Monday. The plaintiffs on the Monday morning at 9.42 telegraphed to the defendant: 'Please wire whether you would accept forty for delivery over two months, or if not, longest limit you could give.' The defendant sent no answer to this telegram, and after its receipt on the same day he sold the warrants, and at 1.25 p.m. telegraphed to the plaintiffs that he had done so. Before the arrival of his telegram to that effect, the plaintiffs having at 1 p.m. found a purchaser for the iron, sent a telegram at 1.34 p.m. to the defendant stating that they had secured his price. The defendant refused to deliver the iron, and thereupon the plaintiffs brought an action against him for non-delivery thereof. The jury found at the trial that the relation between the parties was that of buyer and seller, not of principal and agent.

LUSH J: ... It is apparent throughout the correspondence, that the plaintiffs did not contemplate buying the iron on speculation, but that their acceptance of the defendant's offer depended on their finding someone to take the warrants off their hands. All parties knew that the market was in an unsettled state, and that no one could predict at the early hour when the telegram was sent how the prices would range during the day. It was reasonable that, under these circumstances, they should desire to know before business began whether they were to be at liberty in case of need to make any and what concession as to the time or times of delivery, which would be the time or times of payment, or whether the defendant was determined to adhere to the terms of his letter; and it was highly unreasonable that the plaintiffs should have intended to close the negotiation while it was uncertain whether they could find a buyer or not, having the whole of the business hours of the day to look for one. Then again, the form of the telegram is one of inquiry. It is not 'I offer forty for delivery over two months'. Here there is no counter proposal. The words are, 'Please wire whether you would accept forty for delivery over two months, or, if not, the longest limit you would give.'

There is nothing specific by way of offer or rejection, but a mere inquiry, which should have been answered and not treated as a rejection of the offer. This ground of objection therefore fails.

4 Communication of acceptance

The question of communication is a complex topic and needs to be looked at under a number of headings:

4.1 General principle

The general principle is that 'An acceptance must be communicated to the offeror'. Using this principle it is clear that in bilateral contracts silence is not sufficient: *Felthouse* v *Bindley* (1862). As we shall see below the law is slightly different in relation to unilateral contracts.

A good illustration of the operation of this principle is instantaneous communication through the use of telex machines. Although there is in fact a slight delay between the message being sent and received, the law treats the communication as being instantaneous. The same arguments apply to communication by telephone but not to the postal service. In *Entores Ltd* v *Miles Far East Corporation* (1955) it was held that acceptance only took place when the message was received on the plaintiff's telex machine.

Entores Ltd v *Miles Far East Corporation*
[1955] 2 QB 327

The plaintiff company in London made an offer by telex to the agents in Holland of the defendant corporation, whose headquarters were in New York, for the purchase of a quantity of copper cathodes, and their offer was duly accepted by a communication received on the plaintiffs' telex machine in London.

The plaintiff company sought leave to serve notice of a writ on the defendant corporation in New York claiming damages for breach of the contract so made.

DENNING LJ: ... When a contract is made by post it is clear law throughout the common law countries that the acceptance is complete as soon as the letter is put into the post box, and that is the place where the contract is made. But there is no clear rule about contracts made by telephone or by telex. Communications by these means are virtually instantaneous and stand on a different footing.

Now take a case where two people make a contract by telephone. Suppose, for instance, that I make an offer to a man by telephone and, in the middle of his reply, the line goes 'dead' so that I do not hear his words of acceptance. There is no contract at that moment. The other man may not know the precise moment when the line failed. But he will know that the telephone conversation was abruptly broken off: because people usually say something to signify the end of the conversation. If he wishes to make a contract, he must therefore get through again so as to make sure that I heard. Suppose next, that the line does not go dead, but it is nevertheless so indistinct that I do not catch what he says and I ask him to repeat it. He then repeats it and I hear his acceptance. The contract is made, not on the first time when I do not hear, but only the second time when I do hear. If he does not repeat it, there is no contract. The contract is only complete when I have his answer accepting the offer.

Lastly, take the telex. Suppose a clerk in a London office taps out on the teleprinter an offer which is immediately recorded on a teleprinter in a Manchester office, and a clerk at that end taps out an acceptance. If the line goes dead in the middle of the sentence of acceptance, the teleprinter motor will stop. There is then obviously no contract. The clerk at Manchester must get through again and send his complete sentence. But it may happen that the line does not go dead, yet the message does not get through to London. Thus the clerk at Manchester may tap out his message of acceptance and it will not be recorded in London because the ink at the London end fails, or something of that kind. In that case, the Manchester clerk will not know of the failure but the London clerk will know of it and will immediately send back a message 'not receiving'. Then, when the fault is rectified, the Manchester clerk will repeat his message. Only then is there a contract. If he does not repeat it, there is no contract. It is not until his message is received that the contract is complete.

The same decision was reached by the House of Lords in *Brinkibon Ltd v Stahag Stahl und Stahlwarenhandelsgesellschaft mbH* (1983) however, *obiter* statements in the case suggested that the principle may not be an absolute one. Two examples need to be mentioned. First, it may be that the two parties contracting are from different sides of the world, consequently any acceptance would be received outside normal office hours. Depending upon the intention of the parties it could be that acceptance takes place when the communication is printed on the machine not when it is read by the offeror when the office opens in the morning.

Secondly, what happens if the communication of acceptance is not received? The principle would indicate then there is no contract but would that be the case if the offeree had sent the communication and the reason for it not being printed on the offeror's telex machine was due to a fault in the latter's machine? It can be argued that the courts in such a case would uphold a binding contract.

Self check questions
1. What is the general principle of communication of acceptance?
2. Give three examples of methods of acceptance to which the general principle applies.
3. X, in London, at 5.00 pm (assume GMT for all times) offers to sell Y in Australia a consignment of steel. Y at 4.00 am the next day, knowing that X's office will be shut, sends a telex to X accepting the offer which is correctly recorded on X's machine. X reads the acceptance at 9.00 am when the office is opened. When does acceptance take place?
4. A, in Preston, makes an offer to B, in Manchester. B sends a telex to A accepting the offer, but due to a fault in A's telex machine the message is not received. Is there a contract?

Answers
1. Acceptance must be communicated.
2. Telex, telephone and word of mouth.
3. The answer depends very much on the intention and commercial expectation of the parties. If the parties have dealt with each other before then acceptance would take place at 4.00 am when the message is sent and received.
4. If A knew there was a fault on his machine then it may well be that following *Brinkibon* (above) despite the message not being received acceptance has taken place.

4.2   Acceptance by post
Acceptance by post is an exception to the general principle of acceptance discussed above. The so-called postal rule is that a postal acceptance takes effect when the letter is posted. The first authority for this rule is the decision in *Adams v Lindsell* (1818). However, as the postal rule is an exception to the general principle of communication it is hedged around with a number of prerequisites. The first of these is that it must be reasonable to use the post as a method of communication. Read the extract below:

Henthorn v Fraser
[1892] 2 Ch 27

H, who lived at Birkenhead, called at the office of a land society in Liverpool, to negotiate for the purchase of some houses belonging to them. The secretary signed and handed to him a note giving him the option of purchase for 14 days at £750.

On the next day the secretary posted to H a withdrawal to the offer. This withdrawal was posted between 12 and 1 p.m., and did not reach Birkenhead till after 5 p.m. In the meantime H had, at 3.50 p.m., posted to the secretary an unconditional acceptance of the offer, which was delivered in Liverpool after the society's office had closed, and was opened by the secretary on the following morning:

LORD HERSCHELL: I should prefer to state the rule thus: Where the circumstances are such that it must have been within the contemplation of the parties that, according to the ordinary usages of mankind, the post might be used as a means of communicating the acceptance of an offer, the acceptance is complete as soon as it is posted. It matters not in which way the proposition be stated, the present case is in either view within it.

Therefore it could be argued that if the original offer was made by telex for the sake of speed then it may not be reasonable to use the post as the mode of communication. In such a case acceptance would only take place when the letter was received and not posted.

Secondly, the offeror can exclude the operation of the postal rule by the wording of the offer. In *Holwell Securities Ltd* v *Hughes* (1974) the wording was held sufficient to exclude the operation of the postal rule.

Holwell Securities Ltd v *Hughes*
[1974] 1 All ER 161

By cl 1 of an agreement dated 19th October 1971 made between the defendant of the one part and the plaintiffs of the other, the plaintiffs were granted an option to purchase certain freehold property from the defendant. Clause 2 of the agreement provided: 'The said option shall be exercisable by notice in writing to the (defendant) at any time within six months from the date hereof . . .'. On 14th April 1972 the plaintiffs' solicitors wrote a letter to the defendant giving notice of the exercise of the option. The letter was posted, properly addressed and prepaid, on 14th April, but it was never in fact delivered to the defendant or to his address. No other written communication of the exercise of the option was given or sent to the defendant before the expiry of the time-limit on 19th April. In an action against the defendant seeking specific performance of the option agreement, the plaintiffs contended that, since a contractual offer could be accepted by posting a letter of acceptance, the time of acceptance being the moment of posting, the option had been validly exercised when their letter of 14th April was posted.

LAWTON LJ: . . . Counsel for the plaintiffs submitted that the option was exercised when the letter was posted, as the rule relating to the acceptance of offers by post did apply. The foundation of his argument was that the parties to this agreement must have contemplated that the option might be, and probably would be, exercised by means of a letter sent through the post. I agree. This, submitted counsel, was enough to bring the rule into operation. I do not agree. . . . [After citing Lord Herschell's statement in *Henthorn* v *Fraser* (above) Lawton LJ continues:]

Does the rule apply in all cases where one party makes an offer which both he and the person with whom he was dealing must have expected the post to be used as a means of accepting it? In my judgment, it does not. First, it does not apply when the express terms of the offer specify with this exception to the general rule through their handling of football pool coupons. Secondly, it probably does not operate if its application would produce manifest inconvenience and absurdity.... In my judgment, the factors of inconvenience and absurdity are but illustrations of a wider principle, namely, that the rule does not apply if, having regard to all the circumstances, including the nature of the subject-matter under consideration, the negotiating parties cannot have intended that there should be a binding agreement until the party accepting an offer or exercising an option had in fact communicated the acceptance or exercise to the other. In my judgment, when this principle is applied to the facts of this case it becomes clear that the parties cannot have intended that the posting of a letter should constitute the exercise of the option.

The reason for the offeror wanting to exclude the postal rule is clear. If the rule were to operate a contract is formed when the letter is posted and it is irrelevant that the letter of acceptance is lost in the post: *Household Fire and Carriage Accident Insurance Co. Ltd v Grant* (1879). The decision in *Holwell Securities Ltd v Hughes* reflects commercial attitude to the operation of the postal rule — that is, that businessmen wish to exclude it and the courts will uphold the parties' intention.

Self check questions
1.   What is the postal rule? State its relationship to the general principle of acceptance.
2.   X makes an offer by telephone and Y purports to accept the offer by post. When does acceptance take place?
3.   X makes an offer to Y by post and states in his offer that he wishes to 'receive a reply'. Y posts a letter of acceptance which is lost in the post. Is there a contract?

Answers
1.   The postal rule states that acceptance takes place when the letter is posted. The rule is, however, an exception to the general principle relating to communication.
2.   As X has made his offer by telephone is it then reasonable (see *Henthorn v Fraser* (1892)) to accept the offer by post? It may well not be reasonable and therefore the acceptance takes place when the letter arrives, that is actual communication, rather than when it is posted.
3.   The crucial words are 'receive and reply'. These words would exclude the operation of the postal rule (*Holwell Securities Ltd v Hughes* (1974)), therefore as the letter is lost no acceptance has taken place.

4.3 *Method of acceptance prescribed by the offeror*

The offeror is able to stipulate the way in which the acceptance is to be communicated. What happens if the offeree does not use the method prescribed? The courts have drawn a distinction between mandatory and directory modes of acceptance. These categories have been drawn from public law and roughly can be equated with compulsory and optional — the authority for this principle is *Yates Building Co. Ltd* v *R. J. Pulleyn and Sons (York) Ltd* (1975).

The courts have given two guidelines in order to help us make this distinction. First, for the method to be construed as mandatory, the wording of the offer must be clear and any doubt will be construed against the offeror. Secondly, if an alternative method is adopted and such a method is no less disadvantageous to either party then the law will construe the method as directory only: *Manchester Diocesan Council for Education* v *Commercial and General Investments Ltd* (1970).

4.4 *Acceptance in unilateral contracts*

The question of acceptance in such contracts relates to performance, as already mentioned above. The oft-quoted example relates to a reward situation: Suppose A offers £100 to anyone who walks from the University in Preston to the University of Lancaster. B, having seen the notice, sets off but just before he reaches the University A revokes the offer. Can A do this? Three possibilities as to when acceptance takes place need to be examined:

Figure 7.1

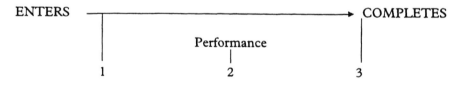

In our example does the student have to complete performance, that is arrive at the University, before A's offer is accepted? In *Carlill* v *Carbolic Smoke Ball Co.* (1893), Mrs Carlill by using the smokeball three times daily and for the two weeks accepted the offer. In the terms of Figure 7.1 we are talking of stage 3, that is she had entered and fully completed performance. Note below the words of Bowen LJ in *Carlill* v *Carbolic Smoke Ball Co.* (1893) — (see also 2.2.3, above).

> BOWEN LJ: It was said that there was no notification of the acceptance of the contract. One cannot doubt that, as an ordinary rule of law, an acceptance of an offer made ought to be notified to the person who makes the offer, in order that the two minds may come together. Unless this is done the two minds may be apart, and there is not that consensus which is necessary according to the English law — I say nothing about the laws of other countries — to make a contract. But there is this clear gloss to be made upon

that doctrine, that as notification of acceptance is required for the benefit of the person who makes the offer, the person who makes the offer may dispense with notice to himself if he thinks it desirable to do so, and I suppose there can be no doubt that where a person in an offer made by him to another person, expressly or impliedly intimates a particular mode of acceptance as sufficient to make the bargain binding, it is only necessary for the other person to whom such offer is made to follow the indicated method of acceptance; and if the person making the offer, expressly or impliedly intimates in his offer that it will be sufficient to act on the proposal without communicating acceptance of it to himself, performance of the condition is a sufficient acceptance without notification. . . .

Now, if that is the law, how are we to find out whether the person who makes the offer does intimate that notification of acceptance will not be necessary in order to constitute a binding bargain? In many cases you look to the offer itself. In many cases you extract from the character of the transaction that notification is not required, and in the advertisement cases it seems to me to follow as an inference to be drawn from the transaction itself that a person is not to notify his acceptance of the offer before he performs the condition, but that if he performs the condition notification is dispensed with. It seems to me that from the point of view of common sense no other idea could be entertained. If I advertise to the world that my dog is lost, and that anybody who brings the dog to a particular place will be paid some money, are all the police or other persons whose business it is to find lost dogs to be expected to sit down and write me a note saying that they have accepted my proposal? Why, of course, they at once look for the dog, and as soon as they find the dog they have performed the condition. The essence of the transaction is that the dog should be found, and it is not necessary under such circumstances, as it seems to me, that in order to make the contract binding there should be any notification of acceptance. It follows from the nature of the thing that the performance of the condition is sufficient acceptance without the notification of it, and a person who makes an offer in an advertisement of that kind makes an offer which must be read by the light of that common sense reflection. He does, therefore, in his offer impliedly indicate that he does not require notification of the acceptance of the offer.

A slightly different approach was adopted in *Errington* v *Errington* (1952). The decision in *Errington* clearly fits into our second category, that is by entering into and continuing performance the couple were said to have accepted the offer or at least the offer could not be revoked. Therefore, in relation to our example A cannot revoke the offer and B could claim the £100.

Errington v *Errington*
[1952] 1 KB 290

A father, wishing to provide a home for his son, who had recently married, purchased a dwelling-house through a building society, paying a lump sum and leaving the balance on mortgage to be paid by weekly instalments. He retained the conveyance in his own name and paid the rates, but promised that if the son and daughter-in-law continued in occupation and duly paid the instalments until the last one was paid, he would then transfer the property to them. He was on affectionate terms with the daughter-in-law and handed her the building society's book, directing her not to part with it. When the father died he, by his will, left all his property, including the house in question, to his widow. Up to that time the son and the son's wife had together occupied the dwelling-house and paid the instalments, but the son then left his wife and went to live with his widowed mother. The wife continued to occupy the dwelling-house and to pay the instalments.

DENNING LJ: . . . It is to be noted that the couple never bound themselves to pay the instalments to the building society; and I see no reason why any such obligation should be implied. It is clear law that the court is not to imply a term unless it is necessary; and I do not see that it is necessary here. Ample consent is given to the whole arrangement by holding that the father promised that the house should belong to the couple as soon as they paid off the mortgage. The parties did not discuss what was to happen if the couple failed to pay the instalments to the building society, but I should have thought it clear that, if they did fail to pay the instalments, the father would not be bound to transfer the house to them. The father's promise was a unilateral contract — a promise of the house in return for their act of paying the instalments. It could not be revoked by him once the couple entered on performance of the act, but it would cease to bind him if they left it incomplete and unperformed, which they have not done. If that was the position during the father's lifetime, so it must be after his death. If the daughter-in-law continues to pay all the building society instalments, the couple will be entitled to have the property transferred to them as soon as the mortgage is paid off; but if she does not do so, then the building society will claim the instalments from the father's estate and the estate will have to pay them. I cannot think that in those circumstances the estate would be bound to transfer the house to them, anymore than the father himself would have been.

A final point to note is that while situations 2 and 3 in figure 7.1 would lead to acceptance, merely entering performance would not be sufficient.

Self check question
1. In *Carlill* v *Carbolic Smoke Ball Co.* what would have happened if Mrs Carlill had caught influenza after only the end of the first week?

Answer
1. Despite the decision in *Errington* v *Errington* it is quite clear from the wording of the advertisement in *Carlill* v *Carbolic Smoke Ball Co.* that in order to accept the offer Mrs Carlill had to fully perform the conditions laid down, that is three times daily for a fortnight.

4.5   Battle of the forms

A problem which has arisen in recent years relates to the exchange of standard forms. The courts have had difficulty in deciding when acceptance takes place. A number of solutions have been suggested: first, the so-called 'last shot' doctrine, i.e., the party who fires last is the party on whose terms the contract is made. Secondly, Lord Denning in *Butler Machine Tool Co. Ltd v Ex-Cell-O Corporation (England) Ltd* (1979) suggested that in order to find whether the parties intended to contract, the correspondence/communications between the parties should be looked at as a whole in order for the decision to be made.

Thirdly, the courts in *Gibson v Manchester City Council* (1979) (see below) re-affirmed the use of the traditional devices of offer and acceptance to solve the problem. It would appear that parties are now attempting to resolve the issues between themselves or through arbitration as there has been little recent case law in this area.

Gibson v *Manchester City Council*
[1979] 1 All ER 972

LORD DIPLOCK: . . . Lord Denning MR rejected what I have described as the conventional approach of looking to see whether on the true construction of the documents relied on there can be discerned an offer and acceptance. One ought, he said, to 'look at the correspondence as a whole and at the conduct of the parties and see therefrom whether the parties have come to an agreement on everything that was material'. . . . There was, however, no reference to this standard form of agreement in any of the documents said to constitute the contract relied on in the instance case, nor was there any evidence that Mr Gibson had knowledge of its terms at or before the time that the alleged contract was concluded. . . .

Geoffrey Lane LJ in a dissenting judgment which for my part I find convincing, adopted the conventional approach. He found that on the true construction of the documents relied on as constituting the contract, there never was an offer by the council acceptance of which by Mr Gibson was capable in law of constituting a legally enforceable contract. It was but a step in the negotiations for a contract which, owing to the change in the political complexion of the council, never reached fruition.

My Lords, there may be certain types of contract, though I think they are exceptions which do not fit easily into the normal analysis of a contract as being constituted by offer and acceptance; but a contract alleged to have been made by an exchange of correspondence between the parties in which the successive communications other than the first are in reply to one another is not one of these. I can see no reason in the instance case for departing from the conventional approach of looking at the handful of documents relied on as constituting the contract sued on and seeing whether on their true construction there is to be found in them a contractual offer by the council to sell the house to Mr Gibson and an acceptance of that offer by Mr Gibson. I venture to think that it was by departing from this conventional approach that the majority of the Court of Appeal was led into error.

5   Termination of offer

An offer can be terminated in a number of ways, for example by a counter-offer. The most important method of termination is however revocation.

5.1   Revocation of the offer

The general principle is that an offer may be revoked at any time before acceptance. Obviously it is crucial to decide when this occurs. Added to this there is a further requirement that the revocation must be communicated. In this context the postal principle does not apply: *Byrne & Co. v Van Tienhoven & Co.* (1880). On the facts of the case the revocation only became effective on the date when it was received.

Byrne & Co. v Van Tienhoven & Co.
(1880) 5 CPD 344

By letter of the 1st October the defendants wrote from Cardiff offering goods for sale to the plaintiffs at New York. The plaintiffs received the offer on the 11th and accepted it by telegram on the same day, and by letter on the 15th. On the 8th of October the defendants posted to the plaintiffs a letter withdrawing the offer. This letter reached the plaintiffs on the 20th. Held, by Lindley J, that the withdrawal was inoperative, a complete contract binding both parties having been entered into on the 11th of October when the plaintiffs accepted the offer of the 1st, which they had no reason to suppose was withdrawn.

Therefore an offer can be withdrawn at any time before it is accepted by the offeree but the revocation must be communicated to the offeree before such purported acceptance. Thus the offeree must know of the revocation of the offer but it need not come directly from the offeror.

Clearly the principle is an important one and two further points can be made about communication. First, the communication need not be sent by the offeror, it is sufficient that a third party communicates: *Dickinson v Dodds* (1876). Secondly, the duty imposed to communicate is judged from an objective point of view; thus the duty is not an absolute one but a reasonable one. Therefore, if the communication of revocation is made in the same form as that of the offer then this will be held to be sufficient communication: *Shuey v United States* (1875).

Problem

		Nature of
Wording to	Richard places the following *advertisement* _____	*advertisement*
exclude	in his local newsagent's window at 9.00 am:	
postal rule	'1993 Volkswagen Polo *will be sold* for _____	*Intention*
	—£3,000 to the first person *contacting*	
	Richard at his home address below …	
	cash only'. _____	*Mode of acceptance*

Peter *posts* a letter at *9.30 am* to
Richard enclosing a *cheque* for £2,000.
John, at 1.00 pm, tries to contact
Richard by phone; however Richard is
out, but John leaves a message on
Richard's answering machine saying
he will be round the next morning _____ *Acceptance*
with the cash.
At *4.00 pm* Richard sells the car to
Ewan and he places a notice to *that*
effect in the newsagent's window. _____ *Revocation*
Richard returns home at *5.00 pm*
where he finds Peter's letter and
hears John's message.

Discuss.

Suggested answer

The problem concerns the issue of agreement. The courts have traditionally used the devices of offer and acceptance and despite the judgment of Lord Denning in *Butler Machine Tool Co. Ltd* v *Ex-Cell-O Corporation (England) Ltd*, the use of these devices was recently re-affirmed by the House of Lords in *Gibson* v *Manchester City Council*.

The first question to answer is whether the advert amounts to an offer, the acceptance of which creates a contract, or merely an invitation to treat which starts the bargaining process. Generally newspaper adverts are seen as invitations to treat: *Partridge* v *Crittenden*. However, on the facts of the problem it may be possible to distinguish that case on two grounds. First, the advert says 'will be sold' which seems to indicate an intention to be bound and is similar to the wording of the offer in *Carlill* v *Carbolic Smoke Ball Co.* where it was held that such wording amounted to an offer, the offer being to the whole world. Secondly, one of the main objections in *Partridge* v *Crittenden* was that the supply and demand were unlimited whereas here the supply is limited — therefore this objection does not apply and added to this Richard stipulates it is the first person contacting him.

We have established that the advert is an offer. The next question relates to acceptance of the offer and in particular the law relating to communication of acceptance. The general principle is that the acceptance must be communicated in order to be effective. One exception to this is the postal rule which states that the offer is accepted when the letter is posted — does that principle apply to Peter's letter? Clearly it is reasonable for Peter to use the post, therefore, the principle to that effect from *Henthorn* v *Fraser* is satisfied. However, the offer says the first person *contacting* Richard: following the principle from *Holwell Securities Ltd* v *Hughes* the offeror by using the appropriate wording can exclude the postal rule. On the facts here the word 'contacting' is sufficient to do this.

A further point to note about Peter's letter is that he includes a cheque rather than cash as prescribed in the offer. Here we are talking about the mode of acceptance prescribed by the offeror. In *Yates Building Co. Ltd* v *R. J. Pulleyn and Sons (York) Ltd* a distinction was drawn between mandatory and directory modes of acceptance and a two-fold test was suggested to help us make this distinction. First, was the wording of the offer sufficient to indicate that the mode was mandatory? Here Richard says 'cash only' and this could well be held to be clear enough wording. Secondly, the courts will ask themselves whether by using an alternative mode this has prejudiced the other party; if it has not then the mode will be directory: *Manchester Diocesan* case. In this case it can be argued that Richard has asked for cash because of the uncertainty inherent in cheques and therefore the mode will be construed as mandatory.

Secondly, under the heading of acceptance we need to consider John's action of leaving a message on Richard's answering machine for 1.00 pm. In such situations, following the decisions in *Entores Ltd* v *Miles Far East Corporation* and the *Brinkibon* case, it is clear that the general principle of communication applies there and it can be argued that the acceptance does not take place until Richard hears the message at 5.00 pm. However, following dicta by Lord Wilberforce in the *Brinkibon* case it may be that acceptance can take place at an earlier time but this depends on the intention of the parties. Certainly it can be argued that John has done everything within his power to accept and added to this fact is the nature of the possible contract in question, i.e., unilateral. Acceptance in such contracts can take place through performance and following *Errington* v *Errington* it could be said that as John has entered into and clearly wishes to continue performance then acceptance may have taken place in this context.

The final issue to discuss is whether Richard has revoked the offer by placing the advert in the window. Two principles apply: first, revocation cannot take place after acceptance and from the above it may well be that John has accepted the offer. Secondly, any revocation must be communicated: *Byrne & Co.* v *Van Tienhoven & Co.* however, the duty is only to do everything that is reasonable (*Shuey* v *United States*) and on the facts Richard may have discharged this duty.

6   Intention to create legal relations

A brief mention must be made about the second basic element of a contract. The courts adopt an objective test in deciding whether or not there was this intention. The law draws a distinction between social, family or other domestic arrangements and commercial agreements. In the former the presence or absence of an intention to create legal relations depends upon the inference to be drawn by the court from the language used by the parties and the circumstances in which they used it. The presumption generally taken by the courts in such circumstances is that the parties do not intend to create legal relations. The general principle can be rebutted in certain cases: for example, in *Simpkins* v *Pays* (1955) the agreement between the parties attracted legal relations despite its seemingly domestic nature. The defendant owned a house in which she lived with X her granddaughter, and the plaintiff, a paying boarder. All three jointly took part in the weekly newspaper competition. The entries were made in the defendant's name but there was no regular rule as to who should pay postage and other expenses. One week they were successful and the defendant received £750. The plaintiff lodger claimed a third of this sum. The defendant said that there was no intention to contract. The court held that it was a joint enterprise to which each contributed in the expectation of sharing any prize that was won. The lodger got her third.

A comparison may be made with commercial agreements. In such agreements the intention is presumed and must be rebutted by the party seeking to deny it. The parties, in trying to rebut this presumption, use the device of 'honour clauses', that is 'the agreement is binding in honour only'. Although the onus is a heavy one such clauses have been upheld. In *Rose and Frank Co.* v *J. R. Crompton and Bros Ltd* (1925), the agreement contained the following clause: 'This arrangement is not entered into . . . as a formal or legal agreement, and shall not be subject to legal jurisdiction in the law courts . . . but it is only a definite expression and record of the purpose and intention of the . . . parties concerned, to which they each honourably pledge themselves'. The House of Lords held that the agreement was not legally binding.

Activity
The next time you are filling in your pools coupon read the wording carefully. What is the legal effect of that wording?

7 Consideration

The third, and final, requirement for there to be a binding contract in English law is that of consideration. Of the three requirements consideration is often the most difficult to grasp due to its abstract nature and this is often reflected in the case law to be discussed below.

First, a straightforward example: A offers to buy a chocolate bar from B, a shopkeeper, for 20 pence. B accepts the offer. Clearly there is an offer, acceptance and intention to create legal relations. The consideration in this case would be the 20 pence, that is the price for the promise. Therefore we have a legally binding contract. This example gives no problems. However, the requirement for consideration has led the courts to make some interesting decisions. To take a further example: A, the father of an illegitimate child, offers the mother £1 a week if she keeps the child 'happy and well'. Suppose the mother is under a duty to maintain the child. Has she provided any consideration to enforce the promise of the father? The answer, as we shall see below, is yes and it is cases like this which cause the difficulty.

Finally, by way of introduction, all contracts in English law have to be supported by consideration, other than those made under seal. The exception to the general rule is of little importance for our purposes.

7.1 Definitions

There has been much academic debate as to the definitive definition of consideration. For our purposes we shall use the definition from *Currie* v *Misa* (1875) — that of benefit and detriment.

Figure 7.2

Promisor	Exchange of	Promisee
(Person giving	←————————————————→	(Person receiving
the promise)	Promises	the promise)

The essence of the analysis is that we are looking at the benefit/detriment for each promise. Equally, given the mutual exchange of promises, the roles of the promisor and promisee are in fact reversed as both parties suffer benefit detriment. Therefore in our chocolate bar example the benefit received by A is the obtaining of the chocolate bar and the detriment is the giving up of the 20 pence. Clearly the benefit/detriment for the shopkeeper is the other way round. As we shall see it is not often as clear cut as this.

Two further established definitions or more strictly, types of consideration, need to be mentioned. First, *executed consideration* which is performance of an act in return for a promise. Executed consideration is typified by unilateral contracts. Secondly *executory consideration* which is consideration where there has been a mutual exchange of promises and is found in the majority of bilateral contracts. These two definitions are useful when discussing the concept of past consideration below.

7.2 Adequacy or sufficiency of consideration

In order to support a promise does consideration have to reflect the economic value of the exchange taking place? For example: A offers B ten pence for a ring worth £1,000 and B accepts the offer. The law, in the absence of some form of duress, would uphold this bargain as it is supported by a sufficient rather than adequate consideration.

In *Chappell & Co. Ltd* v *Nestlé Co. Ltd* (1960) the chocolate wrappers were said to be a part of the consideration as Nestlé received benefit from the purchase of the extra chocolate bars.

Chappell & Co. Ltd v *Nestlé Co. Ltd*
[1960] AC 87

The H Co. manufactured and sold to the N Co., who were manufacturers of milk chocolate, a number of gramophone records of a work which was 'musical' within the meaning of the Copyright Act 1956, and the copyright of which belonged to the appellants. The recording was made on a thin film of cellulose acetate adapted for mounting on cardboard discs which were supplied by the N Co. and bore matter advertising their chocolate, the price charged to N Co. being 4d. per record. The N Co. advertised the records for sale to the public at the price of 1s. 6d. each, but with a stipulation to the effect that intending purchasers must in respect of each record send, in addition, three wrappers from 6d. packets of their milk chocolate. The company made a profit on each transaction. The wrappers when received were worthless and were thrown away.

The appellants sought to restrain the two companies from manufacturing and selling the records on the ground that the transactions involved breaches of copyright in that in the circumstances they were not protected by the provisions of section 8 of the Copyright Act 1956:   –

LORD REID: ... I can now turn to what appears to me to be the crucial question in this case: was the 1s. 6d. an 'ordinary retail selling price' within the meaning of section 8? That involves two questions, what was the nature of the contract between the Nestlé Co. and a person who sent 1s. 6d. plus three wrappers in acceptance of their offer, and what is meant by 'ordinary retail selling price' in this context?

To determine the nature of the contract one must find the intention of the parties as shown by what they said and did.

... The respondents avoid this difficulty by submitting that acquiring and delivering the wrappers was merely a condition which gave a qualification to buy and was not part of the consideration for sale. Of course, a person may limit his offer to persons qualified in a particular way, e.g., members of a club. But where the qualification is the doing of something of value to the seller, and where the qualification only suffices for one sale and must be re-acquired before another sale, I find it hard to regard the repeated acquisitions of the qualification as anything other than parts of the consideration for the sales. The purchaser of records had to send three wrappers for each record, so he had first to acquire them. The acquisition of wrappers by him was, at least in many cases, of direct benefit to the Nestlé Co., and required expenditure by the acquirer which he might not otherwise have incurred. To my mind the acquiring and delivering of the wrappers was certainly part of the consideration in these cases, and I see no good reason for drawing a distinction between these and other cases.

The case is clear authority for the principle that sufficiency rather than adequacy is the requirement for consideration. However, what the case does not clarify is whether or not the consideration 'must be something of value'. To return to the second example, in the introduction, that of the father of the illegitimate child making the promise of £1 per week, if the child is kept happy and well; in *Ward v Byham* (1956) (see page 79) the court held that such consideration was not only sufficient but also of value in the eyes of the law. In conclusion it can be said that the law will uphold most things as being sufficient consideration; the only exception being mere moral obligations. However, in *Ward v Byham* the keeping of the child 'happy and well' was not merely a moral obligation but amounted to consideration.

In a recent decision of the Court of Appeal: *Williams v Roffey Brothers and Nicholls (Contractors) Ltd* (1990), the court placed particular emphasis on the avoidance of a disbenefit amounting to consideration. The theory being that by avoiding a penalty the promisor had obtained 'benefit in practice'. The wider implications of this case will be discussed below.

Williams v Roffey Brothers and Nicholls (Contractors) Ltd
[1990] 1 All ER 512

The defendant, a building contractor, entered into a contract to refurbish a block of 27 flats and subcontracted the carpentry work to the plaintiff for £20,000. The defendant agreed to make interim payments for work completed. After 80% of the interim payments were made the plaintiff found that the price was too low and further as he had failed to supervise his workmen properly he was in financial difficulties. The defendant, who was subject to a penalty clause for non-completion in the main contract, realised the subcontract had been underpriced. The defendant then agreed to pay the plaintiff a further £575 per flat on completion to ensure that the work would be completed on time. The plaintiff finished eight further flats but the defendants only paid £1,500. The plaintiffs claimed the money owed.

Held: Where one party to a contract agreed, in the absence of economic duress or fraud, to make a payment to the other party in order to ensure completion of the contract and thereby obtained a benefit, such as the avoidance of a penalty payable to a third party if the contract was not completed on time, the obtaining of that benefit could amount to consideration for the payment of the additional sum.

You should, therefore, think carefully of the idea of 'benefit in practice' in assessing whether or not there is consideration to enforce a promise.

The concept of 'benefit in practice' or 'practical benefit' is further illustrated by the recent case of:

Pitt v PHH Asset Management Ltd
[1993] 4 All ER 961

The defendant, as agent of mortgagees in possession, placed a property on the market through a firm of estate agents (the selling agent) at £205,000. The plaintiff and B were both interested in purchasing the property and B made a written offer of £185,000. The plaintiff made an offer of £190,000 which was accepted by the estate agents but B increased her offer to £195,000 and the acceptance of the plaintiff's offer was withdrawn. The plaintiff then increased his offer to £200,000, which B promptly matched, but the plaintiff's offer was the one accepted subject to contract. B increased her offer to £210,000 and the next day the estate agents told the plaintiff that the acceptance of his offer had again been withdrawn. The plaintiff threatened the selling agent that he would seek an injunction to prevent the sale to B and that he would tell B that he was withdrawing so that she would lower her offer. The plaintiff and selling agent then reached an oral agreement (the agreement) that the defendant would sell the property to the plaintiff for £200,000 and would not consider any further offers provided the plaintiff exchanged contracts within two weeks of receipt of a draft contract. That agreement was recorded in a letter from the plaintiff to the selling agent. The defendant confirmed the terms of the agreement by a letter the same day to the selling agent, a copy of which was sent to the plaintiff. The defendant sent a draft contract to the plaintiff and eight days later the plaintiff indicated that he was ready to exchange. However, on the same day the defendant's principals wrote to the plaintiff's solicitors stating their intention to proceed with B's offer of £210,000 but giving the plaintiff the opportunity to exchange contracts that day at the increased price. The plaintiff refused and the property was sold to B. Amongst other contentions concerning the enforceability of the agreement, the defendant claimed that the plaintiff had given no consideration for the agreement.

Held: The plaintiff had provided valuable consideration for the agreement since (a) although the threat of an injunction was only of nuisance value as it had no chance of succeeding, the plaintiff had by entering into the agreement removed that nuisance and the threat of his withdrawing and suggesting to B that she lower her offer and (b) his promise to limit himself to two weeks for the exchange of contracts was of value to the defendant as it knew that if it gave the plaintiff a draft contract to agree there would be no delay by the plaintiff beyond two weeks.

The decision is interesting as it confirms the trend, started by the decision in *Williams* v *Roffey Brothers and Nicholls (Contractors) Ltd* (1990), towards the increasing liberalisation of the requirement of consideration. If the 'avoidance of nuisance' amounts to consideration; it rather begs the question what is not consideration?

7.3   Past consideration
The general principle is that a promise as to payment made subsequent to and independent of the act does not amount to valid consideration. In *Re McArdle* (1951) as the promise was made to the daughter-in-law after the work had been undertaken it was held to be past consideration and therefore no consideration.

Re McArdle
[1951] 1 All ER 905

A man left a house by will to his widow for life and then to his children. During the widow's life her daughter-in-law (who lived in the house) made various improvements to the house. After this work had been done all the children signed a document addressed to the daughter-in-law stating that 'in consideration of your carrying out certain alterations and improvements to the property . . . we hereby agree that the executors . . . shall repay to you from . . . the estate, when . . . distributed, the sum of £488 in settlement of the amount spent on such improvements'. The Court of Appeal held this was past consideration.

The courts have, however, made an exception to this principle. The exception has to satisfy the following requirements:

(a)   the act must be done at the request of the promisor;
(b)   it must have been understood that payment would be made;
(c)   the payment, if it had been promised in advance, must have been legally recoverable.

In *Re Casey's Patents* (1892) the court implied a promise, as to payment, before the work was undertaken.

Re Casey's Patents
[1892] 1 Ch 104

A and B, joint owners of certain patents, wrote to C as follows: 'In consideration of your services as the practical manager in working both our patents . . . we hereby

agree to give you one-third share of the patents, the same to take effect from this date.'
A and B afterwards deposited the letters patent with C to assist him in effecting a sale
of the patents, which however did not take place. C registered the above letter, and
claimed to retain possession of the letters patent as a co-owner of a third share therein.

BOWEN LJ: ... But then it was said by Mr Daniel, 'But there is no consideration, and this document is not under seal'. We will see if there is consideration. The consideration is stated, such as it is. It is, 'in consideration of your services as the practical manager in working our patents as above for transit by steamer'. ... Mr Daniel said, 'Oh! but it is past services that it means, and past services are not a consideration for anything'. Well, that raises the old question — or might raise it, if there was not an answer to it ... a subject of great interest to every scientific lawyer, as to whether a past service will support a promise... . But the answer to Mr Daniel's point is clear. Even if it were true, as some scientific students of law believe, that a past service cannot support a future promise, you must look at the document and see if the promise cannot receive a proper effect in some other way. Now, the fact of a past service raises an implication that at the time it was rendered it was to be paid for, and, if it was a service which was to be paid for, when you get in the subsequent document a promise to pay that promise may be treated either as an admission which evidences or as a positive bargain which fixes the amount of that reasonable remuneration on the faith of which the service was originally rendered. So that here for past services there is ample justification for the promise to give the third share. Therefore, this is an equitable assignment which cannot be impeached.

The major difference between this case and *Re McArdle* (above) is the nature of the situation. In *Re Casey* it was a commercial one whereas in *Re McArdle* it was a domestic one. An analogy can be drawn with the law on intention to create legal relations — that is, there is a presumption of an implied promise in a commercial situation as opposed to a domestic one.

Self check questions
1.   What type of consideration was it in *Re Casey's Patents*? Explain.
2.   A helps B, an old person, across the road. B then offers A £1. Can A enforce the promise?
3.   X, a window cleaner, asks Y if he wants his windows cleaning. Y answers in the affirmative. X does the work satisfactorily but when X demands £2, Y refuses to pay. Is Y entitled to do this?

Answers
1.   The consideration in *Re Casey* was executed consideration as the work had been done in response to a promise, albeit an implied one.
2.   A cannot enforce the promise as to payment as it had been made independent to and subsequent of the act. Also such a situation would be classified as a social one and there would be no implied promise as to payment before the work was done.

3. Y is not entitled to refuse to pay. Such a situation would fit into the principle from *Re Casey*.

7.4 Consideration must move from the promisee

Figure 7.3

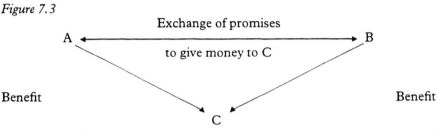

In figure 7.3 what is the position of C if either A or B default on payment? C cannot enforce the promises between A and B for two reasons. First, C is not a party to the agreement — this is the privity rule. The privity rule is fundamental in English law and states that a person must be a party to the bargain in order to enforce it. Secondly, C has provided no consideration as A and B are the people in our diagram who have exchanged promises and it is irrelevant that C may benefit.

In *Tweddle* v *Atkinson* (1861) the plaintiff could not enforce the agreement as he was not a party to the agreement nor had he provided any consideration, that is consideration had not moved from the promisee.

Tweddle v *Atkinson*
(1861) 1 B & S 393

The declaration stated that the plaintiff was the son of John Tweddle, deceased, and, before the making of the agreement hereafter mentioned, married the daughter of William Guy, deceased; that, before the said marriage, John Tweedle and William Guy each orally promised to give a marriage portion to his child in consideration of the marriage, which promises were unperformed; that after the marriage, John Tweedle and William Guy, as a mode of giving effect to their said oral promises, entered into an agreement in writing.

The plaintiff claimed that afterwards and before this suit, he and his wife ratified the agreement, that August 21, 1855, passed and all things necessary to entitle the plaintiff to have the £200 in the agreement paid by William Guy or his executor had happened; but that the money remained unpaid.

CROMPTON J: ... The modern cases have, in effect, overruled the old decisions; they show that the consideration must move from the party entitled to sue upon the contract. It would be a monstrous proposition to say that a person was a party to the contract for the purpose of suing upon it for his own advantage, and not a party to it for the purpose of being sued. It is said that the father in the present case was agent for the son in making the contract, but that argument ought also to make the son liable upon it. I am prepared to overrule the old decisions, and to hold that, by reason of the principles which now govern the action of assumpsit, the present action is not maintainable.

Problem
1. Put *Tweddle* v *Atkinson* into diagrammatical form using figure 7.3 as the basis for it.

Suggested answer

Figure 7.4

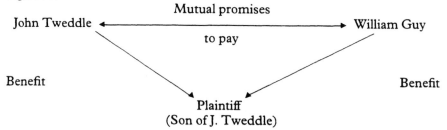

7.5 *Performance of existing duties as consideration*
The general principle — but again there are exceptions — is that merely to perform an existing duty does *not* amount to consideration for a fresh promise. Suppose that A gets paid £3 per hour for his job and his employer offers him a bonus, although A does not have to do any extra duties. The law would say that A is merely performing his existing duty and therefore no consideration has been provided for the new promise.

This subject is examined under three headings:

7.5.1 *Duty imposed by law* Here we are talking about duties imposed by the general law, that is public duties. For example, a person could not enforce a promise relating to payment in attending as a witness if he had already been subpoenaed (public duty): *Collins* v *Godefroy* (1831). The decision in *Collins* v *Godefroy* is based on public policy arguments, but what happens if the person/group exceeds their public duty — can the promise then be enforced?

In *Glasbrook Brothers Ltd* v *Glamorgan County Council* (1925) the court held that by providing the garrison/billeted force, the police had exceeded the existing duty imposed on them by law and were therefore entitled to payment.

Glasbrook Brothers Ltd v *Glamorgan County Council*
[1925] AC 270

On the occasion of a strike a colliery manager applied for police protection for his colliery and insisted that it could only be efficiently protected by billeting a police force on the colliery premises. The police superintendent was prepared to provide what in his opinion was adequate protection by means of a mobile force, but refused to billet police officers at the colliery except on the terms of the manager agreeing to pay for the force so provided at a specified rate:

VISCOUNT CAVE: . . . If in the judgment of the police authorities, formed reasonably and in good faith, the garrison was necessary for the protection of life and property, then they were not entitled to make a charge for it, for that would be to exact a payment for the performance of a duty which they clearly owed to the appellants and their servants; but if they thought the garrison a superfluity and only acceded to Mr James' request with a view to meeting his wishes, then in my opinion they were entitled to treat the garrison duty as special duty and to charge for it . . .

Upon this point Sir John Simon in his powerful argument for the appellants contended that the true inference to be drawn from the evidence was that the police authority, having a discretion to elect between protecting the collieries (which admittedly required protection in some form) by means of the 'mobile body' to which Colonel Smith referred or by means of a garrison, chose the latter alternative in consideration of payment, and they could not so (as he put it) 'sell their discretion'. Upon the evidence, I do not think that they did anything of the kind. Colonel Smith said clearly that the police garrison was no part of his scheme of protection and did not help him in his scheme at all; that he had an ample force by which to protect the collieries from outside and was well able to cope with the situation. It does not appear that the provision of the garrison, who were brought in from distant parts of the county, relieved the force on the spot from any of their duties, or that the local force was reduced in consequence; and I think that the true inference is that the garrison formed an additional and not a substituted or alternative means of protection.

The courts, however, may well have taken this idea of exceeding the existing duty a step further by the decision in *Ward* v *Byham* (1956).

Ward v *Byham*
[1956] 2 All ER 318

After the unmarried parents of a child had separated, the mother became housekeeper to a man who was ready to let the child live with them, and she wrote asking the father to let her have the child and to pay her the £1 a week he was paying a neighbour to maintain it. She received a letter from the father in reply saying 'I am prepared to let you have (the child) and pay you up to £1 a week allowance for her providing you can prove that she will be well looked after and happy and also that she is allowed to decide for herself whether or not she wishes to come and live with you'. It was agreed that she should have the child who went to live with her. She received the £1 a week until seven months later when she married the man for whom she was acting as housekeeper, when the father stopped the payments. The mother brought an action for the £1 per week based on the father's undertaking.

DENNING LJ: . . . By statute the mother of an illegitimate child is bound to maintain it, whereas the father is under no such obligation (see s. 42 of the National Assistance Act 1948). . . .

I approach the case, therefore, on the footing that, in looking after the child, the mother is only doing what she is legally bound to do. Even so, I think that there was sufficient consideration to support the promise. I have always thought that a promise to perform an existing duty, or the performance of it, should be regarded as good consideration, because it is a benefit to the person to whom it is given. Take this very case. It is as much a benefit for the father to have the child looked after by the mother as by a neighbour. If he gets the benefit for which he stipulated, he ought to honour his promise, and he ought not to avoid it by saying that the mother was herself under a duty to maintain the child.

MORRIS LJ: . . . The father was saying, in effect: Irrespective of what may be the strict legal position, what I am asking is that you shall prove that the child will be well looked after and happy, and also that you must agree that the child is to be allowed to decide for herself whether or not she wishes to come and live with you. If those conditions were fulfilled the father was agreeable to pay. On those terms, which in fact became operative, the father agreed to pay £1 a week. In my judgment, there was ample consideration there to be found for his promise, which I think was binding.

We have already discussed *Ward* v *Byham* above, when talking of sufficiency of consideration and you must also read the case in this context. Clearly from the judgments there is a divergence of opinion. Morris LJ takes the more traditional approach, that is, the mother had exceeded her existing duty and therefore had provided consideration, albeit by keeping the child happy and well. The judgment of Denning LJ is more interesting as he is suggesting that merely to perform an existing duty is sufficient. In a later case, *Williams* v *Williams* (1957), Denning LJ added the proviso that there must be 'nothing in the transaction which is contrary to the public interest'. The last statement is obviously dealing with the situation in *Collins* v *Godefroy* above.

The statements of Denning LJ are strictly *obiter*, for example, in *Ward* the other two judges used different reasoning to reach their decisions. How then have these statements been received by other judges? In *North Ocean Shipping Co. Ltd* v *Hyundai Construction Co. Ltd* (1979) the court was of the opinion that there must be *extra* consideration in order for the promise to be enforced and that the views of Denning LJ should not be followed. This would appear to be the present position of the law.

7.5.2 Duty imposed by contract with promisor Again the general principle is that to merely perform an existing duty, imposed by contract, does not amount to consideration for a fresh promise. In *Stilk* v *Myrick* (1809) the court clearly thought that the crew, despite the changed circumstances, were merely performing their existing duty. The decision itself seems a little harsh but given the date of the decision it is not surprising. The case is still authority for the general principle but it may well be that if the same factual situation arose today the court would hold that the seamen had gone beyond their existing duty.

Stilk v Myrick
(1809) 2 Camp 317

This was an action for seamen's wages, on a voyage from London to the Baltic and back.

By the ship's articles, executed before the commencement of the voyage, the plaintiff was to be paid at the rate of £5 a month; and the principal question in the cause was, whether he was entitled to a higher rate of wages? In the course of the voyage two of the seamen deserted; and the captain, having in vain attempted to supply their places at Cronstadt, there entered into an agreement with the rest of the crew, that they should have the wages of the two who had deserted equally divided among them, if he could not procure two other hands at Gottenborg. This was found impossible; and the ship was worked back to London by the plaintiff and eight more of the original crew, with whom the agreement had been made at Constadt.

LORD ELLENBOROUGH: . . . Here, I say, the agreement is void for want of consideration. There was no consideration for the ulterior pay promised to the mariners who remained with the ship. Before they sailed from London they had undertaken to do all that they could under all the emergencies of the voyage. They had sold all their services till the voyage should be completed. If they had been at liberty to quit the vessel at Cronstadt, the case would have been quite different; or if the captain had capriciously discharged the two men who were wanting, the others might not have been compellable to take the whole duty upon themselves, and their agreeing to do so might have been a sufficient consideration for the promise of an advance of wages. But the desertion of a part of the crew is to be considered an emergency of the voyage as much as their death; and those who remain are bound by the terms of their original contract to exert themselves to the utmost to bring the ship in safely to her destined port. Therefore, without looking to the policy of this agreement, I think it is void for want of consideration, and that the plaintiff can only recover at the rate of £5 a month.

7.5.3 *Contractual duty owed to a third party* In 7.5.1 and 7.5.2 above, it is quite clear that in order for there to be consideration for a fresh promise the promisee must go beyond the existing duty. The position is however different when talking of performance of an existing duty owed to a third party. Look at the decision in *Scotson v Pegg* (1861). P had contracted with a third party, A, to deliver a cargo of coal to A or to the order of A. A sold the cargo to D and directed P to deliver it to D as per contract. D then made an agreement with P in which 'in consideration that P, at the request of D, would deliver to D' the cargo of coal, then D promised to unload it at a stated rate. P sued D for failure to honour this promise and D pleaded lack of consideration, as P was already under an existing duty of delivery with A. It was held promise supported by consideration as P, by parting with the cargo, was benefit to D.

Figure 7.5

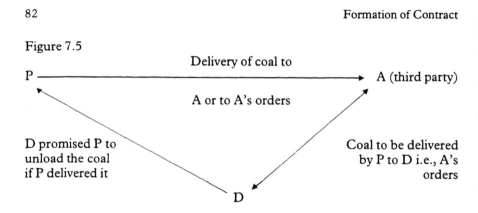

The argument in the case is as follows. P's existing duty was with A which A has transferred by contract to D. P is bound by the contract to deliver the coal but what consideration has he provided to be able to enforce D's promise? In a two-party situation, discussed above, P would have to show that he has gone beyond his existing duty. However, in a three-party situation the mere fact that D has received some benefit is sufficient for the promise to be enforced.

The decision seems to conflict with the normal two-party situation. It was thought that the principle might not be followed but it has been recently confirmed. In *New Zealand Shipping Co. Ltd* v *A. M. Satterthwaite & Co. Ltd* (1975) the principle is taken as being quite clearly established despite the fact that it is very difficult to reconcile with the two-party situation.

New Zealand Shipping Co. Ltd v *A. M. Satterthwaite & Co. Ltd* [1975] AC 154

LORD WILBERFORCE: In their Lordship's opinion consideration may quite well be provided by the appellant to discharge to the carrier. (There is no direct evidence of the existence or nature of this obligation, but their Lordships are prepared to assume it.) An agreement to do an act which the promisor is under an existing obligation to a third party to do, may quite well amount to valid consideration and does so in the present case: the promise obtains the benefit of a direct obligation which he can enforce. This proposition is illustrated and supported by *Scotson* v *Pegg* (1861) which their Lordships consider to be good law.

The decision in *Williams* v *Roffey Brothers and Nicholls (Contractors) Ltd* (1990) (see 7.2, above) means that the differences between the two-party and three-party situations have been reconciled.

GLIDEWELL LJ: ... the present state of the law on this subject can be expressed in the following proposition: (i) if A has entered into a contract with B to do work for, or to supply goods or services to, B in return for payment by B and (ii) at some stage before A has completely performed his obligations under the contract B has reason to doubt whether A will, or will be able to, complete his side of the bargain and (iii) B thereupon promises A an additional payment in return for A's promise to perform his contractual obligations on time and (iv) as a result of giving his promise B obtains in practice a benefit, or obviates a disbenefit, and (v) B's promise is not given as a result of economic duress or fraud on the part of A, then (vi) the benefit to B is capable of being consideration for B's promise, so that the promise will be legally binding.

As I have said, counsel for the defendants accepts that in the present case by promising to pay the extra money the defendants secured benefits. There is no finding, and no suggestion, that in this case the promise was given as a result of fraud or duress.

If it be objected that the propositions above contravene the principle in *Stilk* v *Myrick* I answer that in my view they do not: they refine and limit the application of that principle, but they leave the principle unscathed, e.g., where B secures no benefit by his promise. It is not in my view surprising that a principle enunciated in relation to the rigours of seafaring life during the Napoleonic wars should be subjected during the succeeding 180 years to a process of refinement and limitation in its application in the present day.

It is therefore my opinion that on his findings of fact in the present case, the judge was entitled to hold, as he did, that the defendants' promise to pay the extra money was supported by valuable consideration, and thus constituted an enforceable agreement.

Therefore, if 'benefit in practice' has been received by the promisor then this is sufficient for the promisee to enforce the promise. You may care to ask yourself when there will not be a benefit in practice and therefore will it always be the case that the promisee exceeds the duty imposed on him?

Self check questions
1.   What is the general principle concerning performance of an existing duty amounting to consideration for a fresh promise?
2.   A has a service contract with B for his T.V. The contract guarantees repair within 24 hours. A is a tennis fanatic and on the day of the Wimbledon final his set breaks down. A contacts C, one of B's engineers, and tells him that he will give him an extra £5 if he repairs the set before the final. C does the work as requested. A now refuses to pay. Advise C, using diagrams in your answer.

Answers
1.   To merely perform an existing duty does not amount to consideration for a fresh promise.

2. *Figure 7.6*

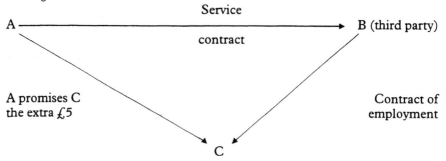

The question can be looked at in two ways. First, it can be argued that C has gone beyond his existing duty in coming out straightaway in order to repair the television. Therefore he has provided consideration for the promise to be enforced. Secondly, as can be seen from the diagram, because of the contractual relationships between the parties concerned it could well fit into a third-party situation (*Scotson* v *Pegg*), and therefore there may be no need for C to show that the existing duty has been exceeded. Further, A has received benefit in practice: see *Williams* v *Roffey Brothers and Nicholls (Contractors) Ltd.*

7.6   Part payment of a debt

The final issue to discuss concerns whether merely paying part of a debt owed discharges the whole of the debt. The general common law principle is that a debt can only be discharged if there is 'full accord and satisfaction' — this is known as the rule in *Pinnel's Case* (1602). What the rule is saying is that there must be agreement (accord) and satisfaction (consideration). Therefore, if A owes B £10 to be paid on a certain day and on that day A only pays £5 the common law will allow B to sue for the balance. The principle was re-affirmed in the case of *Foakes* v *Beer* (1884).

Foakes v Beer
(1884) 9 App Cas 605

An agreement between judgment debtor and creditor, that in consideration of the debtor paying down part of the judgment debt and costs and on condition of his paying to the creditor or his nominee the residue by instalments the creditor will not take any proceedings on the judgment, is without consideration, and does not prevent the creditor after payment of the whole debt and costs from proceeding to enforce payment of the interest upon the judgment.

EARL OF SELBORNE LC: What is the consideration? On the face of the agreement none is expressed, except a present payment of £500, on account and in part of the larger debt then due and payable by law under the judgment. The appellant did not contract to pay the future instalments of £150 each, at the times therein mentioned; much less did he give any new security, in the shape of negotiable paper, or in any other form. The promise *de futuro* was only that of the respondent, that if the half-yearly payments of £150 each were regularly paid, she would 'take no proceedings whatever on the judgment'. No doubt if the appellant had been under no antecedent obligation to pay the whole debt, his fulfilment of the condition might have imported some consideration on his part for that promise. But he was under that antecedent obligation; and payment at those deferred dates, by the forbearance and indulgence of the creditor, of the residue of the principal debt and costs, could not (in my opinion) be a consideration for the relinquishment of interest and discharge of the judgment, unless the payment of the £500, at the time of signing the agreement, was such a consideration. As to accord and satisfaction, in point of fact there could be no complete satisfaction, so long as any future instalment remained payable; and I do not see how any mere payments on account could operate in law as a satisfaction *ad interim*, conditionally upon other payments being afterwards duly made, unless there was a consideration sufficient to support the agreement while still unexecuted. Nor was anything, in fact, done by the respondent in this case, on the receipt of the last payment, which could be tantamount to an acquittance.

The decision has not been without its critics as it was felt that the earlier decision should have been changed. Instead a number of exceptions have developed to the general principle and a few brief introductory points should be made. It should be remembered that the common law exceptions to the principle are based on consideration. However, the equitable exceptions are not based on consideration but on more general equitable principles (see earlier notes) and therefore close examination must be made of them.

7.6.1   Common law exceptions   There are three common law exceptions to the general principle all of which are based on the doctrine of consideration. It must be noted that the three (below) must all be done at the creditor's request.

(a)   Payment, before the due date, of a smaller sum. Therefore if A owes £10 to be paid on April 1st and the creditor asks for £5 on March 15th, then that will be sufficient to discharge the debt.

(b)   Payment at a different place. If the creditor asks A to pay a debt in another place then the debt will be discharged.

(c)   Finally, payment by different means. If the creditor asks A for an article instead of the money owed, this again will discharge the debt.

7.6.2   Equitable exceptions   The nature of common law rules is that they tend to be inflexible and as a result can lead to unfair and often unworkable results. The above exceptions all require some form of consideration. What would happen if the creditor simply told A to 'forget the debt'. At common law, as A has provided no consideration, the debt would still be enforceable. Equity has, however, provided a further exception to the general principle based on the doctrine of promissory estoppel. The source of the doctrine of promissory estoppel is debatable but what is clear is that the leading case on the subject is

Central London Property Trust Ltd v *High Trees House Ltd*(1947). An initial point
to mention about the case is that extracts of the judgment of Denning J are all
obiter dicta and therefore, show the very persuasive nature of such statements.
Look at the case in the form of a diagram (figure 7.7).

Figure 7.7

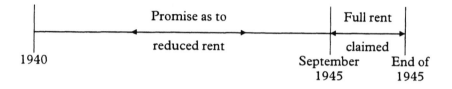

From figure 7.7 it can be seen that the effect of the promise was that back rent
could not be claimed between January 1940 and September 1945. However,
when wartime conditions ceased to exist the full rent became payable again.

Central London Property Trust Ltd v *High Trees House Ltd*
[1947] 1 KB 130

*By a lease under seal dated September 24, 1937, the plaintiff company let to the
defendant company (a subsidiary of the plaintiffs) a block of flats for a term of
ninety-nine years from September 29, 1937, at a ground rent of £2,500 a year. In
the early part of 1940, owing to war conditions then prevailing, only a few of the
flats in the block were let to tenants and it became apparent that the defendants
would be unable to pay the rent reserved by the lease of the rents of the flats.
Discussions took place between the directors of the two companies, which were
closely connected, and, as a result, on January 3, 1940, a letter was written by the
plaintiffs to the defendants confirming that the ground rent of the premises would be
reduced from £2,500 to £1,250 as from the beginning of the term. The defendants
thereafter paid the reduced rent. By the beginning of 1945 all the flats were let but
the defendants continued to pay only the reduced rent. In September, 1945, the
plaintiffs wrote to the defendants claiming that rent was payable at the rate of
£2,500 a year and subsequently, in order to determine the legal position, they
initiated friendly proceedings in which they claimed the difference between the rent
and the rates of £2,500 and £1,250 for the quarters ending September 29 and
December 25, 1945. By their defence the defendants pleaded that the agreement for
the reduction of the ground rent operated during the whole term of the lease and, as
alternatives, that the plaintiffs were stopped from demanding rent at the higher rate
or had waived their right to do so down to the date of their letter of September 21,
1945.*

DENNING J: . . . But what is the position in view of developments in the law
in recent years? The law has not been standing still since *Jorden* v *Money.*

There has been a series of decisions over the last fifty years which, although they are said to be cases of estoppel are not really such. They are cases in which a promise was made which was intended to create legal relations and which, to the knowledge of the persons making the promise, was going to be acted on by the person to whom it was made, and which was in fact so acted on. In such cases the courts have said that the promise must be honoured.... As I have said they are not cases of estoppel in the strict sense. They are really promises — promises intended to be binding, intended to be acted on, and in fact acted on. *Jorden* v *Money* can be distinguished, because there the promisor made it clear that she did not intend to be legally bound, whereas in the cases to which I refer the proper inference was that the promisor did intend to be bound. In each case the court held the promise to be binding on the party making it, even though under the old common law it might be difficult to find consideration for it. The courts have not gone so far as to give a cause of action in damages for the breach of such a promise, but they have refused to allow the party making it to act inconsistently with it. It is in that sense, and that sense only, that such a promise gives rise to an estoppel. The decisions are a natural result of the fusion of law and equity.... In my opinion, the time has now come for the validity of such a promise to be recognised. The logical consequence, no doubt is that a promise to accept a smaller sum in discharge of a larger sum, if acted upon, is binding notwithstanding the absence of consideration: and if the fusion of law and equity leads to this result, so much the better. That aspect was not considered in *Foakes* v *Beer*. At this time of day however, when law and equity have been joined together for over seventy years, principles must be reconsidered in the light of their combined effect. It is to be noticed that in the Sixth Interim Report of the Law Revision Committee, paras. 35, 40, it is recommended that such a promise as that to which I have referred, should be enforceable in law even though no consideration for it has been given by the promisee. It seems to me that, to the extent I have mentioned, that result has now been achieved by the decisions of the courts. I am satisfied that a promise such as that to which I have referred is binding and the only question remaining for my consideration is the scope of the promise in the present case.... under the law as I hold it, it seems to me that rent is payable at the full rate for the quarters ending September 29 and December 25, 1945. If the case had been one of estoppel, it might be said that in any event the estoppel would cease when the conditions to which the representation applied came to an end, or it also might be said that it would only come to an end on notice. In either case it is only a way of ascertaining what is the scope of the representation. I prefer to apply the principle that a promise intended to be binding, intended to be acted on and in fact acted on, is binding so far as its terms properly apply. Here it was binding as covering the period down to the early part of 1945, and as from the time full rent is payable.

Promissory estoppel has developed in an *ad hoc* manner and various require-ments/difficulties can be outlined concerning the doctrine:

(a)   There must be a clear promise which is intended to affect the legal relationship between the parties, and indicates that the promisor will not enforce his strict legal rights. There has not been much debate about this and it can usually be assumed in most situations.

(b)   The general principle is that as a result of the promise the promisee must either act to his detriment or alter his position. An example of alteration would be shown as follows: A owes B £50; B promises not to enforce the debt and as a result A spends the money on a radio. In our example B has altered his position and this general requirement is supported by decisions such as *Ajayi* v *R. T. Briscoe (Nig.) Ltd* (1964). An alternative approach has been suggested: in *Brikom Investments Ltd* v *Carr* (1979) Lord Denning is saying that it is sufficient merely for the promisor to intend that the promisee should rely on the promise and therefore no actual alteration is necessary.

Brikom Investments Ltd v *Carr*
[1979] 2 All ER 75

LORD DENNING: Counsel for the landlords submitted that Mrs Dufton (now Mrs Carr) could not rely on the principle in the High Trees case, because it was essential that she should have acted on the representation; and here she had not acted on it. On her own admission, he said she would have gone on and taken the lease even if she had not been told about the roof. In all the cases said the counsel for the landlords, the courts had said that the party must have acted on the promise or representation in the sense that he must have altered his position on the faith of it, meaning that he must have been led to act differently from what he would otherwise have done. This argument gives, I think, too limited a scope to the principle. The principle extends to all cases where one party makes a promise or representation, intending that it should be binding, intending that the others should rely on it, and on which that other does in fact rely, by acting on it, by altering his position on the faith of it, by going ahead with a transaction under discussion, or by the other way of reliance.... So it seems to me that the judge was quite right in the way he put the case. He said that in all these cases the landlords could not go back to the strict rights under the lease. They had given the tenants their promise or representation to repair the roofs at their own cost, and the tenants relied on it. That gives rise to an equity which makes it unjust and inequitable for the landlords to seek to charge the tenants for a contribution; and the benefit of this equity avails the assignees of the tenants also.

There is obviously a conflict and you should be aware of the alternatives as it is necessary to discuss both views.

(c)   The third problem concerns the issue of whether the promise merely suspends the debt and therefore, by giving adequate notice the debt is enforceable again, or whether the debt is extinguished by the promise. The general view is that the promise merely suspends the debt, however look at the decision in *Central London Property Trust Ltd* v *High Trees House Ltd* more closely. The effect of the flats becoming fully let again meant that the full rent became payable and therefore, in that sense the promise was merely suspensory. However, the back rent between January 1940 and September 1945 (see figure 7.7) could not be claimed. The effect of the promise in the latter case being to extinguish the debt.

It is important to understand the nature of an equitable doctrine. Inherent in such a doctrine is flexibility which in legal terms leads to uncertainty and therefore the fact that there are alternatives should not concern the reader. It should also be noted that the doctrine is essentially of a defensive nature and cannot be used to found an action, that is, it is to be used 'as a shield and not a sword'. Authority for this statement is *Combe* v *Combe* (1951).

Finally, the equitable nature of the doctrine should be emphasised. Therefore, if any of the equitable principles are broken by the person seeking to rely on the doctrine, the promise will have no legal effect. In *D & C Builders Ltd* v *Rees* (1966) the equitable maxim 'he who comes to equity must do so with clean hands' was clearly broken.

Self check questions
1. What is the general common law principle relating to part payment of a debt?
2. What are the common law exceptions to this principle? What is the common theme running throughout them?
3. What is the major difference between the equitable exception and the common law exceptions?

Answers
1. The general principle is that a debt must be discharged with 'full accord and satisfaction'.
2. The common law exceptions are based on the creditor requesting payment at an earlier time, different place or by different means. The common theme throughout the three is that the debtor has provided consideration.
3. The major difference between the two is that in the equitable exception a promise is being given legal effect, albeit as a defence to a claim, when it is unsupported by consideration.

Problem

Debt owed
————Shirley has *borrowed one hundred pounds*
from her boyfriend, John, to be repaid
by *June 1st*, *Shirley* offers to repay
Promise ———— fifty pounds of the sum on *April 30th*,   *Possible common*
but *John refuses* saying that Shirley   *law exceptions*
need not repay the money due to the
amount of washing and ironing Shirley has
done for John *in the past.*

Has S relied
on the promise?   *Shirley decides not to spend the money*
                    but put it all in a building society
                    account which she has specially *opened*
                    to keep the one hundred pounds.

                    John and Shirley fall out, due to
                    the latter's drinking habits, and John   *What is the effect*
                    demands his one hundred pounds back. ⟍ ───── *of the promise?*
                    Shirley refuses, saying she regarded ⟋
                    the debt as extinguished.
                    Advise John.

Suggested answer
The problem is concerned with the law relating to discharge of debt. The general principle — the rule in *Pinnel's Case* — is that to discharge a debt it must be done with full accord and satisfaction. The principle is a common law one and any common law or equitable exceptions need to be discussed in the context of this problem.

John tells Shirley that she can forget the debt because of the washing done in the past. It is clear, from *Pinnel's Case*, that discharge can take place through performance by different means. Here we are talking about a common law exception based on consideration but the fatal flaw in any argument which Shirley may put forward is that the promise was made after the washing had taken place. The principle is that past consideration is no consideration: *Re McArdle*. There is however an exception to this based on a promise being implied, as to payment, before the work is done even though the express promise is made afterwards: *Re Casey's Patents*.

On the facts it can be argued that the exception from *Re Casey* will not apply as such an exception seemingly only applies in commercial situations. Drawing an analogy with the law relating to intention to create legal relations, as this is a 'domestic' situation then the law will not imply such a promise as to payment on the facts; therefore Shirley's plea will fail in this respect.

The second defence which Shirley may have to John's action is based on the equitable principle of promissory estoppel. The principle is an exception to the rule in *Pinnel's Case* and is one of the very few examples in English law where a promise unsupported by consideration will be enforced. In order for the concept to operate, three criteria must be satisfied: first, there must be a clear promise; secondly, the promisee must alter his position and finally one must decide whether the doctrine merely suspends or extinguishes the debt.

On the facts it would appear that John has made a clear promise to bring it within the scope of the doctrine. However, what is far less clear is whether or not Shirley has relied on the promise. The majority of cases indicate that the promisee must have altered his position as a result of the promise: *Ajayi* v *R. T. Briscoe (Nig.) Ltd*. Therefore it would appear that as Shirley has merely placed the money in a new account she has not altered her position. Lord Denning, however, in *Brikom Investments Ltd* v *Carr* took a different approach. The essence of his dicta is that the courts should take an objective view in deciding whether or not there has been reliance and he argues that the mere fact the promise has been made would mean that the promise is intended to be relied upon and subjective reliance by the promisee is not required. It is submitted that although this approach would clearly fit Shirley's situation the courts may well be reluctant to follow the approach of Lord Denning.

The final factor to be noted concerns the effect of the doctrine and again there is a divergence of judicial opinion. The roots of estoppel lie in the doctrine of waiver and in the latter doctrine the effect is to merely suspend the obligation; therefore if adequate notice is given the obligation becomes operational again. The problem here is neatly illustrated by the *High Trees House* case. While the obligation to pay full rent was only suspended as to the future, the arrears of rent during the wartime years could not be claimed i.e., they were extinguished. The position is unclear but it can be argued, quite strongly, that as the obligation in the problem is merely a one-off and not a continuing one, then the courts could hold that the effect of the promise is to discharge the debt.

But as the second criteria, above, has not been fulfilled, it is unlikely that Shirley has a defence in any case.

8 TERMS OF THE CONTRACT

1 Introduction

In the previous unit chapters we have talked about the requirements necessary to create a contract in English law. In this, and the next chapter the contents of the contract will be considered. The chapter will be divided into three parts: terms and representations; implied terms and classification of terms.

2 Terms and representations

The question of whether something is a term of the contract has caused some problems, although with the increasing use of standard form contracts there is invariably a section listed 'Terms of the Contract'. Suppose, though, that A is selling B his car and A describes it as 'a good little runner'. B buys the car and it is anything but a good little runner. The law, in this example, would have to decide whether this statement is a term of the contract or merely a representation; this decision affects the nature of the remedy available. If the statement is held to be a term then damages will be automatically available, whereas if it is merely a representation then the requirements of misrepresentation (see ch. 10) will have to be satisfied.

How then does the law make this decision? The overall test is that there must be 'evidence of an intention by one or both parties that there should be contractual liability in respect of the accuracy of the statement'. In order to help them operate this test the courts have developed a number of criteria or guidelines to aid its operation. Three of these guidelines can be discussed briefly. First, if one party can show that the statement was of importance, for example the way in which the negotiations were conducted, then the statement will be held to be a term: *Bannerman v White* (1861). Secondly, if there has been a lapse of time between the making of the statement and the final entering into the contract then it is more likely to be held to be merely a representation.

Thirdly, if the parties make a formal contract in writing and the statements are not contained in this contract then again it is more likely that the statements will be seen as mere representations: *Heilbut Symons & Co.* v *Buckleton* (1913).

The fourth, and by far the most important guideline, is the strength or degree of knowledge possessed by one party to the contract. In *Oscar Chess Ltd* v *Williams* (1957) and *Dick Bentley Productions Ltd* v *Harold Smith (Motors) Ltd* (1965) the degree of knowledge possessed was obviously crucial. Clearly this test cannot be used in all cases but what it does show is that the law is willing to take into account the bargaining strength of the parties. In *Oscar Chess* v *Williams* the knowledge of the car dealers was equated with this strength and as we shall see, this is a theme running throughout this area of the law.

Oscar Chess Ltd v *Williams*
[1957] 1 WLR 370

In 1955 the defendant entered into a hire-purchase transaction through the plaintiff car dealers to acquire a new car, the car dealers agreeing through their salesman to take in part-exchange a second-hand 10-horse-power Morris car acquired by the defendant's mother for £300 in 1954. The registration book of the Morris car showed it as having been first registered in 1948, with five changes of ownership between 1948 and 1954. The salesman, who was personally familiar with the particular Morris car, after ascertaining from a trade reference book the current price for a 1948 Morris of that model, allowed £290 for it; and the hire-purchase transaction was concluded on that basis. Eight months later the car dealers found out from the manufacturers that the Morris was a 1939 model; the outward appearance of that model had not been altered between 1939 and 1948. The current price for a second-hand 1939 model would have been £175.

The car dealers thereupon brought an action to recover from the defendant as damages £115, the difference in value between a 1939 and a 1948 Morris, claiming that it was an express condition of the contract, or alternatively a warranty, that the Morris car was a 1948 model.

DENNING LJ: . . . Once the fact is put on one side I ask myself: What is the proper inference from the known fact? It must have been obvious to both that the seller had himself no personal knowledge of the year when the car was made. He only became owner after a great number of changes. He must have been relying on the registration book. It is unlikely that such a person would warrant the year of manufacture. The most he would do would be to state his belief, and then produce the registration book in verification of it. In these circumstances the intelligent bystander would, I suggest, say that the seller did not intend to bind himself so as to warrant that it was a 1948 model. If the seller was asked to pledge himself to it, he would at once have said 'I cannot do that. I have only the log-book to go by, the same as you.' . . .

One final word: It seems to me clear that the motor dealers who bought the car relied on the year stated in the log-book. If they had wished to make sure of it, they could have checked it then and there, by taking the engine number and chassis number and writing to the makers. They did not do so at the time, but only eight months later. They are experts, and, not having made that check at that time, I do not think they should now be allowed to recover against the innocent seller who produced to them all the evidence he had, namely, the registration book.

Dick Bentley Productions Ltd v Harold Smith (Motors) Ltd
[1965] 1 WLR 623

The plaintiff B, who was a customer of the defendant car dealers and had told them that he wanted to buy a well-vetted car (a 'quality' British car, the history of which could be obtained from its makers), was told by S, on behalf of the dealers that he had found such a car. B inspected it on the morning of January 23, 1960. The speedometer showed a mileage of 20,000. S, during the inspection, stated, inter alia, *that the car had done only 20,000 miles since being fitted with a replacement engine and gearbox; that the price was £1,850; and that he would guarantee it for 12 months. In the afternoon B, brought his wife to see the car and repeated to her in S's presence the statement by S that it had done only 20,000 miles. B bought and paid for the car. Troubles began almost at once and continued throughout and beyond the guarantee period.*

In an action brought by B claiming damages for breach of the warranty as to mileage, the dealers, while admitting a statement as to mileage, claimed that it was made in the belief that it was true, and denied that it was in law a warranty or that B was induced thereby to buy the car.

The county court judge, having inferred from the history of the car supplied by the makers and other evidence that the mileage done was nearer 100,000 held that the statement as to the mileage was a warranty and that it had been broken; and he awarded damages to the plaintiff.

LORD DENNING MR (On appeal by the defendants): I endeavoured to explain in *Oscar Chess Ltd* v *Williams* that the question whether a warranty was intended depends on the conduct of the parties, on their words and behaviour, rather than on their thoughts. If an intelligent bystander would reasonably infer that a warranty was intended, that will suffice. What conduct, then? What words and behaviour lead to the inference of a warranty? . . . [I]t seems to me that if a representation is made in the course of dealings for a contract for the very purpose of inducing the other party to act upon it, and actually inducing him to act upon it, by entering into the contract, that is prima facie ground for inferring that it was intended as a warranty. It is not necessary to speak of it as being collateral. Suffice it that it was intended to be acted upon and was in fact acted on. But the maker of the representation can rebut this inference if he can show that it really was an innocent misrepresentation, in that he was in fact innocent of fault in making it, and that it would not be reasonable in the circumstances for him to be bound by it. In the *Oscar Chess* case the inference was rebutted . . . He honestly believed on reasonable grounds that it was true. He was completely innocent of any fault. There was no warranty by him, but only an innocent misrepresentation. Whereas in the present case it is very different. The difference is not rebutted. Here we have a dealer, Smith, who was in a position to know, or at least to find out, the history of the car. He could get it by writing to the makers. He did not do so. Indeed, it was done later. When the history of this car was examined, he ought to have known better. There was reasonable foundation for it.

Self check questions
1. Why is it necessary to draw a distinction between terms and representations?
2. What is the general test used by the court in helping them to make this decision?
3. What role does knowledge of the parties have to play?

Answers
1. The distinction between the two has to be drawn as it affects the nature of the remedy available to the innocent party.
2. The general test is based upon the intention of the parties, although the courts have developed guidelines in helping them to make the decision.
3. Knowledge is important as if a party who is deemed to have more knowledge makes a representation then it is more likely to be a term of the contract, and vice versa.

3   Implied terms

During the discussion of terms/representations, if the court decided that the statement did amount to a term then it would be an express term. The nature of express terms means that the parties cannot foresee every eventuality or alternatively the law is prepared to imply terms in a contract on more general considerations. The courts have moved away from basing their test on the intention of the parties to a test based on wider policy grounds. However, the modern test, which is based on necessity, means that the courts are not willing to imply terms readily. A mention should be made of the large number of terms which are implied through the operation of statute, for example the Sale of Goods Act, 1979. These implied terms will be dealt with in chapter 17 below.

The leading case on the way in which terms are to be implied by the courts is *Liverpool City Council v Irwin* (1976). The House of Lords implied a number of terms because it was necessary to do so because of the nature of the contract. The court looked at other landlord/tenant arrangements in order to imply the terms. The nature of the terms implied, however, is important. The court did not impose absolute obligations on the council, but merely to do what was reasonable in the circumstances and on the facts of the case the court held that the council had discharged this duty.

Liverpool City Council v Irwin
[1977] AC 239

The tenants of a council maisonette on the ninth and tenth floors of a 15-storey tower block withheld their rent as a protest against conditions in the building and in their maisonette. In an action by the council for possession the tenants counter-claimed nominal damages, alleging, inter alia, *that the council were in breach of their duty to repair and maintain the common parts of the building of which they retained control, including lifts, staircases, rubbish chutes and passages, and were also, in relation to the demised maisonette, in breach of their covenant for quiet enjoyment and of the implied covenant under section 32(1) of the Housing Act 1961 to keep in repair and proper working order the structure and specified installations. The council denied the existence of the duty alleged and denied breach of covenant. There was no formal demise of the maisonette but merely a document described as 'conditions of tenancy' with a form attached signed only by the tenants stating that they accepted the tenancy on those conditions, which related to obligations only on the part of the tenants and not on the part of the council.*

LORD WILBERFORCE: The present case, in my opinion, represents a fourth category, or I would rather say a fourth shade on a continuous spectrum. The court here is simply concerned to establish what the contract is, the parties not having themselves fully stated the terms. In this sense the court is searching for what must be applied.

What then should this contract be held to be? There must first be implied a letting, that is, a grant of the right of exclusive possession to the tenants. With this there must, I would suppose, be implied a covenant for quiet enjoyment, as a necessary incident of the letting. The difficulty begins when we consider the common parts. We start with the facts that the demise is useless unless access is obtained by the staircase; we can add that, having regard to the height of the block, and the family nature of the dwellings, the demise would be useless without a lift service; we can continue that, there being rubbish chutes built into the structures and no other means of disposing of light rubbish, there must be a right to use the chutes. The question to be answered — and it is the only question in this case — is what is to be the legal relationship between the landlord and tenant as regards these matters.

The House of Lords continued to hold that so far as the common parts were concerned there had to be implied an easement for the tenants and their licensees to use the stairs, a right in the nature of an easement to use the lifts and easement to use the rubbish chutes; that the obligation to be read into the contract on the part of the council was such as the nature of the control itself implicitly required; that where an essential means of access to units in a building in multiple occupation was retained in the landlord's occupation then unless the obligation to maintain that means of access was placed in a defined manner on the tenants individually or collectively the nature of the contract and the circumstances required that it be placed on the landlord; that the standard of obligation was what was necessary having regard to circumstances, namely, an obligation to take reasonable care to keep the means of access in reasonable repair and usability with the recognition that the tenants themselves had their responsibilities according to what a reasonable set of tenants would do for themselves; that the obligation applied to local authority lettings as well as to private lettings and also applied to the lighting of the common parts of the building: but that in the present case it had not been shown that there had been any breach of the obligation.

Finally, in *Shell UK Ltd* v *Lostock Garage Ltd* (1976) Lord Denning saw two broad categories of implied terms and the way in which the courts made their decision depended on whether the contract was of common occurrence or not. What is, however clear, is that the overall test for implication is that of necessity and not whether it is reasonable to imply a term.

Shell UK Ltd v *Lostock Garage Ltd*
[1976] 1 WLR 1187

LORD DENNING MR: . . . This submission makes it necessary once again to consider the law as to implied terms. I venture with some trepidation to suggest that terms implied by law could be brought within one comprehensive category — in which the courts could imply a term such as was just and reasonable in the circumstances. But, as I feared, the House of Lords in *Liverpool City Council* v *Irwin* have rejected it as quite unacceptable. As I read the speeches, there are two broad categories of implied terms.

(i)   The first category

The first category comprehends all those relationships which are of common occurrence. Such as the relationship of seller and buyer, owner and hirer, master and servant, landlord and tenant, carrier by land or by sea, contractor for building works, and so forth. In all those relationships the courts have imposed obligations on one party or the other, saying they are 'implied terms'. These obligations are not founded on the intention of the parties actual or presumed, but on more general considerations . . . In such relationships the problem is not to be solved by asking what did the parties intend? Or would they have unhesitatingly agreed to it, if asked? It is to be solved by asking: has the law already defined the obligation or the extent of it? If so let it be followed. If not, look to see what would be reasonable in the general run of such cases . . . and then say what the obligation shall be. The House in *Liverpool City Council* v *Irwin* went through that very process. They examined the existing law of landlords and tenants, in particular that relating to easements, to see if it contained the solution to the problem: and, having found that it did not, they imposed an obligation on the landlord to use reasonable care. In these relationships the parties can exclude or modify the obligations by express words: but unless they do so, the obligation is a legal incident of the relationship which is attached by the law itself and not by reason of any implied term.

(ii)   The second category

The second category comprehends those cases which are not within the first category. These are cases — not of common occurrence — in which from the particular circumstances a term is to be implied. In these cases the implication is based on an intention imputed to the parties from their actual circumstances: Such an imputation is only to be made when it is necessary to imply to give efficacy to the contract and make it a workable agreement in such manner as the parties would clearly have done if they had applied their mind to the contingency which has arisen. These are the 'officious bystander' types of case. In such cases a term is not to be implied on the ground that it would be reasonable: but only when it is necessary and can be formulated with a sufficient degree of precision. This was the test applied by the majority of this court in *Liverpool City Council* v *Irwin* and they were emphatically upheld by the House on this point.

4 Classification of terms

The final question in this chapter and by far the most difficult, is to decide upon the classification of the term once it is incorporated in the contract. Let us suppose one of the parties to the contract is in breach of one of the terms. What is the innocent party entitled to do? There are two main options open: first, he can repudiate the contract or alternatively he can claim damages. How is this decision made?

The final question requires us to decide upon the classification of the term. Traditionally terms were classified either as: a *condition* which entitles the innocent party to repudiate the contract and/or claim damages or as a *warranty* which merely entitles the innocent party to claim damages. The distinction between the two concepts is shown by the decisions in *Bettini* v *Gye* (1876) and *Poussard* v *Spiers* (1876).

In the former case the rehearsal requirement was seen merely as a warranty whereas the performance on the opening and subsequent nights in the latter case was held to be a condition.

Bettini v *Gye*
(1876) 1 QBD 183

BLACKBURN J: . . . If the plaintiff's engagement had been only to sing in operas at the theatre, it might very well be that previous attendance at rehearsals with the actors in company with whom he was to perform was essential. And if the engagement had been only for a few performances, or for a short time it would afford a strong argument that attendance for the purpose of rehearsals during the six days immediately before the commencement of the engagement was a vital part of the agreement. But we find, on looking to the agreement, that the plaintiff was to sing in theatres, halls, and drawing-rooms, both public and private, from the 30th of March to the 13th of July, 1875, and that he was to sing in concerts as well as in operas, and was not to sing anywhere out of the theatre in Great Britain or Ireland from the 1st of January to the 31st of December, 1875, without the written permission of the defendant, except at a distance of more than fifty miles from London.

The plaintiff, therefore, has, in consequence of this agreement, been deprived of the power of earning anything in London from the 1st of January to the 30th of March; and though the defendant has, perhaps, not received any benefit from this, so as to preclude him from any longer treating as a condition precedent what had originally been one, we think this at least affords a strong argument for saying that subsequent stipulations are not intended to be conditions precedent, unless the nature of the thing strongly shows they must be so.

In *Poussard* v *Spiers* (1876) it was held that the plaintiff's inability to perform on the opening and early performances went to the root of the matter, and justified the defendants in rescinding the contract.

The two cases are, I think, relatively straightforward to understand. The increasing complexity of contractual provisions, however, has created problems for the courts. The courts perceived themselves as making the distinction between the conditions and warranties by looking at the contract in the light of surrounding circumstances and deciding the intention of the parties from the contract itself. It is clear from the above that the decision, as to the nature of the term, is being decided upon without looking at the *effect* of the breach upon the contract. Therefore, it is based upon the intention of the parties indicated either before or at the time the contract was entered into.

The courts have had great difficulty with using the above approach and certainly it can be argued that the effect of the breach was being looked at. There was, however, a substantial shift in emphasis following the decision in *Hongkong Fir Shipping Co. Ltd* v *Kawasaki Kisen Kaisha Ltd* (1962). (NB. The judgment of Diplock LJ is important and should be read.)

Hongkong Fir Shipping Co. Ltd v *Kawasaki Kisen Kaisha Ltd*
[1962] 2 QB 26

By a time charterparty, dated December 26, 1956, shipowners let and charterers hired the Hongkong Fir, *built in 1931, for a period of 24 calendar months. Clause 3 of the charterparty provided that the owners should '... maintain her in a thoroughly efficient state in hull and machinery during service'. The vessel was delivered to the charterers on February 13, 1957, and on that day sailed in ballast from Liverpool to Newport News, Virginia, to pick up a cargo of coal and carry it to Osaka. The vessel's machinery was in reasonably good condition at Liverpool but by reason of its age needed to be maintained by an experienced engine room staff. When she sailed the chief engineer was inefficient and addicted to drink, and the engine room complement insufficient, and, chiefly for that reason, there were many serious breakdowns in the machinery. On the voyage from Liverpool to Osaka she was at sea eight and a half weeks, off hire for about five weeks and had about £21,400 spent on her for repairs. She reached Osaka on May 25 when a further period of about 15 weeks and an expenditure of £37,500 were required to make her ready for sea. In June 1957, the charterers repudiated the charterparty: they had no reasonable grounds for thinking that the owners would be unable to make her seaworthy by mid-September, at the latest, and in fact the vessel sailed from Osaka on September 15 with an adequate and competent engine room staff and was then admittedly in all respects seaworthy. In an action by the owners for damages for wrongful repudiation of the charterparty in which the charterers contended that they were entitled to repudiate by reason of a breach by the owners of their obligation to deliver a seaworthy vessel and that the charterparty was frustrated by the delays and breakdowns.*

DIPLOCK LJ: ... There are ... many contractual undertakings of a more complex character which cannot be categorised as being 'conditions' or 'warranties'. Of such undertakings all that can be predicted is that some breaches will and others will not give rise to an event which will deprive the party not in default of substantially the whole benefit which it was intended that he should obtain from the contract; and the legal consequences of a breach of such an undertaking, unless provided for expressly in the contract, depend upon the nature of the event to which the breach gives rise and do not follow automatically from a prior classification of the undertaking as a 'condition' or a 'warranty'.... . The common law evolves not merely by breeding new principles but also, when they are fully grown, by burying their progenitors.

As my brethren have already pointed out, the shipowners' undertaking to tender a seaworthy ship has, as a result of numerous decisions as to what can amount to 'unseaworthiness', become one of the most complex of contractual undertakings. It embraces obligations with respect to every part of the hull of machinery, stores and equipment and the crew itself. It can be broken by the presence of trivial defects easily and rapidly remediable as well as by defects which must inevitably result in a total loss of the vessel.

Consequently the problem in this case is, in my view, neither solved nor soluable by debating whether the shipowner's express or implied undertaking to tender a seaworthy ship is a 'condition' or a 'warranty'. It is like so many other contractual terms an undertaking, one breach of which may give rise to an event which relieves the charterer of further performance of his undertakings if he so elects and another breach of which may not give rise to such an event but entitle him only to monetary compensation in the form of damages. It is, with all deference to Mr Ashton Roskill's skilful argument, by no means surprising that among the many hundreds of previous cases about the shipowner's undertaking to deliver a seaworthy ship there is none where it was found profitable to discuss in the judgments the questions whether that undertaking is a 'condition' or a 'warranty'; for the true answer, as I have already indicated, is that it is neither, but one of that large class of contractual undertakings one breach of which may have the same effect as that ascribed to a breach of 'condition' under the Sale of Goods Act 1893, and a different breach of which may have only the same effect as that ascribed to a breach of 'warranty' under that Act.

What the judge had to do in the present case, as in any other case where one party to a contract relies upon a breach by the other party as giving him a right to elect to rescind the contract, and the contract itself makes no express provision as to this, was to look at the event which had occurred as a result of the breach at the time at which the charterers purported to rescind the charterparty and to decide whether the occurrence of those events deprived the charterers of substantially the whole benefit which it was the intention of the parties, expressed in the charterparty, that the charterers should obtain from the further performance of their own contractual undertakings.

On the facts the court of appeal decided that the breach was not sufficient to allow repudiation.

In *Hongkong Fir Shipping Co. Ltd* v *Kawasaki* the court is saying that to decide what remedy the innocent party can have one should wait and see; look at the effect of the breach and decide whether it deprives the innocent party of substantially the whole benefit. Obviously if the breach does deprive the innocent party of substantially the whole benefit then the innocent party can repudiate the contract.

The arguments, to date, can be summarised in the form of a diagram (figure 8.1).

Figure 8.1

Time when classification is made	Before or at the time the contract is made	Wait and see and look at the effect of the breach
Nature of term	Condition/ Warranty	Innominate term

The term in *Hongkong Fir Shipping Co. Ltd* v *Kawasaki* is an *innominate term*. It is of importance to understand that the innominate term creates a *separate* category of its own; that is it is neither a condition nor a warranty. Therefore, referring to the grid diagram above, the courts are in effect saying that if they are unable to decide upon the nature of the term through prior classification, then they will look at the effect of the breach through the use of the innominate term.

Before discussing the concept further a number of general points need to be made. The main advantage of the innominate term is that of flexibility in that the courts can give what they think to be the appropriate remedy given the circumstances of the case. On the other hand this flexibility takes away the certainty that is often required in business contracts in particular. The certainty/flexibility debate is still a very real one but the courts will not accept a label put on a term, for example as a condition, if it does not reflect both the commercial expectation of the parties and also the business context in which a particular contract is made.

A number of cases need to be looked at in order to develop this theme. Firstly, in *The Mihalis Angelos* (1971) it is quite clear from the judgment that the commercial expectations of the parties were closely looked at in order to decide upon the nature of the term. Not only was it the commercial expectation of the parties but of the field of commerce as a whole that was held to be important.

The Mihalis Angelos
[1971] 1 QB 164

By a charterparty dated May 25, 1965, the Mihalis Angelos *was chartered to proceed to Haiphong and there load a cargo of mineral ore for a North European port. The charterparty described the vessel as 'now trading and expected ready to load under this charter about July 1, 1965'. Clause 11 of the charterparty provided 'Should the vessel not be ready to load (whether in berth or not) on or before July 20, 1965, charterers have the option of cancelling this contract, such option to be declared, if demanded, at least 48 hours before the vessel's expected arrival at port of loading.' On June 23, 1965, the charterers purported to cancel the charterparty on grounds of force majeure, claiming that there was no ore available at Haiphong as a result of warlike activities over North Vietnam. The owners at once accepted the charterers' conduct as a repudiation of the contract. The owner's claim for damages for loss of profit was referred to arbitrators who found that (a) at the date of the charterparty the owners could not reasonably have expected that the vessel would be ready to load at Haiphong about July 1, 1965; (b) on July 17, 1965, the charterers were not entitled to terminate the charterparty on grounds of force majeure; (c) if the vessel had proceeded to Haiphong she would not have been ready to load there until after July 20, 1965, and the charterers would have exercised their option under clause 11 to cancel the charterparty. The arbitrators held that on July 17, 1965, the charterers committed an anticipatory breach of contract which was accepted by the owners as a repudiation but that, by reason of finding (c), above, the owners were only entitled to nominal damages.*

Held: that the 'expected readiness' clause was a condition and, the owners having broken it in that on May 25, 1965, they could not reasonably have expected that the ship would be ready to load in Haiphong on July 1, 1965 the charterers were entitled to terminate the contract on July 17, 1965.

MEGAW LJ: . . . In my judgment, such a term in a charterparty ought to be regarded as being a condition of the contract, in the old sense of the word 'condition': that is, that when it has been broken, the other party can, if he wishes, by intimation to the party in breach, elect to be released from performance of his further obligations under the contract; and he can validly do so without having to establish that on the facts of the particular case the breach has produced serious consequences which can be treated as 'going to the root of the contract' or as being 'fundamental', whatever other metaphor may be thought appropriate for a frustration case. I reach that conclusion for four interrelated reasons.

First, it tends towards certainty in the law. One of the essential elements of law is some measure of uniformity. One of the important elements of the law is predictability. At any rate in commercial law, there are obvious and substantial advantages in having, where possible, a firm and definite rule for a particular class of legal relationship: for example, as here, the legal categorisation of a particular, definable type of contractual clause in common use. Where justice does not require greater flexibility, there is everything to be said for, and nothing against, a degree of rigidity in legal principle.

Second, it would, in my opinion, only be in the rarest case, if ever, that a shipowner could legitimately feel that he had suffered an injustice by reason of the law having given to a charterer the right to put an end to the contract because of the breach by the shipowner of a clause such as this. If a shipowner has chosen to assert contractually, but dishonestly or without reasonable grounds, that he expects his vessel to be ready to loan on such-and-such a date, wherein does the grievance lie?

Third, it is, as Mocatta J. held clearly established by authority binding on this court that where a clause 'expected ready to load' is included in a contract for the sale of goods to be carried by sea, that clause is a condition, in the sense that any breach of it enables the buyer to reject the goods without having to show that the dishonest or unreasonable expectation of the seller has in fact been prejudiced to the buyer.

Compare the above with the decision in *L. Schuler AG* v *Wickman Machine Tool Sales Ltd* (1974) where merely because one of the parties labelled the term a 'condition' did not mean that any breach of that term allowed the innocent party to repudiate the contract. The decision is very interesting in that Schuler, in calling the term a condition, tried to avoid the court using the innominate term approach. Clearly the nature of the contract did not allow the court to hold that commercial expectation/usage was available to them in order to uphold the arguments of Schuler. The case, therefore, shows that the court is quite prepared to look behind the wording of the contract and instead look at the effect of it on the contract as a whole. Consequently merely using the word condition does not by itself lead to predictability and certainty.

L. Schuler AG v *Wickman Machine Tool Sales Ltd*
[1974] AC 235

LORD REID: ... In the present case it is not contended that Wickman's failures to make visits amounted in themselves to fundamental breaches. What is contended is that the terms of clause 7 'sufficiently express an intention' to make any breach, however small, of the obligation to make visits a condition so that any breach shall entitle Schuler to rescind the whole contract if they so desire.

Schuler maintains that the use of the word 'condition' is in itself enough to establish this intention. No doubt some words used by lawyers do have a rigid inflexible meaning. But we must remember that we are seeking to discover intention as disclosed by *the contract as a whole*. Use of the word 'condition' is an indication — even a strong indication — of such an intention but it is by no means conclusive.

The fact that a particular construction leads to a very unreasonable result must be a relevant consideration. The more unreasonable the result the more unlikely it is that the parties can have intended it, and if they do intend it the more necessary it is that they shall make the intention abundantly clear.

Clause 7(b) requires that over a long period each of the six firms shall be visited every week by one or other of two named representatives. It makes no provision for Wickman being entitled to substitute others even on the death or retirement of one of the named representatives. Even if one could imply some right to do this, it makes no provision for both representatives being ill during a particular week. And it makes no provision for the possibility that one or other of the firms may tell Wickman that they cannot receive Wickman's representative during a particular week. So if the parties gave any thought to the matter at all they must have realised the probability that in a few cases out of the 1,400 required visits a visit as stipulated would be impossible. But if Schuler's contention is right, failure to make even one visit entitled them to terminate the contract however blameless Wickman might be.

This is so unreasonable that it must make me search for some other possible meaning of the contract. If none can be found then Wickman must suffer the consequences. But only if that is the only possible interpretation.

If I have to construe clause 7 standing by itself then I do find difficulty in reaching any other interpretation. But if clause 7 must be read with clause 11 the difficulty disappears. The word 'condition' would make any breach of clause 7(b), however excusable, a material breach. That would then entitle Schuler to give notice under clause 11(a)(i) requiring the breach to be remedied. There would be no point in giving such a notice if Wickman were clearly not in fault but if it were given Wickman would have no difficulty in showing that the breach had been remedied. If Wickman were at fault then on receiving such a notice they would have to amend their system so that they could show that the breach had been remedied. If they did not do that within the period of the notice then Schuler would be entitled to rescind.

In my view, that is a possible and reasonable construction of the contract and I would therefore adopt it. The contract is so obscure that I can have no confidence that this is its true meaning but for the reasons which I have given I think that it is the preferable construction. It follows that Schuler was not entitled to rescind the contract as it purported to do. So I would dismiss this appeal.

Finally, the decision of *Bunge Corporation* v *Tradax Export SA* (1981) needs to be discussed. The case is important for a number of reasons. First, the courts rejected the use of the innominate term despite the fact that the effect of the breach obviously did not deprive the innocent party of substantially the whole benefit of the contract. Secondly, the courts looked at the trade expectation not only of the parties but of the contractual area as a whole. The shipping industry had also seen such clauses as conditions and this was implicitly understood by both parties and to upset well established precedents in the area would have lead to chaos, let alone uncertainty.

How can this area of law be seen as operating at present? What the courts are saying is this. First, there are three types of terms: conditions, warranties and innominate. If *all* the surrounding circumstances are looked at and it can be ascertained what the parties intend then the court will call the term either a condition or warranty. Secondly, the courts now, as compared to the mid-1970s, are less likely to interfere with the contract where the parties have expressed their intention expressly or implicitly through trade usage. The reluctance of the judiciary to intervene is shown in other areas of contract law as well and it may be that certainty has been reintroduced at the expense of fairness which in the business world is perhaps a good thing.

A useful summary of the area covered above is the following article:

Kay, 'The Relative Importance of Contractual Terms'
Preston Law Review [1981] PLR 73

Contractual terms, before 1963, were seen either as 'conditions' or 'warranties'. However, in that year, the Court of Appeal in *Hongkong Fir Shipping Co. Ltd* v *Kawasaki Kisen Kaisha Ltd* introduced a third category of terms: that is to say the 'innominate term' or 'intermediate stipulation'.

Following the decision in *Hongkong Fir* the courts have seemingly had great problems as to which category a term belongs. The recent decisions of the Court of Appeal and the House of Lords in *Bunge Corporation* v *Tradax Export SA* have hopefully shed some light upon this problem.

The facts of the case

Under a contract which incorporated GAFTA form 119, the buyers agreed to purchase from the sellers 15,000 tons of soya bean meal. By agreement between the parties one of the shipments was to be made during June 1975. The buyers were to provide a vessel at the nominated port, and by virtue of clause 7 of form 119, as completed by the parties, they were required to 'give at least 15 consecutive days' notice' of the probable readiness of the vessel. The buyers were two days late with their notice and thus in breach of clause 7. One of the questions to be answered by the courts was whether or not clause 7 amounted to a 'condition', 'warranty' or 'innominate term'.

In discussing the approach taken by the courts in the instant case the writer shall focus upon the judgments of three of the judges involved: Lord Justice Megaw; Lords Roskill and Wilberforce. The reason for this is two-fold: first the three seem to give the leading judgments in their respective courts: Megaw LJ in the Court of Appeal; Lords Roskill and Wilberforce in the House of Lords. Secondly, the above-mentioned judges have sat in previous cases discussing this area of the law and it would appear to be a useful exercise to detect any judicial trend emanating from the three.

A.   *The judgment of Megaw LJ*

It is perhaps worth reflecting upon Megaw LJ's previous views on this subject before discussing this judgment in this case. In *The Mihalis Angelos* he stated:

One of the important elements of the law is predictability. At any rate in commercial law there are obvious and substantial advantages in having, where possible, a firm and definite rule for a particular class of legal relationships . . .

Megaw LJ has previously shown little enthusiasm for the 'innominate term' and it will come as no surprise that clause 7 was construed as a condition by the Lord Justice. The conclusion is based on 'commercial usage' and here the arbitrator's report is used as evidence for this proposition: 'such a provision is customarily treated in the trade as being for the purpose of giving to sellers sufficient time to make necessary arrangements to get the goods to the port of loading on board the nominated vessel.' Given this trade practise insight, the Lord Justice saw the term as a condition, as clearly the parties intended it to be so. The court was then left in no doubt by the weight placed on this observation of the arbitrator by Megaw LJ:

> It would, in my opinion, be arrogant and unjustifiable for a court to substitute any view of its own for the view of the parties themselves as to what was a reasonable time for this purpose.

So where do these remarks leave the innominate term from *Hongkong Fir?* The relevant part of Diplock LJ's speech in *Hongkong Fir* was cited by Megaw LJ:

> ... breach of such an undertaking must give rise to an event which will deprive the party now in default of *substantially the whole benefit* which it was intended that he should obtain from the contract.

Clearly the buyers argued that as, on the facts, the notice of readiness was only two days late then this did not amount to a breach of clause 7 akin to 'substantially the whole benefit'. Megaw LJ dismissed this argument with five reasons, one of which will be focused upon here. The literal interpretation of the words would mean it would be very difficult to show that in such cases the innocent party was ever deprived of 'substantially the whole benefit'. Consequently, given the Lord Justice's reading of a literal interpretation, such a clause would be of little use and it would also run against the intention of the parties and trade usage.

If, as again, to emphasise this point of intention of the parties and surrounding circumstances, dicta of Bowen LJ in *Bentsen* v *Taylor, Sons and Co.* are used as authority for such a proposition:

> There is no way of deciding that question (i.e., the nature of the term) except by looking at the contract in the light of the surrounding circumstances, and then making up one's mind whether the intention of the parties, as gathered from the instrument itself, will best be carried out by treating the promise as a warranty sounding only in damages, or as a condition precedent by the failure to perform ...

Conclusion

The importance of Megaw LJ's judgment cannot be under-estimated as shall be seen below when looking at the judgments from the House of Lords. Two main points arise from the leading judgment of the Court of Appeal: first, there is a great deal of emphasis placed on certainty within the law and to this end the innominate term poses a threat.

Secondly, if the innominate term is to be used it is only after either the intention of the parties or the surrounding circumstances of the contract do not point to a condition or warranty; and given Megaw LJ's diligence for finding the two this will rarely happen.

B.   *The judgment of Lord Roskill*

Lord Roskill when he sat in the Court of Appeal had given judgment on the question of terms in *The Hansa Nord*:

> In my view, a court should not be over ready, unless required by statute or authority so to do, to construe a term in a contract as a 'condition' any breach of which gives rise to a right to reject rather than as a term any breach of which sounds in damages ... I think the court should tend to prefer that construction which will ensure performance and not encourage avoidance of contractual obligations.

Clearly from the above Lord Roskill approves of the innominate term and can it not be argued that we are here talking of a situation in which its use would be appropriate given that the buyer's notice was only two days late? Lord Roskill, however, does say that clause 7 of form 119 is a condition, despite the above, and distinguishes Lord Justice Diplock's judgment in *Hongkong Fir* in two ways.

First, Lord Roskill states:

> But I do not believe he (Diplock LJ) ever intended his judgment to afford an easy escape route from the normal consequences of recission to a contract for a party who had broken what was, on its true construction, clearly a condition of the contract by claiming that he had only broken an innominate term.

Here Lord Roskill is making the same point as Megaw LJ; that is to say if a term points to a condition either through the intention of the parties or trade practice then the courts should leave well alone.

The second factor which Lord Roskill has to distinguish from *Hongkong Fir* concerns further words used by Diplock LJ in that case:

> ... and the legal consequences of a breach of such an undertaking, unless provided for expressly in the contract, depend upon the nature of the event to which the breach gives rise ...

Thus as counsel for the buyer argued, as 'condition' was not expressly mentioned in clause 7 it should be treated as an innominate term. Lord Roskill answers this by calling upon words used by Lord Diplock himself in the later case of *Photo Production Ltd* v *Securicor Transport Ltd*.

> ... whether by express words or by implication of law, failure by one part to perform a particular primary obligation ('Condition' in the nomenclature of the Sale of Goods Act 1893), irrespective of the gravity of the event that has in fact resulted from the breach, shall entitle the other party to put an end to all primary obligations of both parties remaining unperformed ...

Lord Roskill draws an analogy between the two dicta of Lord Diplock and assumes that the words 'or by implication' from *Photo Production* may be added to the words in *Hongkong Fir*. Consequently, the result reached means that intention of the parties and/or trade usage can be implied in the absence of express words.

Conclusion

Lord Roskill has thus seemingly put a check on his own enthusiasm for the 'innominate term' preferring to follow the pre-1962 approach in this case.

C.   *The judgment of Lord Wilberforce*

Lord Wilberforce has sat in two previous cases in this area and seemingly two different approaches come from his Lordship. First in *L. Schuler AG* v *Wickman Machine Tool Sales Ltd* Lord Wilberforce dissented from the majority in not declaring the term in the contract concerned innominate. The nature of the dissent can be seen from the following part of his judgment:

> The use as a promissory term of 'condition' is artificial, as is that of 'warranty' in some contexts. But in my opinion this use is now too deeply embedded in English law to be uprooted by anything less than a complete revision.

A change of mind regarding the efficacy of the 'innominate' term can perhaps be seen from Lord Wilberforce's statements in *Reardon Smith Line Ltd* v *Hansen-Tangen*.

> The general law of contract has developed along more rational lines (e.g., *Hongkong Fir* ...) in attending to the nature and gravity of a breach or departure rather than in accepting rigid categories which do or do not automatically give a right to rescind, and if the choice were between extending cases under the Sale of Goods Act 1893 into other fields, or allowing more modern doctrine to infect those cases, my preference would be clear.

Whether or not this is a change of Lord Wilberforce's attitude on this subject is not altogether clear but one may argue that unlike Lord Justice Megaw and Lord Roskill there is an indication of considering both approaches.

Lord Wilberforce follows Lord Roskill and the Court of Appeal in calling the term a condition. The views of their Lordships may be indicated by the following statement of Lord Wilberforce:

> But I do not doubt that, in suitable cases, the courts should not be reluctant, if the intentions of the parties as shown by the contract so indicate, to hold that an obligation has the force of a condition, and that indeed they should usually do so in the case of time clauses in mercantile contracts. To such cases the 'gravity of the breach' approach of *Hongkong Fir*, would be unsuitable.

Conclusion

Lord Wilberforce clearly wants to uphold the intention of the parties as far as possible — in *Schuler* by express agreement and here in *Tradax* by implication. Thus his Lordship wants the best of both worlds and which of the two tests applies depends upon the facts of the case.

Overall Conclusion

Three points may be drawn from looking at the case as a whole. First, there are still three, as opposed to one (the 'innominate') classifications into which terms of the contract can fit: conditions, warranties and innominate terms.

Secondly, the courts will now only construe the term as being in the latter category if there is ambiguity or doubt, and seemingly this must be of a manifest nature. Thus one can argue strongly there is now more certainty in this area of law.

Finally the decision reflects a trend, previously shown by the House of Lords in *Photo Production* v *Securicor*, of non-intervention by the judiciary. Therefore, as in *Tradax*, if the parties are of equal bargaining strength then the courts should let any results of the bargain/contract made stand: even though the breach may only be a 'minor' one in the circumstances. Thus the courts are giving priority to the 'freedom of contract' principle again.

Activity

The next time you enter into a written standard form contract look carefully at the terms incorporated therein. Can you decide upon the nature of those terms and those implied by statute (see chapter 17)?

Self check questions

1.   What is the effect of a breach of condition?
2.   What is the effect of a breach of warranty?
3.   What is an innominate term and how do the courts decide what rights an innocent party has in such cases?
4.   What is the relationship between conditions/warranties and innominate terms?

Answers

1.   Entitles the innocent party to repudiate and/or claim damages.
2.   Entitles the innocent party to only claim damages.
3.   An innominate term is based upon the effect of the breach on the contract. The court will wait and see if the breach deprives the innocent party of substantially the whole benefit of the contract. If the latter applies then the innocent party may repudiate the contract; for anything less than repudiation, damages are the only remedy.
4.   The two categories must be seen as being mutually exclusive of one another. Conditions/warranties can be determined from the intention of the parties, trade usage etc. whereas innominate terms depend upon the effect of the breach.

Problem

The use of a promissory term of 'condition' is artificial, as is that of 'warranty' in some contexts. But in my opinion this use is now too deeply embedded in English law to be uprooted by anything less than a complete revision. (Per Lord Wilberforce in *L. Schuler AG* v *Wickman Machine Tool Sales Ltd* (1974).)

To what extent is this a true reflection of judicial attitudes toward the interpretation of terms of a contract?

Suggested answer

The essay concerns the nature of contractual terms in English law. Traditionally terms were divided into either conditions or warranties, as indicated by Lord Wilberforce. However, a third category of term has developed which needs to be linked to the statement of Lord Wilberforce.

The courts would decide the nature of the term before or at the time the contract was entered into. Therefore, if the term was held to be a condition it would entitle the innocent party to repudiate the contract and/or claim damages, whereas if the term was a warranty, damages were the only remedy. Although the courts seemingly took the decision at an earlier stage, it can be argued from cases such as *Bettini* v *Gye* and *Poussard* v *Spiers* that the effect of the breach was in fact being looked at.

The decisions as to when the nature of the term should be decided upon was further discussed by the Court of Appeal in the *Hongkong Fir Shipping Case*. The essence of the judgment of Diplock LJ is that the courts in making this decision should 'wait and see' and 'look at the effects of the breach'. Once the court has done this then if the breach 'deprives the innocent part of the whole benefit' then the courts will allow repudiation. In taking this approach the courts are not saying the term is either a condition or warranty but is an innominate term and the courts decide whether or not there should be repudiation or merely damages.

The decision in *Hongkong Fir Shipping* goes against the statement of Lord Wilberforce. However, *Hongkong Fir Shipping* was decided in 1962 and therefore we need to see the way in which the innominate term principle has developed in relation to the traditional approach. A number of authorities may be called to support the innominate term: *The Hansa Nord* and *Reardon Smith Line Ltd* v *Hansen-Tangen* being two. The peak of the principle was reached by the majority of the House of Lords in *L. Schuler AG* v *Wickman Machine Tool Sales Ltd*, Lord Wilberforce dissenting, where the House decided a term was innominate despite the fact that the parties had labelled it a condition. The main advantage of such an approach is one of flexibility as the courts are able to do some kind of notional justice between the parties. However, from a commercial perspective, and this is inherent in the statement of Lord Wilberforce, there is a need for certainty therefore the innominate term did not receive universal support.

The main driving force behind the use of the traditional method was Megaw LJ. In *The Mihalis Angelos* the Lord Justice emphasised the need for predictability and thought the innominate term approach was not appropriate in certain types of contractual situations, for example charter parties. The above approach was approved, albeit implicitly, by the House of Lords in *Bunge* v *Tradax*. The case concerned a time clause and it may be argued that the ratio of the case merely states that such clauses should be treated as conditions.

It is quite legitimate, however, to take a much wider view of the case. The judiciary following the decision in *Photo Production Ltd* v *Securicor Transport Ltd* are much more likely to give effect to the intention of the parties whether express or implied — in *Bunge Corporation* v *Tradax Export SA* the intention was implied through trade usage. Therefore, it could be that the courts are now much less willing to use the innominate term approach where the intention of the parties can be found. The quote of Lord Wilberforce, despite being a dissenting judgment, could well reflect the present state of the law.

9 EXEMPTION CLAUSES

1 Introduction

Exemption clauses are used frequently in the course of business; for example 'The company does not accept liability . . .' is an exemption clause which will have been seen by many. The law, however, has traditionally tried to control the use of exemption clauses through common law and statutory devices. Parliament, in 1977, introduced the Unfair Contract Terms Act which places severe restrictions on the use of such clauses mainly because the drafters of exemption clauses had been able to avoid the common law rules. Further controls have been added by the Unfair Terms in Consumer Contracts Regulations 1994 which apply to other 'unfair terms' as well as exemption clauses. The effect of these additional provisions will be dealt with at the end of this chapter.

A final point should be made by way of introduction. It should not be thought that the law dislikes all forms of exemption clauses, as when two business organisations contract. Exemption clauses are often used to apportion risk between the parties. Therefore, the law will uphold the clause, assuming that it is negotiated between the parties.

This subject will be considered under two headings: common law controls and statutory controls.

2 Common law control

Common-law control can in turn be sub-divided into two: incorporation of the term into the contract and construction of the term.

2.1 Incorporation into the contract
We have discussed incorporation in a more general way when talking of how a pre-contractual statement becomes a term of the contract. There, the overall

test was based on the intention of the parties with a number of guidelines developed by the judiciary. In this area an exemption may be incorporated either by signature or alternatively by notice.

2.1.1 Incorporation by signature The general principle is that a person signing a document is bound by the provisions of that document even though the document has not been read: *L'Estrange* v *F. Graucob Ltd* (1934).

L'Estrange v *F. Graucob Ltd*
[1934] 2 KB 394

The buyer of an automatic slot machine signed and handed to the sellers an order form containing in ordinary print and writing the essential terms of the contract, and in small print certain special terms one of which was 'any express or implied condition, statement, or warranty, statutory or otherwise not stated herein is hereby excluded'. The sellers thereupon signed and handed to the buyers a printed order confirmation assenting to the terms in the order form. The machine was delivered by the sellers to the buyer, who paid to the sellers an instalment of the price. The machine did not work satisfactorily, and the buyer brought an action against the sellers claiming damages for breach of an implied warranty that the machine was fit for the purpose for which it had been sold. The sellers pleaded that the contract provided for the exclusion of all implied warranties. The buyer replied that at the time when she signed the order form she had not read it and knew nothing of its contents, and that the clause warranties could not easily be read owing to the smallness of the print.

Held: by the Divisional Court reversing on this point the judgment of the county court judge, that as the buyer had signed the written contract, and had not been induced to do so by any misrepresentation, she was bound by the terms of the contract, and it was wholly immaterial that she had not read it and did not know its contents; and that the action failed and the sellers were entitled to judgment.

There is, however, one clear exception to this principle and that is where the nature of the terms have been misrepresented to the party who is being bound by the exemption clause. In *Curtis* v *Chemical Cleaning and Dyeing Company* (1951) it was held that even an innocent misrepresentation as to the nature of the written document would deprive the party seeking to rely on the exemption clause of the benefit of it, despite signature.

Curtis v *Chemical Cleaning and Dyeing Company*
[1951] 1 All ER 631

The plaintiff took to the defendants, a firm of dyers and cleaners, a white satin wedding dress for cleaning. She was asked to sign a document which contained a clause that the dress 'is accepted on condition that the company is not liable for any damage howsoever arising.' Before signing the document the plaintiff asked why she had to sign it, and she was told by one of the defendants' servants that the defendant would not accept liability for damages done to beads or sequins on the dress. The plaintiff then signed the document without having read all of it. When the dress was returned, there was a stain on it. The county court judge found that there was no stain on the dress when the plaintiff left it with the defendants for cleaning, that the burden of proof was on the defendants to show that the stain had not been caused by their negligence, and that the defendants had failed to discharge that burden. The defendants did not challenge that finding, but sought to rely on the exemption clause in the document which the plaintiff had signed.

Held: since the plaintiff had been induced to sign the document by an innocent misrepresentation as to the extent of the exemption clause, the exception never became part of the contract between the parties, and, therefore, the defendants were liable to the plaintiff.

2.1.2   Incorporation by notice   Let us take a common day example. Suppose you go to your local leisure centre and there is displayed over the counter, where payment is made, the following sign 'The Local Authority accept no responsibility for any loss or damage to users' personal belongings'. Is that clause incorporated into your contract with the Local Authority? In order for a clause to be incorporated by notice a number of criteria must be satisfied.

First, the document must be of a contractual nature. In *Chapelton* v *Barry UDC* (1940) the judge held that as the ticket merely amounted to a receipt the document was not of a contractual nature.

Chapelton v *Barry UDC*
[1940] 1 KB 532

The plaintiff who wished to hire a deck chair on a beach went to a pile of deck chairs belonging to the defendant council near to which was displayed a notice in the following terms: 'Barry Urban District Council. Cold Knap. Hire of chairs 2d. per session of 3 hours.' The notice went on to state that the public were requested to obtain tickets for their chairs from the chair attendants and that those tickets should be retained for inspection. There was nothing on the notice relieving the defendant council from liability for any accident or damage arising out of the hire of a chair. The plaintiff obtained two chairs from the attendant for which he paid 4d. and received two tickets therefor. The plaintiff glanced at the tickets and slipped them into his pocket and had no idea that they contained any conditions. On one side of the tickets were the words: 'Barry Urban District Council. Cold Knap. Chair Ticket 2d. Not transferable.' On the other side of the tickets were the words: 'Available for three hours. Time expires where indicated by cut-off and should be retained and shown on request. The council will not be liable for any accident or damage arising from the hire of the chair.' The plaintiff put the chairs up in the ordinary way on a flat part of the beach, and then sat down on a chair which gave way, the canvas having come away from the top of the chair. In an action against the defendants the county court judge found that the accident was due to the negligence of the defendants, but that the defendants were exempted from liability as the plaintiff had sufficient notice of the special contract printed on the ticket. On appeal:

SLESSER LJ: . . . I think that the object of the giving and taking of this ticket was that the person taking might have evidence at hand by which he could show that the obligation he was under to pay 2d. for the use of the chair for three hours had been duly discharged, and I think it is altogether inconsistent, in the absence of any qualification of liability in the notice put up near the pile of chairs, to attempt to read into it the qualification contended for. In my opinion, this ticket is no more than a receipt, and is quite different from a railway ticket which contains upon it the terms upon which a railway company agrees to carry the passenger.

In the extracted judgment above the judge makes a comparison with railway tickets. In *Thompson* v *London Midland and Scottish Railway Co.* (1930) it was held that a railway ticket amounted to a contractual document. The dividing line between the two seems a little thin but it has become accepted law.

Secondly, the notice must be contemporaneous. What the law is saying here is that in order for the document to be incorporated it must be brought to the attention of the other party before or at the time the contract was made. In *Olley* v *Marlborough Court Ltd* (1949) the fact that the notice was only brought to the party's attention after the contract was made meant that the clause was not incorporated.

Olley v *Marlborough Court Ltd*
[1949] 1 KB 532

A notice in the bedroom of a private residential hotel stated: 'The proprietors will not hold themselves responsible for articles lost or stolen, unless handed to the manageress for safe custody. Valuables should be deposited for safe custody in a sealed package and a receipt obtained.' A notice pursuant to s. 3 of the Innkeepers' Liability Act 1863, was conspicuously displayed in the hall of the hotel.

A man and his wife, on arrival at the hotel as guests, in accordance with the custom of the hotel paid for a week's board and residence in advance. They then went upstairs to the bedroom allotted to them, where the first-mentioned notice was displayed.

The guests lost valuable personal possessions and the hotel sought to exclude its liability by reference to the exclusion notice.

Held: That the terms of the notice in the bedroom formed no part of the contract made between the guests and the proprietors of the hotel. The contract had been made before the guests could see the notice. It was for an indeterminate period, to which an end could be put by notice on either side, and the terms of the notice in the bedroom could form no part of the contract until that contract had been terminated.

Activity
When going on holiday, in this country, look closely where the exemption clause is displayed in the hotel.

Self check question
A books a room in B's hotel by phone. A pays a deposit. When A registers there is an exemption clause over the desk. Is the clause incorporated into the contract?

Answer

The question you have to decide upon is when the contract was made? A by phoning and sending a deposit has created a contract and therefore the notice is brought to the attention of A after the contract was made. Therefore B cannot rely on it.

Thirdly, there must be 'reasonable notice' when the law imposes a duty on a person to act in a 'reasonable fashion'; much confusion and hence uncertainty is created. Again the courts have drawn up a number of guidelines in order to help us make this decision. The most important of these, originally stated in *Parker v South Eastern Railway Co.* (1877), is that the party seeking to rely on the clause must give the other party reasonable sufficiency of notice. In *J. Spurling Ltd v Bradshaw* (1956) Lord Denning is clearly suggesting that the more onerous the nature of the clause the greater the sufficiency of notice required. Quite whether there is a need for red ink however is debatable.

J. Spurling Ltd v Bradshaw
[1956] 1 WLR 461

The defendant, a wholesale factor, who had had previous business dealings with the plaintiff warehousemen, delivered to them eight barrels of orange juice for storage, and a few days later received a 'landing account' which on its face referred to conditions printed in small type on the back. These included the London lighterage clause, which exempted the plaintiffs, inter alia, from liability for any loss, damage or detention, in respect of goods entrusted to them in the course of their business, occasioned by the negligence, wrongful act or default of themselves, their servants, or agents. The barrels, when collected, were found to be either empty or in such damaged condition as to be useless. In an action by the warehousemen to recover charges due for storage, the defendant counterclaimed for damages for alleged breach of an implied term of the contract of bailment to take reasonable care of the barrels. The plaintiffs denied negligence and relied on the exemption clause. The county court judge, after hearing the evidence for the defendant only, found that the plaintiffs had been negligent; he dismissed the counterclaim, holding that the exemption clause applied. On appeal by the defendant:

DENNING LJ: . . . This brings me to the question whether this clause was part of the contract. Mr Sofer urged us to hold that the warehousemen did not do what was reasonably sufficient to give notice of the conditions. I quite agree that the more unreasonable a clause is, the greater the notice which must be given of it. Some clauses which I have seen would need to be printed in red ink on the face of the document with a red hand pointing to it before the notice could be held to be sufficient.

A final method of incorporation which must be discussed is whether a previous course of dealings between the parties incorporates the clause into the contract. Suppose that A and B have traded with each other over a number of years. A hires something from B but B did not send details of the contract, including an exemption clause, until after the contract was made. If we follow *Olley* v

Marlborough Court (above) then the clause will not be incorporated but the question of course of dealing must be then looked at.

The law draws a distinction between two types of contractual situation. First, where one party is dealing in the course of business and the other is dealing as a consumer. Secondly, where both parties are dealing in the course of business. Obviously the question of bargaining strength as between the parties is seen as a crucial factor. In *McCutcheon v David MacBrayne Ltd* (1964) and *British Crane Hire Corporation Ltd v Ipswich Plant Hire Ltd* (1975) the crucial factor was the amount of knowledge possessed by the parties as a consequence of the course of dealings between them. The knowledge in the *British Crane Hire* case comes from trade usage, that is the nature of the trade, as much as the express knowledge of the parties. What also must be emphasised is the strength of the bargaining position of the parties as in *British Crane Hire* this was assumed to be equal by the courts.

McCutcheon v David MacBrayne Ltd
[1964] 1 WLR 125

A motor car was delivered to a shipping company at its pier for carriage from the Hebrides to the mainland, the owner's agent receiving a receipt for the freight paid. The ship sank through the negligence of the company's servants and the car was a total loss. In an action by the owner to recover its replacement value the company contended that they were absolved from liability for negligence in accordance with the terms of the conditions of carriage displayed at their office. Their normal practice in accepting goods for shipment was to give the consignor a receipt for the freight paid and 'risk note'. The receipt stated: 'Passengers, passengers' luggage and livestock are carried subject to the conditions specified in the company's sailing bills, notices and announcements.' The 'risk note' consisted of a print of the conditions of carriage with a docket signed by the consignor agreeing to ship the goods 'on the conditions stated above'. In previous similar transactions with the company the car owner or his agent had sometimes signed a 'risk note', but on the present occasion no risk note was issued or signed. Although both the car owner and his agent knew that certain conditions of carriage were normally imposed, neither knew specifically what they were.

LORD DEVLIN: ... In my opinion, the bare fact that there had been previous dealings between the parties does not assist the respondents at all. The fact that a man had made a contract in the same form 99 times (let alone three or four times which are here alleged) will not of itself affect the hundredth contract in which the form is not used. Previous dealings are relevant only if they prove knowledge of the terms, actual and not constructive, and assent to them. If a term is not expressed in a contract, there is only one other way in which it can come into it and that is by implication. No implication can be made against a party of a term which was unknown to him. If previous dealings show that a man knew of and agreed to a term on 99 occasions there is a basis for saying that it can be imported into the hundredth contract without an express statement. It may or may not be sufficient to justify the importation, that depends on the circumstances: but at least by proving knowledge the essential beginning is made. Without knowledge there is nothing. The respondents in the present case have quite failed to prove that the appellant made himself acquainted with the conditions they had introduced into previous dealings. He is not estopped from saying that, for good reasons or bad, he signed the previous contracts without the slightest idea of what was in them. If that is so, previous dealings are no evidence of knowledge and so are of little or no use to the respondents in this case.

I say 'of little or no use' because the appellant did admit that he knew that there were some conditions, though he did not know what they were. He certainly did not know that they were conditions which exempted the respondents from liability for their own negligence, though I suppose, if he had thought about them at all, he would have known that they probably exempted the respondents from the strict liability of a carrier. Most people know that carriers exact some conditons and it does not matter in this case. Mr McCutcheon's knowledge was general knowledge of this sort or was derived from previous dealings. Your lordships can therefore leave previous dealings out of it and ask yourself simply what is the position of a man who, with that amount of general knowledge, apparently makes a contract into which no conditions are expressly inserted?

The answer must surely be that either he does not make a contract at all because the parties are not *ad idem*, or he makes the contract without the conditions. You cannot have a contract subject to uncommunicated conditions the terms of which are known only to one side.

British Crane Hire Corpn Ltd v Ipswich Plant Hire Ltd
[1975] QB 303

The defendant, a plant hire company engaged in drainage and other engineering works on the marsh land, arranged by telephone to hire a dragline crane from the plaintiffs. The crane was delivered and subsequently the plaintiffs sent a printed form setting out the conditions of hire, including the conditions that the defendants should be responsible for the recovery of the crane from soft ground and that the defendants should be responsible for, and indemnify the plaintiffs against, all expenses arising out of the use of the crane. The defendants neither signed nor returned the form to the plaintiffs. Meanwhile, the defendants gave the plaintiffs' driver directions as to the route he should drive the crane over the marsh to the site but warned him of the need to use 'navimats'. The driver did not wait for the defendants to supply the 'navimats' but drove the crane on to the marsh with the result that it sank into the marsh. The defendants managed to get the crane out. On the following day, the crane again sank into the marsh although on that second occasion the driver was using 'navimats' and had followed the instructions of the defendant's site agent.

The plaintiffs sued for the recovery of the crane on the second occasion and the defendants counterclaimed for the cost of recovery of the crane on the first occasion. Deputy Judge Kenneth Jones found that the printed conditions were not incorpor-

ated into the oral contract but held that the defendants were liable for the recovery of the crane on the second occasion on the ground, inter alia, that there was an implied term in the contract that the defendants would return the crane at the end of the hiring. He allowed the defendants' counterclaim for the recovery of the crane on the first occasion on the ground that the plaintiffs' driver had been negligent.

On the defendants' appeal and the plaintiffs' cross appeal:

LORD DENNING MR: But here the parties were both in the trade and were of equal bargaining power. Each was a firm of plant hirers who hired out plant. The defendants themselves knew that firms in the plant-hiring trade always imposed conditions in regard to the hiring of plant: and that their conditions were on much the same lines. The defendants' manager, Mr Turner (who knew the crane), was asked about it. He agreed that he had seen these conditions or similar ones in regard to the hiring of plant. He said that most of them were, to one extent or another, variations of a form which he called 'the Contractors' Plant Association form'. The defendants themselves (when they let out cranes) used the conditions of that form. The conditions on the plaintiffs' form were in rather different words, but nevertheless to much the same effect . . .

From the evidence it is clear that both parties knew quite well that conditions were habitually imposed by the supplier of these machines: and both parties knew the substance of those conditions. In particular that if the crane sank in soft ground it was the hirer's job to recover it: and that there was an indemnity clause. In these circumstances, I think the conditions on the form should be regarded as incorporated into the contract. I would not put it so much on the course of dealing, but rather on the common understanding which is to be derived from the conduct of the parties, namely, that the hiring was to be on the terms of the plaintiffs usual conditions.

A further factor to take into account is the nature of the clause. In particular the more onerous or unusual the clause the more notice and/or greater consistency in the course of dealing is required. For example:

Interfoto Picture Library Ltd v Stiletto Visual Programmes Ltd
[1988] 1 All ER 349

The defendant telephoned the plaintiffs, who ran a library of photographic transparencies, in order to hire certain transparencies. The parties had not dealt with each other before. The defendant hired 47 transparencies. The transparencies were packed into a bag which contained a delivery note. Condition 2 of the terms stated:

A holding fee of £5.00 plus VAT per day will be charged for each transparency which is retained by you longer than the said period of 14 days.

The defendant accepted delivery but did not read any of the conditions contained in the delivery note. The transparencies were returned some two weeks late and the plaintiff claimed £3,783 by way of a holding charge as per Condition 2 of the delivery note.

Held: Where a term in a contract was particularly onerous or unusual and would not be generally known to the other party the party seeking to enforce that condition had to show that it had been fairly and reasonably brought to the other party's attention. Condition 2 was an unreasonable and extortionate clause which the plaintiff had not brought to the attention of the defendant and therefore it did not become part of the contract.

Self check question
X has taken his car to Y garage for a regular service over the past two years. X receives an invoice which states that 'Y garage do not accept any liability for any loss or damage to customer's cars howsoever caused'. The next time X takes his car in it is destroyed. At no time has X read the invoice or had the terms brought to his attention. Is X bound by the exclusion clause?

Answer
Assuming that X is dealing as a consumer it is doubtful that the course of dealing between the parties would be sufficient to incorporate the clause into the contract. However, if X was dealing in the course of business the reasoning in *British Crane Hire* could apply. The facts do not provide sufficient information to give a definitive answer.

2.2 Construction of the exemption clause
The common law imposes a second test which must be satisfied in order for the clause to be valid. The wording of the clause must cover the loss, therefore the courts will construe the clause to see if it covers the loss, if not then the clause will fail. The second test is independent of the first test and even though the first test is satisfied it does not effect the way in which the second one is applied.

The main rule in this area is the *contra proferentem* rule; that is the courts will construe the clause against the person seeking to rely on it. Consequently if there is any doubt or ambiguity the clause will fail. The best illustration of how this rule has operated is in the way the exclusion of negligence liability has or has not been allowed. As we shall see this provides us with an interesting insight into judicial attitudes of dealing with such clauses. The starting point for such a discussion is the decision in *Canada Steamship Lines Ltd* v *The King* (1952) where the following guidelines were suggested:

(a)   If the clause contains language which expressly exempts the person in whose favour it is made from the consequence of negligence of his own servants, effect must be given to that provision.
(b)   If there is no express reference to negligence, the court must consider whether the words used are wide enough in their ordinary meaning to cover negligence on the part of the person seeking to rely on the clause.
(c)   If the words are wide enough for (a), the court must then consider whether the head of damage may be based on some ground other than that of negligence. Thus if the words used cover another head as well as negligence then the clause will fail.

The decision has received much judicial interpretation. There has been a change in the way in which these principles have been applied. A good illustration of the strict application of the principles is the decision in *Smith* v *South Wales Switchgear Ltd* (1978) where it is quite clear that the absence of the word 'negligence' was fatal to the clause.

Smith v *South Wales Switchgear Ltd*
[1978] 1 WLR 165

In May 1970, a motor manufacturing company ('the purchaser') contracted with an electrical company ('the supplier') for maintenance work to be carried out at its factory 'subject to our general conditions of contract obtainable on 'request'. There were in existence three versions of the conditions, the original headed 'General Conditions of Contract 24001' and two others bearing respectively the additions 'Revised January 1969' and 'Revised March 1970'. The supplier did not request a copy, but in July 1970 received a copy of the 1969 conditions printed on the back of a purchase order amendment. By clause 23 of the conditions of 1970:

In the event of the order involving the carrying out of work by the supplier and its subcontractors on land and/or premises of the purchaser, the supplier will keep the purchaser indemnified against: (a) all losses and costs incurred by reason of the supplier's breach of any statute, by-law or regulation; (b) any liability, loss, claim or proceedings whatsoever under statute or common law (i) in respect of personal injury to, or death of any person whomsoever, (ii) in respect of any injury or damage whatsoever to any property, real or personal, arising out of or in the course of or caused by the execution of this order. The supplier will insure against and cause all subcontractors to insure against their liability hereunder.

In carrying out the work at the purchaser's premises an employee of the supplier suffered injury by accident caused by the purchaser's negligence and breach of statutory duty. The purchaser claimed to be indemnified in respect of the liability by virtue of the indemnity clause in the general conditions.

LORD FRASER: ... I do not see how a clause can 'expressly' exempt or indemnify the proferens against his negligence unless it contains the word 'negligence' or some synonym for it.... The word 'whatsoever' occurs in paragraph (b) of clause 23 here, but in my opinion it is no more than a word or emphasis and it cannot be read as equivalent to an express reference to negligence. To hold that it could, would be to invest it with the same sort of magic property as the word 'allenarly' used to have in relation to an alimentary liferent in Scotland and there is no justification for that. In the present case I am clearly of opinion that there is no express provision that the respondents are to be indemnified against the results of their own negligence and that the Second Division were right in so holding.

The decision in *Smith* v *South Wales Switchgear* concerns an indemnity clause but the principles apply to exemption clauses as well. Recent decisions, however, have moved away from this strict approach and a distinction has been drawn between different types of exemption clauses.

Exemption clauses may be divided into two broad categories; exclusion and limitation clauses. Exclusion clauses attempt to exempt *all* liability whereas limitation clauses attempt to limit liability to a set sum. An example of the latter would be: '... liability is limited to £500'. Case law from 1982 indicates that the wording in limitation clauses should not be construed as strictly as exclusion clauses because limitation clauses reflect the commercial expectation of the parties.

The distinction between the two different types of exemption clause was illustrated in *Ailsa Craig Fishing Co. Ltd* v *Malvern Fishing Co. Ltd* (1983) and was re-affirmed by the important House of Lords decision in *George Mitchell (Chesterhall) Ltd* v *Finney Lock Seeds Ltd* (1983). A number of introductory points need to be made about the case before it is read. First, although the clause satisfied the common-law tests it did not satisfy the statutory tests (see below) applicable to exemption clauses. The case is the first judgment of the House of Lords on the relationship between statutory and common law controls and we shall return to this relationship later. Secondly, the decision is clear authority for the more relaxed approach to the construction of limitation clauses in particular and exemption clauses in general. The extracted judgment of Lord Bridge makes it quite clear that the courts are no longer prepared to use strained construction in relation to limitation clauses when the wording and the intention of the parties is clear. Therefore, the absence of the word 'negligence' from an exemption clause does not automatically mean that it will fail.

George Mitchell (Chesterhall) Ltd v Finney Lock Seeds Ltd
[1983] 2 AC 803

In December 1973 the plaintiffs orally ordered 30 lb of Finney's Late Dutch Special cabbage seed from the defendant seed merchants from whom they had purchased seed for many years. The plaintiffs knew that the sale was subject to some conditions of sale. The defendants delivered seeds to the plaintiffs in February 1974 with an invoice in their customary form describing the goods delivered in accordance with the oral order. The conditions of sale on the back of the invoice provided, inter alia, (1) that if the seeds sold or agreed to be sold did not comply with the express terms of the contract or proved defective in varietal purity the liability of the defendant vendors was limited to their replacement or to refund of the price paid, (2) for the total exclusion of all liability for any loss or damage arising from the use of any seeds supplied save their replacement or price refund, (3) for the exclusion of any express or implied condition of warranty, statutory or otherwise, and they stated (4) that the price of seeds supplied was based upon the stated limitations upon liability.

Owing to errors by the defendants' suppliers and employees the seed supplied was not late cabbage seed and was unmerchantable. After the seed was planted in an area of over 60 acres by the plaintiffs, it germinated and grew but was commercially useless and had to be ploughed in. The price of the seed was £201.60. The loss to the plaintiffs was over £61,000.

Two issues were raised on appeal:

(1) Did the limitation clause satisfy the common law rules of construction?
(2) Did the clause satisfy the statutory criteria? (Extracts on this point are examined later.)

At first instance the trial judge held that this clause could not cover loss which was caused by the delivery of something completely different. The defendants appealed against this decision.

Held: Dismissing the appeal, that on their true construction the conditions limited the liability of the defendants to a refund of the price paid or replacement of the seeds and that the ambit of the conditions could not be confined to breaches of contract arising without negligence on the part of the defendants.

LORD BRIDGE: Clause 2 is perfectly clear and unambiguous. The reference to 'seed agreed to be sold' as well as to 'seeds sold' in clause 1 reflects the same dichotomy as the definition of 'sale' in the Sale of Goods Act 1979 as including a bargain and sale as well as a sale and delivery. The defective seeds in this case were seeds sold and delivered, just as clearly as they were seeds supplied, by the appellants to the respondents. The relevant condition, read as a whole, unambiguously limits the appellants' liability to replacement of the seeds or refund of the price. It is only possible to read an ambiguity into it by the process of strained construction which was deprecated by Lord Diplock in *Securicor 1* and by Lord Wilberforce in *Securicor 2*. In holding that the relevant condition was ineffective to limit the appellants' liability for a breach of contract caused by their negligence, Kerr LJ applied the principles stated by Lord Morton of Henryton giving the judgment of the Privy Council in *Canada Steamship Lines Ltd* v *The King*. The learned Lord Justice stated correctly that this case was also referred to by Lord Fraser of Tullybelton in *Securicor 2*. He omitted, however, to notice that, as appears from the passage from Lord Fraser's speech which I have already cited, the whole point of Lord Fraser's reference was to express his opinion that the very strict principles laid down in the *Canada Steamship Lines* case as applicable to exclusion and indemnity clauses cannot be applied in their full rigour to limitation clauses. Lord Wilberforce's speech contains a passage to the like effect, and Lord Elwyn-Jones, Lord Salmon and Lord Lowry agreed with both speeches. Having once reached a conclusion in the instant case that the relevant condition unambiguously limited the appellants' liability, I know of no principle of construction which can properly be applied to confine the effect of the limitation to breaches of contract arising without negligence on the part of the appellants. In agreement with Lord Denning MR, I would decide the common law issue in the appellants' favour.

It should be noted that the clause in fact failed because it did not satisfy the statutory criteria (see 3.1 below).

Self check questions
1. What is the name of the general rule of construction for exemption clauses? What does this rule say?

2.   Name two different types of category of exemption clauses. Why and how does the rule of construction differ between the two?

Answers
1.   The *contra proferentem* rule. The rule states that any doubt or ambiguity in the wording of a clause will be construed against the person seeking to rely on it.
2.   Exemption clauses may be divided into exclusion or limitation clauses. The former attempts to exempt all liability whereas the latter limits the liability to a set sum. The category depends on the wording of the clause. The law imposes a less strict application of the rule of construction in relation to limitation clauses as they reflect the commercial expectation of the parties and the law should give effect to it.

A final point needs to be made under this heading relating to the doctrine of fundamental breach and exemption clauses. Previously it was thought that if a breach was of a fundamental nature (quite what is the meaning of this is debatable) then a clause should not be allowed to exempt liability as a rule of law. However, the courts changed their mind in the case of *Photo Production* v *Securicor* (1980) where it was held that whether or not a clause could exempt liability for a fundamental breach depended on the wording of the clause, i.e., it is a rule of construction.

The decision in *Photo Production* is interesting in a number of ways. On a narrow interpretation it merely established that a fundamental breach of contract can be exempted but the wider implications of the case are more interesting. The attitude of the judges is very much a *laissez-faire* one towards the interpretation of the clause. Therefore, it can be argued that the case shows a change in judicial attitude in that before the decision the courts were more prepared to intervene if they thought that terms, in general, were unfair. What is of particular interest in this context is that the court in *Photo Production* were mindful of the fact that they thought the parties were of equal bargaining strength and therefore the clause should be upheld. The last theme is one which we shall develop below.

Photo Production Ltd v *Securicor Transport Ltd*
[1980] AC 827

The plaintiffs contracted with the defendants for the provision of a night patrol service for their factory of four visits a night. The main perils which the parties had in mind were fire and theft. The contract was on the defendants' printed form incorporating standard conditions which provided: '1. Under no circumstances shall the company be responsible for any injurious act or default by any employee of the company unless such act or default could have been foreseen and avoided by the exercise of due diligence on the part of the company as his employer; nor, in any event, shall the company be held responsible for: (a) Any loss suffered by the customer through ... fire or any other cause, except insofar as such loss is solely attributable to the negligence of the company's employees acting within the course of their employment.' Condition 2 limited the defendants' potential liability under the terms of the contract 'or at common law'.

On a Sunday night one of the defendants' employees entered the factory on duty patrol and then lit a fire which burned down the factory. The employee, who had satisfactory references and had been employed by the defendants for some three months, later said that he had only meant to start a small fire but that it got out of control.

The plaintiffs claimed damages, particularised at over £648,000, based on breach of contract and/or negligence. MacKenna J rejected allegations against the defendants of want of care and failure to use due diligence as employers, and held that condition 1 of the contract excluded them from responsibility for his act in setting fire to the factory and that the doctrine of fundamental breach did not prevent judgment being given for the defendants. The Court of Appeal reversed his decision.

On appeal by the defendants: Held, allowing the appeal, (1) that the doctrine of fundamental breach by virtue of which the termination of a contract brought it, and, with it, any exclusion clause to an end was not good law; that the question whether and to what extent an exclusion clause was to be applied to any breach of contract was a matter of construction of the contract and normally when the parties were bargaining on equal terms they should be free to apportion the risks as they thought fit, making provision for their respective risks according to the terms they chose to agree; (2) that the words of the exclusion clause were clear and on their true construction covered deliberate acts as well as negligence so as to relieve the defendants from responsibility for their breach of the implied duty to operate with due regard to the safety of the premises.

3 Statutory control

The Unfair Contract Terms Act 1977 (UCTA) introduced further control on the validity of exemption clauses. The Act gives the judiciary the ability to either strike down clauses completely or subject other types of clauses to the test of 'reasonableness'.

The Act does not affect the common law rules on the subject and they still have to be satisfied as well as the statutory test. The judiciary have, however, not applied the common law tests with the same rigour since the introduction of the Act as it gives them much more flexibility. Two cases can be cited as authority for this proposition: *George Mitchell v Finney Lock Seeds* (above) and *Phillips Products Ltd v Hyland* (1987). In *George Mitchell* the court was quite categorical that the clause satisfied the common law tests whilst failing the statutory test. Secondly, in the *Phillips Products* case the judge virtually ignored the common law tests and the judgment was centred almost entirely around the statutory issues.

3.1 The Provisions of the Act
It is necessary to go through the extracted provisions of the Act before considering any relevant case law on the subject.

(a) *Requirements:* the provisions of the Act on which we shall concentrate only apply to people seeking to exempt liability while they are 'dealing in the course of business'. Exemption clauses can either be between business/business or alternatively business/consumer. The term 'deals as a consumer' is also defined in the Act and it is crucial to look at the relationship of the contracting parties as the Act treats the two situations differently.

(i) *Business liability, s. 1(3):* In the case of both contract and tort, sections 2 to 7 apply (except where the contrary is stated in section 6(4) only to business liability), that is liability for breach of obligation and duties arising—

(a) from things done or to be done by a person in the course of a business (whether his own business or another); or
(b) from the occupation of premises used for business purposes of the occupier;

and references to liability are to be read accordingly.

Section 14: In this Part of this Act—
'business' includes a profession and the activities of any government department or local or public authority.

(ii) *Deals as a consumer, s. 12:* (1) A party to a contract 'deals as consumer' in relation to another party if—

(a) he neither makes the contract in the course of a business nor holds himself out as doing so; and
(b) the other party does make the contract in the course a business: and
(c) in the case of a contract governed by the law of sale of goods or hire-purchase, or by section 7 of this Act, the goods passing under or in pursuance of the contract are of a type ordinarily supplied for private use or consumption.

(b) *Ineffective terms:* s. 2(1) is self-explanatory but note that the death or personal injury must result through negligence.

Section 2(1): A person cannot by reference to any contract term or to a notice given to persons generally or to particular persons exclude or restrict his liability for death or personal injury resulting from negligence.

(c) *Terms subject to the test of reasonableness:* s. 2(2) applies to liability, other than death or personal injury, caused by negligence. Section 3 applies to business/consumer contracts and also business/business contracts where the contract is made through the use of standard forms. Research has shown that at least 99% of all contracts are made by the use of standard form and therefore s. 3 has a wide application. Section 3(2)(a) deals with the situation of a clause which tries to exempt a breach of contract and s. 3(2)(b) covers a slightly more complex situation which requires further explanation. Sub-section (1) is the one which causes problems and is intended to deal with the following situation: let us say that A books a holiday in Resort X at Hotel Y. At the last moment A gets moved to Resort R and Hotel S and there is a clause allowing the holiday firm to do that. The clause would have to satisfy the test of reasonableness as it seeks to render contractual performance substantially different from that which was reasonably expected.

Section 2(2): In the case of other loss or damage, a person cannot exclude or restrict his liability for negligence except insofar as the term or notice satisfies the requirement of reasonableness.

Section 3(1): This section applies as between contracting parties where one of them deals as consumer or on the other's written standard terms of business.

(2)   As against that party, the other cannot by reference to a contract term—

(a)   when himself in breach of contract, exclude or restrict any liability of his in respect of the breach; or
(b)   claim to be entitled—

(i)   to render a contractual performance substantially different from that which was reasonably expected of him, or
(ii)   in respect of the whole or any part of his contractual obligation, to render no performance at all,

except in so far as (in any of the cases mentioned above in this subsection) the contract term satisfies the requirements of reasonableness.

(d)   *The test of reasonableness:* section 11 and sch. 2 should be read together in order to help you make a decision as to reasonableness. Although sch. 2 only, in theory at least, applies to certain sections it appears that the judiciary have not interpreted the statute literally in this case.

What is meant by reasonableness?
Section 11—(1)   In relation to a contract term, the requirement of reason-ableness for the purposes of this Part of this Act, section 3 of the Misrepresentation Act 1967 and section 3 of the Misrepresentation (North-ern Ireland) Act 1967 is that the term should have been a fair and reasonable one to be included having regard to the circumstances which were, or ought reasonably to have been, known to or in the contemplation of the parties when the contract was made.
(2)   In determining for the purposes of section 6 or 7 above whether a contract term satisfies the requirement of reasonableness regard shall be had in particular to the matters in Schedule 2 to this Act; but this subsection does

not prevent the court or arbitrator from holding, in accordance with any rule of law, that a term which purports to exclude or restrict any relevant liability is not a term of the contract.

(3)   In relation to a notice (not being a notice having contractual effect), the requirement of reasonableness under this Act is that it should be fair and reasonable to allow reliance on it, having regard to all the circumstances obtaining when the liability arose or (but for the notice) would have arisen.

(4)   Where by reference to a contract term or notice a person seeks to restrict liability to a specified sum of money, and a question arises (under this or any other Act) whether the term or notice satisfies the requirement of reasonableness, regard shall be had in particular (but without prejudice to subsection 3 above in the case of contract terms) to—

(a)   the resources which he could expect to be available to him for the purpose of meeting the liability should it arise; and

(b)   how far it was open to him to cover himself by insurance.

(5)   It is for those claiming that a contract term or notice satisfies the requirement of reasonableness to show that it does.

Schedule 2
'Guidelines' for Application of Reasonableness Test

The matters to which regard is to be had in particular for the purposes of sections 6(3), 7(3) and (4), 20 and 21 are any of the following which appear to be relevant—

(a)   the strength of the bargaining positions of the parties relative to each other, taking into account (among other things) alternative means by which the customer's requirements could have been met;

(b)   whether the customer received an inducement to agree to the term, or in accepting it had an opportunity of entering into a similar contract with other persons, but without having to accept a similar term;

(c)   whether the customer knew or ought reasonably to have known of the existence and extent of the term having regard, among other things, to any custom of the trade and any previous course of dealing between the parties;

(d)   where the term excludes or restricts any relevant liability if some condition is not complied with, whether it was reasonable at the time of the contract to expect that compliance with that condition would be practicable;

(e)   whether the goods were manufactured, processed or adopted to the special order of the customer.

A number of points need to be made about s. 11. First s. 11(1) states that the test is based on the knowledge of the parties and surrounding circumstances when the contract was made and s. 11(5) indicates that the burden of proof is on the person seeking to rely on the clause, that is that person must show it is reasonable and it is not for the other party to show the clause is unreasonable.

Secondly, the provisions of s. 11(4) should be noted; the subsection applies to limitation clauses and the discussion in *George Mitchell* (see below) is interesting on this issue. Finally the Court of Appeal decision in *Stewart Gill Ltd v Horatio Myer & Co. Ltd* (1992) clarifies two further issues about the operation of s. 11. As previously stated above, the reasonableness of the clause must be determined at the time when the contract was made. Consequently the subsequent operation or effect of the exemption clause is not a relevant consideration to take into account. This led one of the judges in the *Stewart Gill* case to the conclusion that an exemption stands or fails as a whole. Therefore the courts will not sever (see chapter 11.4) the part of the clause which is being relied upon and the court will not allow the non-reasonable part of the cause to stand.

The provisions of sch. 2 also need to be discussed. As stated above the schedule only strictly applies to certain sections of the Act but we shall consider it in relation to the sections under discussion. In *George Mitchell v Finney* the judgment clearly looks at paragraph (a) in the schedule. Obviously the strength of the parties in this case is equated with the ability or more precisely non-ability, to negotiate the terms on which the contract was made. Therefore in any problem situation you will have to try and assess this question of bargaining strength. Secondly, the ability to insure was seen as a critical factor in that the farmers were either unable to insure or found it so expensive that it was prohibitive to do so. The question of insurance is a relevant factor when discussing limitation clauses: s. 11(4).

Finally two further, more general points can be noted from the case. First, Lord Bridge thought it should only be in exceptional circumstances that the appellate courts should overrule the initial finding as to 'reasonableness' by the trial judge. Secondly, the case shows the relationship between the common-law tests and the statutory test. In the case the common-law tests were satisfied but not the statutory criteria.

NB. Part of the judgment, on the common-law issues, has been extracted (2.2, above). Although Lord Bridge is referring to s. 55 of the Sale of Goods Act 1893 as substituted by the Supply of Goods (Implied Terms) Act 1973, that section is now incorporated into UCTA and therefore the principles he discusses are relevant to the question of 'reasonableness' in UCTA.

George Mitchell (Chesterhall) Ltd v Finney Lock Seeds Ltd
[1983] 2 AC 803

LORD BRIDGE: The question of relative bargaining strength under paragraph (a) and of the opportunity to buy seeds without a limitation of the seedsman's liability under paragraph (b) were inter-related. The evidence was that a similar limitation of liability was universally embodied in the terms of trade between seedsmen and farmers and had been so for very many years. The limitation had never been negotiated between representative bodies, but, on the other hand, had not been the subject of any protest by the National Farmers Union. These factors, if considered in isolation, might have been equivocal. The decisive factor, however, appears from the evidence of four witnesses called for the appellants, two independent seedsmen, the chairman of the appellant company, and a director of a sister company (both being wholly-owned subsidiaries of the same parent). They said that it had always been their practice, unsuccessfully attempted in the instant case, to negotiate settlements of farmers' claims for damages in excess of the price of the seeds, if they thought that the claims were 'genuine' and 'justified'. This evidence indicated a clear recognition by seedsmen in general, and the appellants in particular, that reliance on the limitation of liability imposed by the relevant condition would not be fair or reasonable.

Two further factors, if more were needed, weight the scales in favour of the respondents. The supply of autumn, instead of winter, cabbage seeds was due to the negligence of the appellants' sister company. Irrespective of its quality, the autumn variety supplied could not, according to the appellants' own evidence, be grown commercially in East Lothian. Finally, as the trial judge found, seedsmen could insure against the risk of crop failure caused by supplying the wrong variety of seed without materially increasing the price of seeds.

My Lords, even if I felt doubts about the statutory issue, I should not, for the reasons explained earlier, think it right to interfere with the unanimous original decision of that issue by the Court of Appeal. As it is, I feel no such doubts. If I were making the original decision, I should conclude without hesitation that it would not be fair or reasonable to allow the appellants to rely on the contractual limitation of the liability.

I would dismiss the appeal.

Further guidelines as to the operation of the reasonableness test come from the judgment of Lord Griffiths in *Smith* v *Bush, Harris* v *Wyre Forest District Council* (1989). Both cases concern the tortious liability of surveyors to prospective purchasers of houses when preparing valuation reports for a building society and local authority respectively. The House of Lords held that in both cases a duty of care was owed by the surveyors to prospective purchasers. The question then arose whether any exemption clause would satisfy the test of reasonableness. Lord Griffiths thought that four factors were relevant.

(a) *Equality of bargaining power.* On the facts the disclaimer was imposed; clearly the reasoning from *George Mitchell* v *Finney* is again relevant.

(b) *The availability to mortgagors (prospective purchasers) of alternative advice.* Such advice whilst available would be expensive and force people to pay twice for the same service.

(c) *Special difficulties associated with the task undertaken.* The work was said to be 'at the lower end of the surveyor's field of professional expertise'. Therefore, there were no special difficulties.

(d) *The practical consequences of the decision.* Lord Griffiths stated that it was for surveyors to bear any loss of this kind through their indemnity insurance. Any increase in premiums would not be acceptable.

Applying the above criteria the House of Lords held that the test of reasonableness was not satisfied.

Self check questions
1.   Why is it important to know whether the parties acted in the course of business or not?
2.   What type of loss cannot be exempted under the Act?
3.   What factors are taken into account when deciding the test of reasonableness?
4.   What is the relationship between the statutory and common-law controls on exemption clauses?

Answers
1.   The Act only applies where a person is seeking to exempt liability while acting in the course of business. The Act then draws a further distinction between business/consumer dealings in that certain types of liability cannot be exempted against the latter but can be against the former assuming the test of reasonableness is satisfied. The position of the parties is also relevant when deciding upon the question of reasonableness.
2.   Death or personal injury resulting from negligence cannot be excluded.
3.   Section 11(4) and sch. 2 lists the factors to be taken into account when making the decision. In *George Mitchell* the court looked at the bargaining positions of the parties and the role of insurance as being the relevant factors to be taken into account.
4.   An exemption clause must satisfy both the common law and statutory criteria. The courts in recent cases have, however, tended to concentrate on the statutory criteria. But for the purposes of answering an examination question both sets of principles must be examined.

4   Exemption clauses and third parties

A brief word must be said about third parties getting the benefit of exemption clauses.

Figure 9.1

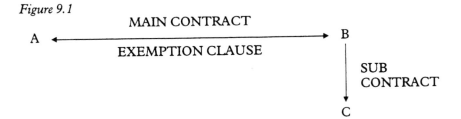

In figure 9.1, C, the third party, is trying to obtain the benefit of the exemption clause in the contract between A and B. The cases on this issue concern stevedores trying to get the benefit of exemption clauses. The main contract is the bill of lading and the stevedores, who are unloading the cargo, are trying to get the benefit of the exemption clause.

In *Scruttons Ltd* v *Midland Silicones Ltd* (1962) a number of requirements were laid down in order for a stevedore to get the benefit of a clause:

(a)   the bill of lading must make it clear that the stevedore is to be protected;
(b)   the carrier is not only contracting on his behalf, but also as the agent for the stevedore;
(c)   the carrier has authority to do so;
(d)   any consideration problems must be solved. (See earlier notes in the consideration unit on performance of an existing duty with a third party, para: 7.4.)

In *New Zealand Shipping Co. Ltd* v *Satterthwaite* (1975) and *Port Jackson Stevedoring* v *Salmond* (1981) the courts, instead of concentrating on the technical requirements listed above, looked at the commercial reality of the situation. The courts clearly thought that by giving effect to the commercial expectation of the parties then the stevedores (third party) should gain the benefit of the exemption clause in both cases.

Problem
Bob, a self-employed builder, regularly hires a rubbish skip from Tidyskips. On the last five occasions, the invoice, received afterwards, has had the following printed on the reverse:

Tidyskips shall not be liable for any loss or damage howsoever caused to customers' premises and if, notwithstanding the foregoing, any liability for damage to customers' property should arise, that liability shall be limited to £100.

Bob telephones Tidyskips and orders a skip to be delivered to his home on the following day. Sid, an employee of Tidyskips, negligently drives the delivery vehicle into Bob's garden wall causing it to collapse onto Bob's new car. The wall costs £500 to rebuild and the repairs to the car cost £800. Advise Bob.

Suggested answer
(NB The answer does not make reference to the 1994 Regulations.)
    The problem raises the question as to the validity of exemption clauses. Three issues have to be discussed. First, is the clause incorporated into the contract; secondly, does the wording of the clause cover the loss and finally does the clause satisfy the tests laid down by UCTA 1977.
    The clause to be incorporated must satisfy the various common-law tests. One of the major problems is that Bob does not receive the actual clause until after the contract was made and following the decision in *Olley* v *Marlborough Court* there would not be sufficient notice. On the facts, however, it states that Bob has regularly dealt with Tidyskips and therefore incorporation could take

place through a course of dealing between the parties. The law is not altogether clear on this point as, for example, in *McCutcheon* v *MacBrayne* as the party did not know the details of the clause, despite regular dealings between the parties, there was not incorporation. Contrast this with *British Crane Hire* v *Ipswich Plant Hire* where incorporation took place because both parties were aware of the terms and each party had dealt in the trade regularly. It is difficult to draw a firm conclusion on the facts and would be for the court to decide.

The second common-law test to be satisfied is that of construction, that is does the wording cover the nature of the loss? An initial point to note is that the liability is caused by the negligence of Sid, an employee, who is clearly a third party to the contract. The general principle is that third parties do not, because of the privity principle, get the benefit of exemption clauses. The law has become more relaxed in this respect, for example *Port Jackson Stevedoring* v *Salmond*, but again the position of Sid is unclear.

The courts have developed various criteria under the construction test: the *contra proferentem* rule being one. The clause may be seen as having two parts to it: firstly, an exclusion clause and secondly, a limitation clause. The wording of the exclusion states 'any loss or damage howsoever caused' and following the decision in *Smith* v *South Wales Switchgear* it may be that these words are too wide — and therefore would fail under the *contra proferentem* rule — to exclude negligence. The courts in recent years have taken a more relaxed attitude to the construction test, and even though the exclusion clause wording may be too wide the courts have taken an even more relaxed approach to limitation clauses. The essence of the reasoning from cases such as *Ailsa Craig* v *Malvern Fishing* and *George Mitchell* v *Finney Lock Seeds* is that limitation clauses reflect commercial efficacy and therefore the courts do not interfere with these clauses.

The implications of UCTA 1977 need to be discussed. Two preliminary points have to be made. First, although UCTA does not change the common-law rule the courts have obviously been prepared to rely more on statute than the common law in controlling exemption clauses (*George Mitchell*). Secondly, the appellate courts are reluctant to overrule any finding of the trial judge at first instance unless there is clear absurdity (*George Mitchell*) and this must be taken into account in advising Bob. The Act requires that the exemption clause satisfies the requirement of reasonableness, s. 2(2); the burden of proof being on Tidyskips as they are seeking to rely on the clause.

Above, we discussed whether the clause should be seen as one or two separate ones. If we treat them differently then the Act does give slightly different guidelines for exclusion clauses as opposed to limitation clauses. Although the guidelines in schedule 2 are only said to apply to ss. 6 and 7 the courts have clearly taken them into account in helping them make this decision in the context of s. 2. One of the key factors seems to be whether or not the term has been imposed, as opposed to negotiated, between the parties — see the reasoning in *Smith* v *Bush* and *George Mitchell* v *Finney*. On the facts here it is difficult to draw conclusions either way. In relation to the limitation clause s. 11(4) states that the courts should look at the resources of the parties and the position of insurance. Bob may well have the house and the car insured in order to cover such loss but it is clear from *George Mitchell* v *Finney* that the courts do see this as being important. The courts have left this issue deliberately vague and it is very difficult to give a definitive answer as to the question of reasonableness.

5   Unfair Terms in Consumer Contracts Regulations 1994

5.1   Background

The Unfair Terms in Consumer Contracts Regulations 1994 were made to implement the EC directive on unfair terms in consumer contracts (93/13/EEC). As to the general applicability of EC directives see chapter 3.

Although we are dealing with these Regulations in a chapter on exemption clauses it must be emphasised that the Regulations do not merely apply to exemption clauses, but to contractual terms in general. This point, in itself, will lead to confusion as the Regulations are an addition to existing common law and statutory controls. Therefore an exemption clause will not only be subject to the requirements of UCTA 1977, but also to the criteria contained in the 1994 Regulations. There has been much criticism of this piecemeal approach to legislative provision. A more logical approach would have been to incorporate the Directive into English law, together with existing provisions, in a new Act of Parliament. The government chose not to follow this route.

A number of the concepts contained in the Regulations, particularly the requirement of 'good faith' (see reg. 4(1)) are virtually unknown to English law. However, these concepts are by no means uncommon in other European States' domestic jurisdictions, and it will be interesting to see whether or not any of this thinking finds its way into English law. By way of example, the 1994 Regulations are not dissimilar to those contained in the German Civil Code, 1976.

The Regulations came into force on 1 July 1995.

Unfair Terms in Consumer Contracts Regulations 1994 (SI 1994/3159)

Citation and commencement

1.   These Regulations may be cited as the Unfair Terms in Consumer Contracts Regulations 1994 and came into force on 1st July 1995.

Interpretation

2.—(1)   In these Regulations—

'business' includes a trade or profession and the activities of any government department or local or public authority;

'the Community' means the European Economic Community and the other States in the European Economic Area;

'consumer' means a natural person who, in making a contract to which these Regulations apply, is acting for purposes which are outside his business;

'court' in relation to England and Wales and Northern Ireland means the High Court, and in relation to Scotland, the Court of Session;

'Director' means the Director General of Fair Trading;

'EEA Agreement' means the Agreement on the European Economic Area signed at Oporto on 2 May 1992 as adjusted by the protocol signed at Brussels on 17 March 1993;

'member State' shall mean a State which is a contracting party to the EEA Agreement but until the EEA Agreement comes into force in relation to Liechtenstein does not include the State of Liechtenstein;

'seller' means a person who sells goods and who, in making a contract to which these Regulations apply, is acting for purposes relating to his business.

(2)   [Relates to Scotland.]

Terms to which these Regulations apply

3.—(1)   Subject to the provisions of Schedule 1, these Regulations apply to any term in a contract concluded between a seller or supplier and a consumer where the said term has not been individually negotiated.

(2)   In so far as it is in plain, intelligible language, no assessment shall be made of the fairness of any term which—

(a)   defines the main subject-matter of the contract, or

(b)   concerns the adequacy of the price or remuneration, as against the goods or services sold or supplied.

(3)   For the purposes of these Regulations, a term shall always be regarded as not having been individually negotiated where it has been drafted in advance and the consumer has not been able to influence the substance of the term.

(4)   Notwithstanding that a specific term or certain aspects of it in a contract has been individually negotiated, these Regulations shall apply to the rest of a contract if an overall assessment of the contract indicates that it is a pre-formulated standard contract.

(5)   It shall be for any seller or supplier who claims that a term was individually negotiated to show that it was.

Unfair terms

4.—(1)   In these Regulations, subject to paragraphs (2) and (3) below, 'unfair term' means any term which contrary to the requirement of good faith causes a significant imbalance in the parties' rights and obligations under the contract to the detriment of the consumer.

(2)   An assessment of the unfair nature of a term shall be made taking into account the nature of the goods or services for which the contract was concluded and referring, as at the time of the conclusion of the contract, to all circumstances attending the conclusion of the contract and to all the other terms of the contract or of another contract on which it is dependent.

(3)   In detemining whether a term satisfies the requirement of good faith, regard shall be had in particular to the matters specified in Schedule 2 to these Regulations.

(4)   Schedule 3 to these Regulations contains an indicative and non-exhaustive list of the terms which may be regarded as unfair.

Consequence of inclusion of unfair terms in contracts

5.—(1)   An unfair term in a contract concluded with a consumer by a seller or supplier shall not be binding on the consumer.

(2)   The contract shall continue to bind the parties if it is capable of continuing in existence without the unfair term.

Construction of written contracts

6.   A seller or supplier shall ensure that any written term of a contract is expressed in plain, intelligible language, and if there is doubt about the meaning of a written term, the interpretation most favourable to the consumer shall prevail.

Choice of law clauses

7.   These Regulations shall apply notwithstanding any contract term which applies or purports tp apply the law of a non-member State, if the contract has a close connection with the territory of the member States.

Prevention of continued use of unfair terms

8.—(1)   It shall be the duty of the Director to consider any complaint made to him that any contract term drawn up for general use is unfair, unless the complaint appears to the Director to be frivolous or vexatious.

(2)   If having considered a complaint about any contract term pursuant to paragraph (1) above the Director considers that the contract term is unfair he may, if he considers it appropriate to do so, bring proceedings for an injunction (in which proceedings he may also apply for an interlocutory injunction) against any person appearing to him to be using or recommending use of such a term in contracts concluded with consumers.

(3)   The Director may, if he considers it appropriate to do so, have regard to any undertakings given to him by or on behalf of any person as to the continued use of such a term in contracts concluded with consumers.

(4)   The Director shall give reasons for his decision to apply or not to apply, as the case may be, for an injunction in relation to any complaint which these Regulations require him to consider.

(5)   The court on an application by the Director may grant an injunction on such terms as it thinks fit.

(6)   An injunction may relate not only to use of a particular contract term drawn up for general use but to any similar term, or a term having like effect, used or recommended for use by any party to the proceedings.

(7)   The Director may arrange for the dissemination in such form and manner as he considers appropriate of such information and advice concerning the operation of these Regulations as may appear to him to be expedient to give to the public and to all persons likely to be affected by these Regulations.

SCHEDULE 1   CONTRACTS AND PARTICULAR TERMS
EXCLUDED FROM THE SCOPE OF THESE REGULATIONS

Regulation 3(1)

These Regulations do not apply to—

(a)   any contract relating to employment;

(b)   any contract relating to succession rights;

(c)   any contract relating to rights under family law;

(d)   any contract relating to the incorporation and organisation of companies or partnerships; and

(e)   any term incorporated in order to comply with or which reflects—

(i)   statutory or regulatory provisions of the United Kingdom; or

(ii)   the provisions or principles of international conventions to which the member States or the Community are party.

SCHEDULE 2   ASSESSMENT OF GOOD FAITH
Regulation 4(3)

In making an assessment of good faith, regard shall be had in particular to—

(a)   the strength of the bargaining positions of the parties;

(b)   whether the consumer had an inducement to agree to the term;

(c)   whether the goods or services were sold or supplied to the special order of the consumer, and

(d)   the extent to which the seller or supplier has dealt fairly and equitably with the consumer.

SCHEDULE 3   INDICATIVE AND ILLUSTRATIVE LIST OF TERMS WHICH MAY BE REGARDED AS UNFAIR
Regulation 4(4)

1.   Terms which have the object or effect of—

(a)   excluding or limiting the legal liability of a seller or supplier in the event of the death of a consumer or personal injury to the latter resulting from an act or omission of that seller or supplier;

(b)   inappropriately excluding or limiting the legal rights of the consumer vis-à-vis the seller or supplier or another party in the event of total or partial non-performance or inadequate performance by the seller or supplier of any of the contractual obligations, including the option of offsetting a debt owed to the seller or supplier against any claim which the consumer may have against him;

(c)   making an agreement binding on the consumer whereas provision of services by the seller or supplier is subject to a condition whose realisation depends on his own will alone;

(d)   permitting the seller or supplier to retain sums paid by the consumer where the latter decides not to conclude or perform the contract, without providing for the consumer to receive compensation of an equivalent amount from the seller or supplier where the latter is the party cancelling the contract;

(e)   requiring any consumer who fails to fulfil his obligation to pay a disproportionately high sum in compensation;

(f)   authorising the seller or supplier to dissolve the contract on a discretionary basis where the same facility is not granted to the consumer, or permitting the seller or supplier to retain the sums paid for services not yet supplied by him where it is the seller or supplier himself who dissolves the contract;

(g)   enabling the seller or supplier to terminate a contract of indeterminate duration without reasonable notice except where there are serious grounds for doing so;

(h)   automatically extending a contract of fixed duration where the consumer does not indicate otherwise, when the deadline fixed for the consumer to express this desire not to extend the contract is unreasonably early;

(i)   irrevocably binding the consumer to terms with which he had no real opportunity of becoming acquainted before the conclusion of the contract;

(j)   enabling the seller or supplier to alter the terms of the contract unilaterally without a valid reason which is specified in the contract;

(k)   enabling the seller or supplier to alter unilaterally without a valid reason any characteristics of the product or service to be provided;

(l)   providing for the price of goods to be determined at the time of delivery or allowing a seller of goods or supplier of services to increase their price without in both cases giving the consumer the corresponding right to cancel the contract if the final price is too high in relation to the price agreed when the contract was concluded;

(m)   giving the seller or supplier the right to determine whether the goods or services supplied are in conformity with the contract, or giving him the exclusive right to interpret any term of the contract;

(n)   limiting the seller's or supplier's obligation to respect commitments undertaken by his agents or making his commitments subject to compliance with a particular formality;

(o)   obliging the consumer to fulfil all his obligations where the seller or supplier does not perform his;

(p)   giving the seller or supplier the possibility of transferring his rights and obligations under the contract, where this may serve to reduce the guarantees for the consumer, without the latter's agreement;

(q)   excluding or hindering the consumer's right to take legal action or exercise any other legal remedy, particularly by requiring the consumer to take disputes exclusively to arbitration not covered by legal provisions, unduly restricting the evidence available to him or imposing on him a burden of proof which, according to the applicable law, should lie with another party to the contract.

2.   Scope of subparagraphs 1(g), (j) and (l)

(a)   Subparagraph 1(g) is without hindrance to terms by which a supplier of financial services reserves the right to terminate unilaterally a contract of indeterminate duration without notice where there is a valid reason, provided that the supplier is required to inform the other contracting party or parties thereof immediately.

(b)   Subparagraph 1(j) is without hindrance to terms under which a supplier of financial services reserves the right to alter the rate of interest payable by the consumer or due to the latter, or the amount of other charges for financial services without notice where there is a valid reason, provided that the supplier is required to inform the other contracting party or parties thereof at the earliest opportunity and that the latter are free to dissolve the contract immediately.

Subparagraph 1 (j) is also without hindrance to terms under which a seller or supplier reserves the right to alter unilaterally the conditions of a contract of indeterminate duration, provided that he is required to inform the consumer with reasonable notice and that the consumer is free to dissolve the contract.

(c)   Subparagraphs 1 (g), (j) and (l) do not apply to:

—transactions in transferable securities, financial instruments and other products or services where the price is linked to fluctuations in a stock exchange quotation or index or a financial market rate that the seller or supplier does not control;

—contracts for the purchase or sale of foreign currency, traveller's cheques or international money orders denominated in foreign currency;

(d)   Subparagraph 1 (l) is without hindrance to price indexation clauses, where lawful, provided that the method by which prices vary is explicitly described.

5.2   Comment on the Regulations
A number of comments will now be made on the contents of the Regulations. For the sake of convenience these will be made regulation by regulation.

5.2.2   Regulation 2 (interpretation)   The definition of 'consumer' raises some interesting points. UCTA 1977 applies (albeit differently in some sections) to both business — consumer and business — business contracts. The 1994 Regulations only apply to business — consumer contracts. Therefore a director of a company who buys a car would have to show that it was bought for private use in order for the Regulations to apply. It is by no means clear who the burden of proof is on in such a situation. However, if the company was to buy the car for the private use of the director then it is quite clear that such a contract would not be covered by the 1994 Regulations, whereas, under the current interpretation of UCTA 1977 that Act would govern any exemption clause contained in the contract (see R & B Customs Brokers Ltd v United Dominions Trust Ltd [1988] 1 WLR 321).

5.2.3   Regulation 3 (terms to which the Regulations apply)   The presumption is that it is non-negotiation of a particular term or terms which is important rather than the negotiation of the contract as a whole. An example of a non-individually negotiated contract would be when contracting to travel by British Rail or booking a package holiday.

Regulation 3(2) is more difficult to interpret. The concept of 'plain, intelligible language' is a novel principle in English law. It may be, of course, that it is merely saying that the two categories of terms listed have to satisfy the contra proferentem test (see earlier in this chapter). However, what is unfortunate in the context of consumer protection is the fact that the Regulations do not apply to what is often the most contentious term of a contract, the price.

Schedule 1 to the Regulations specifically excludes a number of contracts and terms from being covered by the Regulations. There is some divergence from UCTA 1977 in this respect in that insurance contracts are not covered by UCTA 1977 but by the 1994 Regulations.

5.2.4 Regulation 4 (unfair terms) Regulation 4(1) states that in order for a term to be unfair it must be both contrary to the requirement of 'good faith' and cause a 'significant imbalance'. Much of the discussion, below, will focus upon the meaning of 'good faith'. However, two preliminary points should be mentioned. First there is no definition of 'significant imbalance', although sch. 3 does provide a 'non-exhaustive' list of terms which may be regarded as unfair, secondly, it is not clear who the burden of proof is on, whereas UCTA 1977, s. 11, places the burden of proof firmly on the person seeking to rely on the term. Regulation 6 states that if there is any doubt or ambiguity then the interpretation most favourable to the consumer shall prevail. Does this therefore mean that the same burden of proof will apply to the assessment of 'good faith' etc? It can be argued that the burden of proof is a neutral one.

The principle of 'good faith' is a new one in English law. A few cases, for example, *Interfoto Picture Library Ltd* v *Stiletto Visual Programmes Ltd* [1988] 1 All ER 349 (see above) have discussed and seemingly applied the principle but it is not generally applicable in English law. During consultation on drafting the Regulations it was suggested that 'good faith' should be replaced by 'reason-ableness', but this was rejected. The factors contained in sch. 2, however, do bear a remarkable resemblance to those contained in UCTA 1977 as guidelines for the application of the reasonableness test.

In sch. 2 the only unfamiliar guideline is (d), the concept of dealing 'fairly and equitably with the consumer'. Quite what this adds over and above the existing guidelines is unclear but it could well be that the English courts will merely apply a slightly modified reasonableness test in this context and the rights of consumers will not be enhanced.

5.2.5 Regulation 5 (consequence of inclusion of unfair terms in contracts) The effect of a term being an unfair one is merely to render that term voidable and the contract will continue in existence if it is capable of doing so without that term being enforceable. There are clear differences with UCTA 1977, which renders certain types of exemption clauses void (see, for example, UCTA 1977, s. 2(1)). One can only assume that there will be a lot of litigation before it becomes clear what are unfair terms.

5.2.6 Regulation 8 (prevention of continued use of unfair terms) Finally Regulation 8 gives the Director General of Fair Trading (the Director) powers to seek an injunction in his own right to prevent the use of certain terms. It will be interesting to see how these provisions are used, if they are used at all.

10　MISREPRESENTATION

1　Introduction

This chapter looks at a principle which, if shown, renders a contract voidable. We shall discuss what is meant by voidable later but at this stage one should be aware that a misrepresentation does *not* automatically bring a contract to an end. Misrepresentation is defined as:

> A statement of *fact* made by one party to the contract (the representor) to the other (the representee) which, while not forming a term of the contract, is one of the reasons that *induces* the representee to enter into the contract.

A number of issues arise from this definition. First, the relationship with terms of the contract needs to be discussed. When you are dealing with pre-contractual statements the first question to ask yourself is whether or not the statement has become a term of the contract. In the chapter on terms we saw that the courts had developed a test based on the intention of the parties with a number of guidelines in order to help them make this decision. Some of the decisions made by the court were not easy to follow but the development of negligent misrepresentation (both at common-law and through statute) has meant that the courts will not go to great lengths to incorporate a statement as a term, as misrepresentation will provide a remedy. Therefore, when dealing with a question it is still necessary to distinguish between a pre-contractual statement which has been incorporated (a term) and a statement which has not (a misrepresentation). In both cases the law will provide a remedy.

The law, however, requires a number of factors to be satisfied in order for a misrepresentation to be actionable. These are, first, that the statement is one of fact and secondly, that it has induced the other party to enter into the contract. Once we have established this then the nature of the misrepresentation needs to be discussed in order for the type of remedy to be ascertained.

2   Requirements for an effective misrepresentation

2.1   Statement of fact

A statement of fact is one relating to the past or present and needs to be distinguished from a number of different forms of statement.

2.1.1   Fact, not opinion

The statement must be one of fact, not opinion, and a number of cases need to be discussed in order to establish this distinction. In *Bisset* v *Wilkinson* (1927) the court thought that the statement was merely one of opinion as the amount of knowledge possessed by the representor meant that the statement could not be one of fact.

Bisset v *Wilkinson*
[1927] AC 177

A representation of fact may be inherent in a statement of opinion; in any case the existence of the opinion in the person expressing it is a question of fact. When it is sought to rescind a contract on the ground of the falseness of a statement of opinion it was induced, it must be inquired what was the meaning of the statement made, and whether it was true. Relevant to those enquiries are, the material facts of the transaction, the knowledge of the parties, the words used, and the actual conditions of the subject-matter.

In an action by a vendor of land in New Zealand to recover under the contract, the purchaser claimed to rescind the contract on the ground of the falseness of a statement as to the carrying capacity of the land for sheep.

Held: On the evidence, applying the above considerations, that the statement was merely of an opinion which the vendor honestly held; and accordingly that the defence failed.

The judgment of the Court of Appeal was reversed.

The decision in *Bissett* can be contrasted with the earlier one in *Smith* v *Land and House Property Corporation* (1884). In this case the landlord knewn about the state of the finances of the tenant and even though the statement was seemingly expressed as opinion the knowledge of the representor meant it became a statement of fact.

Smith v *Land and House Property Corporation*
(1884) 28 ChD 7

The Plaintiffs put up a hotel for sale on the 4th August, 1882, stating in the particulars that it was let to 'F (a most desirable tenant), at a rental of £400 for an unexpired term of 27½ years.' The L Co. sent M their secretary, to inspect the property. M reported that F from business he was doing could hardly pay his rent, and that the town in which it was situated seemed to be 'in the last stage of decay'. The directors on receiving this report, directed M to bid up to £5,000. M went and bought for £4,700. Before completion, F went into liquidation, and the L Co. refused to complete. The Plaintiffs sued for specific performance. It was proved that

on the 1st May 1882, the Lady Day quarter's rent was wholly unpaid. That a
distress was then threatened, and that F paid £30 on the 6th May, £40 on the 13th
June, and the remaining £30 shortly before the auction, and that no part of the
quarter's rent due at Midsummer had been paid. The Chairman of the company
was orally examined, and deposed most positively, that the company would not
have bought but for the representation in the particulars that F was a most desirable
tenant. Mr Justice Denman held that there was a material misrepresentation, and
that the contract had been entered into in reliance upon it. His lordship accordingly
dismissed the action, and on a counter claim by the defendants, rescinded the
contract. On appeal:

BOWEN LJ: . . . In considering whether there was a misrepresentation, I will
first deal with the argument that the particulars only contain a statement of
opinion about the tenant. It is material to observe that it is often fallaciously
assumed that a statement of opinion cannot involve the statement of fact. In
a case where the facts are equally well known to both parties, what one of
them says to the other is frequently nothing but an expression of opinion.
The statement of such opinion is in a sense a statement of fact, about the
condition of the man's own mind, but only of an irrelevant fact, for it is of no
consequence what the opinion is. But if the facts are not equally known to
both sides, then a statement of opinion by the one who knows the facts best
involves very often a statement of material fact, for he impliedly states that he
knows facts which justify his opinion. Now a landlord knows the relation
between himself and his tenant, other persons either do not know them at all
or do not know them equally well, and if the landlord says that he considers
that the relations between himself and his tenant are satisfactory, he really
avers that the facts peculiarly within his knowledge are such as to render that
opinion reasonable. Now are the statements here statements which involve
such a representation of material facts? They are statements on a subject as
to which prima facie the vendors know everything and the purchasers
nothing. The vendors state that the property is let to a most desirable tenant,
what does that mean? I agree that it is not a guarantee that the tenant will go
on paying his rent, but it is to my mind a guarantee of a different sort, and
that amounts at least to an assertion that nothing has occurred in the
relations between the landlord and the tenant which can be considered to
make the tenant an unsatisfactory one. That is an assertion of a specific fact.
Was it a true one? Having regard to what took place between Lady Day and
Midsummer, I think that it was not. In my opinion a tenant who had paid last
quarter's rent by driblets under pressure must be regarded an undesirable
tenant. (The appeal was dismissed.)

In the *Smith* case, above, the landlord had express knowledge of the tenant's
position. The law has, however, taken this principle a step further by implying
knowledge to the representor because of the position in which the representation was made. The decision in *Esso Petroleum Co. Ltd v Mardon* (1976)
illustrates the principle. The court is saying that because of the special
knowledge and skill of Esso's representative that the petrol company was in a

much better position to realise what the sales of petrol would be. The decision is important as again the law is making professional people liable, in this case through their statements, because of the amount of bargaining skill and power they possess as against the non-professional person in the particular context in which they are operating.

Esso Petroleum Co. Ltd v *Mardon*
[1976] 1 QB 801

In 1961 the plaintiffs, a large oil company, found a site on a busy main street which they considered suitable for a filling station as an outlet for their petrol sales. One of their servants with some 40 years' experience of the trade calculated that the potential throughput was likely to reach 200,000 gallons by the third year of operation. On the basis of that estimate they bought the site and started to build the station; but the local planning authority refused permission for the pumps to front on to the main street and the station had to be built back to front. Despite that fundamental alteration in siting, the plaintiffs early in 1963 interviewed the defendant, a prospective tenant, and the same experienced servant together with a local colleague gave him the same estimated throughput of 200,000 gallons. The defendant suggested that 100,000 to 150,000 was more likely; but his doubts, as the judge found, were quelled by his trust in the greater experience and expertise of the plaintiffs' servants; and on April 10, 1963, he entered into a written tenancy agreement for three years at a rent of £2,500 for the first two years and £3,000 for the third.

Despite his best endeavours the throughput in the first 15 months was only 78,000 gallons, mainly because the pumps were screened from the main street passing public. In July 1964, after he had sunk all his capital in the business — £6,270, provided by a private limited company in which he and his wife held all the shares — and had incurred a large bank overdraft he gave the plaintiffs notice. As they wanted to keep the station open and controlled by a good tenant they offered him a new tenancy agreement at a yearly rent of £1,000 plus a surcharge on petrol sold and he entered into it on September 1, 1964. But the losses continued; the plaintiffs gave the defendant no real help and when he could not pay cash for the petrol supplied they cut off his supplies. In December 1966 they issued a writ claiming possession of the premises, moneys owed, and mesne profits. The defendant gave up possession in March 1967 and he counterclaimed for damages for breach of the warranty as to the potential throughput, and alternatively for negligent misrepresentation by virtue of which he had been induced to enter into the contract of April 10, 1963, and the second agreement of September 1, 1964.

Held, that the statement as to potential throughput was a contractual warranty for it was a factual statement on a crucial matter made by a party who had, or professed to have, special knowledge and skill with the intention of inducing the other party to enter into the contract of tenancy; that it did induce the defendant to enter into the contract and therefore the plaintiffs were in breach of the warranty and liable in damages for the breach.

LORD DENNING MR: Now I would quite agree with Mr Ross-Munro that it was not a warranty — in this sense — that it did not *guarantee* that the throughput *would be* 200,000 gallons. But, nevertheless, it was a forecast made by a party — Esso — who had special knowledge and skill. It was the yardstick (the e.a.c.) by which they measured the worth of a filling station. They knew the facts. They knew the traffic in the town. They knew the throughput of comparable stations. They had much experience and expertise at their disposal. They were in a much better position than Mr Mardon to make a forecast. It seems to me that if such a person makes a forecast, intending that the other should act upon it — and he does act upon it, it can well be interpreted as a warranty that the forecast is sound and reliable in the sense that they made it with reasonable care and skill. It is just as if Esso said to Mr Mardon: 'Our forecast of throughput is 200,000 gallons. You can rely upon it as being a sound forecast of what the service station should do. The rent is calculated on that footing.' If the forecast turned out to be an unsound forecast such as no person of skill or experience should have made, there is a breach of warranty.

It is very different from the New Zealand case where the land had never been used as a sheep farm and both parties were equally unable to form an opinion as to its carrying capacity: see particularly *Bisset* v *Wilkinson* [1927] AC 177, 183-184.

In the present case it seems to me that there was a warranty that the forecast was sound, that is, Esso made it with reasonable care and skill. That warranty was broken. Most negligently Esso made a 'fatal error' in the forecast they stated to Mr Mardon, and on which he took the tenancy. For this they are liable in damages.

2.1.2   Fact, not intention Remember our definition of fact was that the statement must either relate to the past or the present. Consequently statements as to the future do not amount to ones of fact. Again there is an exception to this principle where it can be shown that the representor never had any intention of carrying out his future statements. In *Edgington* v *Fitzmaurice* (1885) as the representor never had any intention of using the money for the purpose stated the statement was one of fact.

Edgington v *Fitzmaurice*
(1885) 29 ChD 459

The directors of a company issued a prospectus inviting subscriptions for debentures, and stating that the objects of the issue of debentures were to complete alterations in the buildings of the company, to purchase horses and vans, and to develop the trade of the company. The real object of the loan was to enable the directors to pay off pressing liabilities. The Plaintiff advanced money on some of the debentures under the erroneous belief that the prospectus offered a charge upon the property of the company, and stated in his evidence that he would not have advanced his money but for such belief, but that he also relied upon the statements contained in the prospectus. The company became insolvent.

Held, that the misstatement of the objects for which the debentures were issued was a material misstatement of fact, influencing the conduct of the Plaintiff, and rendered the directors liable to an action for deceit, although the Plaintiff was also influenced by his own mistake.

BOWEN LJ: The state of a man's mind is as much a fact as the state of his digestion. It is true that it is difficult to prove what the state of a man's mind at a particular time is, but if it can be ascertained it is as much a fact as anything else. A misrepresentation as to the state of a man's mind is, therefore, a misstatement of fact.

2.1.3   Non-disclosure as a fact   The general principle is that silence does not amount to misrepresentation: that is non-disclosure and is not actionable. There are again exceptions to this principle. First, there are a group of contracts classified as being *uberrimae fidei* (of the upmost good faith) for example contracts of insurance. The nature of these contracts requires complete disclosure and a fact not being disclosed amounts to misrepresentation.

Secondly, where a statement which was true when made later becomes false, the representor is under a duty to disclose the alteration. The exception is based on the principle that a statement, once made, continues to operate until the time of contracting. The principle is illustrated by the decision in *With* v *O'Flanagan* (1936) where the notion of the representation being a continuing one is emphasised.

With v *O'Flanagan*
[1936] Ch 575

In January, 1934, negotiations were entered into for the sale of a medical practice, and the vendor then represented to the purchasers that the takings of the practice were at the rate of £2,000 per annum. The contract was signed on May 1, 1934, but by that date the circumstances had changed, as the practice had fallen owing to the illness of the vendor and the employment of several local tenants. The change of circumstances was not disclosed to the purchasers, and when they took possession on that date they found that the practice was almost non-existent. They thereupon commenced an action for rescission of the contract.

Bennett J held that, as the contract was not a contract uberrimae fidei, *the case was the ordinary one of parties to a contract having to prove, before they could obtain rescission, that the representations which induced them to act were in fact untrue at the time when they were made; that in this case the representation was true at the time when it was made, and the action failed.*

On appeal:

LORD WRIGHT MR: . . . The matter, however, may be put in another way though with the same effect, and that is on the ground that a representation made as a matter of inducement to enter into a contract is to be treated as a continuing representation. That view of the position was put in *Smith* v *Kay* by Lord Cranworth. He says of a representation made in negotiation sometime before that date of a contract: 'It is a continuing representation. The representation does not end for ever when the representation is once made; it continues on. The pleader who drew the bill, or the young man himself, in stating the case, would say, "Before I executed the bond I had been led to believe, and I therefore continued to believe, that it was executed pursuant to the arrangement." ... this doctrine is not limited to a case of contracts *uberrimae fidei* or to any cases in which owing to confidential relationships there is a peculiar duty of disclosure ...'. With the greatest respect to the learned judge, I cannot find in the authorities, so far as I know them or so far as they have been brought to my attention, any justification for these limitations.

The appeal was upheld.

2.2   Inducement

The second requirement is that the statement of fact must induce the representee to enter into the contract. In order for this requirement to be satisfied it is essential that the misrepresentation operated on the mind of the representee and the burden of proof is on the representee to show this. The above principle is illustrated by the decision in *Smith v Chadwick* (1884) where the plaintiff was unable to discharge the burden imposed on him.

Smith v Chadwick
(1884) 9 App Cas 187

The prospectus of a company which was being formed to take over iron-works, contained a statement that 'the present value of the turnover or output of the entire works is over £1,000,000 sterling per annum.'

If that statement meant that the works had actually in one year turned out produce worth at present prices more than a million, or at that rate per year, it was untrue. If it meant only that the works were capable of turning out that amount of produce it was true.

In an action of deceit for fraudulent misrepresentation whereby the plaintiff was induced to take shares he swore in answer to interrogatories that he 'understood the meaning' of the statement 'to be that which the words obviously conveyed', and at the trial was not asked either in examination or cross-examination what interpretation he had put upon the words.

Held, by the House of Lords that the statement taken in connection with the context was ambiguous and capable of the two meanings; that it lay on the plaintiff to prove that he had interpreted the words in the sense in which they were false and had in fact been deceived by them into taking the shares, and that as he had as a matter of fact failed to provide this the action could not be maintained.

Finally, in this context, it should be noted that the representee is under no duty to check the validity of the statement made by the representor. The principle was established by the decision in *Redgrave v Hurd* (1881).

Self check questions

1.   What is the difference between terms of the contract and an actionable misrepresentation?
2.   What are the requirements for an actionable misrepresentation?   –

3. What is the difference between a statement of fact as opposed to one of opinion? How do the courts make this decision?

4. What is the test to decide whether or not the representee has been induced by the statement of fact?

Answers

1. A misrepresentation while *not* being a term of the contract is actionable because various criteria have been satisfied. An initial decision must be made as to the nature of a pre-contractual statement and various guidelines have been suggested by the courts to help determine whether or not the statement is incorporated or not.

2. A misrepresentation must be a statement of *fact* which *induced* the representee to enter into the contract.

3. A statement of fact relates to the past or present and is actionable whereas a mere statement of opinion is not. In order to decide whether or not the statement is one of opinion the courts look at the amount of knowledge, either express or implied, held by the representor. The decision in *Esso Petroleum Co. Ltd v Mardon* is important in this context as here the court implied knowledge to the representor because of the expertise held.

4. The burden of proof is on the representee to show that the statement operated on his mind and induced him to enter into the contract.

3 Types of misrepresentation

There are three type of misrepresentation: fraudulent, negligent and innocent. The importance of the decision as to the type of misrepresentation affects the remedy available to the innocent party. The two remedies available to the innocent party are rescission (putting the contract to an end) and damages. Therefore as a pre-requisite to a discussion on remedies the nature of the misrepresentation has to be decided.

The most important development as to type of misrepresentation came in the 1960s from two sources. First, the House of Lords in the case of *Hedley Byrne & Co. Ltd v Heller and Partners Ltd* (1964) stated that a duty of care was owed, in certain situations, as to the nature of representations made. Secondly, Parliament passed the Misrepresentation Act 1967 which gives further protection to contracting parties in a misrepresentation situation. Both of these will be discussed further below. The types of misrepresentation need to be discussed.

3.1 Fraudulent misrepresentation

The burden of proof is on the plaintiff (representee) to show that the representor acted in a fraudulent manner. In *Derry v Peek* (1889) the court said that in order to prove fraud the statement must be made knowingly or without belief in its truth, or recklessly. As the burden of proof is on the representee it is often very difficult to show fraud and as a consequence of the decision in *Derry v Peek* the remedy of misrepresentation was severely limited. Developments below have overtaken this problem.

Derry v *Peek*
(1889) 14 App Cas 337

A special Act incorporating a tramway company provided that the carriages might be moved by animal power, and, with the consent of the Board of Trade, by steam power. The directors issued a prospectus containing a statement that by their special Act the company had the right to use steam power instead of horses. The plaintiff took shares on the faith of this statement. The Board of Trade afterwards refused their consent to the use of steam power and the company was wound up. The plaintiff having brought an action of deceit against the directors founded upon the false statement.

LORD HERSCHELL ... Having now drawn attention, I believe, to all the cases having a material bearing upon the question under consideration, I proceed to state briefly the conclusions to which I have been led. I think the authorities establish the following propositions: First, in order to sustain an action of deceit, there must be proof of fraud, and nothing short of that will suffice. Secondly, fraud is proved when it is shown that a false representation has been made (1) knowingly, or (2) without belief in its truth, or (3) recklessly, careless whether it be true or false. Although I have treated the second and third as distinct cases, I think the third is but an instance of the second, for one who makes a statement under such circumstances can have no real belief in the truth of what he states. To prevent a false statement being fraudulent, there must, I think, always be an honest belief in its truth. And this probably covers the whole ground, for one who knowingly alleges that which is false, has obviously no such honest belief. Thirdly, if fraud be proved, the motive of the person guilty of it is immaterial. It matters not that there was no intention to cheat or injure the person to whom the statement was made.

It was held reversing the decision of the Court of Appeal that the defendants were not liable, the statement as to steam power having been made by them in the honest belief that it was true.

3.2   Negligent misrepresentation
This concept will be looked at under two sub-headings.

3.2.1   Common law
The subject of common law negligent misrepresentation will be dealt with more fully in the section on torts. We, however, need to deal with it here as it still has ramifications in the area of contract. The decision in *Hedley Byrne & Co. Ltd* v *Heller and Partners Ltd* (1964) imposes liability for negligent misrepresentations made by a person in the course of business or professional affairs.

Hedley Byrne & Co. Ltd v *Heller and Partners Ltd*
[1964] AC 465

The appellants were advertising agents, who had placed substantial forward advertising orders for a company on terms by which they, the appellants, were personally liable for the cost of the orders. They asked their bankers to inquire into the company's financial stability and their bankers made inquiries of the respondents, who were the company's bankers, the respondents gave favourable references but stipulated that these were 'without responsibility'. In reliance on these references the appellants placed orders which resulted in a loss of £17,000. They brought an action against the respondents for damages for negligence.

Held, that a negligent, though honest, misrepresentation, spoken or written, may give rise to an action for damages for financial loss caused thereby, apart from any contract or fiduciary relationship, since the law will imply a duty of care when a party seeking information from a party possessed of a special skill trusts him to exercise due care, and that party knew or ought to have known that reliance was being placed on his skill and judgment. However, since here there was an express disclaimer of responsibility, no such duty was, in any event, implied.

LORD REID: ... Wherever in the course of business or professional affairs in response to a request a person gives advice or information, in circumstances in which a reasonable man would know that he could be relied on and without clearly denying responsibility for his words, a duty of care arises to exercise such care as is reasonable in the circumstances. If this care is not exercised and damage results an action for damages will be at common law in accordance with the usual principle of negligence.

A number of points need to be noted about this principle. First, liability only arises where there is a 'special relationship' between the parties and this should be seen as limited to somebody acting in the capacity outlined above. Secondly, the burden of proof is on the plaintiff (representee) to show that the representor acted in a negligent manner, again this burden is often difficult to discharge. Finally, the concept applies generally to all negligent advice and not merely to pre-contractual situations. Therefore, the representee is actually suing in tort for damages and the remedy of rescission is not available.

3.2.2 Statute Section 2(1) of the Misrepresentation Act 1967 provides a statutory form of negligent misrepresentation. The wording of s. 2(1) is, to say the least, convoluted and as a result has caused a number of problems in its interpretation. The section establishes an action for negligent misrepresentation in that even though there has not been fraudulent misrepresentation, a cause of action may still exist provided a number of criteria are satisfied. First, the representee must enter into the contract with the representor as a result of the misrepresentation. Secondly, the burden of proof is on the representor to show that 'he had reasonable ground to believe ... the facts represented were true'.

Section 2(1) Misrepresentation Act 1967

Where a person has entered into a contract after a misrepresentation had been made to him by another party thereto and as a result thereof he has suffered loss, then, if the person making the misrepresentation would be liable to dmages in respect thereof had the misrepresentation been made fraudulently, that person shall be so liable notwithstanding that the misrepresentation was not made fraudulently, unless he proves that he had reasonable ground to believe and did believe up to the time the contract was made that the facts represented were true.

The two criteria, above, can be compared with the *Hedley Byrne* principle in that the common law principle does not require a contract to be entered into and the burden of proof is different. The burden being on the representor in s. 2(1) makes it advantageous as compared to the common-law principle. A final comparison can be mentioned in that s. 2(1) does not require there to be a special relationship between the parties as compared to the common-law principle. (NB. The other provisions of the Act will be dealt with below.)

The interpretation of s. 2(1) by the courts must now be looked at. In *Howard Marine v Ogden* (1978) the court indicated that the onus of proof was on Howard Marine to show that their representative, Mr O'Loughlin, had reasonable ground to believe in the truth of the statement. The crucial part of the judgment is at the bottom of paragraph two where the judge says 'In the course of negotiations leading to a contract the statute imposes an absolute obligation not to state facts which the representor cannot prove he had reasonable ground to believe'. The decision is interesting as the court is interpreting s. 2(1) in such a way that the representor would find it difficult to discharge the burden of proof imposed on him.

Howard Marine v *Ogden*
[1978] QB 574

During extended negotiations between the defendants, civil engineering contractors, and the plaintiffs, owners of two German-built sea-going barges, for the hire of barges for carrying heavy clay in vast quantities out to sea and dumping it, the barge owners' marine manager answered questions put by the contractors to him and representatives of competing firms at a meeting of July 1, 1974. To the question: 'What is the capacity of each barge?' he replied orally '850 cubic metres' and that that was equivalent to about 1,600 tonnes deadweight carrying capacity, subject to weather, fuel load, and time of year. He based that figure of 1,600 tonnes on his recollection of an entry in Lloyd's Register which gave the capacity of the barges as 1,800 tonnes. Owing to a mistake in the Register that figure of 1,800 tonnes was unfortunately incorrect. The correct deadweight capacity — 1,055 tonnes — could have been ascertained from the ship's documents in the owners' possession. The contractors continued the negotiations for hiring the barges without obtaining any other figure for the vital matter of deadweight capacity, and took the barges into use in October 1974 under the terms of a charterparty which in its final agreed form included an exception clause that 'charterers' acceptance of handing over the vessel shall be conclusive that they have examined the vessel and found her in all respects fit for the intended and contemplated use by the charterers . . . '

The contractors took delivery of the barges and used them for some six months. But they had soon become doubtful about the stated deadweight capacity and when in March 1975 they discovered that the correct capacity was only 1,055 tonnes they paid £20,000 for hire and refused to pay any more. The owners withdrew the barges and issued a writ claiming £93,183 for outstanding hire charges. The contractors denied liability and counter-claimed for damages, alleging breaches of collateral warranties in the representations of fact, as to deadweight capacity made before contract; breach of the duty of care to give correct pre-contract information arising from the special relationship between the parties where the contractors relied on the barge owners' expert knowledge; and liability to damages under section 2(1) of the Misrepresentation Act 1967 by reason of the innocent but incorrect representation as to the barge owners.

BRIDGE: ... The first question then is whether Howards would be liable in damages in respect of Mr O'Loughlin's misrepresentation if it had been made fraudulently, that is to say, if he had known that it was untrue. An affirmative answer to that question is inescapable. The judge found in terms that what Mr O'Loughlin said about the capacity of the barges was said with the object of getting the hire contract for Howards, in other words, with the intention that it should be acted on. This was clearly right. Equally clearly the misrepresentation was in fact acted on by Ogdens. It follows, therefore, on the plain language of the statute that, although there was no allegation of fraud, Howards must be liable unless they proved that Mr O'Loughlin had reasonable ground to believe what he said about the barges' capacity.

It is unfortunate that the judge never directed his mind to the question whether Mr O'Loughlin had any reasonable ground for his belief. The question he asked himself, in considering liability under the Misrepresentation Act 1967, was whether the innocent misrepresentation was negligent. He concluded that if Mr O'Loughlin had given the inaccurate information in the course of the April telephone conversations he would have been negligent to do so but that in the circumstances obtaining at the Otley interview in July there was no negligence. I take it that he meant by this that on the earlier occasions the circumstances were such that he would have been under a duty to check the accuracy of his information, but on the later occasions he was exempt from any such duty. I appreciate the basis of this distinction, but it seems to me, with repect, quite irrelevant to any question of liability under the statute. If the representee proves a misrepresentation which, if fraudulent, would have sounded in damages, the onus passes immediately to the representor to prove that he had reasonable grounds to believe the facts represented. In other words the liability of the representor does not depend upon his being under a duty of care the extent of which may vary according to the circumstances in which the representation is made. In the course of negotiations leading to a contract the statute imposes an absolute obligation not to state facts which the representor cannot prove he had reasonable ground to believe.

It was held on appeal that the contractors could not establish any claim in contract for there was nothing in the pre-contract negotiations which could amount to a collateral warranty.

3.3   Innocent misrepresentation

A brief note must be made of innocent misrepresentation. The advent of negligent misrepresentation, in particular the interpretation of s. 2(1) in *Howard Marine* v *Ogden* (above) had limited the use of this category. In this case the representator had available to him, through the ship's documents, the carrying capacity of the barges. Assuming this information had indicated that the carrying capacity was in fact 1,055 tonnes then it could well be that the representor had discharged his duty under s. 2(1). The court would not have required the representor to actually check the carrying capacity, because of the complexity and cost involved, and therefore the burden would have been discharged. If the above analysis is correct then the appropriate course of action would have been in innocent misrepresentation.

Self check questions
1.   Why is it important to decide upon the nature of the misrepresentation?
2.   What are the requirements for the different types of misrepresentation and on whom is the burden of proof?

Answers
1.   The decision is important as the remedy available to the innocent party varies according to the type of misrepresentation.

2.

TYPE	REQUIREMENTS	BURDEN OF PROOF
Fraudulent	Acting knowingly or recklessly or without belief in its truth	On the representee
Negligent — common-law	Duty of care as a result of a special relationship between the parties	On the representee
Negligent — s. 2(1) of MRA, 1967	Representor must show reasonable grounds to believe in the truth of the statement.	On the representor

4   Remedies

In the introduction it was stated that a misrepresentation merely renders the contract voidable. The onus is on the representee to put the contract to an end through the remedy of *rescission* which, in theory at least, is available in all types of misrepresentation. The second remedy is that of *indemnity/damages* and there the type of misrepresentation is crucial to decide which applies. We shall look at each remedy in turn.

4.1 Rescission

Rescission is an equitable remedy and therefore it is both discretionary and can be lost through actions of the innocent party. Section 2(2) of the 1967 Act also imposes limits on the operation of the remedy. The limitations are listed below.

4.1.1 Affirmation of the contract
The representee by his actions can affirm the contract, and therefore lose the right to rescind. In *Long* v *Lloyd* (1958) the representee finally lost his right to rescind by taking his lorry to Middlesbrough — indeed if you read the judgment carefully the right to rescind could well have been lost at an earlier date. The decision in *Long* is the clearest example of affirmation available.

Long v Lloyd
[1958] 1 WLR 753

On October 19, 1956, the plaintiff, a haulage contractor, saw a newspaper advertisement inserted by the defendant offering for sale at £850 a 1947 Dennis 12/14 ton lorry described as in 'exceptional condition'. On the telephone that evening the defendant told the plaintiff that the lorry was in 'first-class condition'. On the next day the plaintiff saw the vehicle at the defendant's premises. The defendant said that the lorry was capable of a speed of 40 miles an hour. On October 22, 1956, the plaintiff, accompanied by the defendant, took the lorry for a trial run on the road. The defendant made various representations as to the lorry, one of which was that its fuel consumption was 11 miles to the gallon. The plaintiff there and then bought the lorry for the reduced price of £750, paying half the purchase price and leaving the balance to be paid later. On October 23, 1956, a receipt was posted to the plaintiff by the defendant: 'Received from (the plaintiff) the sum of £375 by cheque being half payment of Dennis vehicle DDW 864 as tried and approved by the above. Balance remaining £375.'

On October 24, 1956, the plaintiff drove the lorry from Sevenoaks, where he carried on business, to Rochester to pick up a small load. On the journey the dynamo ceased to function and the plaintiff was advised to fit a reconstructed dynamo. He noticed also that an oil seal was allowing oil to escape, that there was a crack in one of the wheels, and that the vehicle had consumed 8 gallons of fuel for a journey of about 40 miles. That night he told the defendant of these defects. The defendant said that the dynamo was 'all right' when the lorry left him and offered to pay half the cost of the reconstructed dynamo. This the plaintiff accepted. The defendant denied any knowledge of the broken oil seal. The next day the dynamo was fitted and the lorry was driven to Middlesbrough by the plaintiff's brother. On October 26, 1956, the plaintiff learnt from his brother that the lorry had broken down on its journey. In consequence, the plaintiff wrote to the defendant complaining of leakage or consumption of oil from the sump, of a fuel consumption of only 9 miles a gallon, and of the fact that instead of the lorry being a 40-mile-an-hour vehicle it was an effort to keep it at 25 miles an hour with the 4-ton load.

The plaintiff brought an action for rescission of the contract on the ground of innocent misrepresentation.

PEARCE LJ: Thus, to recapitulate the facts, after the trial run the plaintiff drove the lorry home from Hampton Court to Sevenoaks, a not inconsiderable distance. After that experience he took it into use in his business by driving it on the following day to Rochester and back to Sevenoaks with a load. By the time he returned from Rochester he knew that the dynamo was not charging, that there was an oil seal leaking, that he had used 8 gallons of fuel for a journey of 40 miles, and that a wheel was cracked. He must also, as we think, have known by this time that the vehicle was not capable of 40 miles per hour. As to oil consumption, we should have thought that, if it was so excessive that the sump was practically dry after 300 miles, the plaintiff could have reasonably been expected to discover that the rate of consumption was unduly high by the time he had made the journey from Hampton Court to Sevenoaks and thence to Rochester and back.

On his return from Rochester the plaintiff telephoned to the defendant and complained about the dynamo, the excessive fuel consumption, the leaking oil seal and the cracked wheel. The defendant then offered to pay half the cost of the reconstructed dynamo which the plaintiff had been advised to fit, and the plaintiff accepted the defendant's offer. We find this difficult to reconcile with the continuance of any right of rescission which the plaintiff might have had down to that time.

But the matter does not rest there. On the following day the plaintiff, knowing all that he did about the condition and performance of the lorry, dispatched it, driven by his brother, on a business trip to Middlesbrough. That step, at all events, appears to us to have amounted in all the circumstances of the case, to a final acceptance of the lorry by the plaintiff for better or for worse, and to have conclusively extinguished any right of rescission remaining to the plaintiff after completion of the sale.

Accordingly, even if the plaintiff should be held to have had a right to rescission which survived the completion of the contract, we think that on the facts of this case he lost any such right before his purported exercise of it.

For these reasons we would dismiss this appeal.

4.1.2 Lapse of time   The representee can lose the right to rescind through a lapse of time. There are no hard and fast rules as to what amounts to a lapse of time sufficient for these purposes. In *Leaf* v *International Galleries* (1950) the court held that the lapse here meant that the remedy was lost. Clearly each case turns on its own particular facts.

Leaf v *International Galleries*
[1950] 2 KB 86

In 1944 the defendants sold to the plaintiff for £85 a picture which they represented to have been painted by J. Constable. In 1949 the plaintiff tried to sell it at Christies and was then informed that it had not been painted by Constable. He thereupon took it back to the defendants who retained it for investigation. As they still maintained that it was painted by Constable, the plaintiff brought an action in which he claimed rescission of the contract and repayment of the £85. The county court judge found that the defendants had made an innocent misrepresentation and that the picture had not been painted by Constable, but he gave judgment for the defendants on the ground that the remedy of rescission was not available where a contract had been executed.

Held, assuming the equitable remedy of rescission for an innocent misrepresentation to be open to a buyer of goods, that it was not open to the buyer in this case as it had not been exercised within a reasonable time.

N.B. Misrepresentation renders the contract voidable at the option of the representee but where he affirms the contract he loses his option to avoid. Moreover, though lapse of time is not of itself a bar to rescission it may indicate a waiver of the right to rescind and in all cases of delay equitable remedies may be withheld.

4.1.3 Section 2(2) of the Misrepresentation Act, 1967 Rescission as we have said, is available in all types of misrepresenation. Section 2(2) gives the court a discretion, in non-fraudulent situations, to award damages instead of rescission. The court might think that where there is an innocent misrepresentation damages would be more appropriate than putting the contract to an end.

Section 2(2) Misrepresentation Act, 1967

Where a person has entered into a contract after a misrepresentation has been made to him otherwise than fraudulently, and he would be entitled, by reason of the misrepresentation, to rescind the contract, that the contract, then, if it is claimed, in any proceedings arising out of the contract, that the contract ought to be or has been rescinded, the court or arbitrator may declare the contract subsisting and award damages in lieu of rescision, if of opinion that it would be equitable to do so, having regard to the nature of the misrepresentation and the loss that would be caused by it if the contract were upheld, as well as to the loss that rescission would cause to the other party.

Rescission can also be lost in two further situations, which can be dealt with briefly. First, where the subject matter of the contract cannot be restored to the representor. Secondly, where a third party has gained an interest in the goods.

4.2 Indemnity/Damages
Damages are not available for all types of misrepresentation subject to s. 2(2) of the Act: for example, at common law in innocent misrepresentation the non-statutory remedies available are rescission and an indemnity which we shall discuss below.

4.2.1 Damages Damages can be assessed in two ways: either on a reliance basis or on an expectation basis. The difference between the two can be illustrated by the following example: Assume P would have made a good bargain if the representation had been true. P bought something for £100 which would have been worth £150 if the representation had been true — but which is in fact only worth £90.

We need to examine the difference between reliance and expectation. If the damages are assessed on the reliance theory then the damages would be the amount paid — £100 minus the actual value £90: that is,

$$£100 - £90 = £10$$

Compare this with the expectation theory which is based on the idea of performance of the contract. The actual value would have been £150 and therefore the expectation damages would be assessed as below:

$$£150 - £90 = £60$$

Expectation damages are available for breach of contract but here the damages should be assessed on a reliance (tortious) basis. There are a number of reasons for this: in fraudulent misrepresentation the representee is pursuing his remedy in the tort of deceit. Therefore in *Doyle* v *Olby* (1969) the court made it quite clear that damages should be assessed on a tortious and not contractual basis. The case is interesting as all damages directly flowing from the fraud were allowed, less any benefits received.

Doyle v *Olby*
[1969] 2 QB 158

The plaintiff saw an advertisement of an ironmongers' business for sale at £4,500 for the lease, business and goodwill, the stock to be taken at a valuation. He made inquiries, and the company's director produced accounts for the preceding three years which showed considerable annual profits. The director's brother told the plaintiff, inter alia, that all the trade was over the counter. The plaintiff agreed to buy and went into occupation under a new lease at a higher rent, but with a covenant that the vendors would not engage in similar business within a 10-mile radius for five years. Having undertaken liabilities of some £7,000, he soon found that the turnover had been misrepresented and in particular, that half the trade had been obtained by the director's brother acting as part-time traveller at £555 a year; and shortly after he took over, an associated company began to canvass the vendors' former customers in the district.

The plaintiff began an action against the two companies, the director, and his brother, for damages for fraud and conspiracy. Meanwhile, after three years' disastrous efforts to trade, he sold the business, but was left with liabilities of some £4,000. At the trial Swanwick J found all the defendants guilty of fraud and conspiracy and awarded the plaintiff damages of £1,500, two and a half times the cost of employing a part-time traveller at £600 a year, as equivalent to the cost of making good the representation or the reduction in the value of the goodwill.

The plaintiff appealed against the amount of damages.

Held, allowing the appeal:

(1)   That the court could apply the proper measure of damages for deceit despite the fact that the wrong measure was proposed by the plaintiff's counsel at the trial, for the court would not let a man with a just claim suffer by reason of his counsel's

mistake unless it were shown that to take a different course would do injustice to the defendants; and that had not been shown.

(2)   That the proper measure of damages for deceit, as distinct from damages for breach of contract, was all the damage directly flowing from the tortious act of fraudulent inducement which was not rendered too remote by the plaintiff's own conduct, whether or not the defendants could have foreseen such consequential loss. The plaintiff's position before the fraudulent inducement should be compared with his position at the end of the transaction. As in the instant case the plaintiff had been tricked into buying a business which he would otherwise not have bought at all, the court should award him his overall loss up to his final disposal of the business, less any benefits he had received.

(3)   That as the evidence before the court was limited, the court should estimate the damages by treating the matter as one for a jury, and on that broad approach a proper round figure would be £5,500.

There has been much debate as to how damages should be assessed under s. 2(1) of the Act. The reason for this debate is the confusion over whether s. 2(1) gives the same remedy as if the misrepresentation had been made fraudulently, in which case the reasoning in *Doyle* v *Olby* should apply, or whether damages should be assessed on the same basis as under the *Hedley Byrne* (see above) principle. Three cases, below, illustrate the continuing difficulties in trying to answer this question.

Royscot Trust Ltd v *Rogerson*
[1991] 3 All ER 294

The first defendant (the customer) agreed to buy a second-hand car for £7,600 from the second defendant, a dealer in used cars. The car was bought on hire-purchase through the plaintiff, a finance company, the customer paying a deposit of £1,200. In order to meet the finance company's condition that at least 20% of the purchase price be paid by way of deposit, the dealer represented to the finance company that the purchase price was £8,000 and that the customer had paid a deposit of £1,600, leaving a balance of £6,400, which was the same as the true balance while at the same time satisfying the 20% deposit requirement. The hire-purchase agreement was entered into between the customer and the finance company on that basis and the finance company paid the dealer £6,400. The customer paid instalments amounting to £2,774.76 and then dishonestly sold the car for £7,200 to a private purchaser, who obtained good title to it by virtue of the Hire-Purchase Act 1964, s. 27. The finance company issued proceedings against both the customer and the dealer. Judgment was entered in default against both defendants for damages, which were assessed against the customer for the amount outstanding under the hire-purchase agreement, and against the dealer for £1,600, which was the difference between the £6,400 the finance company had paid to the dealer and the £4,800 it would have paid had it known that the deposit was only £1,200. The dealer appealed against the assessment of the damages, contending that the finance company had suffered no loss because it had obtained title to a car worth at least £6,400. The finance company cross-appealed, contending that its loss was £3,625.24, being the difference between the amount paid to the dealer and the amount received from the customer before he defaulted.

Held: Since the Misrepresentation Act 1967, s. 2(1) provided that a person making an innocent misrepresentation which induced another to enter into a contract as a result of which that other person suffered loss should be 'so liable' to pay damages as if the representation had been made fraudulently, the measure of damages for an innocent misrepresentation giving rise to an action under s. 2(1) was the measure of damages in tort for fraudulent misrepresentation, with the result that the innocent party was entitled to recover any loss which flowed from the misrepresentation, even if the loss could not have been foreseen. Accordingly, the finance company was entitled to claim from the dealer any loss arising from the dealer's misrepresentation even if that loss was unforeseeable provided it was not otherwise too remote and since, having regard to the reality of the transaction, the customer's action in fraudulently disposing of the car was a reasonably foreseeable act, which was not novus actus interveniens breaking the chain of causation, the finance company was entitled to damages of £3,625.24, being the difference between the amount paid by it to the dealer and the amount received from the customer before defaulting, although the finance company would have to give credit for any sums which it recovered from the customer under the judgment against him. The dealer's appeal would therefore be dismissed and the finance company's cross-appeal allowed.

Although the decision has been criticised it has not been overruled and remains unaltered. However, if the principle of the decision is that the damages in an action under the Misrepresentation Act 1967, s. 2(1), are the same as in an action for fraudulent misrepresentation, two cases, on the effect of contributory negligence (see further chapter 15) illustrate that this is not in fact the case.

Alliance and Leicester Building Society v *Edgestop Ltd*
[1994] 2 All ER 38

L, an employee of the defendant estate agents and valuers, was convicted of four offences of procuring the execution of a valuable security by deception, contrary to the Theft Act 1968, s. 20. In each case the valuable security consisted of documents authorising the telegraphic transfer of substantial sums of money from the plaintiffs, a building society and a finance company, to a client account of a firm of solicitors. The plaintiffs brought actions against the defendants, who had fraudulently overvalued certain hotels in order to procure the plaintiffs to make substantial loans for the purchase and on the security of the hotels. It was alleged that the defendants were vicariously liable for the actions of L, who was their servant and agent acting within the scope of his actual or ostensible authority and on the defendants' behalf, and therefore the defendants were liable in deceit. The defendants pleaded contributory negligence to the finance company's claim and applied for leave to amend their defence to the society's claim to plead contributory negligence to that claim pursuant to s. 1(1) of the Law Reform (Contributory Negligence) Act 1945. The particulars of contributory negligence alleged were that the plaintiffs had failed to ascertain that L was not qualified to make the valuations and had acted outside the scope of his authority.

Held: Contributory negligence was not a defence to an action for deceit at common law and nothing in the 1945 Act affected that position. Accordingly, a person liable for deceit, whether personally or vicariously, was not entitled to deny, by way of a plea of contributory negligence, that his deceit was the sole effective cause of the damage suffered by the victim. It followed that the defendants were not entitled to plead contributory negligence to the plaintiffs' claims.

The decision is quite clear in that the court stated that contributory negligence does not apply to claims in deceit.

The reason why contributory negligence can be pleaded under s. 2(1) is due to the interpretation of 'fault' in the Law Reform (Contributory Negligence) Act 1945 — see generally chapter 15. The view expressed in *Gran Gelato* is that in order for there to be liability under s. 2(1) some element of fault must be present. This view is contentious in that s. 2(1) is often thought of as being a 'fiction of fraud'. Therefore as contributory negligence does not apply to fraudulent misrepresentation, due to its basis in deceit, it is argued that as s. 2(1) gives the same remedies as fraudulent misrepresentation then the answer should be the same in both.

Gran Gelato Ltd v *Richcliff (Group) Ltd*
[1992] 1 All ER 865

In 1984 the first defendant granted the plaintiff an underlease of basement and ground-floor shop premises for a term of almost 10 years, the underlease being carved out of two head leases. The plaintiff paid the first defendant a premium of £30,000 for the underlease and then spent almost £100,000 on alterations and shopfittings. Unknown to the plaintiff and its solicitors, both head leases contained redevelopment break clauses giving the head lessor the right to terminate the head leases for redevelopment by giving 12 months' notice expiring in or after June 1989. In the course of the negotiations leading to the grant of the underlease the plaintiff's solicitors sent 'inquiries before lease' to the first defendant's solicitors (the second defendants). Inquiry 3(A) asked whether there were 'any . . . rights affecting the . . . superior leasehold titles which would . . . in any way inhibit the enjoyment of the property by the Tenant in accordance with the terms of the present draft lease', to which the answer was, 'Not to the Lessor's knowledge'. In November 1988 the head lessor exercised the break clause option when the paintiff's underlease still had about 4½ years to run. The plaintiff brought an action claiming damages for negligence against both defendants for breach by the first defendant under the Misrepresentation Act 1967, s. 2(1). The plaintiff alleged that the answer to inquiry 3(A) constituted a representation that there was no provision for early termination in the two head leases, that the representation was false and made negligently, that the representation had been intended to induce the plaintiff to take the underlease and that the plaintiff had done so in reliance on the representation. The first defendant claimed that the plaintiff had been contributorily negligent in proceeding without first seeing the head leases and also counterclaimed for unpaid rent of £50,420. The plaintiff contended that s. 1 of the Law Reform (Contributory Negligence) Act 1945 did not apply to a claim for damages under the 1967 Act.

Held: (1) In normal conveyancing transactions the solicitor acting for the seller did not in general owe the buyer a duty of care when answering inquiries before contract or the like, because in the context of a contract for the sale of land the answers given on his behalf and, furthermore, where an agent had acted within the scope of his authority on behalf of a known principal and the principal himself owed a duty of care to a third party, it was not in general necessary for the reasonable protection of the third party that a further duty of care, owed by the agent to the third party and independent of the duty he owed to his principal, be imposed on the agent. However, where a solicitor stepped outside his role as solicitor for his client and accepted direct responsibility towards the third party with whom his client was dealing he did owe such a duty to the third party. In the circumstances, in which there were no special features giving rise to a duty of care owed by the second defendants to the plaintiff, the plaintiff's claim against them would be dismissed.

(2) Since the break clauses in the head leases were rights affecting the superior leasehold titles which would inhibit the plaintiff's enjoyment of the property as tenant, as had in fact happened, the answer to inquiry 3(A) that there were no such rights to the first defendant's knowledge was a misrepresentation, on which the plaintiff had relied and for which, subject to proof of loss, it was entitled to damages from the first defendant.

(3) Where a plaintiff brought concurrent claims against the defendant in negligence at common law and under the 1967 Act the defence of contributory negligence under the 1945 Act applied to both claims and the damages recoverable by the plaintiff could be reduced by reason of his contributory negligence. Accordingly, the defence of contributory negligence was available to the first defendant in respect of the claim made against it under s. 2(1) of the 1967 Act. However, on the facts, it would not be just or equitable to make any reduction in the plaintiff's damages since the first defendant had intended that the plaintiff would act in reliance on the accuracy of the answers provided on the first defendant's behalf and the plaintiff had in fact so acted and any carelessness on its part in failing to make other inquiries was no answer to its claim against the first defendant. On the issue of damages, the plaintiff was entitled to recover, and set off against the counterclaim for unpaid rent, the rent payable after September 1987 when the existence of the break clauses was discovered together with 50% of the premium and the legal costs of the acquisition and all costs of abortive attempts to dispose of the property, but not the alteration and shopfitting costs.

The decision states that contributory negligence does apply to both claims and therefore affects damages recoverable under the Misrepresentation Act 1967, s. 2(1). The decision in either the *Royscot* case or *Gran Gelato* is wrong. At present we need to be aware of both decisions and understand their contradictory nature.

4.2.2 Indemnity Damages are not available, subject to s. 2(2) of the Act, for innocent misrepresentation. Instead the court will grant an indemnity. The principle is that an indemnity only relates to loss incurred as a result of entering into the contract. The operation of this principle is shown by the decision in *Whittington* v *Seale-Hayne* (1900).

Whittington v Seale-Hayne
(1900) 82 LT 49

W took a lease of land after negotiations with the agent of S-H who had said that the premises were in a sanitary condition and good state of repair. The lease did not contain these statements but it did provide that the tenants (W) should pay rent, rates, do repairs or any work required by the local authority. W started a poultry farm employing a manager and buying stock. As a result of poor drains the stock died, the manager became ill and the local authority required the drains to be put in order.

W claimed compensation, inter alia, *for:*

(1)   value of stock lost
(2)   loss of profits
(3)   medical expenses
(4)   rates
(5)   rent
(6)   cost of repairs ordered by L.A.

The court held that (1), (2) and (3), although a result of the contract were not necessarily incurred under it. Items (4), (5) and (6) were necessarily incurred because if W had not expended money on these they would have been in breach of the covenants in the lease. They could not claim to be indemnified by way of compensation for injuries sustained by the insanitary condition of the premises and occasioned by their entering into the contract. Such compensation is in reality damages pure and simple, and is not the proper consequence of rescinding the contract.

Self check questions
1.   Why and in what ways can the remedy of rescission be lost?
2.   On what basis should damages for misrepresentation be assessed?
3.   What is the difference between indemnity and damages?
4.   Draw a diagram to illustrate the remedies for each type of misrepresentation

Answer
1.   Rescission is an equitable remedy and therefore discretionary. It can be lost because of affirmation, lapse of time, restitution is no longer possible and a third party has gained an interest. Added to the above, s. 2(2) of the Act gives the court the ability to award damages in lieu of rescission.
2.   Damages for misrepresenation should be assessed on a reliance (tortious) basis.
3.   An indemnity can only be claimed for loss arising from the entering into the contract and not for any consequential loss which can only be claimed as damages.

4.   TYPE OF MISREPRESENTATION   REMEDIES AVAILABLE

Fraudulent	Rescission and Damages
Negligent — *Hedley Byrne & Co. Ltd* v *Heller and Partners Ltd*	Damages only
Negligent — s. 2(1) MRA, 1967	Rescission and Damages
Innocent	Rescission and Indemnity — subject to s. 2(2) MRA, 1967

Problem

Statement of fact? ——— Alex is negotiating to lease a new grocer's shop from Bond plc, which owns a number of similar shops. *Bond's area manager*

Knowledge of representor —— states that the turnover of the shop *would reach £20,000 per annum.* Bond plc invites Alex to have an independent valuation

Duty to inspect? ——— carried out, but Alex sees no need for this.   *Inducement*
Alex enters into a *seven year lease* with Bond plc — the rent being £2,000 per annum. *No*   *Is statement*
mention is made in the lease of the likely ——— *incorporated*

Purchased in reliance on —— turnover. Alex buys new equipment, including an *electronic till and display into the contract?*
statement material, for a *further £1,000.* After *two years* Alex realises that the turnover of the —— *Time and*
shop is no more than £8,000 per annum *rescission*
and that his expected profit of *£5,000 per annum* has not *materialised.* ——————— *Able to claim*
Discuss.   *loss of profit?*

Suggested answer
The question concerns the law on misrepresentation. Before we discuss the requirements and effects of that concept it is necessary to establish why the question does not concern terms of the contract.

The court looks at the intention of the parties in order to decide whether or not a statement has been incorporated as a term of the contract on the facts; because the statement has *not* been mentioned in the lease this would seem to indicate that the statement is a non-contractual one and therefore if it is to have legal effect it must satisfy the requirements of misrepresentation.

A misrepresentation is a statement of fact which induced the representee to enter into the contract. Once we have established this, the type of misrepresentation needs to be decided upon as this effects the remedy available to the innocent party. On the facts it would appear that the statement made by the area manager of Bond is merely one of opinion and following *Bissett* v *Wilkinson* would not be actionable. The law has, however, developed from this, and will impose liability on an expert in such situations. In *Esso Petroleum Co. Ltd* v *Mardon* a statement made by Esso's representative was held to be fact and not opinion because of the skill/expertise held by the representor. Therefore, in our case it could well be argued that because of the implied bargaining skill of Bond's area manager the statement is one of fact and therefore actionable.

The second requirement is that the statement induced Alex to enter into the contract. The only issue raised on the facts is whether Alex was under a duty to have an independent valuation as it is clear that the representation acted on his mind. The law, following the decision in *Redgrave* v *Hurd* (1881) does not impose a duty on the representee to check the validity of the statement. Therefore the inducement requirement is satisfied.

An actionable misrepresentation has been established. The type of misrepresentation now has to be discussed. In order for it to amount to a fraudulent misrepresentation the representee (Alex) must show that Bond plc acted recklessly or dishonestly or without belief in the truth of the statement. Applying this test to the facts it would be very difficult for Alex to show that Bond plc acted in a fraudulent manner. Alex would be far better to use s. 2(1) of the Misrepresentation Act 1967; as he can show he entered into the contract as a result of Bond's representation the onus then shifts to the representor.

Section 2(1) requires the representor to show he had reasonable grounds to believe in the truth of the statement. The court, in *Howard Marine* v *Ogden*, interpreted the section as imposing an absolute obligation to this effect. Using this interpretation on the facts it would appear very difficult for Bond plc to discharge the onus of proof imposed on them. It is worth mentioning the possibility of liablity under the *Hedley Byrne* principle but as the onus is on Alex under the principle it seems unnecessary to pursue the matter.

Assuming there is liability under s. 2(1) the two remedies available to Alex are rescission and damages. Rescission is an equitable remedy and therefore can be lost in a number of circumstances. Alex only realised that the representation was wrong after two years and this lapse of time, following *Leaf* v *International Galleries*, could prove fatal to Alex's claim to rescind the contract. Alternatively, it could be agreed that through his actions he has affirmed the contract (*Long* v *Lloyd*), and again the right to rescind is lost. The above can be contrasted with the argument that he would have only realised that Bond plc had misrepresented the situation after trading for two years. Therefore the situation is open to argument.

The second remedy available to Alex is damages. There has been much conjecture on what basis damages are assessed under s. 2(1) but it is thought that damages should in fact be assessed on a tortious (reliance) basis. Consequently the damages which can be claimed are those expenses resulting from the misrepresentation. Alex spent £1,000 on an electronic till and display material which on this theory can be claimed. Alex may also try to claim money for loss of profits but such damages would not be available on a tortious basis. Therefore Alex is only able to claim damages which arose from the misrepresentation and these will not include damages for loss of profits.

11   RESTRAINT OF TRADE

1   Introduction

In the previous chapter we dealt with the principle of misrepresentation which renders the contract voidable. This chapter shall examine a category of contract which the law treats as being void. This statement is slightly misleading as if a contract is void then it has no legal effect; it may be more correct to say that in fact if a contract comes into this category it is unenforceable assuming the following criteria are not satisfied:

(a)   does a contract come within the doctrine of restraint of trade?

(b)   if the contract is within the doctrine does it satisfy the test of reasonableness? and

(c)   what is the effect of the contract not satisfying the test of reasonableness?

We shall use the following general principle when dealing with the subject: 'All covenants in restraint of trade are prima facie unenforceable at common-law and are enforceable only if they are reasonable with reference to the interests of the parties concerned and to the public.'

2   Categories of restraint

The courts have developed various tests to decide whether or not a contract comes within the doctrine. The problem is that there is no definitive test and as a result the courts have developed the scope of the doctrine on a case by case basis. This position is unsatisfactory as it means that business organisations, in particular, try to avoid the operation of the doctrine but then find that the contract comes within the doctrine and has to be justified in order to be upheld.

A number of cases have to be examined in order for an idea of the doctrine to be given. In *Nordenfelt v Maxim Nordenfelt Guns and Ammunition Co. Ltd* (1894) the court upheld a complete restraint as it was able to satisfy the test of reasonableness. It is interesting to note the wording of the clause as the effect of it was to stop Nordenfelt from working with anybody else for twenty-five years.

Nordenfelt v Maxim Nordenfelt Guns and Ammunition Co. Ltd
[1894] AC 535

A patentee and manufacturer of guns and ammunition for purposes of war covenanted with a company to which his patents and business had been transferred that he would not for twenty-five years engage except on behalf of the company either directly or indirectly in the business of a manufacturer of guns or ammunition:

LORD MACNAGHTEN: The true view at the present time I think, is this: The public have an interest in every person's carrying on his trade freely: so has the individual. All interference with individual liberty of action in trading, and all restraints of trade of themselves, if there is nothing more, are contrary to public policy, and therefore void. That is the general rule. But there are exceptions: restraints of trade and interference with individual liberty of action may be justified by the special circumstances of a particular case. It is a sufficient justification, and indeed it is the only justification, if the restriction is reasonable, that is, in reference to the interests of the parties concerned and reasonable in reference to the interests of the public, tht it is so framed and so guarded as to afford adequate protection to the party in whose favour it is imposed, while at the same time it is in no way injurious to the public. That, I think, is the fair result of all the authorities.

Held: Affirming the decision of the Court of Appeal, the covenant though unrestricted as to space was not, having regard to the nature of the business and the limited number of the customers (namely the Governments of this and other countries), wider than was necessary for the protection of the company, nor injurious to the public interests of this country. It was therefore valid and might be enforced by injunction.

Therefore it was laid down that a partial restraint is allowable provided that it is reasonable in the interest of the parties and the interest of the public as a whole. But there is a presumption that a restrictive agreement is void and the party wishing to uphold it must establish:

(i)   that there is an interest which merits protection;
(ii)   the restriction is reasonable as between the parties;
(iii)   the restriction is not contrary to the public interest.

The decision in *Nordenfelt* is straightforward in the sense that the clause clearly came within the doctrine. A more complex example is provided by the decision in *Esso Petroleum Co. Ltd v Harper's Garage (Stourport) Ltd* (1968). The case concerned the operation of a solus agreement and it can be seen from the extracted judgment of Lord Reid that his analysis as to why a solus agreement should come within the doctrine is not altogether convincing. Indeed, two other members of the House of Lords suggested alternative tests but for our purposes the judgment of Lord Reid is sufficient. (Note: the *Esso* decision will be discussed further below on the question of reasonableness of restraint.)

Esso Petroleum Co. Ltd v *Harper's Garage (Stourport) Ltd*
[1968] AC 269

The appellants, suppliers of motor fuel to dealers, entered into two sales agreements with the respondents in relation to two garages, M and C, owned by the respondents. The agreements were on the appellants' standard forms.

*Under the agreement dated June 27, 1963, in respect of garage M, the appellants agreed to sell and the respondents agreed to buy from the appellants for a period of four years and five months from July 1, 1963, at the appellants' wholesale schedule prices to dealers ruling at the date of delivery their total requirements of motor fuels for resale at garage M. The appellants further agreed to allow the respondents a rebate of 1 ¼d. a gallon on all fuels bought under the agreement and to extend to the respondents the advantages of their dealer cooperation plan. The respondents agreed (*inter alia*) not to resell motor fuels for use in vehicles holding private licences under the Road Traffic Acts except in accordance with the appellants' retail scheme in connection with resales, to operate the garage in accordance with the dealer cooperation plan, which listed six advantages to dealers and under which the respondents agreed (*inter alia*) to keep the garage open at all reasonable hours, and, if they sold the garage, to get the buyer to enter into a similar sales agreement with the appellants.*

*The agreement dated July 5, 1962, in relation to garage C was for a period of 21 years from July 1, 1962, but otherwise the agreements were identical. Garage C was subject to a mortgage dated October 6, 1962, whereby the appellants advanced, under a loan agreement of July 12, 1962, £7,000 to the respondents, who covenanted (*inter alia*) to repay by instalments over 21 years the sum advanced with interest, charged the garage by way of legal mortgage with payment to the appellants of the sums covenanted to be paid, covenanted to keep the garage open during normal working hours, to purchase their total requirements of motor fuels at the mortgaged premises from the appellants during the continuance of the mortgage so long as the appellants should be ready to supply the same at their usual list price, not to buy, receive or sell any motor fuels other than those purchased from the appellants, not to offer any lubricants for sale unless of corresponding type or the nearest equivalent to those supplied by the appellants, who should be given no less publicity than any other supplier, and not to redeem the mortgage otherwise than in accordance with the covenant for repayment.*

In 1961 low-priced petrol came on the market and the appellants, considering that the resale price maintenance clause in the agreement penalised their dealers, wrote to all their dealers, including the respondents, on December 3, 1963, to the effect that they would not insist on its implementation. In fact they had never done so. The respondents replied on December 4, 1963, to the effect that they deemed the sales agreements null and void by reason of the removal of the resale price maintenance clause, relying on an implied term of the contracts. They began to sell another brand of petrol at the garages. They also announced their intention of redeeming the mortgage which could not be redeemed without their consent, otherwise than in accordance with the covenant for repayment.

The appellants sought injunctions restraining the respondents from buying or selling motor fuels other than those of the appellants at the two garages during the subsistence of the solus agreements and in respect of garage C, during the subsistence of the mortgage.

LORD REID: ... In my view this agreement is within the scope of the doctrine of restraint of trade as it had been developed in English law. Not only have the respondents agreed negatively not to sell other petrol but they have agreed positively to keep this garage open for the sale of the appellants' petrol at all reasonable hours throughout the period of the tie. It was argued that this was merely regulating the respondent's trading and rather promoting than restraining his trade. But regulating a person's existing trade may be a greater restraint than prohibiting him from engaging in a new trade. And a contract to take one's whole supply from one source may be much more hampering than a contract to sell one's whole output to one buyer. I would not attempt to define the dividing line between contracts which are and contracts which are not in restraint of trade, but in my view this contract must be held to be in restraint of trade. So it is necessary to consider whether its provisions can be justified. ...

The decision in *Esso Petroleum Co. Ltd* v *Harper's Garage (Stourport) Ltd* brought a great number of contracts within the doctrine and as a result lawyers tried to find devices in order to avoid the doctrine. In *Alec Lobb (Garages) Ltd* v *Total Oil (Great Britain) Ltd* (1985) the court rejected the argument that a lease and lease-back arrangement did not come within the doctrine. Clearly the court was reluctant to give a free hand to contracting parties in such situations and therefore brought such agreements within the doctrine. Again you will notice that the judge does not give many reasons for his decision, therefore maintaining the flexibility of the court in such matters.

Alec Lobb (Garages) Ltd v *Total Oil (Great Britain) Ltd*
[1985] 1 All ER 303

The plaintiffs were a company and a mother and her son, who were the shareholders and directors of the company, which in 1964 borrowed £15,000 from the defendant, a petrol company, on the security of a legal charge on the premises created by the plaintiff company in favour of the defendant. The charge contained a covenant (a tie covenant) by the plaintiff company to purchase the defendant's petrol exclusively during the continuance of the loan (which was repayable by instalments over 18 years) and for a further period thereafter, and made the charge irredeemable during the period of the loan. By November 1968 the plaintiff company, though trading profitably, was under financial pressure from other creditors. The mother and son stood to lose their livelihood and face personal bankruptcy if the plaintiff company was wound up due to insolvency. The son felt unable to resort to any other petrol company for finance because of the tie with the defendant and negotiations took place between the parties in which the plaintiffs were separately and independently advised by solicitors and accountants. The defendant, although reluctant to enter into any further transaction with the plaintiffs, wished to preserve the garage as an outlet for sales of its petrol. Accordingly, it agreed to put further capital into the plaintiff company by means of a lease and lease-back transaction, comprising a lease of the garage premises to the defendants for 51 years in return for the payment to the plaintiff company of a premium of £35,000 (based on a fair valuation of the premises as a tied site) and the immediate lease-back of the premises by an underlease to the son personally for a term of 2 years at a rent of £2,250, which represented an adequate return on the premium paid by the defendant. The underlease contained a tie covenant by the son to purchase the defendant's petrol exclusively for the 21-year term of the underlease and provisions for a mutual break of the underlease at the end of the seventh and fourteenth years and an absolute prohibition on assignment of the underlease. The transaction extinguished the existing charges. Completion of the transaction took place in July 1969, by which time the current tie covenant under the charges was treated as having three years to run. Payment of the plaintiff company's debts and costs absorbed most of the premium received from the defendant, leaving little of the premium left over for use as working capital. The transaction thus failed in its object of rescuing the company from the constraints of inadequate working capital. However, the plaintiffs took no steps to have the transaction set aside until June 1979, when they issued a writ against the defendant seeking to have the transaction set aside on the grounds, inter alia, *that the bargain was harsh and unconscionable, or alternatively that the tie covenant was void as being an unreasonable restraint of trade which rendered the whole transaction invalid.*

The judge held, inter alia: *(i) that although the tie provision was void as being an unreasonable restraint of trade it was severable from the rest of the transaction which was valid and enforceable, (ii) that on the facts the transaction was not harsh and unconscionable and (iii) that, in any event, the plaintiffs' claim to set aside the transaction was barred by laches. The plaintiffs appealed. The defendant cross-appealed, contending that the underlease was not an agreement in restraint of trade because (i) the underlease derived from the disposal by the company of substantially all its interest in the property by the grant of the 51-year lease to the defendant and (ii) the underlease was granted to the mother and son, and not to the company, or alternatively that, even if the underlease was an agreement in restraint of trade, the restrictions on trading in the underlease were, in all the circumstances, reasonable and were therefore valid.*

DILLON LJ: It is logical to consider the cross-appeal first, and I can deal very shortly with the second of the above arguments. In *Esso Petroleum Co. Ltd v Harper's Garage (Stourport) Ltd* [1968] AC 269 it was held that the doctrine of restraint of trade had no application to restraints imposed on persons who, before the transaction by which the restraints were imposed, had no right whatsoever to trade at all on the land in question. Their Lordships had in mind in particular the case where the owner of land grants a lease of the land to a person who had no previous right to occupy the land, and imposes by the lease restraints on the lessee's power to trade as he likes on the land. Such a lease would ordinarily not be regarded as an agreement in restraint of trade. In the present case however the granting of the lease-back to Mr and Mrs Lobb rather than to the company was a palpable device in an endeavour to evade the doctrine of restraint in trade. Mr and Mrs Lobb were only selected as lessees because they were the proprietors of the company previously in occupation. The court has ample power to pierce the corporate veil, recognise a continued identity of occupation and hold, as it should, that Total can be in no better position *quoad* restraints of trade by granting the lease-back to Mr and Mrs Lobb than if it had granted the lease-back to the company.

As for the argument that the lease-back is not an agreement in restraint of trade because the restrictions on the lease-back derive from a disposal by the company of a large part of its interest in the property, I have had considerable difficulty in understanding the argument. It is of course clear that there is no agreement in restraint of trade where a person deprives himself of all right to trade as he wishes on land by selling all his interest in that land. In the present case, however, that is not what the company did and the whole object was that trade should continue in the property. The lease and lease-back have to be taken together as two essential parts of one transaction, and in my judgment it follows from the reasoning of their Lordships in *Esso* v *Harper's Garage* that the agreement constituted by the lease and lease-back is an agreement in restraint of trade in as much as it subjects the company to a continuation for a longer period of the restraints on trading which had validly been imposed for a much shorter period before 25 July 1969.

We shall see below a number of contracts which have traditionally been subject to the restraint of trade concept: sale of business, employment contracts restraining employees on leaving etc. Finally, to show the width of the doctrine and the reasoning used by the courts the decision in *A. Schroeder Music Publishing Co. Ltd* v *Macaulay* (1974) needs to be discussed. The extracted judgment shows quite clearly the question the judge had to ask himself was whether or not 'the bargain was fair'. The judiciary are deciding upon the validity of the contract using restraint of trade as their vehicle to do so.

A. Schroeder Music Publishing Co. Ltd v Macaulay
[1974] 1 WLR 1308

A song writer, aged 21 and unknown, entered into an agreement with music publishers in their 'standard form' whereby the publishers engaged his exclusive services during the term of the agreement. By clause 1 the agreement was, subject as thereinafter provided, to remain in force for five years. By clause 3(a) the song writer assigned to the publishers the full copyright for the whole world in all his musical compositions during the term. Clauses 5 to 8 dealt with the song writer's remuneration, which was to be by royalties on works published. By clause 9(a) if the total royalties during the term exceeded £5,000 the agreement was automati-

cally extended for a further five years. By clause 9(b) the publishers could determine the agreement any time by one month's written notice. No such right was given to the song writer. By clause 16(a) the publishers had the right to assign the agreement. By clause 16(b) the song writer agreed not to assign his rights under the agreement without the publishers' prior written consent. The song writer brought an action claiming a declaration that the agreement was contrary to public policy and void. Plowman J so held and made the declaration sought, and his judgment was affirmed by the Court of Appeal.

On appeal by the publishers:

LORD DIPLOCK: ... Because this can be classified as a contract in restraint of trade the restrictions that the respondent accepted fell within one of those limited categories of contractual promises in respect of which the courts still retain the power to relieve the promisor of his legal duty to fulfil them. In order to determine whether this case is one in which that power ought to be exercised, what your Lordships have in fact been doing has been to assess the relative bargaining power of the publisher and the song writer at the time the contract was made and to decide whether the publisher had used his superior bargaining power to exact from the song writer promises that were unfairly onerous to him. Your Lordships have not been concerned to inquire whether the public have in fact been deprived of the fruit of the song writer's talents by reason of the restrictions, nor to assess the likelihood that they would be so deprived in the future if the contract were permitted to run its full course.

It is, in my view, salutary to acknowledge that in refusing to enforce provisions of a contract whereby one party agrees for the benefit of the other party to exploit or to refrain from exploiting his own earning power, the public policy which the court is implementing is not some 19th century economic theory about the benefit to the general public of freedom of trade, but the protection of those whose bargaining power is weak against being forced by those whose bargaining power is stronger to enter into bargains that are unconscionable. Under the influence of Bentham and of *laissez-faire* the courts in the 19th century abandoned the practice of applying the public policy against unconscionable bargains to contracts generally, as they had formerly done to any contract considered to be usurious; but the policy survived in its application to penalty clauses and to relief against forfeiture and also to the special category of contracts in restraint of trade. If one looks at the reasoning of 19th century judges in cases about contracts in restraint of trade one finds lip service paid to current economic theories, but if one looks at what they said in the light of what they did, one finds that they struck down a bargain if they thought it was unconscionable as between the parties to it and upheld it if they thought that it was not.

So I would hold that the question to be answered as respects a contract in restraint of trade of the kind with which this appeal is concerned is: 'Was the bargain fair?' The test of fairness is, no doubt, whether the restrictions are both reasonably necessary for the protection of the legitimate interests of the promisee and commensurate with the benefits secured to the promisor under the contract. For the purpose of this test all the provisions of the contract must be taken into consideration.

My Lords, the provisions of the contract have already been sufficiently stated by Lord Reid. I agree with his analysis of them and with his conclusion that the contract is unenforceable. It does not satisfy the test of fairness as I have endeavoured to state it.

Self check questions
1.   What is the effect of a contract coming within the doctrine of restraint of trade?
2.   How do the courts decide whether or not a contract comes within the doctrine?

Answers
1.   The contract is prima facie (on its face) unenforceable unless it satisfies the test of reasonableness.
2.   The courts have developed no single test; although prohibiting a trade or whatever is seen as being crucial. The reason for this is that courts give themselves flexibility as to how the doctrine operates.

3   The test of reasonableness

3.1   *General considerations*
The test of reasonableness can be divided into two: legitimate interests of the parties and the public interest. To be enforceable a contract must satisfy both these criteria; each of which will be dealt with below.

3.1.1   *Legitimate interests of the parties*   Only a number of general points can be made here. The reason for this is that many contracts turn on their own particular factual situation and the courts have given us guidelines rather than definitive statements. The restraint must be *no more* than is reasonably necessary. You will see this statement in many of the case extracts in this book and its application obviously depends on the factual situation under discussion. Secondly, as we shall see in more detail below, the test of reasonableness varies between different types of contract; for example employer/employee restraints are more difficult to show. Finally, under this heading, the burden of proof is on the person seeking to enforce the contract to show that it is reasonable as between the parties and often it is difficult to discharge this burden.

3.1.2   *Public interest*   The first point to note is that the burden of proof shifts from the person seeking to enforce the clause to the person questioning the validity of it. Therefore, in an employer/employee contract it is for the employer to show it is reasonable as between the parties and once this has been established it is then for the employee to show that it is unreasonable as in the public interest.

What is meant by the public interest? In *Texaco Ltd* v *Mulberry Filling Station Ltd* (1972) the judge severely limited the second limb of the test by equating it with the interests of the parties. By ignoring the wider implications of reasonableness — for example, economic criteria — the judge in effect has linked the two limbs together. Therefore, if the contract is reasonable as between the parties it is more than likely to be reasonable as in the public interest.

Texaco Ltd v Mulberry Filling Station Ltd
[1972] 1 WLR 814

By a legal charge made on January 22, 1965, under the terms of which a petrol-supplying company ('Texaco') was to advance moneys repayable over 20 years at a low rate of interest to a petrol retailing company ('Mulberry') for the redevelopment of its garage premises, Mulberry covenanted to purchase its petrol requirements exclusively from Texaco.

By a second legal charge made on January 30, 1968, and securing the balance of moneys repayable under the 1965 charge, the final instalment to be paid by August 1, 1972, Mulberry covenanted not to purchase or sell at its garage any petrol other than that supplied by Texaco. In January 1971 an unofficial strike of tanker drivers prevented delivery of Texaco's petrol to Mulberry, who then took petrol from another supplier and continued to do so after the strike ended and Texaco was willing and able to deliver. In March 1971, Texaco issued a writ claiming that Mulberry's covenants under the 1968 charge were 'valid, binding and enforceable' until redemption of the charge and motioned for an injunction to restrain Mulberry until trial or further order from purchasing, selling or advertising at its garage any petrol other than that supplied by Texaco.

UNGOED-THOMAS J: ... If my analysis and approach are correct, reasonableness in the interests of the public refers to the interests of the public as recognised in a principle of proposition of law and not to the interests of the public at large. The question which such reasonableness raises would thus not be whether the restraint might be less in a different organisation of industry or society, or whether the abolition of the restraint might lead to a different organisation of industry or society and thus, on balance of many considerations, to the economic or social advantage of the country, but whether the restraint is, in our industry and society as at present organised and with reference to which our law operates, unreasonable in the public interests as recognised and formulated in such principle or proposition of law. For my part, I prefer to decide that the restraints relied on in our case are reasonable in the interests of the public, not on balance but because there is, in conditions as they are, no unreasonable limitation of liberty to trade.

Lord Wilberforce stated the public interest in terms relevant to the case before him, in 'the normal proposition that the public has in the absence of countervailing considerations an interest in men being able to trade freely ...'; and I would venture to express the public interest in terms relevant to our case which appear to me to be consonant with Lord Wilberforce's proposition of law, viz. that the public has an interest in men being able to trade freely subject, *inter alia*, to reasonable limitations which conform with the contemporary organisation of trade. The restrictions in our case are reasonable in reference to the interests of the public as expressed in this proposition.... . Thus I decide the restraint of trade issue in favour of the plaintiff.

3.2 Specific types of contract

The general considerations have been examined above. We now need to examine how these factors apply to particular contractual situations.

3.2.1 Employer/Employee contracts

An employer may only protect a *proprietary interest*. In *Morris* v *Saxelby* (1916) this was defined as either business connection (that is where an employee has personal knowledge of and influence over the customers of his employer) or trade secrets which if divulged would create an advantage for a competitor of the employer. Trade secrets, in this context, are wider than merely secret processes.

The rationale for this limitation is that an employee is in a weaker bargaining position, when negotiating his contract of employment, than is the employer. Consequently the law is very reluctant to enforce such types of clause. The law does, however, take a realistic approach and two cases can be given to show situations when restraints have been upheld as being reasonable. In both *Marion White Ltd* v *Francis* (1972) and *Home Counties Dairies Ltd* v *Skilton* (1970) the context of the business relationship between the parties meant that the courts could uphold them as being reasonable.

Marion White Ltd v Francis
[1972] 1 WLR 1423

The plaintiff employers employed the defendant employee as an assistant in one of their hairdressing salons. By clause 5 of the agreement between them she agreed that she would not during the continuance of her employment or within 12 months after it should have ceased directly or indirectly carry on or assist in carrying on either as principal or as manager agent or servant or assistant or in any other capacity whatsoever be in any way engaged or concerned or interested in the business of a ladies' hairdresser within one half mile of her employers' premises. On a claim by the employers against the employee for an injunction to restrain her from being employed by the competitor, from soliciting customers of the employers, and for damages for breach of covenant, the deputy judge granted an injunction restraining her from soliciting customers of the employers and nominal damages for breach of that covenant, but, holding that the covenant in restraint of trade was too wide because it would prevent the employee from acting as a receptionist in a rival hairdressing salon, he refused to grant an injunction against her continued employment by the competitor. The employers appealed.

Held: Since a covenant in restraint of trade must be read in the context of the business in relation to which it was entered into and of the relationship between the parties and of what they might reasonably contemplate, the covenant here was aimed at active participation by the employee in a hairdressing business in a way directly connected with the hairdressing aspects of such a business and so was not too wide. It was therefore a good and valid and effective covenant and the employers were entitled to a declaratory judgment accordingly.

Home Counties Dairies Ltd v Skilton
[1970] 1 WLR 526

A milk roundsman agreed that during his employment and for a year after leaving he would not serve or sell to or solicit orders from any person or company who at any time during the last 6 months of his employment was a customer of his employer and served by the employee in his employment. This was held valid because the employer has a goodwill interest to be protected. It was reasonable as it only prevented the employee from being a milk roundsman. The time limit of 1 year was reasonable especially as it covered customers served in the last 6 months only.

A second factor which has to be taken into account when deciding upon the reasonableness of these contracts concerns limits of time and space. Again it is very difficult to draw hard and fast principles as a wide restraint may be reasonable in certain situations but not in others. In *Forster and Sons v Sugget* (1918) and *Mason v Provident Clothing and Supply Co.* (1913) the application of the principles can be seen.

Forster and Sons v Sugget
(1918) 35 TLR 87

The plaintiff company and the defendant entered into an agreement under which the defendant was to be employed as works engineer at the plaintiff's works and was not to divulge any trade secret during his employment or thereafter except in the proper course of business and on the determination of his employment he was not, for five years, to carry on in the United Kingdom or to be interested in glass bottle manufacture or any other business connected with glass making carried on by the plaintiffs.

Held: That the agreement was not unreasonably in restraint of trade.

Mason v Provident Clothing and Supply Co.
[1913] AC 724

By a contract for the employment of the defendant as canvasser by the plaintiffs, a clothing and supply company having branches all over England, described in the contract as carrying on business on the check and credit system 'at London in the county of Middlesex' (amongst other places), the defendant agreed that he would not within three years after the termination of the employment be in the employ of any person, firm, or company carrying on or engaged in a business the same as or similar to that of the plaintiff company, or assist any person employed or assisting in any such business, 'within 25 miles of London aforesaid where the company carry on business'.

VISCOUNT HALDANE: . . . My Lords, the respondents have to show that the restriction they have sought to impose goes no further than was reasonable for the protection of their business. But even assuming the construction most favourable to them, that which makes the words introducing the 25 miles limit apply to every branch of the restrictive language, I think that they fail to show this. I have examined the evidence as to the character of the business and the document which sets out particularly the duties of these canvassers. I can find nothing to lead me to think that the canvasser could become possessed of any special knowledge of the kind recognised as a trade secret. I doubt whether there were any secrets in this business. The success of the canvasser depended, as I have already said, mainly on his natural aptitude. No doubt he might acquire, in the course of his employment, lists of actual or possible customers in the district in which he had canvassed. I think that under a properly limited clause the employers would have been entitled to restrain him from canvassing such customers. But that is not the clause which the respondents in this case did frame. They have chosen to try to bind the appellant to an extent which might be necessary for their protection if they had been carrying on a business of a different kind. . . . It is no doubt as a general rule wise to leave adult persons to make their own agreements and take the consequences, but in the present class of case considerations of public policy come in and make it necessary for the Court to scrutinise agreements like the one before your Lordships jealously. The practice of putting into these agreements anything that is favourable to the employer is one which the Courts have to check, and the judges have to see that Lord Macnaghten's test is carefully observed. As I do not think that clause 8 complies with that test, I am of opinion that it was void altogether.

In one case 'the whole of the UK' was held to be reasonable, whereas in the other a restraint of 25 miles did not satisfy the test. It is important, therefore, to read each contract in its own context in order to determine whether or not the time and space are reasonable.

3.2.2 Exclusive purchasing contracts: solus petrol agreements We have discussed above the fact that such agreements come within the doctrine of restraint. What factors do the courts take into account when assessing the reasonableness of such contracts? In *Esso Petroleum Co. Ltd v Harper's Garage (Stourport) Ltd* (1968) (see 2, above) the judge obviously thought the interests of the parties and the petrol trade, in general, justified a five-year restraint. The above can be compared with the arguments relating to the 21-year tie which the court thought could not be justified by Esso in the circumstances.

Esso Petroleum Co. Ltd v Harper's Garage (Stourport) Ltd
[1968] AC 269

LORD REID: It is now generally accepted that a provision in a contract which is to be regarded as in restraint of trade must be justified if it is to be enforceable, and that the law on this matter was correctly stated by Lord Macnaghten in the *Nordenfelt* case.

So in every case it is necessary to consider first whether the restraint went farther than to afford adequate protection to the party in whose favour it was granted, secondly whether it can be justified as being in the interests of the party restrained, and, thirdly, whether it must be held contrary to the public interest. I find it difficult to agree with the way in which the court has in some cases treated the interests of a person to agree to suffer a restraint unless he gets some compensating advantage, direct or indirect. And Lord Macnaghten said: '... of course the quantum of consideration may enter into the question of the reasonableness of the contract'.

Where two experienced traders are bargaining on equal terms and one has agreed to a restraint for reasons which seem good to him the court is in grave danger of stultifying itself if it says that it knows that trader's interest better than he does himself. But there may well be cases where, although the party to be restrained has deliberately accepted the main terms of the contract, he has been at a disadvantage as regards other terms: for example where a set of conditions has been incorporated which has not been the subject of negotiation — there the court may have greater freedom to hold them unreasonable.

What were the appellant's legitimate interests must depend largely on what was the state of affairs in their business and with regard to the distribution and sale of petrol generally. And those are questions of fact to be answered by evidence or common knowledge.... In my view there is sufficient material to justify a decision that ties of less than five years were insufficient, in the circumstances of the trade when these agreements were made, to afford adequate protection to the appellants' legitimate interests. And if that is so I cannot find anything in the details of the Mustow Green agreement which would indicate that it is unreasonable. It is true that if some of the provisions were operated by the appellants in a manner which would be commercially unreasonable they might put the respondents in difficulties. But I think that a court must have regard to the fact that the appellants must act in such a way that they will be able to obtain renewals of the great majority of their very numerous ties, some of which will come to an end almost every week. If in such circumstances a garage owner chooses to rely on the commercial probity and good sense of the producer, I do not think that a court should hold his agreement unreasonable because it is legally capable of some misuse. I would therefore allow the appeal as regards the Mustow Green agreement.

But the Corner Garage agreement involves much more difficulty.... A tie for 21 years stretches far beyond any period for which developments are reasonably foreseeable. Restrictions on the garage owner which might seem tolerable and reasonable in reasonably foreseeable conditions might come to have a very different effect in quite different conditions; the public interest comes in here more strongly. And, apart from a case where he gets a loan, a garage owner appears to get no greater advantage from a 20-year tie than he gets from a five-year tie. So I would think that there must be at least some clearly established advantage to the producing company — something to show that a shorter period would not be adequate — before so long a period could be justified. But in this case there is no evidence to prove anything of the kind. And the other material which I have thought it right to consider does not appear to me to assist the appellant here. I would therefore dismiss the appeal as regards the Corner Garage agreement.

The decision in *Esso Petroleum Co. Ltd* v *Harper's Garage (Stourport) Ltd* was interpreted as restricting solus agreements to a maximum of five years. The law, again, has slightly changed its policy on the way in which reasonableness is assessed in such clauses: the decision in *Alec Lobb (Garages) Ltd* v *Total Oil (Great Britain) Ltd* (1985) (see 2 above) bears this out. A number of factors seem to have been relevant in holding that the 21-year tie was reasonable: firstly, it was a rescue operation benefitting the plaintiffs as well as providing an outlet for the defendant's petrol. Secondly, there was ample consideration for the grant of the lease to the defendant. Thirdly, there were break clauses at the end of the seventh and fourteenth year which effectively created a series of three seven-year restraints. Finally, the transaction was of public interest in that it maintained an outlet which benefitted the public at large.

Alec Lobb (Garages) Ltd v *Total Oil (Great Britain) Ltd*
[1985] 1 All ER 303

DILLON LJ: ... The decision in *Esso* v *Harper's Garage* has been generally taken as laying down a rule of thumb that a petrol supply restraint, requiring a dealer to take all his petrol from one petrol company, is reasonable and valid if it will last for no more than 5 years, but if it will last for significantly more than 5 years, e.g., for 21 years, it is unreasonable and invalid unless the petrol company can prove that a tie for the longer period is an economic necessity for it. No such evidence of economic necessity has been put forward by Total in the present case, but the contention that the longer tie is in all the circumstances reasonable has been urged on a different ground.

In *Esso* v *Harper's Garage* [1968] AC 269 at 300, 323 both Lord Reid and Lord Pearce referred with approval to the statement of Lord Macnaghten in *Nordenfelt* v *Maxim Nordenfelt Guns and Ammunition Co. Ltd* [1894] AC 535 at 565, that of course the quantum of consideration may enter into the question of the reasonableness of the contract.

In the present case the consideration for the grant of the lease and thus the consideration for the restraint, since the lease-back was part of the same transaction as the lease, was the payment by Total to the company of the premium of £35,000. That figure was arrived at by a professional valuation as being the value of the 51-year lease, subject to the lease-back, the initial rent under which (£2,250 per annum) was significantly below a full market rent. The lease-back thus had a capital value, but the real value of the property was in the value of the lease, and, because the lease was for such a long term at a peppercorn rent, the value of the reversion on the lease, the company's underlying freehold interest subject to the lease, was of the very slight value of some £600 to £1,000 only.

The choice of 51 years as the term of the lease came about originally because it was common ground that if the term of the lease had not exceeded 50 years the premium of £35,000 would have been taxable as income in the company's hands, and that would have defeated the object of the whole transaction, viz. recapitalising the business of the company in an endeavour to keep it afloat. But despite its provenance the 51-year length of the term is a very real factor in the case, firstly because that is what Total paid for by the premium and secondly because, despite some pressure, Total refused to grant the lease-back for more than 21 years with the mutual breaks which I have mentioned.

Against this background certain factors are clear. The first is that for planning reasons the property is most unlikely to be used, during the 21-year term of the lease-back, for any purpose other than that of a garage and filling station. The next is that it can make no significant difference to the public at large whether the petrol sold there comes from Total or from Esso or Shell or any other major oil company. The next point is that the lessees under the lease-back are not locked into trading in Total's products from the property for 21 years. If they find this unattractive, they are free to exercise the break clause under the lease-back at the end of the seventh or fourteenth years of the term and leave; if it seems harsh that the company may be compelled by adverse conditions to leave the property which it formerly owned the answer is that it has already received the substantial value of the property in the shape of the premium of £35,000 for the grant to Total of the 51-year lease of the property at a peppercorn rent.

Finally, if the lease-back had been granted for 5 years only, with the result that the tie in it would have been unquestionably valid, the lessees would have been left at the end of the 5 years with the choice of either leaving the property or applying for a new tenancy under the Landlord and Tenant Act 1954. But any new tenancy would, like any new tenancy which might be granted under the Act at the end of the 21-year term of the lease-back, have been likely to have been for a maximum of 5 or 7 years only (subject to the possibility of application for a further new tenancy under the 1954 Act) subject to the same tie provisions as are to be found in the lease-back. It was the lessee's interest that required that the lease and lease-back arrangement should be for a significantly long term since the premium payable by Total for a short term, such as a mere 5-year term, could not conceivably have been enough to recapitalise the company and solve the company's financial difficulties.

In the circumstances of this case, and not least because at the time of the grant of the lease and lease-back the company was subject to a valid tie for a term of three to four years, I can see no real significance in the difference between a tie for 5 years and the term of 7 years to the first break under the lease-back.

The reasoning, above, is interesting as the court has taken a fairly liberal interpretation in upholding the validity of the clause.

Self check questions
1.   What are the two factors in the test of reasonableness? What is the burden of proof in the two factors?
2.   What factors do the courts take into account when assessing the public interest criteria?
3.   What may an employer protect in a restraint clause against an employee?
4.   How do the courts work out the reasonableness of time and space?

Answers
1.   A clause must be reasonable as between the parties and reasonable in the public interest. It is for the person seeking to rely on the clause to show it is reasonable as between the parties, in so far as it only goes as far as is necessary to protect the legitimate interests of the parties. Once it has been shown to be reasonable between the parties then the party seeking to challenge the clause must show it is unreasonable.
2.   The courts do not take into account economic or social criteria but limit themselves to the interests of the parties.
3.   An employer may only protect a proprietory interest which is defined as a business connection or trade secrets.
4.   The time and space limits must be no more than is reasonably necessary in the circumstances for the interest to be protected. It is difficult to draw up hard and fast rules, as the reasonableness of time and space depends upon the facts of each case.

4   What is the effect of the contract not satisfying the test of reasonableness?

The effect of the clause not satisfying the test of reasonableness is that the restraint is not enforceable. The courts, however, will sever the offending parts of a clause in order to allow it to be enforced. In *Attwood v Lamont* (1920) the courts laid down various criteria as to how severance should operate. The most important to note is that the courts will not rewrite the contract in order to save it and indeed the courts have applied severance strictly.

Attwood v Lamont
[1920] 3 KB 57

The plaintiff carried on business at Kidderminster as a draper, tailor, and general outfitter. By a contract of employment of the defendant by the plaintiff, after reciting that the defendant had requested the plaintiff to employ him as an assistant in his business at an annual salary and commission on turnover above a certain amount in the tailoring department and that the plaintiff was willing to do so only upon his entering into the agreement not to trade in opposition to him thereinafter expressed, the defendant agreed that he would not at any time thereafter 'either on his own account or on that of any wife of his or in partnership with or as assistant, servant, or agent to any other person, persons or company carry on or be in any way directly or indirectly concerned in any of the following trade or businesses; that is to say, the

trade or business of a tailor, dressmaker, general draper, milliner, hatter, haberdasher, gentlemen's, ladies' or children's outfitter at any place within a radius of ten miles of' Kidderminster.
   Held:

   (a)   That the covenant being a single covenant for the protection of the plaintiff's entire business could not be severed.
   (b)   That even if the covenant could be severed by confining it to the tailoring business it would still be void as being in restraint of competition.

The following points may now be taken to be established by the decisions of the House of Lords in the above cases:

   (i)   It is the covenantee who has to show that the restraint sought to be imposed upon the covenantor goes no further than is reasonable for the protection of his business.
   (ii)   The restraint must be not only in the interests of the covenantee but in the interests of both the contracting parties.
   (iii)   An employer is not entitled by a covenant taken from his employee to protect himself after the employment has ceased against his former servant's competition, although a purchaser of goodwill is entitled to protect himself against such competition on the part of his vendor.
   (iv)   Previously accepted rules as to the doctrine of severance require careful application if not entire reconsideration.

Problem

Kev a footballer, returns from the World ——*Bargaining* Cup in disgrace having been involved in *position* an alleged bribes scandal.   *of Kev*

He decides to leave his First Division Club and return to the first club, Crimethorpe United, who are struggling at the bottom of the Third Division.

Nature of   As he has so much time on his hands Kev
interest to be   enters into a contract with the local
protected   sportswear manufacturers, Slick plc, to
   act as a salesman and *also endorse their goods.* Slick in fact were the only
   company who would offer Kev such a
   contract after his earlier alleged
   activities.

The terms of the contract state:
   'On leaving employment with Slick———*Interest*

Time _____   plc I covenant not to *work for or endorse*
                             the products of another sportswear
                             manufacturer for *2 years* within the
                             United Kingdom.' _____ *Area*

                             Crimethorpe's fortunes change and they
                             win through to the semi-finals of the FA
                             Cup. Slick's sales *multiply tenfold* but   *Change of*
                             Kev decides to leave them *and start*   *circumstances*
                             working for Dodgy plc, a well known
                             national sportswear manufacturer, and
                             agrees to endorse *their new range of*
                             sportswear.

                             Advise Slick.

Suggested answer

The problem concerns the enforceability of a clause which falls within the restraint of trade doctrine. The reason for the clause falling within the doctrine is that it seeks to restrict the way in which Kev carries on his trade or business: *Nordenfelt* v *Maxim Nordenfelt*. The effect of the contract being within the doctrine is that it is prima facie unenforceable unless it satisfies the test of reasonableness.

An initial point to note from the facts is the bargaining position of the parties when the contract was entered into. Kev had returned from the World Cup in disgrace and also joined a Third Division club; these factors would bring into play the decision in *A. Schroeder Music Publishing Co. Ltd* v *Macaulay*. The reasoning in the case is based on the fact that the terms were imposed by one party on the other because of the relative bargaining strength possessed by one party as against the other. Here it can be argued that Slick plc took advantage of Kev's position and this should be a factor taken into account when assessing the reasonableness of the clause.

The nature of the contract is similar to an employer/employee situation. An employer is only entitled to protect a proprietary interest which is defined as either business connections or trade secrets: *Morris* v *Saxelby*. Slick plc would claim that Kev has personal contact with prospective customers of Slick through his work as a salesman and this would amount to a business connection which Slick would be entitled to protect. The position of Kev endorsing goods is less clear as it can be argued that he does not have the same personal contact with customers. It is for Slick to show that there is a proprietary interest to protect and that the clause goes no further than is reasonably necessary in the circumstances.

The second factor as to reasonableness between the parties concerns the time and the area of restraint. The length of the restraint in the problem is two years and it is for Slick to show that it is reasonable in the circumstances. Each case depends very much on its facts and in this context restraints of 12 months have been upheld as being reasonable: *Marion White Ltd* v *Francis*. It can be argued that the clause goes further than is reasonably necessary but to counter that is the fact that Kev's influence may well last for a period of up to two years.

Similar factors govern the reasonableness of the area of restraint. A restraint of the whole of the UK has been upheld as being reasonable in *Forster* v *Sugget*. Slick must show that Kev's influence extends to the whole of the UK in order for it to be enforceable.

Finally, in the context of the reasonableness issue, the different bargaining positions of the parties have been mentioned, above. Clearly the circumstances have changed because of the success achieved by Crimethorpe United. The general principle is that the reasonableness of the clause is assessed when the contract is made; however, if the change in circumstances could be foreseen at the time, then they are relevant factors to be taken into account in the reasonableness question. Clearly at the time the contract was entered into Kev was in a much weaker bargaining position and *A. Schroeder Music Publishing Co. Ltd* v *Macaulay* indicates this is a relevant factor. It can be argued, however, that the change in Crimethorpe's fortunes could have been foreseen and therefore it is a relevant factor.

The final issue to discuss is whether or not the clause could be saved if it did not satisfy the test of reasonableness. A possibility of severance could arise if the words 'work for or endorse' were thought to be too wide. As mentioned above the endorsement of goods may not be held to be a proprietary interest and therefore the principle in *Attwood* v *Lamont* would allow the words 'or endorse' to be severed in order to make it a reasonable reastraint in the circumstances.

-

12 FRUSTRATION OF CONTRACT

1 Introduction

In this chapter we shall be dealing with one way in which a contract can be discharged. A contract can be discharged, put to an end, in a number of ways: breach, performance and agreement. The essence of frustration is that it occurs when a change of circumstances *after the formation* of the contract has rendered it physically or commercially impossible to fulfil.

There are a number of important points to note from the definition. Firstly, the event which is alleged to amount to frustration, must occur after the contract has been made. Therefore, if the contract either fails because of something on the face of the contract or it is in fact impossible to perform — due to an event which has taken place before formation — neither event amounts to frustration. Secondly, our definition talks about the change of circumstances rendering the contract either physically or commercially impossible to fulfil; as will be seen below the courts have had numerous problems trying to define this.

A final point to mention is that neither party must be responsible for the change in circumstances. Therefore, if the alleged frustrating event was self-induced, this does not amount to frustration but discharge by breach of contract. Again we shall expand this concept below.

2 The test for frustration

The first case on frustration was the decision in *Taylor* v *Caldwell* (1863) where the test for frustration was thought to be an implied condition to the effect that a party should be excused where performance has become impossible. The test used in *Taylor* v *Caldwell* is based on the courts implying a term into the contract; however, referring back to the chapter on terms of the contract it was quite clear that the courts had great difficulty in deciding how a term should be implied.

Taylor v *Caldwell*
(1863) 3 B & S 826

It was held that A agreed with B to give him the use of a Music Hall on certain specified days, for the purpose of holding concerts, with no express stipulation for the event of the destruction of the Music Hall by fire. (i) Where there is a positive contract to do a thing, not in itself unlawful, the contractor must perform it or pay damages for not doing it, although in consequence of unforeseen accidents the performance of his contract has become unexpectedly burdensome or even impossible. (ii) But this rule is only applicable when the contract is positive and absolute, and not subject to any condition either express or implied. (iii) Where, from the nature of the contract, it appears that the parties must from the beginning have known that it could not be fulfilled unless when the time for the fulfilment of the contract arrived some particular specified thing continued to exist, so that, when entering into the contract, they must have contemplated such continuing existence as the foundation of what was to be done; there, in the absence of any express or implied warranty that the thing shall exist, the contract is not to be construed as a positive contract, but as subject to an implied condition that the parties shall be excused in case, before breach, performance becomes impossible from the perishing of the thing without default of the contractor. (iv) That both parties were excused from performance of the contract.

The difficulty of the implied term theory led the courts to develop a number of other tests. In *Davis* v *Fareham UDC* (1956) the judge stated that the test depended on whether, from all the surrounding circumstances, there could be said to be a radical change in the obligation. The problem from our point of view is to decide which test to choose. We shall concentrate on the test from *Davis* v *Fareham UDC* as it is easier to use on different factual situations which shall be discussed below.

Davis v *Fareham UDC*
[1956] AC 696

On July 9, 1946, contractors entered into a building contract to build 78 houses for a local authority for a fixed sum within a period of eight months. They had attached to their form of tender a letter, dated March 18, 1946, stating that it was subject to adequate supplies of labour being available as and when required. Owing to the unexpected circumstances, and without fault of either party, adequate supplies of labour were not available and the work took 22 months to complete. The contractors contended that the contract price was subject to there being adequate supplies of labour available by reason of the letter of March 18, 1946, stating that it was subject to adequate supplies of labour being available as and when required. The contractors contended that: the contract price was subject to there being adequate supplies of labour available by reason of the letter of March 18, 1946; that the contract was frustrated; and claimed to be entitled on a quantum meruit *to a sum in excess of the contract price.*

LORD RADCLIFFE: . . . Before I refer to the facts I must say briefly what I understand to be the legal principle of frustration. It is not always expressed in the same way, but I think that the points which are relevant to the decision of this case are really beyond dispute. The theory of frustration belongs to the law of contract and it is represented by a rule which the courts will apply in certain limited circumstances for the purpose of deciding that contractual obligation, *ex facie* binding, are no longer enforceable against the parties. The description of the circumstances that justify the application of the rule and, consequently whether in a particular case those circumstances exist are, I think, necessarily questions of law.

I have pointed out that the descriptions vary from one case of high authority to another.... . So perhaps whenever the law recognises that without default of either party a contracted obligation has become incapable of being performed because the circumstances in which performance is called for would render it a thing radically different from that which was undertaken by the contractor, *Non haec in foedera veni*. It was not this that I promised to do.

There is, however, no uncertainty as to the materials upon which the court must proceed.... . In the nature of things there is often no room for any elaborate inquiry. The court must act upon a general impression of what its rule requires. It is for that reason that special importance is necessarily attached to the occurrence of any unexpected event that as it were, changes the face of things. But, even so, it is not hardship or inconvenience or material loss itself which calls the principle of frustration into play. There must be as well such a change in the significance of the obligation that the thing undertaken would, if performed, be a different thing from that contracted for. (It was held that the contract had not been frustrated.)

Self check questions
1. What is the essence of frustration?
2. Does frustration take place if it is due to the default of either party?
3. Which is the preferred test for frustration?

Answers
1. The essence of frustration is that an event occurs, after the formation of the contract, which renders the contract physically or commercially impossible to fulfil.
2. No, the event must not be due to the default of either party.
3. The preferred test is that the event must mean there is a radical change in the obligation and this is assessed by looking at the surrounding circumstances.

3 Illustrations of the doctrine

3.1 Cancellation of an expected event
Let us take an example to illustrate the principle under discussion. Suppose A hires a coach to take his local rugby team to an international at Twickenham. On the Friday before the game they find that the game has been postponed due

to frost. Is the contract between the coach firm and A frustrated? Two cases need to be examined in order to try and provide an answer.

In *Krell* v *Henry* (1903) and *Herne Bay Steamboat Co.* v *Hutton* (1903) the issue was discussed. It should be noted that the same judge, Vaughan Williams LJ, sat in both cases and therefore his views should be read carefully. In the former case the judge stated that frustration was not limited to destruction of the subject-matter, but depended upon the continued existence of the foundation of the contract. The foundation of the contract was said to be the viewing of the Coronation procession, whereas in the example of the person going to Epsom on Derby Day the race was not thought to be the foundation and cancellation of the race would not amount to frustration.

Krell v *Henry*
[1903] 2 KB 740

By a contract in writing of June 20, 1902, the defendant agreed to hire from the plaintiff a flat in Pall Mall for June 26 and 27, on which days it had been announced that the coronation processions would take place and pass along Pall Mall. The contract contained no express reference to the coronation processions, or to any other purpose for which the flat was taken. A deposit was paid when the contract was entered into. As the procession did not take place on the days originally fixed, the defendant declined to pay the balance of the agreed rent.

VAUGHAN WILLIAMS LJ: I do not think that the principle of the civil law as introduced into the English law is limited to cases in which the event causing the impossibility of performance is the destruction or non-existence of some thing which is the subject-matter of the contract or of some condition or state of things expressly specified as a condition of it. I think that you first have to ascertain, not necessarily from the terms of the contract, but, if required, from necessary inferences, drawn from surrounding circumstances recognised by both contracting parties, what is the substance of the contract, and then to ask the question whether that substantial contract needs for its foundation the assumption of the existence of a particular state of things. If it does, this will limit the operation of the general words, and in such case, if the contract becomes impossible of performance by reason of the non-existence of the state of things assumed by both contracting parties as the foundation of the contract, there will be no breach of the contract thus limited ... in my judgment the taking place of those processions on the days proclaimed along the proclaimed route, which passed 56A, Pall Mall, was regarded by both contracting parties as the foundation of the contract; and I think that it cannot reasonably be supposed to have been in the contemplation of the contracting parties, when the contract was made, that the coronation would not be held on the proclaimed days, or the processions not take place on those days along the proclaimed route; and I think that the words imposing on the defendant the obligation to accept and pay for the use of the rooms for the named days, although general and unconditional, were not used with reference to the possibility of the particular contingency which afterwards occurred. It was suggested in the course of the argument that if the occurrence, on the proclaimed days, of the coronation and the procession in this case were the foundation of the contract, and if the general words are thereby limited or qualified, so that in the event of the non-occurrence of the coronation and procession along the proclaimed route they would discharge both parties from further performance of the contract, it would follow that if a cabman was engaged to take some one to Epsom on Derby Day at a suitable enhanced price for such a journey, say £10, both parties to the contract would be discharged in the contingency of the race at Epsom for some reason becoming impossible; but I do think this follows, for I do not think that in the cab case the happening of the race would be the foundation of the contract. No doubt the purpose of the engager would be to go to see the Derby, and the price would be proportionately high; but the cab had no special qualifications for the purpose which led to the selection of the cab for this particular occasion. Any other cab would have done as well. Moreover, I think that, under the cab contract, the hirer, even if the race went off, could have said, 'Drive me to Epsom; I will pay you the agreed sum; you have nothing to do with the purpose for which I hired the cab', and that if the cabman refused he would have been guilty of a breach of contract, there being nothing to qualify his promise to drive the hirer to Epsom on a particular day. Whereas in the case of the coronation, there is not merely the purpose of the hirer to see the coronation procession, but it is the coronation procession and the relative position of the rooms which is the basis of the contract as much for the lessor as the hirer; and I think that if the King, before the coronation day and after the contract, had died, the hirer could not have insisted on having the rooms on the days named. It could not in the cab case be reasonably said that seeing the Derby race was the foundation of the contract, as it was of the licence in this case. . . . In each case one must ask oneself, first, what, having regard to all circumstances, was the foundation of the contract? Secondly, was the performance of the contract prevented? Thirdly, was the event which prevented the performance of the contract of such a character that it cannot reasonably be said to have been in the contemplation of the parties at the date of the contract? If all these questions are answered in the affirmative (as I think they should be in this case), I think both parties are discharged from further performance of the contract. . . . I think this appeal ought to be dismissed.

Herne Bay Steam Boat Co. v *Hutton*
[1903] 2 KB 683

In consequence of the public announcement of an intended royal naval review at Spithead on June 28, 1902, an agreement in writing was entered into between the plaintiffs and the defendant that the plaintiffs' steamship Cynthia *should be 'at the disposal' of the defendant on June 28 to take passengers from Herne Bay 'for the purpose of viewing the naval review and for a day's cruise round the fleet; also on June 29 for similar purposes: price £250 payable, £50 down, balance before the ship leaves Herne Bay'.*

On the signing of the agreement the defendant paid £50 deposit. On June 25 the review was officially cancelled, whereupon the plaintiffs wired to the defendant for instructions, stating that the ship was ready to start, and also requesting payment of the balance. Receiving no reply, the plaintiffs, on June 28 and 29, used the ship for their own purposes, thereby making a profit. On June 29 the defendant repudiated the contract in toto. During the two days in question the fleet remained anchored at Spithead.

The plaintiffs brought an action to recover the balance less the profits made by their use of the ship during the two days.

VAUGHAN WILLIAMS LJ: ... Mr Hutton in hiring this vessel, had two objects in view: first, of taking people to see the naval review, and, secondly, of taking them round the fleet. Those no doubt, were the purposes of Mr Hutton, but it does not seem to me that because, as it is said, those purposes became impossible, it would be a very legitimate inference that the happening of the naval review was contemplated by both parties as the basis and foundation of this contract, so as to bring the case within the doctrine of *Taylor* v *Caldwell*. On the contrary, when the contract is properly regarded, I think the purpose of Mr Hutton, whether of seeing the naval review or of going round the fleet with a party of paying guests, does not lay the foundation of the contract within the authorities.

Having expressed that view, I do not know that there is any advantage to be gained by going on in any way to define what are the circumstances which might or might not constitute the happening of a particular contingency as the foundation of a contract. I will content myself with saying this, that I see nothing that makes this contract differ from a case where, for instance, a person has engaged a brake to take himself and a party to Epsom to see the races there, but for some reason or other, such as the spread of an infectious disease, the races are postponed. In such a case it could not be said that he could be relieved of his bargain. So in the present case it is sufficient to say that the happening of the naval review was not the foundation of the contract.

The part of the judgment concerning the Derby Day example is difficult to follow but can be explained with reference to the decision in *Herne Bay* v *Hutton*. In this decision it can be seen that the contract had two purposes, seeing the naval review and going round the fleet; therefore as they were seen to be equally as important the contract was not frustrated.

Returning to the opening example; it can be argued that the contract between the coach firm and A is not frustrated. Two reasons can be given for this: firstly, any other coach would have been satisfactory and secondly, a day in London could be said to have its attractions, without a rugby international.

3.2 Delay and time

The question as to whether a delay amounts to frustration has caused problems. Clearly the delay must be abnormal but how is this question decided? In *Pioneer Shipping* v *BTP Tioxide* (1981) the following test was suggested: 'It is not the nature of the cause of delay which matters so much as the effect of that cause upon the performance of the obligations which the parties have assumed one towards the other.'

In *Davis* v *Fareham UDC* (above) the delay was not sufficient to render the obligation 'radically different'. A similar harsh approach was followed in the case of *National Carriers* v *Panalpina* (1981) (see extract below) where a break of 20 months out of 10 years was held not to be sufficient. The case, however, must be put in the context of the type of contractual obligation in question. In *National Carriers* the contract was in the form of a lease and the court had to decide whether or not a lease could be frustrated as previous authority was not clear on this. An explanation of the problems faced by the court on this issue needs to be made.

A lease creates a legal estate in land therefore a right is gained in that land. The reasoning is that the lessee has got what he has bargained for, an interest in land, and it is irrelevant that the land cannot be used for a particular purpose. The problem is that in many short term letting situations it is difficult to distinguish between a lease and a licence; the latter creating no legal estate in the land. An example will illustrate the problem: suppose A rents a cottage for two weeks for his holiday and it is burnt down after the contract is made but before A goes on holiday. Assuming the fire is nobody's fault, following *Taylor* v *Caldwell* (see 2 above) it could well amount to a frustrating event. The problem, at least before *National Carriers* v *Panalpina* was that if the letting amounted to a lease then the contract could not be frustrated whereas if it amounted to a licence (as in *Krell* v *Henry*) it could. The law has had great difficulty in distinguishing between a lease and licence therefore in *National Carriers* v *Panalpina* it was decided that frustration could, in theory at least, apply to a lease albeit in exceptional circumstances.

Returning to the facts of *National Carriers* v *Panalpina* it can be seen that while the judges were prepared, in theory at least, to allow frustration of a lease, the time when the land had to be unavailable for its stated use had to be much longer before it could amount to frustration. Indeed the case does in fact show that the court is unwilling to find a 'radical change' in the obligation.

National Carriers Ltd v *Panalpina (Northern) Ltd*
[1981] AC 675

A warehouse was demised to the defendants for a period of 10 years from January 1, 1974. By the lease, the defendants covenanted not to use it otherwise than for the purpose of a warehouse without the plaintiffs' consent. The only vehicular access to the warehouse was by a street which the local authority closed on May 16, 1979, because of the dangerous condition of a derelict Victorian warehouse opposite to that demised to the defendants. In the events that subsequently happened, the period between the closure of the street and its reopening after demolition of the Victorian warehouse was likely to be about 20 months. During that period, the demised warehouse was rendered useless for the defendants' purposes. In an action by the plaintiffs for recovery of unpaid rent, the defendants claimed that the lease had been frustrated by the events that had happened. Judgment was entered for the plaintiffs.

On the defendants' appeal to the Lords it was held, dismissing the appeal: (1) (Lord Russell of Killowen dissenting) that the doctrine of frustration was in principle applicable to leases, though the cases in which it could properly be applied were likely to be rare; (2) that (per Lord Hailsham of St Marylebone LC, Lord Simon of Glaisdale and Lord Roskill) frustration of a contract occurred when the nature of the outstanding rights and obligations were so significantly changed by some supervening event from what the parties could reasonably have contemplated at the time of its execution that it would be unjust to hold them to its performance and that, having regard in particular to the likely length of continuance of the lease after the interruption of the user in relation to the term originally granted, on the facts the defendants had failed to raise a triable issue as to the applicability of the doctrine of frustration.

LORD WILBERFORCE: I now come to the second question which is whether on the facts of the case the appellant should be given leave to defend the action: can it establish that there is a triable issue? I have already summarised the terms of the lease. At first sight, it would appear to my mind that the case might be one for possible frustration. But examination of the facts leads to a negative conclusion. The circumstances which it is claimed amount to a frustrating event are proved by affidavit evidence supplemented and brought up to date by other documents. They are as follows. The first order closing Kingston Street was made on May 16, 1979, to take effect from May 18. The lease had then four years and six and a half months to run. In his affidavit sworn on September 20, 1979, the appellant's solicitor stated that it was likely that 'well over a year' would have elapsed before a decision could be made as regards the listed Victorian warehouse opposite the appellant's premises, the condition of which made the closure necessary. The town clerk of the city of Kingston-upon-Hull had written on August 7 that it was probably unlikely that the matter could be resolved 'within the next year'. It appears that a local inquiry was held into the future of the listed warehouse, and the Secretary of State on March 20, 1980, approved the inspector's report and granted consent for its demolition. On September 30, 1980, the town clerk informed the lessors that the estimated date for completion of the demolition was 'some time in late December 1980 or early January 1981'. I think it is accepted that the reopening of Kingston Street would immediately follow.

So the position is that the parties to the lease contemplated, when Kingston Street was first closed, that the closure would probably last for a year or a little longer. In fact it seems likely to have lasted for just over 8 months. Assuming that the street is reopened in January 1981, the lease will have three more years to run.

My Lords, no doubt, even with this limited interruption the appellant's business will have been severely dislocated. It will have had to move goods from the warehouse before the closure and to acquire alternative accommodation. After reopening the reverse process must take place. But this does not approach the gravity of a frustrating event. Out of 10 years it will have lost under two years of use: there will be nearly three years left after the interruption has ceased. This is a case, similar to others, where the likely continuance of the term after the interruption makes it impossible for the lessee to contend that the lease has been brought to an end. The obligation to pay rent under the lease is unconditional, with a sole exception for the case of fire, as to which the lease provides for a suspension of the obligation. No provision is made for suspension in any other case: the obligation remains. I am of opinion therefore that the lessee has no defence to the action for rent, that leave to defend should not be given and that the appeal must be dismissed.

Self check questions
1. How many purposes did the contract in *Krell* v *Henry* have as opposed to that in *Herne Bay* v *Hutton*?
2. What is required for a time delay to amount to frustration?

Answers
1. In *Krell* v *Henry* the contract had one purpose, its foundation, which was the viewing of the Coronation procession; whereas in *Herne Bay* v *Hutton* the contract had two equally important purposes.
2. The delay must make the performance of obligations 'radically different'. In this context it is important to note the nature of the contract in question — for example, a lease.

4   Self-induced frustration

We have stated above that the frustrating event must not be due to the 'act or default' of either party. The principle is illustrated by the decision in *Maritime National Fish* v *Ocean Trawlers* (1935) where the contract was ended by the deliberate election of the owners not to give a licence to the boat which was the subject-matter of the contract; therefore that party was in breach. The act above was an intentional one; however, it is not clear whether or not a negligent act amounts to self-inducement. There is no clear authority, but the burden of proof is on the person trying to show that the frustration was self-induced and further guidance has been provided by the decision in *The Super Servant Two* (see below).

Maritime National Fish Ltd v *Ocean Trawlers Ltd*
[1935] AC 524

The respondents were owners and the appellants were charterers of a steam trawler which was fitted with, and could operate as a trawler only with an otter trawl. By the charterparty the vessel could be used only in the fishing industry. The charterparty was renewed for a year from October 25, 1932. At that date both parties knew that a Canadian statute, which was applicable, made it an offence to leave a Canadian port with intent to fish with a vessel using an otter trawl, except under licence from the Minister. In March, 1933, the appellants applied to the

Minister for licences for five trawlers which they were operating. The Minister intimated that only three licences would be granted and requested the appellants to name the three trawlers in respect of which the three licences should be granted. The appellants named three trawlers, excluding the trawler now in question, and accordingly licences were granted for those three only. The appellants thereupon claimed that they were no longer bound by the charterparty, and to an action claiming the charter hire pleaded that the charterparty had become impossible of performance and their obligations under it ended.

LORD WRIGHT: . . . What matters is that they could have got a licence for the *St Cuthbert* if they had so minded. If the case be figured as one in which the *St Cuthbert* was removed from the category of privileged trawlers, it was by the appellants' hand that she was so removed, because it was their hand that guided the hand of the Minister in placing the licences where he did and thereby excluding the *St Cuthbert*. The essence of 'frustration' is that it should not be due to the act of election of the party. . . . Their Lordships are of the opinion that the loss of the *St Cuthbert*'s licence can correctly be described, *quoad* the appellants, as 'a self-induced frustration'. . . . On this ground their Lordships are of the opinion that the appeal should be dismissed with costs.

The limits on the principle of self-induced frustration was one of the issues in the following case.

J. Lauritzen AS v *Wijsmuller BV (The Super Servant Two)*
[1990] 1 Lloyd's Rep 1

By a contract dated July 7, 1980 the defendants (Wijsmuller) agreed to carry the plaintiffs' (Lauritzen's) drilling rig (Dan King) from the Hitachi shipyard at Aryake, Japan to a delivery location off Rotterdam. The drilling rig was to be delivered between June 20, 1981 and August 20, 1981 and was to be carried by using what the contract described as the 'transportation unit'. The unit was defined as meaning Super Servant One *or* Super Servant Two.

The defendants were given the right to cancel the performance under the contract in the event of force *majeure or any other circumstances whatsoever which reasonably prevented the performance of the contract. The defendants also had the right to substitute the transportation unit by other means of transport and there was a duty of care clause in which the defendants agreed to do everything that a good carrier might reasonably be expected to do in order to reach the port of discharge in time and safety.*

On January 29, 1981 Super Servant Two *sank. The defendants had intended to use* Super Servant Two *for this contract; they had entered into other contracts with other persons which they could only perform using* Super Servant One. *On or about February 16, 1981 the defendants informed the plaintiffs that they would not carry out the transportation of the drilling rig with either* Super Servant One *or* Super Servant Two.

In the event a 'without prejudice' agreement was entered into in April, 1981 under which the rig was transported on a barge towed by a tug.

Held: (1) Under the contract the defendants could have satisfied their obligation by using Super Servant One *to carry* Dan King *after* Super Servant Two *had sunk, but they elected not to do so; the doctrine of frustration only availed a party who contracted to perform a contract of carriage with a vessel which through no fault of his own no longer existed; but that was not this case. The* Dan King *contract did provide an alternative; the sinking of* Super Servant Two *did not automatically and without more ado bring the contract to an end by reason of frustration; even after the sinking the defendants could have used* Super Servant One *and this issue (i.e., self-induced frustration), would be answered in the negative.*

(2) The real question was whether the frustrating event relied on was truly an outside event or extraneous change of situation or whether it was an event which the party seeking to rely on it had the means and opportunity to prevent but nevertheless caused or permitted to come about; the plaintiffs had pleaded in some detail the grounds on which they alleged that Super Servant Two *was lost as a result of the carelessness of the defendants, their servants or agents; if those allegations were made good to any significant extent the defendants would be precluded from relying on their plea of frustration and this issue (i.e., self-induced frustration), would also be answered in the negative.*

BINGHAM LJ: The doctrine of frustration depends on a comparison between circumstances as they are or are assumed to be when a contract is made and circumstances as they are when a contract is, or would be, due to be performed. It is trite law that disappointed expectations do not of themselves give rise to frustrated contracts. To frustrate, an event must significantly change—

> ... the nature (not merely the expense or onerousness) of the outstanding contractual rights and/or obligations from what the parties could reasonably have contemplated at the time of [the contract's] execution [*National Carriers Ltd* v *Panalpina (Northern) Ltd* [1981] AC 675 at p. 700, per Lord Simon of Glaisdale].

Had the *Dan King* contract provided for carriage by *Super Servant Two* with no alternative, and that vessel had been lost before the time for performance, then assuming no negligence by Wijsmuller (as for purposes of this question we must), I feel sure the contract would have been frustrated. The doctrine must avail a party who contracts to perform a contract of carriage with a vessel which, through no fault of his, no longer exists. But that is not this case. The *Dan King* contract did provide an alternative. When that contract was made one of the contracts eventually performed by *Super Servant One* during the period of contractual carriage of *Dan King* had been made, the other had not, at any rate finally. Wijsmuller have not alleged that when the *Dan King* contract was made either vessel was earmarked for its performance. That, no doubt, is why an option was contracted for. Had it been foreseen when the *Dan King* contract was made that *Super Servant Two* would be unavailable for performance, whether because she had been deliberately sold or accidentally sunk, Lauritzen at least would have thought it no matter since the carriage could be performed with the other. I accordingly accept Mr Legh-Jones's submission that the present case does not fall within the very limited class of cases in which the law will relieve one party from an absolute promise he has chosen to make.

The decision in the case now makes two things clearer. First, a person who has a choice (in this case between two ships) and exercises it cannot rely on frustration if that choice means the contract cannot be performed. Secondly, frustration cannot be pleaded by a party if the non-performance is due to that party's negligence.

The above seems particularly harsh, given the fact that the other ship (the *Super Servant One*) was unavailable. But the courts are clearly telling the parties that they must try to deal with these matters through express terms of the contract: in this context what are called *force majeure* clauses. The Court of Appeal indicated that an appropriately worded clause, in the absence of negligence, would be sufficient to cover such a situation as occurred in the case above.

5   The legal consequences of frustration

Frustration brings the contract to an end forthwith and both parties are released as to future obligations. The main problems, however, relate to either work done or money paid over before the contract is frustrated. Two examples can illustrate the problem: firstly A is installing a new kitchen in B's house but due to nobody's fault the house is destroyed by fire and the kitchen was only half completed. Obviously the contract is frustrated but what of the work done by A? Secondly, X hires a room from Y for a particular purpose for £50, paying £25 as a deposit. The reason for hiring the room is no longer there and following *Krell* v *Henry* the contract is frustrated. What of the £25 deposit?

The common law, in both examples above, did not provide a satisfactory answer and as a result Parliament intervened through the provisions of the Law Reform (Frustrated Contracts) Act 1943. We need to examine some of the provisions of the Act in some detail and you should not worry if you find the extracted section (below) difficult to follow as you are not alone, in that judicial decisions, which are not included here, make the section even more difficult to follow.

The Law Reform (Frustrated Contracts) Act 1943

1.—(1)   Where a contract governed by English law has become impossible of performance or been otherwise frustrated, and the parties thereto have for that reason been discharged from the further performance of the contract, the following provisions of this section shall, subject to the provisions of section two of this Act, have effect in relation thereto.

(2)   All sums paid or payable to any party in pursuance of the contract before the time when the parties were so discharged (in this Act referred to as 'the time of discharge') shall, in the case of sums so paid, be recoverable from him as money received by him for the use of the party by whom the sums were paid, and, in the case of sums so payable, cease to be so payable:

Provided that, if the party to whom the sums were so paid or payable incurred expenses before the time of discharge in, or for the purpose of, the performance of the contract, the court may, if it considers it just to do so having regard to all the circumstances of the case, allow him to retain or, as the case may be, recover the whole or any part of the sums so paid or payable, not being an amount in excess of the expenses so incurred.

(3)   Where any party to the contract has, by reason of anything done by any other party hereto in, or for the purpose of, the performance of the contract, obtained a valuable benefit (other than a payment of money to which the last foregoing subsection applies) before the time of discharge, there shall be recoverable from him by the said other party such sum (if any), not exceeding the value of the said benefit to the party obtaining it, as the court considers just, having regard to all the circumstances of the case and, in particular —

(a)   the amount of any expenses incurred before the time of discharge by the benefited party in, or for the purpose of, the performance of the contract, including any sums paid or payable by him to any other party in pursuance of the contract and retained or recoverable by that party under the last foregoing subsection, and

(b)   the effect, in relation to the said benefit, of the circumstances giving rise to the frustration of the contract.

The first point to note, s. 1(1), is that the Act *only* applies when the contract has been frustrated; i.e., frustration is a pre-requisite in order for the Act to operate. The second of our examples, concerning the payment of the deposit, is dealt with by s. 1(2) of the Act. Applying the first paragraph to our example X would be able to claim the deposit of £25 from Y. However, in the second paragraph, the proviso in s. 1(2) must be applied; therefore if Y has done some work towards the contract he may be able to claim some expenses for this. We need to expand the facts a little; suppose Y has done some cleaning work in the room costing £10. The court will probably allow Y to keep £5 of the deposit as he has obviously gained some benefit as well and it would not seem equitable for Y to be able to claim all the money incurred by the cleaning costs.

Finally, the first example needs to be dealt with and s. 1(3) is the appropriate subsection. Initially it must be noted that the sub-section does not apply when money has been paid over; this is dealt with by s. 1(2). The major difficulty with our example is whether B has gained a 'valuable benefit' as the wording of s. 1(3) requires. The cases on the issue are by no means clear and it can be argued that B has gained a valuable benefit in that half the work had already been done. A counter argument to the above is that the 'valuable benefit' only accrues when the work is completed but this overlooks the fact that as half the work had been done it would cost less to complete. Finally, it should be noted that any payment under s. 1(3) is discretionary and by taking the above approach it gives the court a wide discretion to apply the subsection.

Self check questions
1.   What is the effect of a frustrating event as to future obligations?
2.   When does the Act apply?
3.   What is the difference between s. 1(2) and s. 1(3)?

Answers
1.   A frustrating event discharges the contract as to the future.
2.   The Act only applies after there has been a frustrating event.
3.   Section 1(2) applies when money has been paid over before the frustrating event and s. 1(3) deals with the situation where a valuable benefit has been gained in performing the contract before that contract is frustrated.

Problem
Fred owns a pair of houses overlooking Aintree Racecourse and in *1976 let* one of them for 25 years to John, a *horse-racing fanatic* retaining the other house for his own use. In January *1985* Fred finds that he will be abroad during the Grand National week and agrees to give *Peter* the use of his house *for that week* for a fee of £500. Peter pays £200 in advance of which Fred spends £50 on having the garden telescope overhauled. In February it is announced that the racecourse has been sold to property developers and that there *will be no further* races at *Aintree*.

Discuss.

Suggested answer
The problem is concerned with the question as to whether the two contracts have been frustrated as a result of no further racing being held at Aintree. Frustration occurs when an event, after the formation of the contract, has rendered the contract physically or commercially impossible to fulfil. An initial point to make is that there is no question of self-inducement as the alleged frustrating event is completely outside the control of the parties.

A test for deciding whether frustration has occurred should be suggested. In *Davis v Fareham UDC* it was stated that the court should look for a radical change in the obligation which can be judged from the surrounding circumstances. This test will be applied to the facts below; if, and only if, a frustrating event is shown can the Law Reform (Frustrated Contracts) Act 1943 be applied.

Firslty look at the contract between Fred and John. The initial point to discuss is the nature of the contractual obligation. The facts of the question do not make this clear but a 25-year letting would normally take the form of a lease and in this context the decision in *National Carriers v Panalpina* must be mentioned. The case states that, in theory at least, a lease can be frustrated but that such situations are rare and this should be born in mind in the subsequent discussion. John is said to be a horse-racing fanatic; he will no doubt argue that this is the reason why he leased the house in 1976 and following *Krell* v *Henry* the contract should be said to be frustrated.

Two arguments can be put to counter this. Firstly, given the length of the contract, it can be argued that it had two purposes of equal importance; that is using the house as well as watching the racing. The authority for this proposition is *Herne Bay Steamboat* v *Hutton* which was distinguished from *Krell* v *Henry* on the ground that if a contract had two purposes of equal importance, and merely one became unobtainable, then the contract would not be frustrated. Secondly, the nature of the contract would further support this argument that frustration would not apply. John has used the house for both purposes for ten years, and following the *National Carriers* v *Panalpina* decision on the application of frustration to leases in only exceptional circumstances it seems that the contract between Fred and John will not be frustrated.

The contract between Fred and Peter needs to be examined. A number of points need to be mentioned from the facts; the contract is only a week long, coinciding with the races; and Peter has paid £500 which is way above the market value for renting a house for such a period. These factors would suggest that watching the racing is the foundation of the contract and following *Krell* v *Henry* the contract is frustrated.

Assuming the contract between Fred and Peter is frustrated, we need to discuss the effect of the frustration. Peter is discharged as to future obligations under the contract and therefore does not have to pay the balance of £300 owed. The difficulty centres around the deposit of £200 and the provisions of the Law Reform (Frustrated Contracts) Act 1943 come into operation. Section 1(2) would seemingly allow Peter to claim all the deposit back but the proviso does allow the courts to award Fred at their discretion, any reasonable expense incurred. Can Fred then claim the whole of the £50? It is probable that the court would allow Fred to only claim half that amount because although the overhauling of the telescope was for the purpose of the contract, Fred has also got the benefit of this in the future. Therefore, it is likely the court will allow Fred to claim £25 in expenses and return the rest of the deposit, £175, to Peter.

13 DURESS, UNDUE INFLUENCE AND INEQUALITY OF BARGAINING POWER

1 Introduction

English law, as a general principle, will not examine the fairness of a contract. There are, however, situations when the law will intervene if a contract has been entered into as a result of pressure which is regarded as illegal. The problem is that the judiciary have had great difficulty in deciding when the pressure is sufficient for them to intervene and this will be examined under the headings of duress, undue influence and inequality of bargaining power. An important aspect of this area is the influence it has on topics already discussed. The bargaining position of the parties was important in deciding whether a statement had become a term of the contract; the validity of an exemption clause and the enforceability, or otherwise, of restraint of trade contracts.

2 Duress

The common law definition of duress is limited to actual violence or threats of physical violence. We shall briefly deal with this concept before looking at the way in which a category of economic duress has been developed in recent years.

Perhaps the most liberal interpretation of duress was given in the decision in *Barton* v *Armstrong* (1975). The court is saying that if the threats of violence were merely one of the reasons why the contract was entered into then that is sufficient for the contract to be rendered void. The decision is open to criticism; however, in practical terms the principle is by no means as important as that of economic duress to be discussed below.

Barton v Armstrong
[1975] 2 All ER 465

A, the former chairman of a company, threatened B, the managing director with death if the company did not agree to pay a large sum in cash and to purchase A's shares in the company. There was evidence that B thought the proposed agreement was a satisfactory business arrangement. B executed a deed on behalf of the company carrying out the agreement.

LORD CROSS: Their Lordships think that the same rule should apply (i.e., misrepresentation) in cases of duress and that if A's threats were 'a reason' for B's executing the deed he is entitled to relief even though he might well have entered into the contract if A had uttered no threats to induce him to do so.

Therefore the contract was held to be void on the facts, given the burden of proof.

The principle of economic duress is a relatively new one in English law; however a number of preliminary points can be made. Firstly, if economic duress is proved it renders the contract *voidable*. Above, we said that common-law duress rendered the contract *void*; therefore it is important to note this distinction. Secondly, the relative newness of the principle has meant that no clear test of what actually amounts to economic duress has emerged. The result of this is a mish-mash of cases some of which are discussed below.

In *The Siboen and the Sibotre* (1976), *North Ocean Shipping* v *Hyundai Construction* (1979), and *Pao On* v *Lau Yiu Long* (1980) the courts have had to distinguish between commercial pressure, which in the eyes of the law at least is legitimate; and economic duress which of course is not. In the former and latter cases the courts thought that contracts negotiated 'at arm's length' (whatever that may mean) were valid, whereas in the middle case, *North Ocean Shipping*, the threat to break the contract amounted to economic duress. The right to rescind in *North Ocean Shipping* was lost as the innocent party had affirmed the contract. The dividing line between legitimate and illegitimate pressure is a fine one which we need to illustrate by reference to two more discussion areas.

Occidental Worldwide Investment Corporation v Skibs A|S Avanti
(The Siboen and The Sibotre)
[1976] 1 Lloyd's Rep 203

D chartered two vessels to the P under separate charterparties. Subsequently P, whose financial position was deteriorating threatened to break the charterparties and gave the impression (false) that they were liable to go bankrupt if the rate of hire was not reduced. As a result the D signed addenda to the charterparties agreeing to reduce the rate of hire. D claimed rescission on grounds of misrepresentation and duress.

Held: Voidable on the ground of misrepresentation but not duress.

KERR J: He was acting under great pressure, but only commercial pressure, and not under anything which could in law be regarded as a coercion of his will so as to vitiate his consent.

Compare this test with *Barton v Armstrong* above. From this it can be seen that the crucial question is how to decide between commercial pressure (which is legitimate) and coercion which is not.

North Ocean Shipping v *Hyundai Construction Co. Ltd*
[1979] QB 705

D agreed to build a tanker for P: a fixed price was to be paid by instalments in US dollars. After the first instalment was paid the US dollar devalued by 10%. D then put forward a claim to an increase of 10% in the remaining instalments, threatening to break the contract unless their demands were met. P, who at the time were negotiating a very lucrative contract for the charter of the tanker, agreed 'without prejudice' to pay the increase. P paid the increased instalment without protest. P then claimed that the agreement was either void, for lack of consideration, or voidable for duress.

Held: On the question of whether or not the acts amounted to duress Mocatta J indicated that three questions should be asked:

(a)   Was there duress? Compulsion may take the form of 'economic duress' if the necessary facts are proved. A threat to break a contract may amount to such 'economic duress'.

(b)   What is the effect of the duress? It renders the contract voidable.

(c)   Was the remedy lost by any actions by the parties i.e., did they affirm the contract?

On the facts it was decided that affirmation had taken place — seemingly the same criteria applied as for affirmation in misrepresentation.

A further decision to be made is the relationship between 'market forces' and coercion when two large companies are involved.

Pao On v *Lau Yiu Long*
[1980] AC 614

P agreed (the main agreement) to sell shares to X Co. and in return were to be allocated shares in X Co. Under the agreement P promised X that they would retain 60% of their newly acquired shares of X for one year. This term was put in at the defendant's request who were majority shareholders in X. Under a subsidiary agreement the defendants agreed to buy back P's shares so as to provide security against fluctuating prices. The agreement however, made no mention of a rise in prices thus P threatened to break the agreement if they (P) were not compensated — the defendants drew up a separate agreement to that effect. The share prices slumped: the defendants refused to honour the agreement and P sued. The defendants claimed agreement for duress.

Held: Although subject to common pressure no coercion of consent i.e., public policy requires a contract negotiated at arm's length to be vitiated.

The first of these areas concerns the influence of pressure exerted in restraint of trade contracts. Obviously the bargaining position of the parties is important in assessing the reasonableness of the contract as between the parties but the facts of the case may also give rise to economic duress arguments as well. The decision in *Alec Lobb* v *Total Oil* (1985) (see below and also section 2, chapter 11) illustrate this point. The court makes a number of interesting points. Firstly, the mere fact that the parties were of unequal bargaining power did not matter as no pressure had been exerted on the plaintiff by the defendant. Added to this the fact that the plaintiffs had no realistic alternative did not matter, the only one being liquidation of the company; furthermore the economic necessity of the plaintiffs action did not seemingly matter.

Alec Lobb (Garages) Ltd v *Total Oil (Great Britain) Ltd*
[1985] 1 All ER 303

Held: Where one party had acted extortionately, oppressively or coercively towards the other, the court would in fairness set aside a transaction so made. However, a transaction was not rendered harsh or unconscionable merely because the parties were of unequal bargaining power and the stronger party had not shown that the terms of agreement were fair, just and reasonable. Furthermore, a transaction was not unconscionable merely because a party was forced by economic necessity to make it. On the facts, although the plaintiffs had no realistic alternative, no pressure had been exerted on them by the defendant, which was reluctant to enter into the transaction, and furthermore the plaintiffs themselves had sought the defendant's assistance to avert financial collapse and had sought the prior advice of their solicitors and accountant, which they had chosen to ignore. Accordingly, the judge had been right to find that the defendant's conduct was not unconscionable or oppressive.

DILLON LJ: I turn therefore to the appellants' case on equitable grounds.

The basis of the contention that the transaction of the lease and lease-back ought to be set aside in equity is that it is submitted, and in the court below was accepted on behalf of Total, that during the negotiations for the lease and lease-back the parties did not have equal bargaining power, and it is therefore further submitted that a contract between parties who had unequal bargaining power can only stand and be enforced by the stronger if he can prove that the contract was in point of fact fair, just and reasonable. The concept of unequal bargaining power is taken particularly from the judgment of Lord Denning MR in *Lloyds Bank Ltd* v *Bundy* [1975] QB 326.

In fact Lord Denning MR's judgment in *Lloyds Bank Ltd* v *Bundy* merely laid down the proposition that where there was unequal bargaining power the contract could not stand if the weaker did not have separate legal advice. In the present case Mr Lobb and the company did have separate advice from their own solicitor. On the facts of this case, however, that does not weaken the appellants' case if the general proposition of law which they put forward is valid. Total refused to accept any of the modifications of the transaction as put forward by Total which the solicitor for the company and Mr Lobb suggested, and in the end the solicitor advised them not to proceed. Mr Lobb declined to accept that advice because his and the company's financial difficulties were so great, and, it may be said, their bargaining power was so small, that he felt he had no alternative but to accept Total's terms. Because of the existing valid tie to Total which had, as I have said, three to four years to run, he had no prospect at all of raising finance on the scale he required from any source other than Total. There is no suggestion that there was any other dealer readily available who could have bought the property from him subject to the tie. The only practical solutions to him were to accept the terms of the lease and lease-back as put forward by Total on which Total was not prepared to negotiate, or to sell the freehold of the property to Total and cease trading. In these circumstances, it would be unreal, in my judgment, to hold that if the transaction is otherwise tainted it is cured merely because Mr Lobb and the company had independent advice.

In the present case there are findings of fact by the deputy judge that the conduct of Total was not unconscionable, coercive or oppressive. There is ample evidence to support those findings and they are not challenged by the appellants. The case is that the judge applied the wrong test; where there is unequal bargaining power, the test is, they say, whether its terms are fair, just and reasonable and it is unnecessary to consider whether the conduct of the stronger party was oppressive or unconscionable. I do not accept the appellants' proposition of law. In my judgment the findings of the judge conclude this ground of appeal against the appellants.

Inequality of bargaining power must anyhow be a relative concept. It is seldom in any negotiation that the bargaining powers of the parties are absolutely equal. Any individual wanting to borrow money from a bank, building society or other financial institution in order to pay his liabilities or buy some property he urgently wants to acquire will have virtually no bargaining power: he will have to take or leave the terms offered to him. So, with house property in a seller's market, the purchaser will not have equal bargaining power with the vendor. But Lord Denning MR did not envisage that any contract entered into in such circumstances would, without more, be reviewed by the courts by the objective criterion of what was reasonable: see *Lloyds Bank Ltd* v *Bundy* [1975] QB 326 at 336. The courts would only interfere in exceptional cases where as a matter of common fairness it was not right that the strong should be allowed to push the weak to the wall. The concepts of unconscionable conduct and of the exercise by the stronger of coercive power are thus brought in, and in the present case they are negatived by the deputy judge's findings.

The decision in *Alec Lobb* v *Total Oil* is of some importance as it shows the present tendency of the courts not to intervene save in exceptional circumstances. Two further cases need to be discussed in order to show the change in attitude of the courts and the rejection of a much wider principle which would have given the court the ability to intervene more freely.

The first case is the decision in *Lloyds Bank* v *Bundy* (1975) and in particular the judgment of Lord Denning. The judgment is suggesting that there should be relief given where a party, without independent advice, has entered into a contract which is unfair for a number of reasons, for example inadequate consideration. Clearly this principle is much wider than economic duress which has been distinguished from commercial pressure by the courts; Lord Denning is seemingly equating some commercial pressure with his general principle of intervention.

Lloyds Bank Ltd v *Bundy*
[1975] QB 326

The defendant, an elderly farmer, and his only son had been customers of the plaintiff bank for many years. The son formed a company which banked at the same branch. In 1966 the defendant guaranteed the company's overdraft for £1,500 and charged the farm to the bank to secure that sum. The company's overdraft increased and the bank required further security. The son said that the defendant would give it. In May 1969 the son saw the defendant with the bank's assistant manager, B, who suggested that the defendant should sign a further guarantee for £5,000 and execute a further charge for £6,000. B left the necessary papers with the defendant's solicitor who advised him that the most the defendant could put into his son's affairs was £5,000, about half the value of his assets, the house in which he lived. The defendant on that advice on May 27, 1969, executed the further guarantee and charge.

The affairs of the son and his company further deteriorated and company cheques were returned unpaid. The son told H, who had succeeded B as assistant bank manager, that his father would give further security if necessary.

On December 17, 1969, the son visited the defendant with H, who had with him a further guarantee for £11,000 and a further charge for £3,500 ready for signature. H said that the bank would continue to allow the company, whose trouble he thought was 'deep seated', to draw money on overdraft up to £10,000 provided 10 per cent of its incomings were paid into a separate account to reduce the overdraft and that the defendant guaranteed the account up to £11,000 and gave the further charge to bring the amount charged on the house up to that sum. The defendant said that he was 100 per cent behind his only son and signed the guarantee and further charge which H produced.

At the end of 1970, after a receiving order had been made against the son, the company ceased to trade. The bank tried to sell the defendant's house for £9,500.

On the bank's claim for possession, H said in evidence that at the meeting of December 17, 1969, he 'would think the defendant relied on me implicitly to advise him about the transaction as bank manager' and that he knew the defendant 'had no other assets except' the house. The defendant said that he 'always trusted' H and 'simply sat back and did what they said'. The county court judge granted the bank an order for possession and dismissed the defendant's counter-claim for the setting aside of the guarantee and legal charge of December 17, 1969.

On appeal by the defendant:

LORD DENNING MR: . . . Now let me say at once that in the vast majority of cases a customer who signs a bank guarantee or a charge cannot get out of it. No bargain will be upset which is the result of the ordinary interplay of forces. There are many hard cases which are caught by this rule. Take the case of a poor man who is homeless. He agrees to pay a high rent to a landlord just to get a roof over his head. The common law will not interfere. It is left to Parliament. Next take the case of a borrower in urgent need of money. He borrows it from the bank at high interest and it is guaranteed by a friend. The guarantor gives his bond and gets nothing in return. The common law will not interfere. Parliament has intervened to prevent moneylenders charging excessive interest. But it has never interfered with banks.

Yet there are exceptions to this general rule. There are cases in our books in which the courts will set aside a contract, or a transfer of property, when the parties have not met on equal terms — when the one is so strong in bargaining power and the other so weak — that, as a matter of common fairness, it is not right that the strong should be allowed to push the weak to the wall. Hitherto those exceptional cases have been treated each as a separate category in itself. But I think the time has come when we should seek to find a principle to unite them. I put on one side contracts or transactions which are voidable for fraud or misrepresentation or mistake. All those are governed by settled principles. I go only to those where there has been inequality of bargaining power, such as to merit the intervention of the court.

Gathering all together, I would suggest that through all these instances there runs a single thread. They rest on 'inequality of bargaining power'. By virtue of it, the English law gives relief to one who, without independent advice, enters into a contract upon terms which are very unfair or transfers property for a consideration which is grossly inadequate, when his bargaining power is grievously impaired by reason of his own needs or desires, or by his own ignorance or infirmity, coupled with undue influences or pressures brought to bear on him by or for the benefit of the other. When I use the word 'undue' I do not mean to suggest that the principle depends on proof of any wrongdoing. The one who stipulates for an unfair advantage may be moved solely by his own self-interest, unconscious of the distress he is bringing to the other. I have also avoided any reference to the will of the one being 'dominated' or 'overcome' by the other. One who is in extreme need may knowingly consent to a most improvident bargain, solely to relieve the straits in which he finds himself. Again, I do not mean to suggest that every transaction is saved by independent advice. But the absence of it may be fatal. With these explanations, I hope this principle will be found to reconcile the cases. Applying it to the present case, I would notice these points:

(1)   The consideration moving from the bank was grossly inadequate. The son's company was in serious difficulty. The overdraft was at its limit of £10,000. The bank considered that its existing security was insufficient. In order to get further security, it asked the father to charge the house — his sole asset — to the uttermost. It was worth £10,000. The charge was for

£11,000. That was for the benefit of the bank. But not at all for the benefit of the father, or indeed for the company. The bank did not promise to continue the overdraft or to increase it. On the contrary, it required the overdraft to be reduced. All that the company gained was a short respite from impending doom.

(2)   The relationship between the bank and the father was one of trust and confidence. The bank knew that the father relied on it implicitly to advise him about the transaction. The father trusted the bank. This gave the bank much influence on the father. Yet the bank failed in that trust. It allowed the father to charge the house to his ruin.

(3)   The relationship between the father and the son was one where the father's natural affection has much influence on him. He would naturally desire to accede to his son's request. He trusted his son.

(4)   There was a conflict of interest between the bank and the father. Yet the bank did not realise it. Nor did it suggest that the father should get independent advice. If the father had gone to his solicitor — or to any man of business — there is no doubt that any one of them would say: 'You must not enter into this transaction. You are giving up your house, your sole remaining asset, for no benefit to you. The company is in such a parlous state that you must not do it.'

These considerations seem to me to bring this case within the principles I have stated. But, in case the principle is wrong, I also say that the case falls within the category of undue influence of the second class stated by Cotton LJ in *Allcard* v *Skinner* (1887) 36 ChD 145, 171. I have no doubt that the assistant bank manager acted in the utmost good faith and was straightforward and genuine. Indeed the father said so. But beyond doubt he was acting in the interests of the bank — to get further security for a bad debt. There was such a relationship of trust and confidence between them that the bank ought not to have swept up his sole remaining asset into its hands — for nothing — without his having independent advice. I would therefore allow this appeal.

The decision in *Lloyds Bank* v *Bundy* can be explained on other grounds, for example undue influence (see 3, below). The importance of the case is the judgment of Lord Denning. However, it has been severely limited by a recent House of Lords decision: *National Westminster Bank* v *Morgan* (1985) (see extract below — for facts and rest of case see 3, below). Lord Scarman is quite clear that no general principle of inequality of bargaining power is required as existing common-law and legislative measures are sufficient. Therefore, the judgment of Lord Denning in *Lloyds Bank* v *Bundy* should not be followed and the courts will stick to existing principles such as economic duress and undue influence.

National Westminster Bank plc v *Morgan*
[1985] AC 686

LORD SCARMAN: Lord Denning MR believed that the doctrine of undue influence could be subsumed under a general principle that English courts will grant relief where there has been 'inequality of bargaining power'. He deliberately avoided reference to the will of one party being dominated or overcome by another. The majority of the court did not follow him; they based their decision on the orthodox view of the doctrine as expounded in *Allcard* v *Skinner* (1887) 36 ChD 145. The opinion of the Master of the Rolls, therefore, was not the ground of the court's decision, which was to be found in the view of the majority, for whom Sir Eric Sachs delivered the leading judgment.

Nor has counsel for the respondent sought to rely on Lord Denning MR's general principle: and, in my view, he was right not to do so. The doctrine of undue influence has been sufficiently developed not to need the support of a principle which by its formulation in the language of the law of contract is not appropriate to cover transactions of gift where there is no bargain. The fact of an unequal bargain will, of course, be a relevant feature in some cases of undue influence. But it can never become an appropriate basis of principle of an equitable doctrine which is concerned with transactions 'not to be reasonably accounted for on the ground of friendship, relationship, charity, or other ordinary motives on which ordinary men act' (Lindley LJ in *Allcard* v *Skinner*). And even in the field of contract I question whether there is any need in the modern law to erect a general principle of relief against inequality of bargaining power. Parliament has undertaken the task — and it is essentially a legislative task — of enacting such restrictions upon freedom of contract as are in its judgment necessary to relieve against the mischief: for example, the hire-purchase and consumer protection legislation, of which the Supply of Goods (Implied Terms) Act 1973, Consumer Credit Act 1974, Consumer Safety Act 1978, Supply of Goods and Services Act 1982 and Insurance Companies Act 1982 are examples. I doubt whether the courts should assume the burden of formulating further restrictions.

Self check questions
1. What is the definition of common-law duress?
2. If proved, what is the effect of duress and economic duress on a contract?
3. How do the courts decide what amounts to economic duress?
4. Why was there found to be no economic duress in the *Alec Lobb* v *Total Oil* case?
5. Is there a general principle of inequality of bargaining power?

Answers
1. Common law duress is limited to violence or threats of physical violence.
2. Duress renders the contract void whereas economic duress merely renders the contract voidable. As economic duress makes a contract voidable the ability to rescind can be lost as in misrepresentation.
3. Economic duress includes threats to break a contract but not merely commercial pressure which is legitimate. The courts, however, have given no absolute definition of the principle and seemingly treat each case on its own facts.   –

4. The defendant did not exert pressure on the plaintiff therefore it was irrelevant that there was no reasonable alternative available to the plaintiff in the case. The case shows that the courts are not willing to intervene on the facts despite the admitted inequality of bargaining power between the parties.
5. After the decision in the *National Westminster* case it is quite clear that there is no general principle of inequality of bargaining power.

3 Undue influence

We shall deal with the area of undue influence known as 'relational'; that is where the court presumes because of the relationship between the parties that the contract is the result of improper pressure even though there has been no actual evidence of it. A good example of the principle is provided by *Allcard* v *Skinner* (1887) where the relationship between the parties led to an assumption of undue influence. The defendant could not discharge the burden of proof imposed on her to the effect that the plaintiff acted voluntarily.

Allcard v *Skinner*
(1887) 36 ChD 145

P was introduced by her spiritual adviser to D who was lady superior of a Protestant institution known as 'The Sisters of the Poor'. Three years later P became a sister and took the vows of poverty, chastity and obedience. By the time P left the 'Sisters' she had given £7,000 to D, of which only £1,671 remained unspent. P claimed back the £1,671 on the ground that it had been procured by undue influence.

Held: Even though no unfair pressure was put on P the money was still recoverable as she had received no independent advice.

In *Lloyds Bank* v *Bundy* (1975) (see above) all three judges stated that because of the relationship of trust and confidence between the Bank and Bundy, undue influence would be assumed and the Bank failed to rebut the burden of proof imposed on them. The principle, though, is limited by the fact that the agreement itself must actually confer an unfair advantage on the party who is exercising the undue influence and this is illustrated by the decision in *National Westminster Bank* v *Morgan* (1985). We have already discussed the case above, the court disapproving of any general principle of inequality; but what is clear in this context is the requirement that there must be an advantage taken by the party seeking to exert the influence. Furthermore, the court held that the banker/client relationship does not ordinarily give rise to the presumption of undue influence.

National Westminster Bank plc v *Morgan*
[1985] AC 686

The husband, who was an unreliable and improvident businessman, was unable to meet the repayments due under a mortgage secured over the home which he owned jointly with his wife. As a result the then mortgagee commenced proceedings to take possession of the home, and to avert that the husband made refinancing arrangements with a bank. The bank was made aware of the urgency of the matter and, after the husband executed a legal charge in favour of the bank, the bank manager, at the husband's request, called at the home to get the wife to execute it. Unlike the previous occasion when she executed a mortgage over the home, independent legal advice was not given to her before she signed the mortgage. The husband was present at the brief meeting between the bank manager and the wife at the home although she made it clear she would have preferred him to be absent. The wife told the bank manager that she had little faith in her husband's business ventures and that she did not want the legal charge to cover his business liabilities. The bank manager assured her in good faith but incorrectly that the charge only secured the amount advanced to refinance the mortgage. In fact the charge did extend to business advances. The bank obtained an order for possession of the home after the husband and wife fell into arrears with payments. Soon afterwards the husband died without any indebtedness owing to the bank for business advances. The wife appealed against the order for possession contending that she had signed the mortgage because of undue influence from the bank and that therefore the legal charge should be set aside. The bank argued that a defence of undue influence could only be raised when a defendant had entered into a transaction which was manifestly disadvantageous to him and, since the husband had died without business debts owing to the bank, the wife was not manifestly disadvantaged but instead had benefited under the transaction because it had averted the proceedings by the prior mortgagee for possession.

Held: Allowing the appeal, that the principle that justified the setting aside of a transaction on the ground of undue influence was the victimisation of one party by the other, and before a transaction could be set aside for undue influence, whether in reliance on evidence or on the presumption of the exercise of undue influence, it had to be shown that the transaction had been wrongful in that it had constituted a manifest and unfair disadvantage to the person seeking to avoid it; that evidence of the mere relationship of the parties was not sufficient to raise the presumption of undue influence without also evidence that the transaction itself had been wrongful in that it had constituted an advantage taken of the person subjected to the influence which, failing proof to the contrary, was explicable only on the basis that undue influence had been exercised to procure it; and that, on the facts, the deputy judge had been entitled to find that the relationship between the wife and the bank had never gone beyond the normal business relationship of banker and customer and that the transaction had not been disadvantageous to the wife.

Per curiam. *(i)   The doctrine of undue influence has been sufficiently developed not to need the support of a principle of 'inequality of bargaining power' which by its formulation in the language of the law of contract is not appropriate to cover transactions of gift where there is no bargain. And even in the field of contract it is questionable whether there is any need in the modern law to erect a general principle of relief against inequality of bargaining power.*

(ii)   There is no precisely defined law setting limits to the equitable jurisdiction of a court to relieve against undue influence.

(iii)   The relationship between banker and customer is not one which ordinarily gives rise to a presumption of undue influence; in the ordinary course of banking

business a banker can explain the nature of the proposed transaction without laying
himself open of a charge of undue influence.

The decision in the *National Westminster* case (above) indicates that a person seeking to have an agreement set aside for undue influence must not only show that it was entered into as a result of the undue influence but also that the transaction itself is manifestly disadvantageous. This is discussed in the next case.

Bank of Credit and Commerce International SA v Aboody
[1992] 4 All ER 955

The defendants, who were husband and wife, were the directors and shareholders of a family company which was effectively run by the husband as a one-man business. The wife signed company documents without question as and when they were put before her by her husband, whom she trusted to run the company for their mutual benefit. In order to secure the company's borrowing from the plaintiff bank the defendants entered into six transactions, comprising three joint and several guarantees and three charges in favour of the bank over a house owned by the wife. On the occasion of the signing of the final charge the bank, on the advice of its own solicitors, arranged for an independent solicitor to advise the wife separately on the nature of the charge but in the course of the solicitor's interview with her the husband burst into the room and after an argument between the husband and the solicitor the wife signed the charge. The company subsequently collapsed, owing over £888,000 to the bank, which brought an action against the defendants to enforce its securities. The bank obtained judgment by default against the husband but the wife challenged the validity of the guarantees and charges on the ground, inter alia, *that they had been obtained by the undue influence of the husband. There was evidence from the independent solicitor that the husband was a bully and that the wife was under pressure and had signed because she wanted peace. The judge found that the husband had used undue influence over the wife to procure the execution of the transactions and that he had acted as the agent of the bank to procure her consent to and execution of the relevant documents but he refused to set aside the transactions, on the ground that there was no proof that the transactions were to the manifest disadvantage of the wife. The wife appealed, contending that a party who proved that a transaction was induced by the actual exercise of undue influence was entitled to have it set aside without also having to prove that the transaction was manifestly disadvantageous and that, in any event, each of the six transactions was manifestly disadvantageous to her.*
   Held: (1)   A party who proved that a transaction was induced by the exercise of actual undue influence was not entitled to have it set aside in reliance on the doctrine of undue influence without also proving that the transaction was manifestly disadvantageous to him or her. In that respect there was no distinction between a plea based on actual undue influence, which would only be upheld if the court was satisfied that such influence had been affirmatively proved on the evidence, and a plea of presumed undue influence, in which the relationship between the parties was such that the court would presume that undue influence had been exerted unless

evidence was adduced proving the contrary, e.g., by showing that the complaining party had received independent advice. However, if the party pleading actual undue influence could also show that there had been an abuse of confidence by the other party he was not then required to prove that the transaction was manifestly disadvantageous to him since the onus was then on the other party to establish the fairness of the transaction: National Westminster Bank plc *v* Morgan [1985] 1 All ER 821 *applied.*

(2)　Manifest disadvantage for the purposes of the doctrine of undue influence had to be a disadvantage which was obvious as such to any independent and reasonable person who considered the transaction at the time with knowledge of all the relevant facts. The fact that the complaining party had been deprived of the power of choice (e.g., because his will had been overborne through the failure to draw his attention to the risks involved) was not of itself a manifest disadvantage rendering the transaction unconscionable. Furthermore, since the giving of a guarantee or charge always involved the risk that the guarantee might be called in or the charge enforced, the question whether the assumption of such a risk was manifestly disadvantageous to the giver of the guarantee or charge depended on balancing the seriousness of the risk of enforcement to the giver, in practical terms, against the benefits gained by the giver in accepting the risk.

(3)　The husband, in inducing his wife to enter into the six transactions, had deliberately acted so as to conceal matters from her in a way which prevented her from giving proper detached consideration to her independent interest in transactions which involved substantial risks to her and the mere fact that he might have had no intention to injure her did not save his conduct from being unconscionable. However, even though the wife had proved actual undue influence on the part of the husband, there were no grounds for disagreeing with the judge's conclusion that on balance a manifest disadvantage had not been shown by the wife in respect of any of the six transactions, since although there were substantial potential liabilities and the family home was at risk as a result of the transactions, that was counterbalanced by the fact that the loans gave the company a reasonably good chance of surviving, in which case the potential benefits to the wife would have been substantial. Moreover, the evidence established that on balance the wife would have entered into the transactions in any event and accordingly it would not be right to grant her equitable relief as against the bank. The wife's appeal would therefore be dismissed.

The *Aboody* case is an example of presumed undue influence. There are dicta in the case to suggest that the requirement of manifest disadvantage also ought to be proved in cases of actual undue influence. This issue was clarified in the House of Lords decision in:

CIBC Mortgages plc v Pitt
[1993] 4 All ER 433

The husband and wife jointly owned the matrimonial home, which was valued at £270,000 in 1986. The only encumbrance on it was a mortgage in favour of a building society for £16,700. In 1986 the husband told the wife that he would like to borrow some money on the security of the house and to use the loan to buy shares on the stock market. The wife was not happy with the suggestion but as the result of pressure by the husband the wife eventually agreed. The husband and wife signed an application form for a loan from the plaintiff mortgagee of £150,000 for a period of 20 years, the purpose of the loan being expressed to be to pay off the existing mortgage and purchase a holiday home. The plaintiff agreed to advance £150,000 for 19 years and the husband and wife signed the mortgage offer and a legal charge prepared by the plaintiff's solicitors. The wife did not read those documents before signing them or receive any separate advice about the transaction nor did anyone suggest that she should do so. She did not know the amount that was being borrowed. The proceeds of the loan after the existing mortgage was paid off were paid into the husband and wife's joint account and the husband used it to speculate on the stock market. When the market crashed in October 1987 the husband was unable to keep up the mortgage payments and the plaintiff applied for an order for possession of the matrimonial home. The wife contested the application on the ground that she had been induced to sign the mortgage charge by misrepresentation, duress and undue influence on the part of her husband.

Held: (1)   A claimant who proved actual undue influence was not under the further burden of proving that the transaction induced by the undue influence was manifestly disadvantageous but was entitled as of right to have it set aside as against the person exercising the undue influence, since actual undue influence was a species of fraud and, like any other victim of fraud, a person who had been induced by undue influence to carry out a transaction which he did not freely and knowingly enter into was entitled to have that transaction set aside as of right. A person guilty of fraud was no more entitled to argue that the transaction was beneficial to the person defrauded than was a person who had procured a transaction by misrepresentation. The effect of the wrongdoer's conduct was to prevent the wronged party from bringing a free will and properly informed mind to bear on the proposed transaction, which accordingly had to be set aside in equity as a matter of justice.

(2)   However, although the wife had established actual undue influence by the husband, the plaintiff was not affected by it because the husband had not, in a real sense, acted as its agent in procuring her agreement and the plaintiff had no actual or constructive notice of the undue influence. So far as the plaintiff was aware, the transaction consisted of a joint loan to the husband and wife to finance the discharge of the existing mortgage on the matrimonial home with the balance to be applied in buying a holiday home. The loan was advanced to both the husband and wife jointly and there was nothing to indicate to the plaintiff that the loan was anything other than a normal advance to a husband and wife for their joint benefit. The mere fact that there was a risk of there being undue influence because one of the borrowers was the wife was, in itself, not sufficient to put the plaintiff on inquiry. The appeal would therefore be dismissed.

The decision is of great importance in that in cases of actual undue influence, such as the solicitor–client relationship, there is no need to prove that the transaction entered into was of manifest disadvantage. It will be interesting to see whether or not more cases will now come forward because of this decision.

4   Inequality of bargaining power

A number of brief points can be made about this principle. Firstly, as mentioned above, inequality of itself cannot be a ground of invalidity as invalidity depends on the stronger party taking unfair advantage of his position. Secondly, equality of bargaining power is rare and often parties negotiating at arm's length are held to be merely exerting legitimate commercial pressure. Finally, inequality of bargaining power can often mean inequality of bargaining skill and the courts do take this into account when making certain decisions: for example, whether or not a pre-contractual statement has been incorporated into the contract.

14 DAMAGES FOR BREACH OF CONTRACT

This chapter will examine the main remedy for breach of contract, that of damages. Other remedies, such as specific performance and injunctions, will be examined in the context of remedies for breaches of contracts of employment.

1 The basic principle

The basic principle was stated by Parke B in *Robinson* v *Harman* (1848): 'The rule of the common law is, that where a party sustains a loss by reason of a breach of contract, he is, so far as money can do it, to be placed in the same situation, with respect to damages, as if the contract has been performed.'

It is clear, therefore, that the purpose of contractual damages is to place the innocent party in the same position as if the contract had been performed. Such damages are often referred to as expectation loss but it must be made clear that the innocent party must be able to show that there was an expectation of profit to be made from the contract. If the innocent party is unable to show this then he will only be able to claim his reliance losses.

Reliance losses relate to expenses or other costs incurred in reliance on entering into the contract. The purpose of reliance damages is to place the innocent party in the position as if the contract have never been entered into. The relationship between expectation and reliance damages is illustrated by the decision in:

McRae v *Commonwealth Disposals Commission*
(1951) 84 CLR 377

The Commonwealth Disposals Commission (CDC) invited leaders 'for the purchase of an oil tanker lying on Jourmaund Reef . . . the vessel is said to contain oil'. McRae brought the tanker for £285 and the sale stated that the goods 'are sold as and where they lie with all faults'. Neither the reef nor the tanker existed. McRae claimed: (i) the cost of that tanker: £285; (ii) the cost of equipping the salvage expedition: £3,000; (iii) the loss of profits if the tanker and oil had existed — £300,000.

DIXON AND FULLAGAR JJ: But this, as a basis of damages [loss of profit], seems manifestly absurd. The Commission simply did not contract to deliver a tanker of any particular size or of any particular value . . . nor did it contract to deliver any oil.

Applying the above principle the court rejected the claim for the expectation loss (£300,000) as the plaintiff could not prove it. However the court did award £3,285 by way of damages which covered the reliance interest, The £3,285 being made up of the price of the tanker (£285) and the cost of equipping the salvage expedition, The innocent party (McRae) being placed in the same position as if the contract had not been entered into.

Self check questions
1.   What is the basic principle relating to the purpose of contractual damages.
2.   What is the purpose of reliance damages and what is their relationship with expectation damages?

Answers
1.   The basic principle is to put the innocent party in the position as if the contract had been performed; thereby allowing expectation damages.
2.   The purpose of reliance damages is to place the innocent party in the position as if the contract had never been entered into. Reliance damages will be claimed and/or awarded when the plaintiff is unable to show his expectation loss.

2   Remoteness of damage

The purpose of the remoteness principle is to limit the amount of profit or expectation loss the plaintiff can claim. The essence of contractual principles is that of agreement based on the knowledge of the parties. Therefore, in order for the person in breach to be made liable for 'unusual' consequences of a breach of contract he must have knowledge of those consequences.

The general principle is that the party in breach (the defendant) can only be liable for losses which were within the reasonable contemplation of the parties at the time the contract was made. The application of this principle is by no means clear and we must examine the appropriate case law. The principle was first enunciated in:

Hadley v Baxendale
(1854) 9 Exch 341

The plaintiffs' mill was brought to a standstill by the breakage of their only crankshaft. The defendants, who were carriers, failed to deliver the crankshaft, which was to be used as a pattern for a new one, to the manufacturers at the time contracted. As a result the plaintiffs' mill was closed longer than they contemplated. The plaintiffs sued the defendants for loss of profits.

ALDERSON B: Now we think the proper rule in such a case as the present is this: Where two parties have made a contract which one of them has broken the damages which the other party ought to receive in respect of such breach of contract should be such as may fairly and reasonably be considered either arising naturally, i.e., according to the usual course of things, from such breach of contract itself, or such as may reasonably be supposed to have been in the contemplation of both parties, at the time they made the contract, as the probable result of the breach of it. Now, if the special circumstances under which the contract was actually made were communicated by the plaintiffs to the defendants, and thus known to both parties, the damages resulting from the breach of such a contract, which they would reasonably contemplate, would be the amount of injury which would ordinarily follow a breach of contract under these special circumstances so known and communicated. But, on the other hand, if these special circumstances were wholly unknown to the party breaking the contract, he, at the most, could only be supposed to have had in his contemplation the amount of injury which would arise generally, and in the great multitude of cases not affected by any special circumstances, from such a breach of contract. For had the special circumstances been known, the parties might have specially provided for the breach of contract by special terms as to the damage in that case: and of this advantage it would be very unjust to deprive them.

Now the above principles are those by which we think the jury ought to be guided in estimating the damages arising out of any breach of contract. It is said that other cases such as breaches of contract in the non-payment of money, or in the not making a good title to land, are to be treated as exceptions from this, and governed by conventional rules. But as in such cases, both parties must be supposed to be cognisant of that well-known rule, these cases may, we think, be more properly classed under the rule above enunciated as to cases under known special circumstances, because there both parties may reasonably be presumed to contemplate the estimation of the amount of damages according to the conventional rule.

Now, in the present case, if we are to apply the principles above laid down we find that the only circumstances here communicated by the plaintiffs to the defendants at the time the contract was made, were that the article to be carried was the broken shaft of a mill, and that the plaintiffs were the millers of the mill. But how do these circumstances show reasonably that the profits of the mill must be stopped by an unreasonable delay in the delivery of the broken shaft by the carrier of the third person? Suppose the plaintiffs had another shaft in their possession put up or putting up at the time, and that they only wished to send back the broken shaft to the engineer who made it: it is clear that this would be quite consistent with the above circumstances, and yet the unreasonable delay in the delivery would have no effect upon the intermediate profits of the mill. Or, again suppose that at the time of delivery to the carrier, the machinery of the mill had been in other respects defective, then, also, the same results would follow. Here it is true that the shaft was actually sent back to serve as a model for a new one, and that the want of a new one was the only cause of the stoppage of the mill, and that the loss of profits really arose from not sending down the new shaft in proper time, and that this arose from the delay in delivering the broken one to serve as a model. But it is obvious that, in the great multitude of cases of millers sending off broken shafts to third persons by a carrier under ordinary circumstances, such consequences would not, in all probability, have occurred: and these special circumstances were here never communicated by the plaintiffs to the defendants.

It follows, therefore, that the loss of profits here cannot reasonably be considered such a consequence of the breach of contract as could have been fairly and reasonably contemplated by both the parties when they made this contract, for such loss would neither have flowed naturally from the breach of this contract in the great multitude of such cases occurring under ordinary circumstances, nor were the special circumstances, which, perhaps, would have made it a reasonable and natural consequence of such breach of contract, communicated to or known by the defendants. . . . There must therefore be a new trial. . . .

Alderson B, by categorising the consequences of a breach of contract into usual and non-usual consequences is emphasising the amount of knowledge possessed by both parties. Where the damages come within the first category of usual consequences, knowledge of those consequences will be imputed to both parties. However, as will be seen below, these consequences must be a 'real danger' or 'serious possibility'. If the damages come with the second category of non-usual consequences both parties must have actual knowledge of those consequences arising as a result of the breach of contract. The principle is well illustrated by the decision in:

Victoria Laundry (Windsor) Ltd v Newman Industries Ltd
[1949] 2 KB 528

The defendants, an engineering company, agreed to sell a new boiler to the plaintiffs. Both parties knew that the plaintiffs wished to expand their business. The defendants did not know, however, that the plaintiffs intended to use the boiler in order to fulfil highly lucrative government dyeing contracts. The boiler was delivered late and the plaintiffs claimed a general loss of profits and loss of profit on the dyeing contracts.

ASQUITH LJ: What propositions applicable to the present case emerge from the authorities as a whole, including those analysed above? We think they include the following: It is well settled that the governing purpose of damages is to put the party whose rights have been violated in the same position, so far as money can do so, as if his rights had been observed. This purpose, if relentlessly pursued, would provide him with a complete indemnity for all loss *de facto* resulting from a particular breach, however improbable, however unpredictable. This, in contract at least, is recognised as too harsh a rule. Hence, in cases of breach of contract the aggrieved party is only entitled to recover such part of the loss actually resulting as was at the time of the contract reasonably foreseeable as liable to result from the breach.

What was all that time reasonably foreseeable depends on the knowledge then possessed by the parties, or at all events, by the party who later commits the breach. For this purpose knowledge 'possessed' is of two kinds — one imputed, the other actual. Everyone, as a reasonable person, is taken to know the 'ordinary course of things' and consequently what loss is liable to result from a breach of that ordinary course. This is the subject-matter of the 'first rule' in *Hadley* v *Baxendale* but to this knowledge, which a contract-breaker is assumed to possess whether he actually possesses it or not, there may have to be added in a particular case knowledge which he actually possesses of special circumstances outside the 'ordinary course of things' of such a kind that a breach in those special circumstances would be liable to cause more loss. Such a case attracts the operation of the 'second rule' so as to make additional loss also recoverable.

In order to make the contract-breaker liable under either rule it is not necessary that he should actually have asked himself what loss is liable to result from a breach. As has often been pointed out, parties at the time of contracting contemplate, not the breach of the contract, but its performance. It suffices that, if he had considered the question, he would as a reasonable man have concluded that the loss in question was liable to result. Nor finally, to make a particular loss recoverable, need it be proved that on a given state of knowledge the defendant could, as a reasonable man, foresee that a breach must necessarily result in that loss. It is enough if he could foresee it was likely to result. It is enough if the loss (or some factor without which it would not have occurred) is a 'serious possibility' or a 'real danger'. For short, we have used the word 'liable' to result. Possibly the colloquialism 'on the cards' indicates the shade of meaning with some approach to accuracy.

Applying this reasoning to the facts of the case the Court of Appeal held that damages could be awarded for general loss of profits because it was within the reasonable contemplation of the parties that the boiler would be used immediately, whereas in the absence of actual knowledge concerning the government dyeing contracts there could be no damages awarded. The reasoning being that these were classed as 'special circumstances' and to be within the reasonable contemplation of the parties there must be actual knowledge of them.

A further comment on the amount of knowledge required for liability was made in *The Heron II* (1969).

The Heron II
[1969] 1 AC 350

LORD REID: I am satisfied that the court did not intend that every type of damage which was reasonably foreseeable by the parties when the contract was made should either be considered as arising naturally, i.e., in the usual course of things, or be supposed to have been in the contemplation of the parties. Indeed the decision makes it clear that a type of damage which was plainly foreseeable as a real possibility but which would only occur in a small minority of cases cannot be regarded as arising in the usual course of things or be supposed to have been in the contemplation of the parties; the parties are not supposed to contemplate as grounds for the recovery of damage any type of loss or damage which on the knowledge available to the defendant, would appear to him as only likely to occur in a small minority of cases.

In the cases like *Hadley* v *Baxendale* or the present case it is not enough that in fact the plaintiff's loss was directly caused by the defendant's breach of contract. It clearly was so caused in both. The crucial question is whether, on the information available to the defendant when the contract was made, he should, or the reasonable man in his position would, have realised that such loss was sufficiently likely to result from the breach of contract to make it proper to hold that the loss flowed naturally from the breach or that loss of that kind should have been within his contemplation.

The modern rule in tort is quite different and it imposes a much wider liablity. The defendant will be liable for any type of damage which is reasonably foreseeable as liable to happen even in the most unusual case, unless the risk is so small that a reasonable man would in the whole circumstances feel justified in neglecting it; and there is good reason for the difference. In contract, if one party wishes to protect himself against a risk which to the other party would appear unusual, he can direct the other party's attention to it before the contract is made, and I need not stop to consider in what circumstances the other party will then be held to have accepted responsibility in that event. In tort, however, there is no opportunity for the injured party to protect himself in that way, and the tortfeasor cannot reasonably complain if he has to pay for some very unusual but nevertheless foreseeable damage which results from his wrongdoing. I have no doubt that today a tortfeasor would be held liable for a type of damage as unlikely as was the stoppage of Hadley's Mill for lack of a crank shaft: to any one with the knowledge the carrier had that may have seemed unlikely, but the chance of it happening would have been seen to be far from negligible. But it does not at all follow that *Hadley* v *Baxendale* would today be differently decided.

It should be noted that again there is an attempt to limit the potential liability of a defendant. Further, Lord Reid talks about the difference between the remoteness test in contract and the remoteness test in tort. The difference is by no means a clear one and this is illustrated by the decision in the following case.

H. Parsons (Livestock) Ltd v *Uttley Ingham & Co. Ltd*
[1978] 1 All ER 526

The plaintiffs, who were pig farmers, bought a food storage hopper from the defendant manufacturers. When they were erecting the hopper, the defendants omitted to unseal a ventilator on top of the hopper; the ventilator could not be seen from the ground. The pignuts stored in the hopper became mouldy, because of the lack of ventilation, and many of the pigs to which the nuts were fed died of a rare intestinal infection — E. coli. *The plaintiffs claimed for the loss of the pigs and lost sales.*

LORD DENNING MR: It seems to me that in the law of contract, too, a similar distinction is emerging. It is between loss of profit consequent on a breach of contract and physical damage consequent on it.

I would suggest as a solution that in the former class of case, loss of profit cases, the defaulting party is only liable for the consequences if they are such as, at the time of the contract, he ought reasonably to have contemplated as a *serious* possibility or real danger.... The law on this class of case is now covered by the three leading cases of *Hadley* v *Baxendale*, *Victoria Laundry (Windsor) Ltd* v *Newman Industries Ltd* and *The Heron II*. These were all 'loss of profit' cases and the test of 'reasonable contemplation' and 'serious possibility' should, I suggest, be kept to that type of loss or, at any rate to economic loss.

In the second class of case, the physical injury or expense case, the defaulting party is liable for any loss or expense which he ought reasonably to have foreseen at the time of the breach as a possible consequence, even if it was only a *slight* possibility. You must assume that he was aware of this breach, and then you must ask: ought he reasonably to have foreseen at the time of the breach that something of this kind might happen in consequence of it? This is the test which has been applied in cases of tort. But there is a long line of cases which support a like test in cases of contract. One class of case which is particularly apposite here concerns latent defects in goods. In modern words: 'product liability'. In many of these cases the manufacturer is liable in contract to the immediate party for a breach of his duty to use reasonable care, and is liable in tort to the ultimate consumer for the same want of reasonable care. The ultimate consumer can either sue the retailer in contract and pass the liability up the chain to the manufacturer, or he can sue the manufacturer in tort and thus by-pass the chain. The liability of the manufacturer ought to be the same in either case. In nearly all these cases the defects were outside the range of anything that was in fact contemplated, or could reasonably have been contemplated by the manufacturer or by anyone down the chain to the retailers. Yet the manufacturer and others in the chain have been held liable for the damage done to the ultimate user....

Instances could be multiplied of injuries to persons or damage to property where the defendant is liable for his negligence to one man in contract and to another in tort. Each suffers like damage. The test of remoteness is, and should be, the same in both.

Coming to the present case, we were told that in some cases the makers of these hoppers supply them direct to the pig farmer under contract with him, but in other cases they supply them through an intermediate dealer who buys from the manufacturer and resells to the pig farmer on the self-same terms, in which the manufacturer delivers direct to the pig farmer. In the one case the pig farmer can sue the manufacturer in contract. In the other in tort. The test of remoteness should be the same. It should be the test in tort.

The present falls within the class of case where the breach of contract causes physical damage. The test of remoteness in such cases is similar to that in tort. . . . [The] makers of the hopper are liable for the death of the pigs.

SCARMAN LJ: . . . My conclusion in the present case is the same as that of Lord Denning MR but I reach it by a different route.

. . . I differ from him only to this extent: the cases do not, in my judgment, support a distinction in law between loss of profit and physical damage. Neither do I think it necessary to develop the law judicially by drawing such a distinction. Of course (and this is a reason for refusing to draw such a distinction in law) the type of consequence, loss of profit or market or physical injury, will always be an important matter of fact in determining whether in all the circumstances the loss or injury was of a type which the parties could reasonably be supposed to have contemplation.

. . . I agree with Lord Denning MR in thinking that the law must be such that in a factual situation where all have the same actual or imputed knowledge and the contract contains no term limiting the damages recoverable for breach, the amount of damages recoverable does not depend on whether, as a matter of legal classification, the plaintiff's cause of action is breach of contract or tort.

Both judges came to the same answer, but by different reasoning. Lord Denning allowed the claim in damages for the loss of the pigs because it was a 'possible consequence/slight possibility' that they arose as a result of eating the mouldy food. However, the claim for loss of profits was not allowed because this was not a serious possibility. Lord Justice Scarman, however, only allowed the damages for the loss of the pigs because it was within the contemplation of the parties that they would become ill if they were fed with mouldy food; whereas it was not within contemplation that they would die as a result and therefore no claim could be made for loss of profits.

The reasoning is difficult to understand but you must appreciate that the remoteness test is far more difficult to satisfy in contract than is that in tort.

Self check questions
1. What is the purpose of the remoteness test?
2. What is the overall guiding principle adopted by the courts?
3. What distinction was drawn by the courts in *Hadley* v *Baxendale*?
4. Why could the plaintiff in the *Victoria Laundry* v *Newman Industries Ltd* not claim for the loss of the Government dyeing contracts?
5. What is the difference between the remoteness tests in contract and tort? On what basis did Lord Denning draw the distinction?

Answers
1. The purpose of remoteness test is to limit the amount of expectation loss the plaintiff can claim.

2. Damages can only be claimed if they are within the reasonable contemplation of the parties.

3. A distinction was drawn between usual and non-usual consequences. In the former knowledge of consequences can be imputed whereas in the latter both parties must have actual knowledge of the consequences in order to be rendered liable.

4. The court held that the Government contracts fell within the category of non-usual or special circumstances and in the absence of actual knowledge the defendant could not be made liable.

5. The test of remoteness in contract is that of reasonable contemplation whereas in tort it is reasonable foreseeability. Lord Denning stated that in contractual loss of profit cases the reasonable contemplation test should apply whereas in physical damage cases the tortious test should operate. The other judges in the court did not agree with the approach of Lord Denning, but it is a principle which must be remembered.

3 Damages for non-pecuniary losses

The general principle is that damages will not be awarded for non-pecuniary losses, such as injury to the plaintiff's feelings or for his mental distress, as a result of a breach of contract.

A number of cases do, however, put pressure on this general principle. It is clear though that the nature of the contractual situation is critical and it may well be that any such losses can only be claimed in 'consumer' type contracts. There is a need, again, to ask what was within the contemplation of both parties at the time the contract was made.

Jarvis v *Swans Tours Ltd*
[1973] 1 All ER 71

The plaintiff booked a winter sports holiday which the defendants advertised in their brochure as 'a House-party in Morliap' with 'special resident host'.... 'Welcome party ... afternoon tea and cakes.... Yodeller evening'. It was stated that ski-packs would be available, and added, 'You will be in for a great time'. The House-party consisted of 13 people for the first week and only the plaintiff for the second, when there was no representative at the hotel; there was no welcoming party; full length skis were only available for two days; the cake for tea was only crisps and dry nutcake; the yodeller was a local man who sang a few songs in his working clothes. The plaintiff claimed damages for breach of a contract to provide the holiday promised. The trial judge awarded him £31.72, and he appealed.

LORD DENNING MR: In a proper case damages for mental distress can be recovered in contract, just as damages for shock can be recovered in tort. One such case is a contract for a holiday, or any other contract to provide entertainment and enjoyment. If the contracting party breaks his contract, damages can be given for the disappointment, the distress, the upset and frustration caused by the breach. I know that it is difficult to assess in terms of money, but it is no more difficult than the assessment which the courts have to make every day in personal injury cases for loss of amenities. Take the present case. Mr Jarvis has only a fortnight's holiday in the year. He books it far ahead, and looks forward to it all the time. He ought to be compensated for the loss of it.

A sum of £125 was awarded.

The above reason must be compared with the reasoning in:

Hayes v *Dodds*
(1988) 138 NLJ 259

The defendant solicitors acted for the plaintiffs in the purchase of premises for a motor repair business. Before the plaintiffs signed the contract of sale the defendants assured them that the property had the benefit of a right of way giving access to the rear of the property but in fact there was no such right of way, as the plaintiffs discovered after the purchase, and without it the plaintiffs were unable to run their business. They brought an action for damages against the defendants for their negligent advice. Hirst J awarded the plaintiffs £105,748 damages which included an amount of £3,000 for anguish and vexation. The defendants appealed against the award of damages, including the award for anguish and vexation.

STAUGHTON LJ: I am not convinced that it is enough to ask whether mental distress was reasonably foreseeable as a consequence or even whether it should reasonably have been contemplated as not unlikely to result from a breach of contract. It seems to me that damages for mental distress in contract are, as a matter of policy, limited to certain classes of case. . . .

But it should not, in my judgment, include any case where the object of the contract was not comfort or pleasure or the relief of discomfort, but simply carrying on a commercial activity with a view to profit. So I would disallow the item of damages for anguish and vexation.

The judge talks of 'certain classes of case'. It would appear that in commercial contracts damages for non-pecuniary losses cannot be claimed for a breach of contract.

Self check questions
1.   What is the general principle for claiming damages for non-pecuniary loss arising from a breach of contract?
2.   Is any exception of general application?

Answers
1.   The general principle is that such non-pecuniary losses cannot be claimed by way of damages.
2.   Any exception to the above general principle, is limited to certain classes of contracts. It would appear given *Hayes* v *Dodds*, that for breach of commercial contracts non-pecuniary losses cannot be claimed.

4 Damages on behalf of another

Here we are talking about a situation where a contract has been breached which is for the benefit of a third party; for example, A enters into a contract with B whereby B will pay C £50 provided A performs a certain act. A performs the required act.

The general principle of English law is that C has no cause of action as he is not a party to the agreement: privity of contract (see *Tweddle* v *Atkinson* (1861) in Chapter 7).

The only person who can seek a remedy is A but the question then arises whether he can only recover for his own loss or that of C as well. The question was discussed in:

Jackson v *Horizon Holidays Ltd*
[1975] 3 All ER 92, CA

The plaintiff booked a holiday for himself and his family (NB the other members of the family were not parties to the contract). The accommodation and facilities provided were not in accordance with the contract. The plaintiff claimed damages not only for himself but also for his wife and two children.

Held: Damages of £1,100 should be awarded of which £500 was for distress and suffering. However, the decision was based on two different sets of reasoning. James LJ allowed the claim on the basis of the plaintiff's loss only. The plaintiff could not recover for his wife and children as well but only on the basis that the defendants had failed to provide the family holiday contracted for.

Lord Denning MR stated that £500 for distress was an excessive amount for the plaintiff alone to be able to claim in his own right. The amount was allowed on the basis that as the contract was one for the benefit of third parties the plaintiff should be allowed to make a claim for the loss of the third parties (in this case the wife and children) as well.

Lord Denning, in his judgment, was attempting to lay down a general principle to the effect that where a contract was made for the benefit of a third party then their loss could be claimed by the innocent party to the contract in breach. The House of Lords have, however, severely limited the application of this principle.

Woodar Investment Development Ltd v *Wimpey Construction UK Ltd*
[1980] 1 All ER 571

The main issue in this case was whether the purchasers had wrongfully repudiated the contract. The House of Lords held there was no wrongful repudiation but it then went on to discuss the measure of damages. The reason for the discussion was that £150,000 of the purchase price was to be paid not to the vendors but to a third party Transworld Trade Ltd, who was not a party to the contract.

LORD WILBERFORCE: ... The second issue in this appeal is one of damages. Both courts below have allowed Woodar to recover substantial damages in respect of condition 1 under which £150,000 was payable by Wimpey to Transworld Trade Ltd on completion. On the view which it takes of the repudiation issue, this question does not require decision, but in view of the unsatisfactory state in which the law would be if the Court of Appeal's decision were to stand I must add three observations.... The majority of the Court of Appeal followed in the case of Goff LJ with expressed reluctance, its previous decision in *Jackson v Horizon Holidays Ltd*. I am not prepared to dissent from the actual decision in that case. It may be supported either as a broad decision on the measure of damages (per James LJ) or possibly as an example of a type of contract, examples of which are persons contracting for family holidays, ordering meals in restaurants for a party, hiring a taxi for a group, calling for special treatment, there are many situations of daily life which do not fit neatly into conceptual analysis, but which require some flexibility in the law of contract. *Jackson's* case may well be one.

Lord Wilberforce expressly disapproved of Lord Denning's reasoning in *Jackson v Horizon Holidays Ltd* and it is therefore the case that that case is limited to a limited class of contracts.

Self check questions
1.   What is the general principle relating to the rights of a third party in a contractual situation.
2.   Is there a difference of reasoning from the judgments in *Jackson v Horizon Holidays*?
3.   Is the decision in *Jackson v Horizon Holidays* of general application?

Answers
1.   The general principle is that of privity of contract; this is as third party has no rights in his own capacity
2.   James LJ based his reasoning on the fact that the plaintiff could only recover loss in his own capacity and for loss suffered by himself. Lord Denning allowed the plaintiff to claim damages for his family as well on the basis that the contract was for the benefit of third parties.
3.   The principle from *Jackson v Horizon Holidays* is applicable to a limited class of contracts; for example family holidays and meals in restaurants.

5   Mitigation

The innocent party must take all reasonable steps to mitigate his loss. The law is therefore imposing an obligation upon the plaintiff to reduce his losses; failure to do so does not mean he incurs any liability but it means that the loss which is attributable to his mitigation is not recoverable. It must be emphasised that the plaintiff need only do what is reasonable in the circumstances. The operation of this principle is illustrated by:

Payzu Ltd v *Saunders*
[1918-19] All ER Rep 219

The defendant had agreed to sell the plaintiffs a quantity of silk on terms that permitted payment a month after delivery, but after some delays in payment she unjustifiably refused to make any further deliveries except for cash. The plaintiffs accepted this repudiation of the contract. The market price had risen considerably, and the plaintiffs were in fact unable to obtain the silk elsewhere. They claimed the difference between the contract price and the market price on the day they accepted the defendant's repudiation.

BANKES LJ: . . . It is plain that the question what is reasonable for a person to do in mitigation of his damages cannot be a question of law, but must be one of fact in the circumstances of each particular case. There may be cases where as matter of fact it would be unreasonable to expect a plaintiff in view of the treatment he has received from the defendant to consider an offer made. If he had been rendering personal services and had been dismissed after being accused in presence of others of being a thief, and if after that his employer had offered to take him back into his service, most persons would think he would be justified in refusing the offer, and that it would be unreasonable to ask him in this way to mitigate the damages in an action of wrongful dismissal. But that is not to state a principle of law, but a conclusion of fact to be arrived at on a consideration of all the circumstances of the case. Counsel for the plaintiffs complained that the defendant had treated her clients so badly that it would be unreasonable to expect them to listen to any proposition that she might make. I do not agree. In my opinion each party to the contract was ready to accuse the other of conduct unworthy of a high commercial reputation, and there was nothing to justify the plaintiffs in refusing to consider the defendant's offer. I think the learned judge came to the right conclusion on the facts, and that the appeal must be dismissed.

Problem

Parties to Contract	Aris books a reception at the Deer Park Hotel for 1,000 guests (third party) for his daughter's (Florence) wedding.
Terms of Contract	The hotel tells Aris that all the guests will be seated in the main dining room which enables all guests to see the top table.
Third Party	On arrival at the reception Zebedee, the groom, finds that his relatives in fact cannot see the top table because a large pillar is in the way, he expresses his disappointment to Aris (Non-pecuniary loss).

Third Parties	During the evening the majority of the guest suffer from food poisoning which is the result of the Hotel failing to cook properly the chicken served at the reception.
Physical Damages	Florence is so ill that she is unable to go on her honeymoon to Bermuda the next day.
Remoteness of Damage	Discuss the potential liability of the Deer Park Hotel.

Answer

The problem concerns the potential liability of the Deer Park Hotel for the various breaches of contract which have occurred. The appropriate remedy is that of damages and the major issues relate to the claims of Aris, Zebedee, the guests and Florence respectively.

The first issue to be discussed is that of privity of contract. The general principle of English law is that only the parties to a contract have a cause of action (see *Tweddle* v *Atkinson*). There are, however, situations where a party to the contract, in this case Aris, will be able to claim damages on behalf of another. The authority for this principle is *Jackson* v *Horizon Holidays*. It must be noted that the principle is not a general application despite the judgment of Lord Denning, but only applies to a limited class of contracts. Examples of such contracts were given in the decision of *Woodar* v *Wimpey* and it can be argued that the contract in our case comes within the principle.

Aris clearly has a claim for the breach relating to the term that all the guests could see the top table; however the question is whether or not he can claim for loss suffered by Zebedee. Previously it was that non-pecuniary loss, in our case the disappointment of Zebedee, could not be claimed as result of a breach of contract. However, if such loss could be thought to have been within the reasonable contemplation of the parties at the time the contract was made then it is recoverable. Authority for this principle is *Jarvis* v *Swans Tours* where, again, the nature of the subject-matter of the contract was crucial. It would appear that non-pecuniary loss can be claimed in consumer-type contracts, although not in commercial ones (*Hayes* v *Dodds*). Applying these criteria it would appear that Aris would be able to claim such loss on behalf of Zebedee and this is further supported by the decision in *Jackson* v *Horizon Holidays*.

The principle of reasonable contemplation has been mentioned above and this is relevant for damages suffered as a result of the food poisoning. The function of the concept of reasonable contemplation is to limit damages to those within the knowledge possessed by the parties. The law has divided the consequences of breach into usual and non-usual (*Hadley* v *Baxendale*) and whilst actual knowledge is needed for the latter, knowledge will be imputed for the former) *Victoria Laundry* v *Newman*. The question is whether or not by serving chicken properly cooked, guests would get food poisoning. Such consequences are clearly usual consequences of such a breach of contract and therefore the hotel will be liable for such loss.

A more difficult question relates to Florence being unable to go on her honeymoon. It can be argued that such loss could be imputed because the hotel should have been aware that the bride would be going on a honeymoon. It can be argued, however, that such loss could fall within the non-usual consequences category and therefore actual knowledge by the hotel was required in order to make it liable. An interesting argument can be used to support the claim for the damages from the judgment of Lord Denning in *Parsons* v *Uttley Ingham*. Lord Denning stated that in physical damage cases the defendant should be liable for any loss or expense which was a slight possibility. It could be argued that this distinction is unnecessary here because such loss is more than a slight possibility and would satisfy the contractual test of reasonable contemplation.

15 NEGLIGENCE

1 Introduction

If a person acts carelessly and as a result of that carelessness another is injured or suffers loss it may be that that person is negligent in the law of tort. Not all careless acts will allow the wronged person to sue the wrongdoer for negligence. Only those acts which satisfy the criteria below will give rise to liability.

The criteria to be satisfied are:

(a) The existence of a duty to take care which was owed by the wrongdoer to the victim.
(b) Breach of this duty of care.
(c) Resulting damage to the victim.

Each of these criteria merits further examination.

2 Duty of care

The plaintiff (victim) must show that the defendant (wrongdoer) owed him a duty of care in law. Whether such a duty of care exists in any individual case is a question of law which the judge will decide by applying the test established by the House of Lords in *Donoghue* v *Stevenson* [1932] AC 562. This test centres around the *foresight of a reasonable man* and has developed from Lord Atkin's 'neighbour test' which he formulated in the case:

> You must take reasonable care to avoid acts or omissions which you can reasonably foresee would be likely to injure your neighbour. Who, then, in law is my neighbour? The answer seems to be — persons who are so closely and directly affected by my act that I ought reasonably to have them in contemplation as being so affected when I am directing my mind to the acts or omissions which are called in question.

The test is an *objective* one. This means that the existence of a duty of care will be established if a reasonable man placed in the defendant's position would have reasonably foreseen that his carelessness would have caused the plaintiff's loss or damage.

It is important in this context for the plaintiff to show that the duty was owed to him. See, for example:

McLoughlin v *O'Brian*
[1982] 2 All ER 298

The plaintiff's husband and three children were involved in a road accident caused by the negligence of the defendants. One of the plaintiff's children was killed and her husband and other two children were severely injured. At the time of the accident the plaintiff was at home two miles away. She was told of the accident by a motorist who had been at the scene of the accident and she was taken to hospital where she saw the injured members of her family and the extent of their injuries and shock and heard that her daughter had been killed. As a result of hearing and seeing the results of the accident the plaintiff suffered severe and persisting nervous shock. The plaintiff claimed damages against the defendants for the nervous shock, distress and injury to her health caused by the defendants' negligence. The judge dismissed her claim on the ground that her injury was not reasonably foreseeable. On appeal, the Court of Appeal held that the plaintiff was not entitled to claim against the defendants either because as a matter of policy a duty of care was not to be imposed on a negligent defendant beyond that owed to persons in close proximity, both in time and place, to an accident, even though the injuries received by the plaintiff might be reasonably foreseeable as being a consequence of the defendant's negligence, or because the duty of care owed by a driver of a motor vehicle was limited to persons on or near the road. The plaintiff appealed to the House of Lords.

Held: The test of liability for damages for nervous shock was reasonable foreseeability of the plaintiff being injured by nervous shock as a result of the defendant's negligence. Applying that test, the plaintiff was entitled to recover damages from the defendants because even though the plaintif was not at or near the scene of the accident at the time or shortly afterwards the nervous shock suffered by her was a reasonably foreseeable consequence of the defendant's negligence.

3   Breach of duty

Once it has been established that a duty of care is owed to the plaintiff by the defendant then it is a question of fact whether or not the defendant is in breach of that duty of care.

Breach of the duty of care will have occurred if the defendant is shown to have acted in an *unreasonable* manner in the circumstances. This raises the issue of what is a reasonable manner. What is reasonable will vary and will depend on a number of factors.

3.1   Social importance of defendant's action
In an emergency it may be reasonable to take less care because speedy action is required. In *Watt* v *Hertfordshire County Council* (1954) heavy lifting gear which

was being transported on a lorry not designed to carry it, injured a fireman. The lorry was the only one available and the lifting gear was needed to free a woman in danger of losing her life. The court held that the defendants had acted reasonably in the circumstances and were not liable to the fireman.

3.2   Magnitude of possible injury

Conversely greater care will be expected where really serious harm may be caused. This is particularly true in circumstances where the plaintiff possesses certain characteristics which make him more susceptible to harm.

In *Paris v Stepney Borough Council* [1951] AC 367 a fitter was employed as a welder. He had only one good eye and the employer failed to provide safety goggles for his use. The plaintiff lost the sight in his good eye following damage from a fragment of hot metal. The court decided that his employer had acted unreasonably and was therefore negligent in not providing safety goggles.

3.3   Magnitude of risk

It must be remembered that the defendant is *not* expected to take precautions against remote risks. So in *Bolton v Stone* [1951] AC 850, where the plaintiff was struck and injured by a cricket ball and it could be demonstrated that a cricket ball had only been hit out of the ground six times in 30 years, the defendants were not liable.

3.4   Res ipsa loquitur

Res ipsa loquitur means the thing or the facts speak for themselves. This rule will be argued by the plaintiff where he believes that the only explanation for the incident occurring is the defendant's negligence.

Where *res ipsa loquitur* is applied the burden of proof will move from the plaintiff to the defendant. So instead of the plaintiff having the responsibility of proving negligence the court will infer this and it becomes the defendant's responsibility to show that he was *not* negligent.

Pearson v North Western Gas Board
[1968] 2 All ER 669

The plaintiff and her husband were injured, and their home was destroyed, by an explosion of gas on January 1, 1963. The plaintiff's husband died as a result of his injuries. The explosion was of gas which had escaped from the 3 inch metal gas main and had accumulated under the floorboards of the house. On the evidence the cause of the escape of gas was fracture of the gas main owing to the movement of earth caused by severe frost. The pipes were at a depth of 2 feet 9 inches beneath the flagstones of the public footway; the main had been laid in 1878; the metal was in good condition and the expectation of life of such a pipe was 120 years. The expert evidence for the defendants, the gas board, who supplied gas through the main, though not to the plaintiff's house, was that no reasonable steps were open to safeguard the public from the consequences of fractured gas mains. In an action by the widow for damages under the Fatal Accidents Act 1846 to 1959 and the Law Reform (Miscellaneous Provisions) Act 1934 and in her own right:

Held: Even if the doctrine of res ipsa loquitur *applied so as to establish a prima facie case of negligence against the defendants, the expert evidence rebutted it, and accordingly negligence was not proved and the action failed.*

4 Resulting damage to the plaintiff

The plaintiff has to show that the loss or damage he has suffered was *caused* by the defendant's breach of duty and that the nature of the loss or damage suffered was foreseeable.

4.1 Causation in fact

The plaintiff must show that the defendant's conduct was the cause of the damage, i.e., by showing that but for the defendant's negligence the damage would not have occurred.

British Road Services Ltd v *Arthur V. Crutchley & Co. Ltd*
[1967] 2 All ER 785

A night-watchman negligently failed to make a fourth inspection tour. Whisky was stolen after the third inspection tour but before the fourth was due. British Road Services accused the defendants of negligence. The court held that the defendants' negligence had not caused the damages. Even had the night-watchman made the fourth inspection the whisky would still have been stolen.

Some situations will be more complex than this and involve overlapping and concurrent causes. In these circumstances the 'but for' test will not work.

Hill v *New River Co.*
(1868) 18 LT 355

Horses were frightened by a water spout which the defendants had negligently allowed to occur. As a consequence the horses fell into an unfenced cutting. The court held that the water spout and lack of fence caused the resulting damage and that persons responsible for both were liable.

4.2 Causation in law

The 'but for' test eliminates certain factors as causes of the plaintiff's damage. It does not identify the causes on which legal liability rests. This is known as the test of remoteness. If the plaintiff's loss or damage is too remote a consequence of the defendant's negligence then the defendant will not be liable. The test for remoteness of damage was established by the Privy Council in:

The Wagon Mound
[1961] 1 All ER 404

The defendants were charterers of the ship, Wagon Mound. *The carelessness of their servants who were ship engineers caused a quantity of furnace oil to spill into*

Sydney harbour. The oil spread to a wharf owned by the plaintiffs and on which the plaintiffs were carrying out welding operations. After taking advice that the oil was not ignitable, the plaintiffs' continued to carry on these operations. The oil was ignited by the fall of hot metal from the wharf and extensive damage by fire occurred to the plaintiffs' wharf. The trial judge found that the defendants were in breach of duty to the plaintiffs since damage to the wharf through the fouling of its slipways by oil was foreseeable and had actually occurred.

Damage by fire was, however, unforeseeable, because furnace oil has a high ignition point, and it was unforeseeable that it would ignite on water.

The presence of the oil was nevertheless found to be the cause of the fire damage.

Held: The defendants were not liable for the damage by fire since it was not a foreseeable consequence of their breach of duty to the plaintiffs.

The decision provides that damages are recoverable for all reasonably foreseeable consequences of a defendant's breach of duty, but not for injury which is not a reasonably foreseeable consequence.

4.3   The concept of foreseeability

Foreseeability is a more flexible notion than causation. The question to be asked now is: Was the plaintiff's damage a foreseeable consequence of the defendant's act?

In deciding whether there has been a breach of duty the court does not simply ask whether the defendant's conduct created a foreseeable risk to the plaintiff. The degree of risk must be sufficiently great that the defendant should have taken steps to prevent its occurrence, bearing in mind also that the defendant's conduct may have social value, or that it may be very difficult to eliminate the risk.

Two different tests of foreseeability are to be applied, one in deciding the issue of breach, and the other the issue of remoteness of damage. The plaintiff must, in order to raise the question of remoteness at all, establish a breach of a duty of care owed to himself by the defendant.

4.4   Eggshell-skull cases

The rule has always been, you must take your victim as you find him. If you injure a person with physical infirmities you are still responsible for all the damage caused. Although the extent of the damage was unforeseeable, it is not too remote.

Smith v *Leech Brain & Co. Ltd*
[1961] 3 All ER 1159

Here the Court of Appeal allowed the deceased's estate to recover damages from the defendants for his death from cancer of the lip. The lip had been in a pre-malignant condition and cancer broke out when the deceased received a burn from molten metal owing to the defendant's negligence. In these circumstances the court held the defendants liable.   –

5 Contributory negligence

This deals with the situation where the plaintiff has suffered damage through the negligence of the defendant, but has contributed to his damage through his own negligence.

This is a fairly recent development as a result of the Law Reform (Contributory Negligence) Act 1945. Prior to this Act only one person could be considered at fault, either the plaintiff or defendant. Where the defendant established contributory negligence it was a complete defence to the plaintiff's action.

Davies v *Mann*
(1842) 10 M & W 546

A donkey was tethered in the middle of the road. A man came along the road in a pony and trap and hit the donkey. Both parties were negligent. However, it was decided that the person who was responsible was the one who could have avoided the accident last.

5.1 *Present state of the law*

Law Reform (Contributory Negligence) Act 1945, section 1(1)

Where any person suffers damage as the result partly of his own fault and partly of the fault of any other person or persons a claim in respect of that damage shall not be defeated by reason of the fault of the person suffering the damage but the damages recoverable in respect thereof shall be reduced to such extent as the court thinks just and equitable having regard to the claimant's share in the responsibility for the damage.

In order that the power of apportionment be exercised in his favour the defendant must show both that the plaintiff was at fault and that his fault contributed to his damage.

Davies v *Swan Motor Co. (Swansea) Ltd*
[1949] 1 All ER 620

P was injured while riding on the back of a dust lorry in an accident caused by the combined negligence of the driver of the lorry and the driver of a bus. Liability was apportioned among the two defendants, the employers of the bus driver and the lorry driver, and it was found that the plaintiff's own negligence contributed to his injury.

5.2 *Basis of apportionment*
A plaintiff's damages will be reduced to such extent as the court thinks just and equitable having regard to the plaintiff's share in the responsibility for the damage. Two tests must be applied. The court must assess: ‾

(a) The causative potency of the acts of the plaintiff and defendant.

(b) The degree of blameworthiness to be attached to these acts — the degree of departure from the requisite standard of care rather than degree of moral blameworthiness.

The mathematics of apportionment are by no means difficult, award reductions being 1/5, 1/3, 1/2 and 3/4. It is unusual for a court to find a plaintiff less than 10% responsible for his damage, or more than 90%.

Although there is no rule that a reduction of less than 10% should be ignored, the courts will apply the *de minimis* principle (*Capps* v *Miller* [1989] 1 WLR 839).

It is of course logically impossible to make the plaintiff 100% contributorily negligent and this concept is banned by the 1945 Act. In this circumstance the court would be compelled to find that the defendant was not negligent and that the plaintiff was the cause of his own injury or loss.

5.3 The standard of care in particular cases of contributory negligence

5.3.1 Workmen In cases of industrial injuries it is important to take into account the responsibilities of the employer under the health and safety legislation. If these were ignored and the principles of contributory negligence applied every time an employee was careless so as to contribute to his own injury, much of the policy behind the health and safety legislation would be defeated.

Staveley Iron & Chemical Co. Ltd v *Jones*
[1956] 1 All ER 403

The respondent was injured as a result of the negligence of the appellant's employee. The appellants argued that the respondent contributed to his own injury when assisting the appellant's employee, a crane driver, to secure a load. The load was improperly secured but the method of loading meant it was difficult for the respondent to be certain the load was properly centred before lifting.

The House of Lords decided that the crane was negligently handled by the crane driver and contributory negligence was not proved against the respondent because it was not shown that his conduct fell below the standard required from a reasonably careful workman from asssisting in such an operation and therefore the respondent was entitled to damages in full against the appellant company.

5.3.2 Children A lower standard of care is expected of children. Thus an act which would mean that an adult had contributed to his own injury may not do so in the case of a child.

5.3.3 The agony of the moment Where the plaintiff has been put into a position of peril by the defendant's negligence, compelling him to choose one of two or more risky alternatives he is not guilty of contributory negligence if his choice turns out to be a mistaken one.

Jones v *Boyce*
(1816) 1 Stark 493

The plaintiff was a passenger in a coach owned and driven by the defendant. He reasonably believed that the coach was about to overturn because of the defendant's negligent driving. The plaintiff jumped from the coach injuring his leg. It was held that the plaintiff did not contribute to his own injury. His actions in the circumstances were reasonable.

6   Consent

A person who voluntarily consents to risk of harm cannot later bring an action to recover damages for any harm actually suffered. This is known by the maxim '*volenti non fit injuria*' (to the willing no injury can be done). Where the '*volenti*' maxim applies the plaintiff will in effect have consented to his own injury.

Two criteria need to be satisfied before '*volenti*' can be argued by the defendant as a defence to the plaintiff's action:

(a)   The plaintiff's consent must be asserted by some positive act, i.e., it must amount to more than mere acquiescence. Consent may be express or implied from conduct by the plaintiff.

Smith v *Charles Baker and Sons*
[1891] AC 325

A workman working under an overhead crane was injured by a falling stone. Although this method of working was dangerous he had not objected.
It was held that his silence was evidence of mere acquiescence not consent.

(b)   The plaintiff's consent must be freely given.

Bowater v *Rowley Regis Corporation*
[1944] KB 476

A carter objected to taking out a horse which he considered to be dangerous. He was ordered to use the horse by his employers, the defendants. He complied and was injured by the horse.
It was held that he had not freely consented to the risk.

Self check questions
1.   Explain the 'neighbour test' formulated in *Donoghue* v *Stevenson*.
2.   What are the criteria which the plaintiff must establish for a successful action in negligence?
3.   What does '*res ipsa loquitur*' mean?
4.   What effect does a successful plea of contributory negligence have in an action for negligence?
5.   What is the meaning of the maxim '*volenti non fit injuria*'?

Answers

1.   The 'neighbour test' requires the defendant to take reasonable care to avoid acts or omissions which he could reasonably forsee would be likely to injure his neighbour.

2.   The criteria to be satisfied are:

   (a)   The existence of a duty to take care which was owed by the wrongdoer to the victim.

   (b)   Breach of this duty of care.

   (c)   Resulting damage to the victim.

3.   The facts speak for themselves.

4.   A successful plea of contributory negligence has the effect of reducing the damages recoverable by the plaintiff to an extent that the court thinks just and equitable having regard to the plaintiff's share of the responsibility for the damage.

5.   To the willing no injury can be done.

16 PROFESSIONAL NEGLIGENCE

1 Introduction

In addition to imposing liability for negligent actions the law will impose liability for negligent misstatements. Damage or loss in the context of negligent misstatements will consist of pure economic loss and not physical injury to the plaintiff as with actions. The law relating to negligent misstatment is particularly important to people whose work involves giving professional business advice.

2 Negligent misstatements

The rules of negligent misstatement owe their existence to Denning LJ's dissenting judgment in *Candler* v *Crane Christmas & Co.* [1951] 2 KB 164. The plaintiffs wished to invest in a company and relied on information prepared by the company's accountants to make his decision. The information was negligently prepared, inasmuch as the accountants failed to check on the ownership of certain assets which appeared in the company's balance sheet. Shortly after the plaintiffs invested the company was wound up because it was insolvent. The majority of the Court of Appeal held that the company's accountants *did not* owe the plaintiffs a duty of care and so were not liable even if negligence could be proved. Denning LJ disagreed and expressed the view that:

> ... accountants owe a duty of care not only to their own clients, but also to those whom they know will rely on their accounts in the transactions for which those accounts are prepared.

The House of Lords in the later decision of *Hedley Byrne & Co. Ltd* v *Heller and Partners Ltd* [1964] AC 465 overruled the majority Court of Appeal decision in

Candler v *Crane Christmas & Co.*, preferring instead to base their decision on the dissenting judgment of Lord Denning. The decision in *Hedley Byrne* established that a duty of care could, in certain circumstances, be owed in relation to negligent misstatements.

Hedley Byrne & Co. Ltd v Heller and Partners Ltd
[1963] 2 All ER 575

A bank inquired by telephone of the respondent merchant bankers concerning the financial position of a customer for whom the respondents were bankers. The bank said that they wanted to know in confidence and without responsibility on the part of the respondents, the respectability and standing of E Ltd and whether E Ltd would be good for an advertising contract for £8,000 to £9,000. Some months later the bank wrote to the respondents asking in confidence the respondents' opinion of the respectability and standing of E Ltd by stating whether the respondents considered E Ltd trustworthy, in the way of business, to the extent of £100,000 per annum. The respondents' replies to the effect that E Ltd was respectably constituted and considered good for its normal business engagements were communicated to the bank's customers, the appellants. Relying on these replies the appellants, who were advertising agents, placed orders for advertising time and space for E Ltd on which orders the appellants assumed personal responsibility for payment to the television and newspaper companies concerned. E Ltd went into liquidation and the appellants lost over £17,000 on the advertising contracts. The appellants sued the respondents for the amount of the loss, alleging that the respondents' replies to the bank's inquiries were given negligently, in the sense of misjudgment, by making a statement which gave a false impression as to E Ltd's credit. Negligence was found at the trial and contested on appeal. The Court of Appeal affirmed the trial judge's holding that the defendants were not liable because they owed no duty of care, but without deciding whether there had or had not been negligence.

An appeal was made to the House of Lords.

Held: Although in the present case, but for the respondents' disclaimer, the circumstances might have given rise to a duty of care on their part, yet their disclaimer of responsibility for their replies on the occasion of the first inquiry was adequate to exclude the assumption by them of a legal duty of care, with the consequence that they were not liable in negligence.

The House of Lords went on to consider the position of a defendant where no such disclaimer was issued:

LORD MORRIS OF BORTH-Y-GEST: My lords, it seems to me that if A assumes a responsibility to B to tender him deliberate advice there could be a liability if the advice is negligently given. I say 'could be' because the ordinary courtesies and exchanges of life would become impossible if it were sought to attach legal obligation to every kindly and friendly act. But the principle of the matter would not appear to be in doubt. If A employs B (who might, for example, be a professional man such as an accountant or a solicitor or a doctor) for reward to give advice, and if the advice is negligently given, there could be a liability in B to pay damages. The fact that the advice is given in words would not, in my view, prevent liability from arising. . . . If someone who was not a customer of a bank made a formal approach to the bank with a definite request that the bank would give him deliberate advice as to certain financial matters of a nature with which the bank ordinarily dealt the bank would be under no obligation to accede to the request: if however they undertook, though gratuitously, to give deliberate advice (I exclude what I might call casual and perfunctory conversations) they would be under a duty to exercise reasonable care in giving it. They would be liable if they were negligent although, there being no consideration, no enforceable contractual relationship was created. . . .

It is said, however, that where careless (but not fraudulent) misstatements are in question there can be no liability in the maker of them unless there is either some contractual or fiduciary relationship with a person adversely affected by the making of them or unless through the making of them something is created or circulated or some situation is created which is dangerous to life, limb or property. In logic I can see no essential reason for distinguishing injury which is caused by a reliance on the safety of the staging to a ship, or by a reliance on the safety for use of the contents of a bottle of hair wash or a bottle of some consumable liquid. It seems to me, therefore, that if A claims that he has suffered injury or loss as a result of acting upon some misstatement made by B who is not in any contractual or fiduciary relationship with him the inquiry that is first raised is whether B owed any duty to A: if he did the further inquiry is raised as to the nature of the duty. There may be circumstances under which the only duty owed by B to A is the duty not only of being honest but also a duty of taking reasonable care. The issue in the present case is whether the bank owed any duty to Hedleys and if so what the duty was.

. . . it is submitted that in the present case the bank knew that some existing (though to them by name unknown) person was going to place reliance on what they said and that accordingly they owed a duty of care to such person. . . .

Independently of contract there may be circumstances where information is given or where advice is given which establish a relationship which creates a duty not only to be honest but also to be careful. . . .

The inquiry in the present case, and in similar cases, becomes therefore an inquiry as to whether there was a relationship between the parties which created a duty and if so whether such duty included a duty of care. . . .

My lords, I consider that it follows and that it should now be regarded as settled that if someone possessed of a special skill undertakes, quite irrespective of contract, to apply that skill for the assistance of another person who relies on such skill, a duty of care will arise. The fact that the service is to be given by means of, or by the instrumentality of, words can make no difference. Furthermore if, in a sphere in which a person is so placed that others could reasonably rely on his judgment or his skill or on his ability to make careful inquiry, a person takes it on himself to give information or advice to, or allows his information or advice to be passed on to, another person who, as he knows or should know, will place reliance on it, then a duty of care will arise.

Hedley Byrne clearly establishes that a duty of care can exist where a *special relationship* exists between the parties. This goes beyond mere foreseeability of harm. What amounts to a special relationship for the purpose of this rule requires further examination.

3   Relationship between the parties

The House of Lords in *Hedley Byrne & Co. Ltd* v *Heller and Partners Ltd* (1963) made it clear that the test of foresight formulated by Lord Atkin in *Donoghue* v *Stevenson* (1932) (see Chapter 15) and which is applied to negligent actions causing physical injury was not appropriate to actions for negligent misstatements. Instead their Lordships decided that the plaintiff would have to show a 'special relationship' with the defendant.

3.1   Special relationship

The meaning of the term 'special relationship' has been examined closely in recent cases, particularly those relating to the liability of auditors for negligent misstatements. The leading case is:

Caparo Industries plc v *Dickman*
[1990] 2 AC 605

The respondents owned shares in a public company, F plc, whose accounts for the year ended 31 March 1984 showed profits far short of the predicted figure which resulted in a dramatic drop in the quoted share price. After receipt of the audited accounts for the year ended 31 March 1984 the respondents purchased more shares in F plc and later that year made a successful takeover bid for the company. Following the takeover, the respondents brought an action against the auditors of the company, alleging that the accounts of F plc were inaccurate and misleading in that they showed a pre-tax profit of some £1.2 million for the year ended 31 March 1984 when in fact there had been a loss of over £400,000, that the auditors had been negligent in auditing the accounts, that the respondents had purchased further shares and made their takeover bid in reliance on the audited accounts, and the auditors owed them a duty of care either as potential bidders for F plc because they ought to have foreseen that the 1984 results made F plc vulnerable to a takeover bid or as an existing shareholder of F plc interested in buying more shares. On the trial of a preliminary issue whether the auditors owed a duty of care to the respondents, the judge held that the auditors did not. The respondents appealed to the Court of Appeal, which allowed their appeal in part on the ground that the auditors owed the respondents a duty of care as shareholders but not as potential investors. The auditors appealed to the House of Lords and the respondents cross-appealed against the Court of Appeal's decision that they could not claim as potential investors.
Held: (1)   The three criteria for the imposition of a duty of care were foreseeability of damage, proximity of relationship and the reasonableness or otherwise of imposing a duty. In determining whether there was a relationship of proximity between the parties the court, guided by situations in which the existence, scope and limits of a duty of care had previously been held to exist rather than by a

single general principle, would determine whether the particular damage suffered was the kind of damage which the defendant was under a duty to prevent and whether there were circumstances from which the court could pragmatically conclude that a duty of care existed.

(2) Where a statement put into more or less general circulation might foreseeably be relied on by strangers for any one of a variety of purposes which the maker of the statement had no specific reason to anticipate there was no relationship of proximity between the maker of the statement and any person relying on it unless it was shown that the maker knew that his statement would be communicated to the person relying on it, either as an individual or as a member of an identifiable class, specifically in connection with a particular transaction or a transaction of a particular kind and that that person would be very likely to rely on it for the purpose of deciding whether to enter into the transaction.

(3) The auditor of a public company's accounts owed no duty of care to a member of the public at large who relied on the accounts to buy shares in the company because the court would not deduce a relationship of proximity between the auditor and a member of the public when to do so would give rise to unlimited liability on the part of the auditor. Furthermore, an auditor owed no duty of care to an individual shareholder in the company who wished to buy more shares in the company, since an individual shareholder was in no better position than a member of the public at large and the auditor's statutory duty to prepare accounts was owed to the body of shareholders as a whole, the purpose for which accounts were prepared and audited being to enable the shareholders as a body to exercise informed control of the company and not to enable individual shareholders to buy shares with a view to profit. It followed that the auditors did not owe a duty of care to the respondents either as shareholders or as potential investors in the company.

LORD BRIDGE OF HARWICH: What emerges [from cases reviewed by his Lordship] is that, in addition to the foreseeability of damage, necessary ingredients in any situation giving rise to a duty of care are that there should exist between the party owing the duty and the party to whom it is owed a relationship characterised by the law as one of 'proximity' or 'neighbourhood' and that the situation should be one in which the court considers it fair, just and reasonable that the law should impose a duty of a given scope upon the one party for the benefit of the other. But it is implicit in the passages referred to that the concepts of proximity and fairness embodied in these additional ingredients are not susceptible of any such precise definition as would be necessary to give them utility as practical tests, but amount in effect to little more than convenient labels to attach to the features of different specific situations which, on a detailed examination of all the circumstances, the law recognises pragmatically as giving rise to a duty of care of a given scope. Whilst recognising, of course, the importance of the underlying general principles common to the whole field of negligence, I think the law has now moved in the direction of attaching greater sigificance to the more traditional categorisation of distinct and recognisable situations as guides to the existence, the scope and the limits of the varied duties of care which the law imposes. . . .

In advising the client who employs him the professional man owes a duty to exercise that standard of skill and care appropriate to his professional status and will be liable both in contract and in tort for all losses which his client may suffer by reason of any breach of that duty.

Lord Bridge refuses to attempt to create an underlying principle which will govern the circumstances in which a special relationship will exist. Instead he makes it clear that the courts should adopt a pragmatic approach and examine each set of circumstances as they occur. At most the law will acknowledge categories of distinct and recognisable situations which will normally give rise to a special relationship. He goes on to point out that:

The salient feature of all these cases is that the defendant giving advice or information was fully aware of the nature of the transaction which the plaitiff has in contemplation, knew that the advice or information would be communicated to him directly or indirectly and knew that it was very likely that the plaintiff would rely on that advice or information in deciding whether or not to engage in the transaction in contemplation. In these circumstances the defendant could clearly be expected, subject always to the effect of any disclaimer of responsibility, specifically to anticipate that the plaintiff would rely on the advice or information given by the defendant for the very purpose for which he did in the event rely on it. So also the plaintiff, subject again to the effect of any disclaimer, would in that situation reasonably suppose that he was entitled to rely on the advice or information communicated to him for the very purpose for which he required it. The situation is entirely different where a statement is put into more or less general circulation and may foreseeably be relied on by strangers to the maker of the statement for any one of a variety of different purposes which the maker of the statement has no specific reason to anticipate. To hold the maker of the statement to be under a duty of care in respect of the accuracy of the statement to all and sundry for any purpose for which they may choose to rely on it is not only to subject him, in the classic words of Cardozo CJ, to 'liability in an indeterminate amount for an indeterminate time to an indeterminate class' (see *Ultramares Corporation* v *Touche* (1931) 174 NE 441 at p. 444); it is also to confer on the world at large a quite unwarranted entitlement to appropriate for their own purposes the benefit of the expert knowledge or professional expertise attributed to the maker of the statement. Hence, looking only at the circumstances of these decided cases where a duty of care in respect of negligent statements has been held to exist, I should expect to find that the 'limit or control mechanism ... imposed upon the liability of a wrongdoer towards those who have suffered economic damage in consequence of his negligence' [*Candlewood Navigation Corportion Ltd* v *Mitsui OSK Lines Ltd* [1986] AC 1 at p. 25] rested on the necessity to prove, in this category of the tort of negligence, as an essential ingredient of the 'proximity' between the plaintiff and the defendant, that the defendant knew that his statement would be communicated to the plaintiff, either as an individual or as a member of an identifiable class, specifically in connection with a particular transaction or transactions of a particular kind (e.g., in a prospectus inviting investment) and that the plaintiff would be very likely to rely on it for the purpose of deciding whether or not to enter upon that transaction or upon a transaction of that kind.

LORD OLIVER OF AYLMERTON: My Lords, the primary purpose of the statutory requirement that a company's accounts shall be audited annually is almost self-evident. The structure of the corporate trading entity, at least in the case of public companies whose shares are dealt with on an authorised stock exchange, involves the concept of a more or less widely distributed holding of shares rendering the personal involvement of each individual shareholder in the day-to-day management of the enterprise impracticable, with the result that management is necessarily separated from ownership. The management is confided to a board of directors which operates in a fiduciary capacity and is answerable to and removable by the shareholders who can act, if they act at all, only collectively and only through the medium of a general meeting.

Hence the legislative provisions requiring the board annually to give an account of its stewardship to a general meeting of the shareholders. This is the only occasion in each year upon which the general body of shareholders is given the opportunity to consider, to criticise and to comment upon the conduct by the board of the company's affairs, to vote upon the directors' recommendation as to dividends, to approve or disapprove the directors' remuneration and, if thought desirable, to remove and replace all or any of the directors. It is the auditors' function to ensure, so far as possible, that the financial information as to the company's affairs prepared by the directors accurately reflects the company's position in order, first, to protect the company itself from the consequences of undetected errors or, possibly wrongdoing (by, for instance, declaring dividends out of capital) and, secondly, to provide shareholders with reliable intelligence for the purpose of enabling them to scrutinise the conduct of the company's affairs and to exercise their collective powers to reward or control or remove those to whom that conduct has been confided. . . .

In my judgment, accordingly, the purpose for which the auditors' certificate is made and published is that of providing those entitled to receive the report with information to enable them to exercise in conjunction with those powers which their respective proprietary interests confer upon them and not for the purposes of individual speculation with a view to profit. The same considerations as limit the existence of a duty of care also, in my judgment, limit the scope of the duty and I agree with O'Connor LJ that the duty of care is one owed to the shareholders as a body and not to individual shareholders.

To widen the scope of the duty to include loss caused to an individual by reliance upon the accounts for a purpose for which they were not supplied and were not intended would be to extend it beyond the limits which are so far deducible from the decisions of this House.

Two different approaches to the issue of what constitutes a special relationship is evident from the judgments of Lords Bridge and Oliver.

Lord Bridge clearly focuses on the commercial nature of the transaction between the plaintiff and the defendant, arguing that in *Candler* v *Crane Christmas & Co.* the defendant knew that Mr Candler would rely on the accounts in making his investment decision and in *Hedley Byrne* the defendants knew the credit reference would be used by the plaintiff in deciding whether to advance credit to Easipower. It was clear in both these cases that the defendant was aware of the nature of the transaction contemplated by the plaintiff, the ultimate use to which the information would be put and that the plaintiff would act in reliance on the information. However, in circumstances where audit information is published in documents which are available to the public no duty of care to that wider public will arise because a special relationship between the defendant and the wider public cannot be established. Lord Bridge could see no difference between the plaintiff in this case and any other member of the investing public.

Lord Oliver's approach is based on the purpose of a company audit under the companies legislation. The legislation makes clear that a duty of care is owed to the shareholders as a body and not to individual shareholders. This relationship will give rise to a special relationship between the auditors and the general body of shareholders but not between the auditors and individual shareholders and more importantly not between the auditors and a member of the public at large. To have held otherwise would result in the auditor having potentially unlimited liability to anyone who relied on the audit for whatever purpose.

However, a special relationship may arise where the auditor *knew* that his statement would be communicated to a person relying on it for a particular purpose. Additionally the court in *Al Saudi Banque* v *Clarke Pixley* [1990] Ch 313 decided that no duty of care was owed by a company's auditors to banks which had made loans to the company using certain bills of exchange as security which subsequently turned out to be worthless. The auditors in that case were unaware of the bank's specific interest in the company although it was accepted that the company was reliant on bank finance generally and it was thus foreseeable that a bank would use audited accounts when deciding whether to advance finance. However, on the facts this was not sufficient to show a special relationship between the parties.

As can be seen from these cases the courts examine each set of facts on their merits. There is no guarantee that any particular professional relationship will always give rise to a special relationship for the purposes of this part of the law of negligence. However, a number of factors are identifiable as being necessary before the relationship is established. It must be shown that:

(a)   the plaintiff relied on the advice provided by the defendant; and

(b)   in the circumstances it was reasonable for the plaintiff to rely on the defendant for the advice; and

(c)   the defendant realised or should have realised that the plaintiff would rely on that advice.

Self check questions

1.   In what circumstances would a defendant owe a duty of care to a plaintiff for a negligent misstatement?   –

2.   Give examples of what amounts to a 'special relationship'.
3.   In what circumstances might a statement put into general circulation give rise to liability if it is negligent?

Answers
1.   Where it could be shown that the defendant had a special relationship with the plaintiff.
2.   Banker/customer, auditor/general body of shareholders.
3.   Where the maker of the statement knew that it would be communicated to a particular person for a particular reason and that person would rely upon it.

Problem
Scruples, who runs a decorating business, is looking for a trustworthy accountant. He receives an application from Comptroller who states that he is employed by Troth, a friend of Scruples.

Scruples writes to Troth to ask Troth's opinion of Comptroller's suitability for the post and whether Troth considers him to be trustworthy.

Troth, who has a large accounting department, cannot recall Comptroller's face, but nevertheless writes to Scruples stating that Comptroller is in every way suitable.

In fact, if Troth had investigated, he would have discovered that Comptroller was about to be dismissed for dishonesty.

Scruples engages Comptroller but, within a month, Comptroller leaves his employment and emigrates to South America with £20,000 of Scruples's money in his possession.

Advise Scruples.

Suggested answer
On the facts of the problem Scruples may be able to bring an action for damages against Troth in the tort of negligent misstatement.

In the House of Lords decision in *Hedley Byrne & Co. Ltd v Heller and Partners Ltd* (1963) it was established that a duty of care could in certain circumstances by owed in relation to negligent misstatements. However, the case clearly establishes that a duty of care can only exist where a special relationship between the parties can be established. In addition it must be shown that the negligent misstatement caused the loss suffered by the plaintiff.

In the present case Scruples must establish that Troth owed him a duty of care and in order to do that he must show that a special relationship existed between them.

One of the issues that may cause difficulty here is the fact that Scruples and Troth are friends. It was made clear in Lord Morris's judgment in *Hedley Byrne* that 'legal obligations should not be attached to kindly and friendly acts'. The advice must be given in some kind of commercial context. It is significant in this particular case that Scruples *wrote* to Troth rather than telephoning or speaking to him in person. This suggests that a formal rather than informal arrangement was envisaged by Scruples and the fact that Troth would be relied on by Scruples in making his decision.   −

Based on the reasoning in *Caparo Industries plc* v *Dickman* (1990) it would seem fair, just and reasonable that the law should impose a duty of given scope on the one party for the benefit of the other. It is suggested that a special relationship existed between the parties.

The misstatement contained in Troth's letter would appear to be negligent inasmuch as Troth cannot recall Comptroller, fails to make the enquiries regarding his suitability that a reasonable man would have made and simply replies to Scruples's letter.

In all the circumstances it would be reasonable to advise Scruples to begin an action against Troth in the law of negligent misstatement.

17 SALE OF GOODS
— IMPLIED TERMS

1 Introduction

As previously mentioned in Chapter 8.3, the Sale of Goods Act 1979 as amended implies various terms into contracts for the sale of goods. We do not intend going into any detail about what exactly a contract for the sale of goods is, but we shall concentrate on the rights and obligations the law implies into such contracts. The discussion in Chapter 8.2 of the nature of contractual terms is relevant here.

2 Implied terms about title and quiet possession

This implied term applies to all sale of goods contracts, irrespective of the status of the parties; that is, there is no requirement that the seller sells in the course of business.

Sale of Goods Act 1979, s. 12

(1) In a contract of sale, . . . There is an implied condition on the part of the seller that in the case of a sale he has a right to sell the goods, and in the case of an agreement to sell he will have such a right at the time when the property is to pass.

(2) In a contract of sale, . . . There is also an implied warranty that—

(a) the goods are free, and will remain free until the time when the property is to pass, from any charge or encumbrance not disclosed or known to the buyer before the contract is made, and

(b)   the buyer will enjoy quiet possession of the goods except so far as it may be disturbed by the owner or other person entitled to the benefit of any charge or encumbrance so disclosed or known.

Two issues should be noted:

(a)   Section 12(1) implies a condition into the contract relating to the right to sell the goods whereas the terms implied by s. 12(2) are warranties.

(b)   The case law on s. 12 relates to the use of goods or repairs made to the goods before it is discovered that the person in possession has to return them to the owner as the seller did not have the right to sell the goods in question.

Rowland v *Divall*
[1923] 2 KB 500

SCRUTTON LJ: The discussion which this case has received in the course of the argument has made it reasonably clear to me that the learned judge below came to a wrong conclusion. The plaintiff purchased a car from the defendant for £334. He drove it from Brighton, where he bought it, to the place where he had a garage, painted it and kept it there for about two months. He then sold it to a third person who had it in his possession for another two months. Then came the police, who claimed it as the stolen car for which they had been looking. It appears that it had been stolen before the defendant became possessed of it, and consequently he had no title that he could convey to the plaintiff. In these circumstances the plaintiff sued the defendant for the price he paid for the car as on a total failure of consideration. Now before the passing of the Sale of Goods Act (1893) there was a good deal of confusion in the authorities as to the exact nature of the vendor's contract with respect to his title to sell. It was originally said that a vendor did not warrant his title. But gradually a number of exceptions crept in, till at last the exceptions became the rule, the rule being that the vendor warranted that he had title to what he purported to sell, except in certain special cases, such as that of a sale by a sheriff, who does not so warrant. Then came the Sale of Goods Act, which re-enacted that rule, but did so with this alteration: it re-enacted it as a condition, not as a warranty. Section 12 says in express terms that there shall be 'An implied condition on the part of the seller that ... he has a right to sell the goods'. It being now a condition, wherever that condition is broken the contract can be rescinded, and with the rescission the buyer can demand a return of the purchase money, unless he has, with knowledge of the facts, held on to the bargain so as to waive the condition. But Mr Doughty argues that there can never be a rescission where a *restitutio in integrum* is impossible, and that here the plaintiff cannot rescind because he cannot return the car. To that the buyer's answer is that the reason of his inability to return it — namely, the fact that the defendant had no title to it — is the very thing of which he is complaining, and that it does not lie in the defendant's mouth to set up as a defence to the action his own breach of the implied condition that he had a right to sell. In my opinion that answer is well founded, and it would, I think, be absurd to apply the rule as to *restitutio in integrum* to such a state of facts. No doubt the general rule is that a buyer cannot rescind a contract of sale and get back the purchase money unless he can restore the subject-matter. There are a large number of cases on the subject, some of which are not very easy to reconcile with others. Some of them make it highly probable that a certain degree of deterioration of the goods is not sufficient to take away the right to recover the purchase money. However I do not think it necessary to refer to them. It certainly seems to me that, in a case of rescission for the breach of the condition that the seller had a right to sell the goods, it cannot be that the buyer is deprived of his right to get back the purchase money because he cannot restore the goods which, from the nature of the transaction, are not the goods of the seller at all, and which the seller therefore has no right to under any circumstances. For these reasons I think that the plaintiff is entitled to recover the whole of the purchase money as for a total failure of consideration, and that the appeal must be allowed.

The decision in *Rowland* v *Divall* establishes the principle that, even though the innocent purchaser is unable to restore the goods in their original form, he is not precluded from getting the contract price back, the reasoning being that the effect of a breach of s. 12(1) is that there has been a total failure of consideration.

The question of repairs was dealt with in:

Mason v *Burningham*
[1949] 2 KB 545

The plaintiff had purchased a typewriter from the defendant for £20. She subsequently spent £11 10s. on overhauling it. Unknown to the parties the typewriter had been stolen and the plaintiff had to return it to the owner. The plaintiff claimed from the defendant, under the warranty that she should have quiet possession implied in the contract of sale by virtue of the provisions of s. 12 of the Sale of Goods Act, repayment first of the sum of £20, the purchase price she had paid, and in addition £11 10s., being the sum she had spent on overhaul. The defendant repaid the £20 but contended that he was not liable for the moneys spent on overhaul. The county court judge held that, although the plaintiff had done 'the ordinary and natural thing' in having the typewriter overhauled, she was not entitled to recover the cost of such overhaul from the defendant, as it was not a loss due to the fact that the defendant had sold an article to which he had no title.

Held: Allowing the appeal, there had been a breach of the warranty, implied in the contract of sale by s. 12 of the Sale of Goods Act, that the buyer should have and enjoy quiet possession of the goods. The plaintiff was entitled under s. 53(1) of the Act to treat the breach of the implied condition that the seller had a right to sell the goods as a breach of warranty. The cost of overhauling the typewriter was a loss 'directly and naturally resulting, in the ordinary course of events, from the breach of warranty' within s. 53(2) which the plaintiff was entitled to recover from the defendant.

The plaintiff was, therefore, entitled to the cost of the repairs, the reasoning being that such work was within the 'reasonable contemplation of the parties' (see generally chapter X above, on remoteness of damages). The decision seems entirely consistent with the regime of the Act.

3 Implied terms about description, quality and fitness for purpose

3.1 Introduction

Before discussing the content of ss. 13 and 14 of the Sale of Goods Act 1979, an important amendment introduced by the Sale and Supply of Goods Act 1994 must be explained.

The terms implied by ss. 13 and 14 were previously conditions of the contract. Consequently a buyer of goods who could show that either term had been breached was entitled to repudiate the contract and therefore reject the goods (subject to the provisions of ss. 34 and 35, see below). The major criticism of this was that relatively minor breaches of the terms were allowing buyers to repudiate, even though the consequences of the breach were not significant. The Law Commission Report No. 160, *Sale and Supply of Goods* (Cm 137, 1987), recommended changes to the nature of these terms in non-consumer contracts. The proposals of the Law Commission have now been inserted into the SGA 1979 by s. 4 of the 1994 Act.

Sale of Goods Act 1979, s. 15A

(1)   Where in the case of a contract of sale—

(a)   the buyer would, apart from this subsection, have the right to reject goods by reason of a breach on the part of the seller of a term implied by section 13, 14 or 15 above, but
(b)   the breach is so slight that it would be unreasonable for him to reject them,
then, if the buyer does not deal as consumer, the breach is not to be treated as a breach of condition but may be treated as a breach of warranty.

(2)   This section applies unless a contrary intention appears in, or is to be implied from, the contract.
(3)   It is for the seller to show that a breach fell within subsection (1)(b) above.

The effect of s. 15A is that in 'non-consumer' contracts, breaches of ss. 13 to 15 will only give rise to damages if 'the breach is so slight that it would be unreasonable for [the buyer] to reject [the goods]'. The new provision seems relatively self-explanatory, but a number of difficulties can be highlighted:

(a)   What is meant by a 'slight' breach is not clear. For example, if I buy a car for my business, a new Lotus Elan, for the sake of an example, and there is a defect in the paintwork, but in every other way the car is in perfect working order, it is clearly debatable whether or not the car is of 'satisfactory quality' (see the discussion of s. 14(2) in 3.3 below). Assuming the car is not of satisfactory quality the next issue is whether or not the breach is so slight that it would be unreasonable for me to reject it? If the nature of my business requires me to portray a certain image, then clearly a car of this nature with defective paintwork may not be a slight breach for the purpose for which I may require it. Note the burden of proof is on the seller, in this instance. While the section introduces an element of flexibility there is no longer any degree of certainty in this area.

(b) As we shall see below, the definition of a 'consumer' contract is still open to discussion despite the definition inserted in the 1979 Act. The definition of s. 61(5A) of the 1979 Act requires the customer to hold herself as dealing as a consumer and further requires that the goods are 'ordinarily' bought for use by a consumer. Clearly, this does clarify a number of constitutional situations.

3.2   Implied term about description

Sale of Goods Act 1979, s. 13

(1)   Where there is a contract for the sale of goods by description, there is an implied term that the goods will correspond with the description.

(1A)   As regards England and Wales and Northern Ireland, the term implied by subsection (1) above is a condition.

(2)   If the sale is by sample as well as by description, it is not sufficient that the bulk of the goods corresponds with the sample if the goods do not also correspond with the description.

(3)   A sale of goods is not prevented from being a sale by description by reason only that, being exposed for sale or hire, they are selected by the buyer.

Two initial points must be noted. First the term applies to private sales as well as those in the course of business. Secondly the 'term' implied is subject to the reasoning contained in s. 15A of the 1979 Act (see above).

Beale v Taylor
[1967] 1 WLR 1193

The defendant, wishing to dispose of his car, which he believed to be a 1961 Triumph Herald 1200, inserted the following advertisement in a trade paper.

Herald convertible, white, 1961, twin carbs., £190 . . .

As a result of that advertisement the plaintiff went to see the car at the defendant's home and had a trial run in it as a passenger. The plaintiff could not drive it because he was not at that time insured for driving motor vehicles. After the trial run he saw on the rear of the car a metallic disc with the figure 1200 on it. After some discussion he agreed to buy the car for £160, paid a deposit of £10, and the balance a few days later when he had arranged insurance for himself, and drove the car away.

He found the car to be unsatisfactory and on examination by a garage it was found to have been made up of two cars. The rear portion consisted of a 1961 Triumph Herald 1200 model, but the front portion consisted of an earlier model. Those two portions had been welded together unsatisfactorily into one structure, and the vehicle was unroadworthy and unsafe.

The plaintiff brought an action against the defendant, inter alia, for damages for breach of the term implied in the contract by s. 13 of the Sale of Goods Act, that the goods delivered should correspond with their description.

Held: There could be a sale by description of a specific chattel even where the chattel was displayed to and inspected by the buyer so long as it was sold not merely as the specific thing but as a thing corresponding to a description, so that the buyer relied in part on a description and that since the plaintiff when he made his offer for the car relied on the description given in the advertisement and on the metallic disc of a 1961 Triumph Herald 1200 car as showing the kind of car he was buying, the sale was a sale by description. Since the car which was delivered did not correspond with its description, the plaintiff was entitled to damages for breach of the term implied by s. 13 of the Sale of Goods Act, which would be £125, being the price of the car less its value as scrap.

SELLERS LJ: I think that on the facts of this case the buyer when he came along to see this car was coming along to see a car as advertised, that is, a car described as a 'Herald convertible, white, 1961'. When he came along he saw what ostensibly was a Herald convertible, white, 1961, because the evidence shows that the '1200' which was exhibited on the rear of the car is the first model of the '1200' which came out in 1961: it was on that basis that he made the offer to purchase it and in the belief that the seller was presenting his car as that which his advertisement indicated. Apart from that, the selling of a car of that make, I would on the face of it rather agree with the submission of the seller that he was making no warranties at all and making no contractual terms. But fundamentally he was selling a car of that description. The facts, as revealed very shortly afterwards, show that that description was false. It was unfortunately not false to the knowledge of the seller nor of the buyer because no one could see from looking at the car in the ordinary sort of examination which would be made that it was anything other than that which it purported to be. It was only afterwards that on examination it was found to be in two parts.

I think that that is sufficient ground on which to decide this case in favour of the buyer.

The crucial factor in the *Beale* case is that the judge deemed the sale to be one by description. This decision can be contrasted with that in:

Harlingdon and Leinster Enterprises Ltd v *Christopher Hull Fine Art Ltd*
[1990] 1 All ER 737

The defendants were a firm of art dealers which was owned and controlled by H and which carried on business from a London gallery. In 1984 H was asked to sell two oil paintings which had been described in a 1980 auction catalogue as being by *Gabriele Münter, an artist of the German Expressionist school. H specialised in young contemporary British artists and had no training, experience or knowledge which would have enabled him to conclude from an examination of the pictures whether they were by Münter. He took the paintings to Christie's, a well-known firm of art auctioneers, who expressed interest in them, and he also contacted the plaintiffs, who carried on business as art dealers at a London gallery to view the paintings. He made it clear that he did not know much about the paintings and that he was not an expert on them. The plaintiffs' employee agreed to buy one of the paintings for £6,000 without asking any questions about the provenance of the paintings or making any further inquiries about them. The invoice for the painting described it as being by Münter. The painting was later discovered to be a forgery and the plaintiffs sought repayment of the purchase price, claiming,* inter alia, *that the contract was for the sale of goods by description within s. 13(1) of the Sale of Goods Act 1979 and could therefore be avoided on the grounds of misdescription.*

Held: The fact that a description was applied to goods either in the course of negotiations or in the contract itself did not necessarily make the contract one for the sale of goods by description for the purposes of s. 13(1) of the 1979 Act, since for the sale to be 'by' description the description had to be influential in the sale so as to become an essential term or condition of the contract. Although it was possible for a description of goods to be an essential term of the contract even if it was not relied on, the court had to be able to impute to the parties a common intention that it should be a term of the contract before the sale could be described as being 'by description' and in determining what the intention of the parties was the presence or absence of reliance on the part of the buyer was a very relevant factor to be taken into account. Accordingly, for all practical purposes there could not be a sale of goods by description if it was not within the contemplation of the parties that the buyer would rely on the description. Since the plaintiffs had not relied on H's description of the painting as being by Münter but had bought the painting as it was, the sale had not been a sale by description for the purposes of s. 13(1).

NOURSE LJ: It is suggested that the significance which some of [the cases reviewed by his Lordship] attribute to the buyer's reliance on the description is misconceived. I think that that criticism is theoretically correct. In theory it is no doubt possible for a description of goods which is not relied on by the buyer to become an essential term of a contract for their sale. But in practice it is very difficult, and perhaps impossible, to think of facts where that would be so. The description must have a sufficient influence in the sale to become an essential term of the contract and the correlative of influence is reliance. Indeed, reliance by the buyer is the natural index of a sale by description. It is true that the question must, as always, be judged objectively and it may be said that previous judicial references have been to subjective or actual reliance. But each of those decisions, including that of Judge Oddie in the present case, can be justified on an objective basis. For all practical purposes, I would say that there cannot be a contract for the sale of goods by description where it is not within the reasonable contemplation of the parties that the buyer is relying on the description. For those purposes, I think that the law is correctly summarised in these words of *Benjamin on Sale*, p. 641, which should be understood to lay down an objective test:

> Specific goods may be sold as such ... where, though the goods are described, the description is to be relied upon, as where the buyer buys the goods such as they are.

In giving his decision on this question Judge Oddie said:

> There can clearly be a sale by description where the buyer has inspected the goods if the description relates to something not apparent on inspection. Every item in a description which constitutes a substantial ingredient in the identity of the thing sold is a condition.

Later, having said that he had not been referred to any similar case where a sale in reliance on a statement that a painting was by a particular artist had been held to be a sale by description, the judge continued:

> In my judgment such a statement could amount to a description and a sale in reliance on it to a sale by description within the meaning of the 1979 Act. However, on the facts of this case, I am satisfied that the description by Mr Hull before the agreement was not relied on by Mr Runkel in making his offer to purchase which was accepted by Mr Hull. I conclude that he bought the painting as it was. In these circumstances there was not in my judgment a sale by description.

I agree. On a view of their words and deeds as a whole, the parties could not reasonably have contemplated that the plaintiffs were relying on the defendants' statement that the painting was by Gabriele Münter. On the facts which he found the judge could not, by a correct application of the law, have come to any other decision.

Clearly the reliance on the description of the goods must be within the 'contemplation of the parties'.

In *Beale* v *Taylor* the defect (i.e., two cars welded together) was not initially apparent at the time of sale. In the *Harlingdon* case the painting was bought 'as seen' and was not, therefore, a sale by description.'

The term 'description' does not relate to the quality of the goods. Therefore if I describe a faulty car as a 'car' I will not be in breach of s. 13 — see generally *Ashington Piggeries Ltd* v *Christopher Hill Ltd* [1972] AC 441.

3.3   Implied term about quality

3.3.1   Introduction   The law in this area has changed as a result of new provisions being substituted into the Sale of Goods Act 1979 by the Sale and Supply of Goods Act 1994, replacing the old provisions relating to 'merchantable quality' with the new concept of 'satisfactory quality' (see below).

The new provisions which are contained in the 1994 amending legislation are largely based on the Law Commission Report No. 160, *Sale and Supply of*

Goods (Cm 137, 1987). The report is worth reading as it gives excellent background material on the likely effect of the new provisions.

Finally some reference will be made to the law before 3 January 1995 in order to try to explain how the new provisions are likely to change the previous law. This is because the new term of satisfactory quality applies only to contracts entered into after that date. It is not being suggested, however, that reference will be made by the courts to these previous decisions when interpreting the new legislation.

Finally by way of introduction it should be emphasised that the general principle, as contained in s. 14(1) of the Sale of Goods Act 1979, is that of *'caveat emptor'* or 'let the buyer beware'. Therefore the only terms which are implied relating to the quality or fitness for purpose of the goods are those contained in s. 14(2) and (3) of the 1979 Act.

3.3.2   The old law (applicable to contracts entered into before 3 January 1995)

Sale of Goods Act 1979, s. 14, as originally enacted

(2)   Where the seller sells goods in the course of a business, there is an implied condition that the goods supplied under the contract are of merchantable quality, except that there is no such condition—

(a)   as regards defects specifically drawn to the buyer's attention before the contract is made; or
(b)   if the buyer examines the goods before the contract is made, as regards defects which that examination ought to reveal.

. . .

(6)   Goods of any kind are of merchantable quality within the meaning of subsection (2) above if they are as fit for the purpose or purposes for which goods of that kind are commonly bought as it is reasonable to expect having regard to any description applied to them, the price (if relevant) and all the other relevant circumstances.

First, it must be noted that this condition applies only to goods sold in the course of a business.

The second point to note is that the exceptions in paras (a) and (b) have not been affected by the changes. The statutory term is not implied if either the defect has been brought to the buyer's attention or the defect should have been revealed by the actual examination carried out by the buyer.

The old s. 14(2) received a number of criticisms. First there was conflicting case law on whether the goods had to be 'usable' in order to be of merchantable quality or whether it was a question of acceptability. The latter means that the goods should be acceptable to a reasonable person. Clearly the latter would give the consumer far greater rights. So, for example, a car would not be of merchantable quality merely because it could be driven from A to B; but would include wider aspects, such as 'appearance and finish', levels of comfort and so on.

Thirdly it was not clear whether a minor defect or defects would in itself render the goods unmerchantable. Case law in this area, for example, *Millars of Falkirk Ltd* v *Turpie* 1976 SLT 66, made the position unclear. Finally there was no clear consensus on whether or not goods had to remain durable; that is whether goods had to be of merchantable quality for a reasonable length of time following purchase. These are some of the defects which the new law aimed to redress.

3.3.3   The new term of satisfactory quality (applies to contracts entered into on or after 3 January 1995)

Sale of Goods Act 1979, s. 14 as amended

(2)   Where the seller sells goods in the course of a business, there is an implied term that the goods supplied under the contract are of satisfactory quality.

(2A)   For the purposes of this Act, goods are of satisfactory quality if they meet the standard that a reasonable person would regard as satisfactory, taking account of any description of the goods, the price (if relevant) and all the other relevant circumstances.

(2B)   For the purposes of this Act, the quality of goods includes their state and condition and the following (among others) are in appropriate cases aspects of the quality of goods—

(a)   fitness for all the purposes for which goods of the kind in question are commonly supplied,
(b)   appearance and finish,
(c)   freedom from minor defects,
(d)   safety, and
(e)   durability.

(2C)   The term implied by subsection (2) above does not extend to any matter making the quality of goods unsatisfactory—

(a)   which is specifically drawn to the buyer's attention before the contract is made,
(b)   where the buyer examines the goods before the contract is made, which that examination ought to reveal, or
(c)   in the case of a contract for sale by sample, which would have been apparent on a reasonable examination of the sample.

Issues to be aware of, in the context of the new definition:

(a)   The notion of 'satisfactory quality' is, according to the Law Commission Report No. 160, said to reflect more common or day-to-day language.

(b)   The new s. 14(2) introduces the standard of the 'reasonable person'. Therefore an objective test is now appropriate in assessing the quality of goods. The suggestion is that this standard will widen the scope of the quality requirement in Sale of Goods contracts.

(c)   The 'description' and 'price' of the goods are still relevant in determining the quality of the goods. Therefore there will be a lesser standard of 'satisfactory quality' in the context of second-hand goods. It must be noted, however, that the old requirement of 'merchantable quality' required second-hand goods to be more than just functional — see *Shine* v *General Guarantee Corporation Ltd* [1988] 1 All ER 911 and *Business Applications Specialists Ltd* v *Nationwide Credit Corporation Ltd* [1988] RTR 332.

(d)   Section 14(2) now requires specific factors to be taken into account in determining whether or not the goods are of satisfactory quality. A number of these factors had become relevant under the previous legislation but it is argued that the intent behind the factors being included is to benefit the consumer.

(i)   Fitness for all purposes. The goods must be more than merely usable and fitness for purpose is now one of five relevant factors.

(ii)   Appearance and finish. The effect of this requirement is to give effect to the decision of *Rogers* v *Parish (Scarborough) Ltd* [1987] 2 All ER 232 in which Mustill LJ made the following remarks (when speaking of a brand-new Range Rover):

... one would include in respect of any passenger vehicle not merely the buyer's purpose of driving the car from one place to another but of doing so with the appropriate degree of comfort, ease of handling and reliability and, one might add, of pride in the vehicle's outward and interior appearance.

Therefore the new requirement of satisfactory quality does require this factor to be satisfied. But it should be noted that Mustill LJ then went on to say that:

What is the appropriate degree and what relative weight is to be attached to one characteristic of the car rather than another will depend on the market at which the car is aimed.

This later statement, if applied, suggests a sliding scale of applicability of this requirement. It is hoped that the price of new goods will not become a factor in assessing the quality of goods.

(iii)   Minor defects may now, in themselves, render the goods of unsatisfactory quality. It was felt that this factor needed spelling out as there were suggestions (see *Millars of Falkirk Ltd* v *Turpie* 1976 SLT 66) that minor defects did not affect the quality of the goods.

(iv)   Safety. Goods, in order to be of satisfactory quality, must be reasonably safe when used for any of their normal purposes. Clearly any safety regulations operating in a particular area will be relevant considerations to be taken into account when looking at this factor.

(v)   Durability. Goods are now required to be of satisfactory quality for a reasonable time. Note the law does not lay down a specific time-limit. A relevant criterion in assessing the requirement of durability may well be to look at the market for those particular goods in making this assessment. The requirement of durability is to be ascertained at the time the goods were supplied.

The new requirement of 'satisfactory quality' therefore introduces some fundamental changes to this area of law.

4   Implied term about fitness for purpose

Sale of Goods Act 1979, s. 14(3)

Where the seller sells goods in the course of a business and the buyer, expressly or by implication, makes known—

(a)   to the seller, or
(b)   where the purchase price or part of it is payable by instalments and the goods were previously sold by a credit-broker to the seller, to that credit-broker,
any particular purpose for which the goods are being bought, there is an implied term that the goods supplied under the contract are reasonably fit for that purpose, whether or not that is a purpose for which such goods are commonly supplied, except where the circumstances show that the buyer does not rely, or that it is unreasonable for him to rely, on the skill or judgment of the seller or credit-broker.

Two initial points are to be noted. First the term is implied only if the seller sells the goods in the course of a business and secondly what is now implied by s. 14(3) is a term.

The case law on this section has centred on whether or not the goods are fit for a particular purpose and whether or not it is reasonable to rely on the skill or judgment of the seller.

Grant v Australian Knitting Mills Ltd
[1936] AC 85

The appellant, who contracted dermatitis of an external origin as the result of wearing a woollen garment which, when purchased from the retailers, was in a defective condition owing to the presence of excess sulphites which, it was found, had been negligently left in it in the process of manufacture, claimed damages against both retailers and manufacturers.

Held: The retailers were liable in contract for breach of implied warranty or condition under exceptions (i) and (ii) of s. 14 of the Sale of Goods Act 1895 of South Australia (equivalent to s. 14(3) of the 1979 Act).

The garment referred to in this case was in fact a pair of underpants and clearly they were not fit for their particular purpose, that is, wearing them. The decision can be compared with that in:

Griffiths v Peter Conway Ltd
[1939] 1 All ER 685

In June 1937, the plaintiff purchased from the defendants, who are retail traders, a Harris tweed coat, which was specially made for her. Shortly after she began to wear the coat, she developed dermatitis. She sought to recover damages from the defendants on the ground that there had been a breach of the condition implied by what is now the Sale of Goods Act 1979, s. 14(3), in that the article was not reasonably fit for the purpose for which it was supplied. At the hearing, it was found as a fact that the plaintiff's skin was abnormally sensitive, and that there was nothing in the cloth which would have affected the skin of a normal person. The abnormality of the plaintiff's skin was not made known to the seller.

Held: What is now the Sale of Goods Act 1979, s. 14(3), did not apply in the present case, as what was being dealt with here was something abnormal, which no seller would assume to exist.

In this case the seller was not in breach of s. 14(3) due to the idiosyncratic condition of the plaintiff. In order to be able to rely on the skill or judgment of the seller she should have disclosed the fact that she suffered from dermatitis.

Henry Kendall and Sons v William Lillico and Sons Ltd
[1969] 2 AC 31

In 1960, the plaintiffs, game farmers in Suffolk, bought from the defendants (SAPPA) quantities of compounded meal for feeding to pheasants and partridges and their chicks, which the plaintiffs reared for stock and sale. As a result of feeding the meal to them, many of the chicks died and others grew up stunted and unfit for breeding purposes owing, as the trial judge found, to the presence in the compounded meal of a proportion of Brazilian groundnut extraction which contained a toxic substance known as 'aflatoxin' produced by a mould or fungal growth which had infected the groundnuts before processing in the country of origin. SAPPA had bought the relevant supplies from the two third parties, L & Co. and G Ltd, under oral contracts evidenced, in accordance with their normal course of dealing, by sale notes containing written conditions of sale which included a clause stating that 'the buyer takes responsibility of any latent defects'. The two third parties had bought the extractions from the two fourth parties, K & Sons and HC Ltd, who had imported them from Brazil. The third and fourth parties were all members of the London Cattle Food Trade Association and had contracted on the terms of that association's standard contract form No. 6 (c.i.f.) which contained, inter alia, a clause (cl. 10) to the effect that the goods were not warranted free from defect rendering them unmerchantable which would not be apparent on any reasonable examination. The extractions sold and delivered by the fourth parties to the third parties under their respective contracts were shipped in five ships. The trial judge found that the goods in all these consignments were infected by the aflatoxin.

The case was eventually decided by the House of Lords. The key to the decision was whether it was reasonable to rely on Kendall's skill and judgment.

LORD REID: The difficult question is whether the circumstances were such as to show that Grimsdale were relying on Kendall's skill and judgment: but before I come to that there are two other matters which require some explanation. If the law were always logical one would suppose that a buyer, who has obtained a right to rely on the seller's skill and judgment, would only obtain thereby an assurance that proper skill and judgment had been exercised, and would only be entitled to a remedy if a defect in the goods was due to failure to exercise such skill and judgment. But the law has always gone farther than that. By getting the seller to undertake to use his skill and judgment the buyer gets under s. 14 an assurance that the goods will be reasonably fit for his purpose and that covers not only defects which the seller ought to have detected but also defects which are latent in the sense that even the utmost skill and judgment on the part of the seller would not have detected them. It is for that reason that, if s. 14 applies, Grimsdale are entitled to relief even although Kendall had no reason to suspect that the goods might be poisoned.

Secondly it is not necessary to decide whether today it would be a sufficiently particular purpose for Kendall to know that Grimsdale intended to resell to compounders of feeding stuffs. Today some compounders are willing to buy infected goods but presumably some are not, and I doubt whether mere knowledge on the part of Kendall that Grimsdale intended to resell would oblige Kendall to supply goods free from this poison. I would readily accept that a customer buying from an apparently reputable shopkeeper or from a manufacturer will normally as a matter of fact be relying on the seller's skill and judgment unless there is something to exclude the inference. But I do not think that the same can be said when two merchants equally knowledgeable deal with each other. Then I can see no reason in law or in fact for any presumption either way.

If one merchant merely acquired from an importer by buying on c.i.f. documents goods from a normal source and then resold to another merchant by transfer of the c.i.f. documents before taking delivery, there might then be little or no reason to suppose that the former merchant had exercised or could have exercised any skill or judgment with regard to the quality of the goods or that the latter was relying on him. But that was not the position in this case. Kendall had acquired these goods from a new source and one would suppose must have exercised skill and judgment in deciding to buy them and put them on the market. And the evidence appears to me to show that Kendall was recommending them to Grimsdale. In order to bring this subsection into operation it is not necessary to show that the parties consciously applied their minds to the question. It is enough that a reasonable seller in the shoes of Kendall would have realised that he was inviting Grimsdale to rely on his skill and judgment and that is what I think that in fact Kendall was doing. And the same applies to Holland Colombo. If that is right then s. 14 did apply to this case.

Lord Morris therefore makes it clear that in commercial situations, that is, both parties dealing in the course of business, there needs to be some evidence of reliance from the case itself in order for the provisions of s. 14(3) to apply.

5 Exemption clauses and the implied terms

Unfair Contract Terms Act 1977, s. 6

(1)   Liability for breach of the obligations arising from:

(a)   section 12 of the Sale of Goods Act 1979 (seller's implied undertakings as to title, etc.);
(b)   section 8 of the Supply of Goods (Implied Terms) Act 1973 (the corresponding thing in relation to hire-purchase),
cannot be excluded or restricted by reference to any contract term.

(2)   As against a person dealing as a consumer, liability for breach of the obligations arising from—

(a)   section 13, 14 or 15 of the 1979 Act (seller's implied undertakings as to conformity of goods with description or sample, or as to their quality or fitness for a particular purpose);
(b)   section 9, 10 or 11 of the 1973 Act (the corresponding things in relation to hire-purchase),
cannot be excluded or restricted by reference to any contract term.

(3)   As against a person dealing otherwise than as consumer, the liability specified in subsection (2) above can be excluded or restricted by reference to a contract term, but only in so far as the term satisfies the requirement of reasonableness.

The effect of the provision is that the implied term as to title can never be excluded and the undertakings implied by ss. 13 to 15 of the SGA 1979 cannot be excluded when the buyer is 'dealing as consumer'. If both parties are dealing 'otherwise than as consumer' then the exemption clause will operate 'only in so far as the term satisfies the requirement of reasonableness'. (For the meaning of 'reasonableness' see Chapter 9 above. Obviously the exemption clause has to satisfy the existing common law tests, which are discussed earlier in that chapter.)

The definition 'dealing as consumer' is crucial to the operation of this section and this term was discussed in:

R & B Customs Brokers Co. Ltd v *United Dominions Trust Ltd*
[1988] 1 All ER 847

The plaintiffs purchased from the defendant finance company a car supplied by the third-party motor dealer. Clause 2(a) of the conditional sale agreement under which the car was purchased purported to exclude any implied conditions as to the condition or quality of the car or its fitness for any particular purpose in relation to business transactions. The car was the second or third vehicle which the plaintiffs had acquired on credit terms. The agreement not executed until some weeks after the plaintiffs had taken delivery of the car. Before signing the contract the plaintiffs discovered that the roof of the car leaked and two days after the contract was signed they returned the car to the motor dealer for repairs. The motor dealer failed to rectify the leakage problem with the result that the plaintiffs rejected the car and brought an action against the defendants to recover the amount paid under the sale agreement. The defendants in turn claimed an indemnity from the motor dealer. The judge held (a) that the contract contained an implied condition, by virtue of s. 14(3) of the Sale of Goods Act 1979, that it was reasonable for the plaintiffs to rely on the motor dealer's skill and judgment, and (b) that in entering into the sale agreement the plaintiffs were 'dealing as consumer' and accordingly, by virtue of s. 6(2) of the Unfair Contract Terms Act 1977, implied conditions as to condition, quality or fitness for purpose could not be excluded by cl. 2(a) of the agreement. The judge accordingly gave judgment for the plaintiffs. The motor dealer appealed.

Held: (1)   The fact that the plaintiffs had discovered the defect in the car roof before the agreement was executed did not mean that the plaintiffs had ceased to rely on the motor dealer's skill and judgment, since the plaintiffs had anticipated that the car roof would be sucessfully repaired in the near future. Accordingly, the judge was right to conclude that, unless excluded by the express terms of the contract, the sale of the car was subject to an implied condition as to fitness under s. 14(3) of the 1979 Act.

(2)   Where a transaction was only incidental to a business activity, a degree of regularity was required before the transaction could be said to be an integral part of the business carried on and so entered into in the course of that business. Since the car was only the second or third vehicle acquired by the plaintiffs on credit terms, there was not a sufficient degree of regularity capable of establishing that the contract was anything more than part of a consumer transaction. Clause 2(a) of the contract accordingly did not apply since it only excluded liability in relation to business transactions. The plaintiffs were accordingly entitled to judgment.

The mere fact that a company was buying the car did not make it a 'non-consumer' sale. The court looked at the purpose for which the car was being bought and the degree of regularity with which the buyers entered into this type of contract. Great emphasis was placed on the question whether the car was going to be used as an 'integral' part of the business. The finding that the company was 'dealing as consumer' was crucial as the court went on to say that if it had found the other way on this question the exemption clause would have satisfied the test of reasonableness.

6 Loss of the right to reject the goods and terminate the contract

If goods are not of satisfactory quality or not fit for purpose the buyer may nevertheless lose the right to reject the goods through the operation of the Sale of Goods Act 1979, s. 35. (Note that in commercial or business contacts there is not an automatic right to reject if the breach is 'so slight that it would be unreasonable for him to reject them': s. 15A, see above).

The onus of proof is on the seller concerning the issue of the loss of the right to reject. It must be remembered that even if the buyer cannot reject there may still be a claim for damages.

Sale of Goods Act 1979, s. 35

(1)   The buyer is deemed to have accepted the goods subject to subsection (2) below—

    (a)   when he intimates to the seller that he has accepted them, or

    (b)   when the goods have been delivered to him and he does any act in relation to them which is inconsistent with the ownership of the seller.

(2)   Where goods are delivered to the buyer, and he has not previously examined them, he is not deemed to have accepted them under subsection (1) above until he has had a reasonable opportunity of examining them for the purpose—

    (a)   of ascertaining whether they are in conformity with the contract, and

    (b)   in the case of a contract for the sale by sample, of comparing the bulk with the sample.

(3)   Where the buyer deals as consumer or (in Scotland) the contract of sale is a consumer contract, the buyer cannot lose his right to rely on subsection (2) above by agreement, waiver or otherwise;

(4)   The buyer is also deemed to have accepted the goods when after the lapse of a reasonable time he retains the goods without intimating to the seller that he has rejected them.

(5)   The questions that are material in determining for the purposes of subsection (4) above whether a reasonable time has elapsed include whether the buyer has had a reasonable opportunity of examining the goods for the purpose mentioned in subsection (2) above.

(6)   The buyer is not by virtue of this section deemed to have accepted the goods merely because—

    (a)   he asks for, or agrees to, their repair by or under arrangement with the seller, or

    (b)   the goods are delivered to another under a sub-sale or other disposition.

(7) Where the contract is for the sale of goods making one or more commercial units, a buyer accepting any goods included in a unit is deemed to have accepted all the goods making the unit; and in this subsection 'commercial unit' means a unit division of which would materially impair the value of the goods or the character of the unit.

A number of points should be noted about the operation of s. 35:

(a) The right to reject cannot be lost by intimation or by an inconsistent act until there has been a reasonable opportunity to examine for the purpose of seeing whether the goods conform to contract or sample (s. 35(2)(a) and (b)).

(b) It is not possible in a 'consumer' contract to exclude the reasonable opportunity to examine (s. 35(3)). Therefore where the buyer is not dealing in the course of a trade or business then this provision will apply. The practical application of this is to delivery notes which state that the goods have been examined.

(c) The most difficult provision relates to the loss of the right to reject after 'a reasonable time has elapsed' (s. 35(5)). The position here is that one of the factors to take into account in determining this question is whether or not 'the buyer has had a reasonable opportunity of examining the goods'. Much controversy was created by the decision, under the previous legislation, in:

Bernstein v Pamson Motors (Golders Green) Ltd
[1987] 2 All ER 220

On 7 December 1984 the plaintiff took delivery of a new motor car from the defendants for a price of just under £8,000. On 3 January 1985, when the car had done about 140 miles, it broke down on a motorway. The car would not restart and had to be collected by the emergency services. The following day the plaintiff advised the defendants in writing that he regarded the car as not being of merchantable quality and that he was rejecting it. Later that month the car was repaired under the manufacturers' warranty at no cost to the plaintiff. After repair the car was as good as new, but the plaintiff still refused to have it back. The cause of the defect was that a piece of sealant had entered the lubrication system and cut off the oil supply to the camshaft, which then seized up. The plaintiff brought an action against the defendants, contending that the car was not of merchantable quality within s. 14(6) of the Sale of Goods Act 1979 and that the defendants were accordingly in breach of s. 14(2) of that Act. He claimed that he was therefore entitled both to recover damages and to rescind the contract of sale. The defendants contended that the car was of merchantable quality and that, in any event, the plaintiff had accepted the car within s. 35(1) of the 1979 Act and was, therefore, by virtue of s. 11(4) of that Act, limited to a claim for damages alone.

Held: (1) When determining whether any particular defect or feature rendered a new car unmerchantable, the court had to consider (a) whether the car was capable of being driven in safety, (b) the ease or otherwise with which the defect could be remedied, (c) whether the defect was of such a kind that it was capable of being satisfactorily repaired so as to produce a result as good as new, taking into account not only the power or parts at the site of the defect but also any other potential damage, (d) whether there was a succession of minor defects to be taken into consideration and (e) in appropriate cases, any cosmetic factors. On the facts, the car could not be said to have been of merchantable quality when it was delivered to the plaintiff, bearing in mind particularly the safety consideration and the extent of the area of potential damage and the consequent risk that such damage might still exist.

(2)   In considering whether a buyer had had goods for a reasonable time, and hence had lost his right to reject them, the nature of the particular defect and the speed with which it might have been discovered were irrelevant, since s. 35 of the 1979 Act was directed solely to what was a reasonably practical interval between a buyer receiving the goods and his ability to return them bearing in mind the desirability of finality in commercial transactions. On the facts, since the plaintiff had driven about 140 miles and had had the car for three weeks, he had had a reasonable time to examine and try out the car and he had therefore lost the right to reject it. The plaintiff was therefore entitled to damages limited to the cost of making his way home after the breakdown, the loss of his full tank of petrol, a sum to compensate him for a spoilt day and for five days' loss of use of the car.

The finding that the car was not of merchantable quality under the old s. 14(2) was not controversial. It is undoubtedly the case that the car would not be of satisfactory quality under the new s. 14(2) (see above).

The real difficulty with the case is that Mr Bernstein lost his right to reject within three weeks of purchase having only driven the car a total of 140 miles on three occasions. The Law Commission Report (1987) (see above) could not comment on this decision as it was thought that it was being appealed to the Court of Appeal but this did not happen. Therefore it is debatable whether the new legislation affects this decision. The legislators deliberately avoided setting a fixed time-limit for this; therefore we shall have to wait for case law in order to be able to interpret the subsection.

(d)   The fact that the buyer asks for, or agrees to, repair by or under an arrangement with the seller does not in itself constitute acceptance. Further acceptance does not take place merely because goods are delivered to another. This clarifies the previous law to the benefit of the buyer.

18 PROPERTY AND RISK IN SALE OF GOODS

1 Introduction

In addition to the implied terms discussed in Chapter 17 a further issue of importance to sellers and buyers is the passing of ownership or property (and consequently risk) in the goods from the seller to the buyer.

Three issues merit further consideration:

(a) When does property pass?
(b) What effect does passing property have as between the seller and the buyer?
(c) Who is entitled to pass property in the goods?

2 When does property pass?

The Sale of Goods Act 1979 (SGA) contains detailed rules on the passing of property, by which we mean ownership of goods. In reality a buyer is concerned to get full possession, use and enjoyment of the goods without which, for many practical purposes, ownership would be worthless. It is important at this point to distinguish between possession and ownership of goods.

A person in possession of goods will not necessarily own them, for example, a thief will possess goods which he does not own. In addition physical delivery of the goods from the seller to the buyer will not necessarily pass ownership from the seller to the buyer.

Conversely, a buyer can become the owner of goods before taking possession of them.

2.1   Consequences of passing property

Two main consequences arise when property passes from the seller to the buyer:

(a)   The seller can only sue to the price of the goods and cannot claim their return, or damages.

(b)   Risk of accidental damage to the goods normally passes with property. (This will be the case unless the parties expressly agree that it does not.)

2.2   When does property pass?

The provisions in the SGA 1979 are important in this respect, because the parties to the contract will rarely express their intentions in the contract and as can be seen the consequences for both the seller and the buyer once property has passed can be serious.

In order to study the rules set out in the Act it is necessary to distinguish between:

(a)   specific goods, and

(b)   unascertained goods.

2.3   Specific goods

These are goods that are identified and agreed upon at the time the contract is made. The basic position is set out in s. 17 which states that property in the goods will pass in accordance with the intentions of the parties. But as we have seen it is unusual for the parties to express such an intention in the contract. In practice the rules contained in s. 18 will govern the situation.

2.3.1   Rule 1   Where there is an *unconditional* contract for the sale of specific goods in a *deliverable state*, property in the goods passes to the buyer *when the contract is made* and it is *immaterial* that the time of payment *or* delivery are postponed.

Thus, under rule 1, property will pass immediately the contract is made. This can mean that the goods are in the possession of the seller at the buyer's risk. Any damage to the goods will have to be borne by the buyer with obvious consequences. This is especially so in the case of a sale between a retailer and a consumer where the consumer will often have to rely on the retailer's expertise in respect of storage and delivery of the goods.

In this context the judgment of Diplock LJ in *R. V. Ward Ltd v Bignall* [1967] 1 QB 534 is important. Diplock LJ stated that in modern times very little is needed to give rise to the inference that property is only to pass on delivery or payment, thus displacing the operation of rule 1.

What amounts to a 'deliverable state' was discussed in:

Underwood v Burgh Castle Brick and Cement Syndicate
[1922] 1 KB 343

The plaintiffs agreed to sell an engine to the defendants. At the time the contract was made the engine was bolted to the concrete floor of the plaintiffs' premises. It was

*necessary to detach the engine before delivery could take place. The engine was
damaged in the course of delivery. The defendants refused to accept the engine. The
plaintiffs argued that property had passed when the contract was made under rule 1.*

*Held: The engine was not in a deliverable state at the time the contract was made.
At that time it was a fixture as it was still attached to the plaintiffs' premises.*

2.3.2 Rule 2 Where there is a contract for the sale of specific goods but the
seller is bound to do something to the goods for the purpose of putting them in
a deliverable state, property does not pass until the thing is done and the buyer
has notice that it has been done.

For example, if a person buys a car from a garage and the garage is bound to
fit a radio to the car, property or ownership will not pass until the radio is fitted
and the buyer has been informed of this.

2.3.3 Rule 3 Where there is a contract for the sale of specific goods in a
deliverable state but the seller is bound to weigh, measure, test or do some
other act or thing with reference to the goods for the purpose of ascertaining the
price, property does not pass until that is done and the buyer has notice thereof.

This rule needs no further explanation.

2.3.4 Rule 4 Where goods are delivered to a buyer at his request on sale or
return or other similar terms property passes to the buyer:

(a)   when he signifies his approval or acceptance to the seller or does any
other act adopting the transaction; or
(b)   if the buyer retains the goods without giving notice of rejection beyond
any time fixed for the return of the goods (if no time is fixed then beyond a
reasonable period of time).

What is a reasonable period of time under rule 4(b) is a question of fact.

Poole v Smith's Car Sales (Balham) Ltd
[1962] 2 All ER 482

*At the end of August 1960, a car dealer supplied two second-hand cars, one of
1956, to a second car dealer 'on sale or return', during a period of absence on
holiday, the arrangement being that if the second dealer did not sell them they should
be returned to the first dealer. One car was sold and paid for on 21 September.
When the 1956 car was not returned by October, the first dealer made repeated but
unavailing telephone requests for its return and on 7 November wrote a letter to the
second dealer stating that, if it was not returned by 10 November, the car would be
deemed to have been sold to the second dealer. The car was not returned until a
considerable time later and, being in a bad condition (through damage by two
employees of the second dealer), was rejected by the first dealer. He brought an
action for the price of the car or alternatively for its return or value, and in an
affidavit on an application for leave to defend, a director of the second dealer said*

he gave instructions for the car to be returned in late September or early October, as there was no prospect of the car being sold.

Held: The first car dealer was entitled to judgment for the agreed price of £325, because:

(a)   The contract was one of delivery 'on sale or return' within rule 4 and in the absence of rejection the property therefore passed to the second dealer on the expiration of a reasonable time under rule 4(b).

(b)   Having regard to all the circumstances, the holiday arrangement nature of the contract, the quick sale of the first car, the known decline in the second-hand car market in September and October (of which the court took judicial notice), the rapid depreciation then of a 1956 car, the second dealer's statement that by October there was no prospect of the car being sold and the first dealer's reported requests for the return of the car in October and his letter of November 7, the proper inference was that a reasonable time had expired without the car being returned.

2.4   Unascertained goods

These are goods which are not identified or agreed upon at the time the contract is made.

Passing of property in unascertained goods is governed by the Sale of Goods Act 1979, s. 18, rule 5, but subject to the operation of s. 16, which provides that:

Where there is a contract for the sale of unascertained good no property in the goods is transferred to the buyer unless and until the goods are ascertained.

The meaning of the section is obvious: whilst the goods remain unascertained they cannot be designated as belonging to the buyer. So for example in:

Healey v Howlett and Sons
[1917] 1 KB 337

The plaintiff, a fish exporter carrying on business at Valentia, Ireland, entered into a contract with the defendants, fish salesmen, of Billingsgate, to sell to them 20 boxes of hard, bright mackerel. The fish were to be sent to the defendants at Billingsgate. On the same day the plaintiff consigned by railway for Valentia to his (the plaintiff's) order in Holyhead 190 boxes of mackerel, and telegraphed instructions to the railway company at Holyhead to deliver 20 of the 190 boxes to the defendants, and of the remaining 170 boxes, 20 and 150 to two other consignees respectively. After the mackerel were placed on rail at Valentia the plaintiff sent to the defendants by post an invoice on which he placed the words 'at sole risk of purchaser after putting fish on rail here'. The train in which the mackerel were carried from Valentia to Dublin was delayed and arrived at Dublin so late that the mackerel missed the boat by which they ought to have been carried from Dublin to Holyhead. Upon arrival of the 190 boxes at Holyhead an official of the railway company, in accordance with the plaintiff's telegraphic instructions, picked out and earmarked 20 boxes for delivery to the defendants and 20 and 150 boxes for delivery to the two others consignees respectively. In consequence of the delay which had occurred, when the mackerel reached the defendants in London they were not in a merchantable condition as hard, bright mackerel, and the defendants refused to accept them. In an action brought by the plaintiff to recover the price:

Held: (1) As the invoice was not sent by the plaintiff until after the contract of sale was complete and the fish were put on rail, it was not part of the contract, and therefore did not operate so as to place the fish at the risk of the defendants.

(2) As there had been no appropriation of the 20 boxes to the defendants at Valentia, the delivery there to the railway company of the 190 boxes did not pass the property in any particular 20 boxes to the defendants, and that they were not bound by the selection and earmarking made at Holyhead after the delay had occurred; consequently the defendants were entitled to reject the mackerel, and the plaintiff could not recover the price from them.

2.4.1 *Rule 5* When goods conforming to contract descriptions are unconditionally appropriated to the contract with the buyer's assent, property in the goods passes to the buyer. The assent may be express or implied and may be given before or after the appropriation is made.

2.4.2 *What is an unconditional appropriation?* This will be a question of fact in every case but it is clear that goods which are set aside or labelled as belonging to the contract would be unconditionally appropriated to it.

National Coal Board v Gamble
[1958] 3 All ER 203

Coal, which was part of a bulk purchase from the National Coal Board, was loaded into a lorry at a colliery for transport by the owners of the lorry to the purchaser. Loading was done through a hopper operated by the board's servants until M, the lorry driver, told them to stop. M took the lorry to the weighbridge. It was found to be loaded above the maximum permitted weight for the lorry. There were facilities for off-loading at the colliery. H, the servant of the Coal Board at the weighbridge, informed M of the overweight and asked whether he intended to take the load. M said that he would risk it. H made out the weight ticket and gave it to M, who drove away. M's employers were subsequently convicted, in consequence of his driving this load, of unlawfully using the lorry on a road. At the hearing of an information against the Coal Board of having aided and abetted the offence, the board called no evidence and were convicted. On appeal,

Held: The Coal Board were rightly convicted of aiding and abetting since, the sale being of unascertained goods, the property in the coal did not pass until the coal on the lorry had been weighed and there had been assent to the quantity in the lorry being taken, such assent being shown by the weight ticket given to and received by M.

3   What effect does passing property have as between the seller and the buyer?

An issue which is important and closely connected with the passing of property is the transfer of risk. Problems in relation to risk and in particular who should insure against the risk arise in the dynamic conditions of sale, where ownership, possession and control over the goods are in motion between seller and buyer, possibly all moving at different times.

The question of who bears the risk is critical in contracts of sale because it raises a number of issues such as:

(a)   Is the buyer liable to pay the price, even though the good are destroyed?

(b)   Is the seller liable to find a replacement to satisfy the contract, or, if he cannot do so, is he liable to the buyer for damages for non-delivery?

3.1   Passing of risk

Section 20 of the Sale of Goods Act 1979 sets out the basic principle relating to risk: risk passes to the buyer at the same time as property passes, irrespective of whether delivery has taken place.

Thus, it is a combination of rules relating to property and risk that gives the clear picture of who is to bear the loss in the event of destruction of the goods.

There are two express exceptions which need to be noted. The first is that if delivery is delayed through the fault of either party then the party at fault bears the risk of loss caused by the delay (s. 20(2)).

Demby Hamilton & Co. Ltd v *Barden*
[1949] 1 All ER 435

A manufacturer contracted to supply 30 tons of apple juice in accordance with sample to a wine merchant, to be delivered in weekly truckloads. He crushed the apples, put the juice in casks, and kept it pending delivery. It was found as a fact that it would have been difficult to supply juice complying with the sample unless all the apples had been crushed at one time and that the juice was rightly and reasonably kept for the fulfilment of the contract, but that the property in it had not passed to the buyer. After 20½ tons had been delivered no further deliveries were made through the delay of the buyer in breach of the contract between the parties and notwithstanding requests for delivery instructions from the seller, and in due course the undelivered juice went putrid and had to be thrown away. It was found that delivery had been delayed through the fault of the buyer within what is now the Sale of Goods Act 1979, s. 20. In an action by the seller for damages for breach of contract or the price of the goods sold:

Held: (1)   'Goods' in the first proviso to s. 20 meant the contractual goods which had been assembled by the seller for the purpose of fulfilling the contract and making delivery and were ready to be delivered.

(2)   After the delay, therefore, the apple juice was at the risk of the buyer who was liable in respect of its loss.

The second exception is that a seller who retains possession of the goods after property has passed to the buyer retains them as bailee. In these circumstances the seller's liability is limited to loss caused by the seller's negligence. For example, the seller would not be liable for loss resulting from accident.

3.2   Risk of loss during delivery

When the seller is required to send the goods to the buyer and delivers them to a carrier for that purpose, then that is treated as delivery to the buyer, though this is so only when the carrier is independent of the seller (s. 32(1)).

However, if the seller is required to deliver to some specified place, e.g., the buyer's business premises, then the goods will not be classed as delivered until they arrive there.

4   Who is entitled to pass property in the goods?

4.1   The general rule

As a general rule, the sale of goods by a person who is not the owner does not give good title to the buyer, even if the buyer bought in good faith and without notice of the seller's lack of title (Sale of Goods Act 1979, s. 21).

This is the maxim 'nemo dat quod non habet' (a person cannot give what he has not got).

The general rule exists to protect the true owner of goods, but there are a number of exceptions to it. These exist to protect innocent buyers from those without title, in certain cases, at the expense of the true owner.

4.2   Exceptions to the nemo dat rule

4.2.1   Agency by estoppel   If the seller of goods does not own them but sells with the consent and authority of the true owner as the true owner's agent then the buyer will get a good title.

Section 21(1) of the Sale of Goods Act 1979 states that the same applies where the seller does not have the consent of the true owner but the true owner has allowed the seller to conduct himself so that it appears he has consent. These circumstances will give rise to an agency by estoppel. This means that the true owner will be estopped from denying the seller's authority to sell the goods.

Eastern Distributors Ltd v *Goldring*
[1957] 2 QB 600

M, the owner of a Bedford van, wished to purchase a Chrysler motor car from C, a dealer, but had insufficient funds to pay the required deposit. To overcome this, C suggested that M should raise the deposit on the security of the Bedford van, and that he, C, should pretend to the plaintiffs, a hire-purchase company, that M wished to purchase both the van and the Chrysler and that M had paid the necessary deposit on both of them. C would keep the balance of the purchase price when he received it from the plaintiffs and M would pay the instalments due under hire-purchase agreements on both vehicles. M agreed and signed in blank four hire-purchase documents, namely, the proposal forms and memoranda of agreement for the Chrysler and the Bedford, and also signed a delivery note stating that he had taken delivery of the Bedford from C. C completed the documents and forwarded them to the plaintiffs who, acting in good faith, accepted the proposal in respect of the Bedford but rejected that in respect of the Chrysler. C had no authority to proceed in respect of the Bedford unless the transaction with the Chrysler also proceeded, but he nevertheless purported to sell the Bedford van to the plaintiffs. The plaintiffs completed the agreement and sent a counterpart to M. C subsequently told M that the whole transaction had been cancelled and M, who had made no payments under the hire-purchase agreement, sold the Bedford van to the defendant. At all times prior thereto the van had been in M's possession. The plaintiffs claimed the return of the van from the defendant.

Held: (1) By common law, as embodied in what is now the Sale of Goods Act 1979, s. 21(1), where goods are sold by a person not the owner thereof but the owner is by his conduct precluded from denying the seller's authority to sell, the effect is to transfer a real title to the buyer, binding a later purchaser for value without notice from the owner, and not merely a metaphorical title by estoppel; accordingly, since C was armed by M with documents which enabled C to represent that he was the owner of the Bedford with the right to sell it, M was precluded from denying C's authority to sell it, and the plaintiffs acquired the title to the van and M had no title left to pass to the defendant.

(2) That although the form of memorandum signed in blank by M was not a note or memorandum of the hire-purchase agreement 'made and signed by the hirer' as required by the Hire Purchase Act 1938, s. 2(2)(a), and the agreement was rendered unenforceable against M by virtue of ss. 2(2) and 17 of the Act, those sections did not take away from the plaintiffs any rights to possession of the vehicle that they had against third parties.

(3) That even if M and not C was considered as being the seller of the van to the plaintiffs, M retained possession of the van not as a seller remaining in possession but as a bailee under the hire-purchase agreement which, although unenforceable, was not void, and therefore M did not pass any title to the van to the defendant by virtue of what is now the Sale of Goods Act 1979, s. 24.

4.2.2 Sale by a mercantile agent A mercantile agent is a person who in the ordinary course of business as an independent agent has authority to sell or otherwise deal in goods. Thus he does not act only on the express authority of an employing principal.

The Factors Act 1889, s. 2(1), provides that where a mercantile agent is, with the consent of the owner, in possession of goods or documents of title to goods, any sale, pledge, or other disposition of the goods, made by him when acting in the ordinary course of business of a mercantile agent is as valid as if he had been expressly authorised by the owner of the goods, provided the buyer had no notice of the seller's lack of authority.

The important points in s. 2(1) are that the agent must be in possession of the goods with the owner's consent and as an agent to sell.

Additionally the sale must be in the ordinary course of business and the buyer must buy in good faith. This means that there should be nothing unusual or suspicious about the sale. If there are unusual or suspicious circumstances surrounding the sale the buyer will be put on notice and will be deemed to be acting in bad faith and thus lose the protection of the section.

4.2.3   Second sale by a seller in possession   Section 24 of the Sale of Goods Act 1979 provides that where the seller, having sold goods, retains possession of them, or documents of title to them, and sells them a second time, the second buyer will get a good title to the goods on taking physical delivery of them.

This rule will apply provided the second buyer is acting in good faith with no knowledge of the first sale.

In these circumstances the only remedy available to the first buyer is to sue the seller and obtain damages for failure to deliver the goods.

4.2.4   Resale by a buyer in possession   Section 25 of the Sale of Goods Act 1979 provides that if a person, having bought or agreed to buy goods, obtains, with the seller's consent, possession of the goods or of documents of title to them, the delivery or transfer of the goods, or the documents of title, to a person who buys the goods in good faith without notice of any rights retained by the original seller has effect as though it were a sale by a mercantile agent in possession with the consent of the owner.

Two important points need to be noted:

(a)   The section only applies where the original buyer resells in the ordinary course of business.

(b)   The original buyer must have obtained possession with the consent of the seller. However, the fact that the seller's consent to possession has been obtained by the deception of the buyer will not affect the operation of s. 25.

4.2.5   Sale by a person with a voidable title   If a buyer buys goods under a contract which is voidable, he can pass on good title to the goods provided the second buyer buys the goods in good faith with no notice of the original problem. In addition the second sale must take place before the original contract is rescinded.

4.2.6   Sale in market overt   This exception to the *nemo dat* rule was removed by the Sale of Goods (Amendment) Act 1994.

Self check questions
1.   What is the difference between the concepts of possession and property in this part of the law?
2.   What is the general rule governing passing of property?

3.   What is the difference between specific and unascertained goods?
4.   What does the maxim '*nemo dat quod non habet*' mean?
5.   List the five exceptions to the 'nemo dat' maxim.

Answers
1.   Possession means that a person has mere physical control over goods. Property means that a person has legal ownership of the goods. A person may have possession of goods without also having property in them. Alternatively a person may have property in goods without having possession of them.
2.   The general rule is contained in s. 17 of the Sale of Goods Act 1979 which states that property in the goods will pass in accordance with the intention of the parties.
3.   Specific goods are goods identified and agreed upon at the time the contract is made. Unascertained goods are goods not identified or agreed upon at the time the contract is made. The seller may have to obtain the goods from a third party or manufacture or produce them.
4.   A person cannot give what he has not got.
5.   (a) Agency by estoppel. (b) Sale by a mercantile agent. (c) Second sale by a seller in possession. (d) Resale by a buyer in possession. (e) Sale by a person with a voidable title.

Problem
In April 1994, Joe bought a Shakespeare power boat from Sea Spray financed by a two-year credit agreement between Joe and Incredible Credit.
    On 10 June 1995, Joe noticed an Arrow Jet Boat for sale on Sea Spray's forecourt. He negotiated to buy the Arrow Jet Boat for £5,500 using his Shakespeare as a deposit and paying £3,500 in cash.
    Sea Spray agreed to continue to pay the remaining instalments under the credit agreement with Incredible Credit and to respray the hull of the Arrow Boat red before Joe took delivery of it.
    On 16 June 1995, Sea Spray sold the Shakespeare Boat to Pat for £4,000 cash. The following day a fire at their premises destroyed their entire stock of power boats including the Arrow Jet Boat which was being resprayed. Sea Spray have as a result ceased trading.
    Incredible Credit have not received the last two payments due and are seeking to repossess the Shakespeare Boat from Pat. Joe wishes to recover the sum of £5,500 from the liquidators of Sea Spray.
    Advise Pat and Joe.

Suggested answer points
The following points should form the basis of any answer to this problem. Try to produce a full answer yourself and ask your tutor to mark it.

(a)   The main issues.

    (i)   The main issue for *Joe* will be who has property in the Arrow Boat and at whose risk the boat is stored is while it is being resprayed.

(ii)   The main issue for Pat is whether he has obtained a good title to the Shakespeare from Sea Spray. Here a consideration of the *nemo dat* maxim and its exceptions will be important.

(b)   Passing of property in the Arrow Boat. Have the parties expressed any intention as to when property in the Arrow Boat is to pass? If they have then property will pass in accordance with the intention of the parties and the normal rule that risk passes with property will apply. If the parties have not expressed any intention then the rules in s. 18 will determine when property will pass. You will need to decide whether the goods are specific or unascertained before you can choose the appropriate rule.

Note Sea Spray's obligation to respray the boat.

(c)   The '*nemo dat*' maxim. It would appear that Sea Spray did not own the boat when it sold it to Pat. The boat was in fact owned at this stage by Incredible Credit. The maxim '*nemo dat quod non habet*' would mean that Pat would not obtain a good title in the boat. Pat's only hope is to argue that the sale falls within an exception to the *nemo dat* maxim. You should examine the nature and scope of the exceptions to decide whether any of them might apply.

19 CONTRACT OF EMPLOYMENT

1 Introduction

The contract of employment is the basis of employment law. It has become of increasing importance in recent years and it is therefore necessary to spend time discussing it. As we shall see below there are special provisions relating to the contract of employment. However, the general contractual provisions, previously discussed, also apply. Indeed the question of the remedies of injunction and specific performance will be looked at in some detail in the context of contracts of employment.

2 The contract of employment/contract for service distinction

An employee is deemed to be a person who works under the provisions of a contract of employment. The distinction with a contract for services must be made as here the person is deemed to be an independent contractor. The essence of a contract for service is that a person performs services for another.

2.1 Why distinguish?
There are three main reasons for this distinction:

(a) Legislative provisions. Certain legislative provisions, for example the provisions relating to redundancy and unfair dismissal protection under the Employment Protection Consolidation Act (EPCA) 1978, only apply to employees. Consequently employees are given greater statutory protection than independent contractors under a contract for services.

(b) Vicarious liability. This principle means that in the employer/employee relationship, created by a contract of employment, an employer is responsible for acts done by an employee in the course of the employment relationship. The principle of vicarious liability does not apply to the relationship between an independent contractor and the person for whom he is working.

(c)   Implied terms: Certain rights and duties are implied in the contract of employment (see 3.4, below). These obligations do not apply to an independent contractor.

2.2   How the distinction is made

The courts have developed various tests in order for this important distinction to be made; legislation does not provide any help. The courts previously used the 'control' and 'integration' tests; that is to say was there control by the employer over the employee's work or alternatively was the employee integrated into the business of the employer? The two tests did not recognise the changing pattern of modern employment relationships and therefore the multiple or economic reality test was adopted by the courts. The operation of this test is illustrated by the decision in:

Ready Mixed Concrete (South East) Ltd v Minister of Pensions and National Insurance
[1968] 2 QB 497

A written contract between a company marketing and selling concrete and L, which declared L to be an independent contractor, provided, inter alia, that for payment at mileage rates L at his own expense would carry concrete for the company and make available throughout the contract period a vehicle bought by him from a finance organisation associated with the company. He was to obtain an 'A' carriers' licence and was to maintain, repair and insure the vehicle (which was to be painted in the company's colours) and an attached mixing unit belonging to the company, and to drive the vehicle himself, but might with the company's consent hire a competent driver if he should be unable to drive at any time. L was obliged to wear the company's uniform and to comply with the company's rules and was prohibited from operating as a carrier of goods except under the contract. The company had control over major repairs to the vehicle and over L's accounts to ensure that they were prepared by an accountant in a form approved by the company.

The Minister of Pensions and National Insurance determined that L was within the class of employed persons under the National Insurance Act 1965 as being an 'employed person' under contract of service with the company.

On appeal, on the contentions that the contract was not a contract of service, and that L was an independent contractor it was held, allowing the appeal:

(1)   That the inference that parties under a contract were master and servant or otherwise was a conclusion of law dependent on the rights conferred and duties imposed by the contract and if the contractual rights and duties created the relationship of master and servant, a declaration by the parties that the relationship was otherwise was irrelevant.

(2)   That a contract of service existed if: (a) the servant agreed in consideration of a wage or other remuneration to provide his own work and skill in the

performance of some service for his master; (b) the servant agreed expressly or impliedly that, in performance of the service he would be subject to the control of the other party sufficiently to make him the master; and (c) the other provisions of the contract were consistent with its being a contract of service, but that an obligation to do work subject to the other party's control was not invariably a sufficient condition of a contract of service, and if the provisions of the contract as a whole were inconsistent with the contract being a contract of service, it was some other kind of contract and that a person doing the work was not a servant; that where express provision was not made for one party to have the right of control, the question where it resided was to be answered by implication, and that since the common law test of the power of control for determining whether the relationship of master and servant existed was not restricted to the power of control over the manner of performing service but was wide enough to take account of investment and loss in determining whether a business was carried on by a person for himself or for another it was relevant to consider who owned the assets or bore the financial risk.

(3)   That the rights conferred and the duties imposed by the contract were not such as to make it a contract of service, and that L had sufficient freedom in the performance of the obligations to qualify him as an independent contractor.

The crucial factor in this decision concerns who owned the assets or bore the financial risk. Added to this L had sufficient freedom in the way he performed his duties, for example the use of a replacement driver. The decision is also interesting as the court was not influenced by the label placed on the agreement by the parties. The logic of this principle is supported by the decision in:

Ferguson v John Dawson and Partners (Contractors) Ltd
[1976] IRLR 346

F was working on a roof when he fell and suffered serious injuries. He was awarded damages of £30,387.88 against the appellants. The award was made for breach of statutory duty on the basis there was no guard rail on the roof as required by the Construction (Working Places) Regulations 1966. The appeal was made on the ground that F was not an employee but self-employed as a result of the label placed on F by mutual agreement.

Held: Notwithstanding that both the plaintiff and the defendants regarded the plaintiff as a self-employed/labour only sub-contractor, the plaintiff was employed under a contract of service. Hence the defendants owed to him the statutory duty of providing a suitable guard rail as required by the Construction (Working Places) Regulations 1966 and were liable for the award of damages made at first instance for their breach of that duty.

Whilst the express intention of the parties may be a relevant factor, it is not a conclusive factor in deciding what is the true nature of the contract. Where there is no written contract, the court is entitled to find contractual intention by implication. On the facts of the present case, the judge below had correctly found that, according to the established tests, in reality the relationship of employer and employee existed.

The decision is at times difficult to understand, particularly when F was paying his tax on the basis of being self-employed. However, what the decision does show is that the courts will look at the reality of the situation and not be swayed by any label placed on the relationship by the parties.

Self check questions
1.   What is the difference between a contract of employment and a contract for services?
2.   Why is the difference in question 1 (above) important?
3.   How do the courts make the distinction between the two?

Answers
1.   A contract of employment is the basis of the employer/employee relationship whereas a contract for services is the relationship which governs the provision of service by an independent contractor.
2.   The difference in question 1 (above) is important because certain legislative provisions, for example redundancy and unfair dismissal protection, only applies to employees. In addition an employer can be made vicariously liable for the acts of his employee whereas the same principle does not apply to any person who hires an independent contractor.
3.   The courts make this distinction by applying a variety of tests. Increasingly the economic reality or multiple test is the one used: *Ready Mixed Concrete Ltd* v *Minister of Pensions*. Further the label placed on the relationship by the parties is not conclusive: *Ferguson* v *John Dawson*.

3   Sources of the terms of the contract

The methods by which terms become incorporated into a contract of employment are numerous as the sources of them are so disparate. Terms of an employment contract, like any other contractual obligation, determine the mutual rights and duties of each party. A number of sources will be looked at below. The list is not exhaustive, but the most important are discussed.

3.1   The written statement
Section 1 of the EPCA 1978 (as amended) provides that employers must provide employees with a written statement containing particulars of certain terms of the contract of employment:

Employment Protection Consolidation Act 1978, s. 1

(1)   Not later than two months after the beginning of an employee's period of employment with an employer, the employer shall give to the employee a written statement which may, subject to subsection (3) of section 2, be given in instalments before the end of that period.

A statement given under s. 1 must contain particulars of:

(a)   the names of the employer and employee;

(b)   the date when the employment began and the date when the employee's period of continuous employment began;

(c)   the scale or rate of remuneration, or method of calculating remuneration;

(d)   the intervals at which remuneration is paid;

(e)   any terms and conditions relating to hours of work;

(f)   any terms and conditions relating to holiday entitlement (these must be sufficiently specific to allow the employee's holiday entitlement to be precisely calculated);

(g)   any terms and conditions relating to incapacity for work due to sickness or injury, including any provisions for sick pay.

(h)   any terms and conditions relating to pensions and pension schemes (although this does not apply to employees of any body or authority if the employee's pension rights are defined by statute and the employer is obliged by that statute to give new employees information concerning their pension rights);

(i)   the length of notice which the employee is obliged to give and entitled to receive to terminate the contract of employment;

(j)   the title of the job which the employee is employed to do;

(k)   as an alternative to the job title, a brief description of the work for which the employee is employed;

(l)   where the employment is not intended to be permanent, the period for which it is expected to continue or, if it is for a fixed term, the date on which it is to end;

(m)   either the place of work or, where the employee is to work at various places, an indication of that and of the address of the employer; and

(n)   any collective agreements which directly affect the terms and conditions of the employment including, where the employer is not a party, the persons with whom they are made.

It is important to understand that the written statement is *not* the contract of employment but merely written evidence of certain parts of the contract. However, it will be regarded as important if no contradictory evidence is available and further any variation in the s. 1 statement must be agreed by both parties.

3.2   Express terms
These are statements made before the contract is entered into and will form the basis of the majority of employment relationships. The legal provisions as to incorporation are the same as those discussed in Part II of the book.

3.3   Collective agreements
A collective agreement is an agreement between a trade union and an employer which can deal with terms of the contract of employment of employees.

Collective agreements are an important source of terms of the contract, indeed upwards of 75% of all employees are covered by such agreements. It should be noted that if the written statement pursuant to s. 1 of the EPCA 1978 (as amended) refers to a collective agreement as being a source of terms of the contract of employment then the collective agreement becomes legally binding between the employer and employee as a term of that contract of employment. The operation of this principle is shown by the decision in:

Robertson v British Gas Corporation
[1983] ICR 351

Two employees received a letter from their employer stating that they had been appointed gas meter readers/collectors and that, inter alia, *incentive bonus scheme conditions would apply to the work. The employees were also given a written statement of terms of employment in accordance with the amended s. 4 of the Contracts of Employment Act 1972 (now s. 1 of the Employment Protection (Consolidation) Act 1978), which stated that the provisions of an agreement between the employer and the union relating to remuneration and increments applied to the two employees and that any payments which might be due in respect of incentive bonuses 'will be calculated in accordance with the rules of the scheme in force at the time'. The scheme negotiated between the union and the employer had no legal force and the employer gave notice to the union terminating the existing bonus scheme on December 31, 1981. No new scheme was negotiated and the employees received no bonus payments after 1981. They brought actions in the county court to recover arrears of wages. The judge, giving judgment for the employees, held that the letter of appointment set out the terms of the contract of employment and not the statutory written notice and, by the terms of the letter, the employees were entitled to bonus payments. The employer appealed.*

Held: The letter and the statutory statement of terms constituted the written contract of employment. Under its terms an incentive bonus was payable in accordance with the terms negotiated between the union and the employer. Although the collective agreement was not binding between the union and the employer, it had been incorporated into the contracts of employment and, therefore, the employer could not unilaterally determine the scheme and the employees were entitled to the bonus payment. The appeal was dismissed.

KERR LJ: Turning to the two sets of contractual documents in this case, and without distinguishing between them, it seems to me to be clear that both of them were designed to operate in the context of some agreed collective scheme concerning bonus payments, with conditions (in the case of the first document) and rules in force (in the case of the second document), whose terms are to be treated as incorporated into the individual contracts evidenced by these documents. Both of them proceed on the basis that there will be an incentive bonus and that its amount and the terms governing it are to be found in an agreed collective scheme in force from time to time. Such an agreement was in force at the time when both these documents came into existence, and from time to time the terms of the scheme were thereafter varied by some further collective agreement between the trade union side and the employer's side. I agree with Mr Sedley's submission that, when the terms of the collective agreements were varied by consent between the two sides, then the new terms clearly became incorporated into the individual contracts of employment. But what does not follow, in my view, is that the contracts of the individual workmen can be carried by some unilateral variation or abrogation or withdrawal from the collective agreement by either side.

It is true that collective agreements such as those in the present case create no legally enforceable obligation between the trade union and the employees. Either side can withdraw. But their terms are in this case incorporated into the individual contracts of employment, and it is only if and when those terms are varied collectively by agreement that the individual contracts of employment will also be varied. If the collective scheme is not varied by agreement, but by some unilateral abrogation or withdrawal or variation to which the other side does not agree, then it seems to me that the individual contracts of employment remain unaffected. This is another way of saying that the terms of the individual contracts are in part to be found in the agreed collective agreements as they exist from time to time, and, if these cease to exist as collective agreements, then the terms, unless expressly varied between the individual and the employer, will remain as they were by reference to the last agreed collective agreement incorporated into the individual contracts.

In the present case this construction is reinforced by the fact that, although it looks from the documents as though the incentive bonus scheme is merely one small part of the total terms of the individual contracts of employment, it provides in fact an integrated and general framework for a very large number of the mutual rights and obligations of the parties. Indeed, it becomes virtually impossible to determine what the full terms of these individual contracts of employment are if you once take away the agreed collective scheme for an incentive bonus as an integral part of these contracts.

For all these reasons I have no doubt that the judge came to the right conclusion, and I would equally dismiss this appeal.

The decision is important as it emphasises the importance of collective agreements as a source of the contract of employment. Therefore, like any other term of the contract, a collective agreement cannot be unilaterally varied.

3.4   Implied terms

The courts will imply terms into a contract where it is necessary to do so. The same principle applies with contracts of employment and the courts will imply terms when they do not contradict existing express terms. Implied terms can be placed in two categories: implied duties of employees and duties of the employer.

3.4.1   Duties of employees   These duties can be placed in five categories:

(a)   to be ready and willing to work;
(b)   to obey lawful orders;

    (c)   to use reasonable care and skill;
    (d)   to take care of the employer's property;
    (e)   to act in good faith.

Space permits only discussion of the first two categories.

(a)   *To be ready and willing to work.*

The fundamental duty which an employee owes to his employer is to present himself at work and to work in accordance with the contract of employment. If the employee carries out this duty then the employer is under the obligation to pay wages. Clearly if the employee does not carry out this duty then the employer does not have to pay wages. The question is whether or not an employee is entitled to any remuneration if he partially performs the contract.

The principle is discussed in the decision of the Court of Appeal in:

Wiluszynski v *Tower Hamlets London Borough Council*
[1989] ICR 493

The plaintiff was employed by the defendant council as an estate officer with duties including the answering of councillors' inquiries on estate matters. In response to a union instruction calling on the council's estate officers not to answer such inquiries during an industrial dispute, the council notified the officers that unless they were prepared to answer the inquiries they would be neither required for work nor paid. For the period 14 August to 17 September 1985, when he carried on his duties on the council's premises other than answering the inquiries, the plaintiff was not paid his salary, for which he brought an action to recover the moneys. The judge held that the salary was payable. The council appealed.

Held: Since the plaintiff was in breach of his contract of employment by not performing all of his duties and the council had made it clear that if he was not prepared to comply with his contract he was not required for work and would not be paid, the plaintiff was not entitled to sue for remuneration in the absence of evidence that he performed any part of his duties at the direction or request of the council. The appeal was allowed.

NICHOLLS LJ: In my view the council was entitled to adopt the stance that, so long as the plaintiff continued to refuse to carry out part of his contractual duties, the council would not accept his services and the plaintiff would not be paid. Replying to inquiries from councillors was a material part of the duties of estate officers such as the plaintiff. The plaintiff's considered statement that he would not discharge this part of his duties was, in law, a repudiatory breach of his contract. Subject to any provision to the contrary in his contract of employment, such conduct entitled the council to treat the contract as terminated and to dismiss the plaintiff. The contrary conclusion would mean that the council would be obliged to continue to employ and pay the plaintiff even though part of the work required of him and others in his position would not be done. That cannot be right.

In my view, however, termination of the contract is not the only remedy available to an employer in such circumstances. A buyer of goods is entitled to decline to accept goods tendered to him which do not conform to a condition in the contract, without necessarily terminating the contract altogether. So with services. If an employee states that for the indefinite future he will not be performing a material part of his contractual services, the employer is entitled in response, and in advance of the services being undertaken, to decline to accept the proferred partial performance. He can hold himself out as continuing to be ready and willing to carry out the contract of employment, and to accept from the employee work as agreed and to pay him for that work as agreed, while declining to accept to pay for part only of the agreed work.

The decision clearly establishes the principle that in order to be legally entitled to wages an employee must be ready and willing to perform the entire contractual obligation. The decision is of great importance as it establishes that part performance of a contract of employment need not be accepted by an employer.

(b)   *To obey lawful orders.*
An employee is under a duty to obey all the lawful orders of his employer — that is those which are within the scope of the contract. The key question is what orders come within the contract of employment. A good example is provided by the introduction of new working methods.

Cresswell v Board of Inland Revenue
[1984] 2 All ER 713

The Board of the Inland Revenue wished to introduce a system of computer operation of the PAYE scheme. Computerisation would have the effect that calculations formerly done manually by tax officers would be done by computer, all necessary documentation following an individual change of coding would be sent out automatically and where there was a universal review of coding e.g., following a Finance Act, all necessary alterations and notifications would be done automatically. The effect for those grades of Inland Revenue involved, namely clerical assistants and tax officers, was that they would be required to enter relevant information into the computer via a visual display unit rather than onto individual cards.

The plaintiffs, a number of clerical assistants and tax officers, objected to the introduction of the scheme for computerisation on the ground that it would be a breach of their terms of service to introduce it without their consent. The board informed the plaintiffs that it was not prepared to continue with the old manual methods and that it would not pay them while they refused to operate the computerised system. The board also made it clear that it was not putting an end to the plaintiffs' contracts of employment or seeking to take disciplinary action against them and that they would be paid if they returned to full-time work using the computerised system.

The plaintiffs brought an action against the board seeking a declaration that the board was in breach of its contract of employment with the plaintiffs in requiring them to operate or use the system and in suspending them without pay while they refused to operate the system. The plaintiffs contended that the introduction of the computerised system would be such a change in the method of performing the tasks for which they had been recruited as to amount to a change in the nature of their jobs and that the plaintiffs were therefore being asked to perform work under wholly different contracts without their consent. The plaintiffs further contended that the board's action in refusing to pay them until they used the computerised system amounted to their suspension without complying with the appropriate disciplinary procedures and that the board was therefore required to pay them until the proper suspension procedures had been carried out.

Held: The plaintiffs' action would be dismissed for the following reason — an employee did not have a vested right to preserve his working obligations completely unchanged as from the moment he first began work, but was expected to adapt himself to new methods and techniques introduced in the course of his employment. The effect of the board's computerised system was not that the plaintiffs would be doing a different job but merely that they would be doing recognisably the same job in a different way. Although the content of some of the jobs might be considerably affected it would not be altered sufficiently to fall outside the original description of the plaintiffs' proper functions, since it could not be said that staff using the computerised system would be anything other than tax officers working the PAYE scheme. The board was therefore entitled to introduce the computerised system and to require the plaintiffs to operate it under their existing contracts of employment.

Obviously the introduction of new technology, in certain circumstances, could be outside the scope of the contract if it is a 'radical' change in the method and nature of working. The decision in *Cresswell* v *Board of Inland Revenue* recognises the need for change within the scope of the existing contract of employment.

3.4.2 Duties of employer The main examples of these duties are:

(a) to pay contractually agreed remuneration;
(b) to treat employees with trust and confidence;
(c) to indemnify employees;
(d) to observe provisions relating to hours of work.

The most interesting relates to the duty of trust and confidence.

Duty of employer to treat employees with trust and confidence
The nature of this duty has come of the need to show a breach of contract in order to establish a claim for constructive dismissal (see below). Further it is an important limitation on the way in which an employer can treat an employee. The operation of the duty is shown by the decision in:

Courtaulds Northern Textiles Ltd v *Andrew*
[1979] IRLR 84

Mr Andrew, an overseer who had worked for the appellant company for 18 years, had an argument with one of the assistant managers, Mr Sneyd. During the course of this argument, there was a certain amount of provocative observation on both sides and at the end of it, Mr Sneyd said to Mr Andrew, 'You can't do the bloody job anyway'. Mr Andrew reacted to this by resigning.

An industrial tribunal held that Mr Andrew had been constructively dismissed.

The EAT held: The respondent overseer was entitled to treat a statement by the appellant company's assistant manager that 'You can't do the bloody job anyway', where that was not a true expression of the manager's opinion, as conduct which justified him in resigning and claiming constructive dismissal.

There is an implied term in a contract of employment that the employers will not, without reasonable and proper cause, conduct themselves in a manner calculated or likely to destroy or seriously damage the relationship of confidence and trust between the parties.

In the present case, telling the respondent that he could not do his job, when that was not a true expression of opinion, amounted to a breach of that implied term. It was conduct which was likely to destroy the trust relationship which was a necessary element in the relationship between this supervisory employee and his employers.

Moreover, the breach was a fundamental one. Any conduct which is likely to destroy or seriously damage the relationship of mutual trust and confidence between employer and employee must be something which goes to the root of the contract.

Thus, notwithstanding that the industrial tribunal's reasoning was slightly different, their decision that the respondent had been constructively dismissed was justified and the appeal would be dismissed.

Self check questions
1. What is the legal status of the written statement given to an employee pursuant to s. 1 EPCA 1978 (as amended)?
2. What is a collective agreement? Is a collective agreement legally binding between an employer and employee?
3. Is an employer legally obliged to pay an employee any wages if he only performs part of his contract of employment?
4. Can an employer introduce new working techniques within the scope of an existing contract of employment?
5. Is there a contractual term which means that a duty of trust and confidence is owed by an employer to its employees?

Answers
1. The written statement is not the contract of employment but is usually seen as strong evidence of the contents of it.
2. A collective agreement is an agreement made between a trade union and an employer which can be used to regulate the relationship between that employer and its employees. A collective agreement can become legally binding between an employer and employee if it is incorporated into the contract of

employment; an example of the operation of this principle is the decision in *Robertson* v *British Gas*.

3. An employee must perform all his contractual obligations in order to be legally entitled to wages. The employer does not have to accept partial performance of the contract of employment: *Wiluszynski* v *Tower Hamlets LBC*.

4. An employee is under a contractual duty to obey lawful orders of the employer. New technology can be introduced only if it is a different way of doing the same job which the employee was required to do under the contract of employment: *Cresswell* v *Board of Inland Revenue*.

5. An employer owes its employees a contractual duty of trust and confidence. Such a term will be implied into a contract of employment in order to limit the powers of an employer over its employees: *Courtaulds Northern Textiles Ltd* v *Andrew*.

4   Remedies for breach of the contract of employment

We shall deal with the statutory consequences of a contract of employment being terminated in the next chapter; i.e., remedies for unfair dismissal and a claim for a redundancy payment. Here we examine the role of the remedies which are available for a breach of any contract, but apply the remedies in the context of employment contracts.

4.1   Damages
The general principles of remoteness and qualification will apply as previously discussed in Part II. In practical terms, however, damages are rarely claimed against an employee who is in breach as either loss is minimal or alternatively it is difficult to qualify.

4.2   Specific performance and injunction
Specific performance is an order of the court directing that the parties to a contract perform their contractual obligations. It is a fundamental principle of employment law that specific performance is not available to compel performance of a contract of employment.

Trade Union and Labour Relations (Consolidation) Act 1992, s. 236

No court shall, whether by way of—

(a)   an order for specific performance or specific implement of a contract of employment, or

(b)   an injunction or interdict restraining a breach or threatened breach of such a contract,

compel an employee to do any work or attend at any place for the doing of any work.

The section is clearly saying that specific performance will not be ordered or an injunction granted to compel an employee to work. The courts have, however, in recent years been prepared to grant an injunction in order to prevent an *employer* acting in breach of contract and thereby maintaining the status quo of the existing situation before the breach occurred. The application of this principle can be illustrated by two decisions:

Powell v *London Borough of Brent*
[1987] IRLR 466

Mrs Powell was employed by the council as a Senior Benefit Officer. She applied for promotion to a post as Principal Benefits Officer (Policy and Training). She was one of several candidates interviewed and after the interviews were concluded on 27.11.86 she was informed by telephone by the Assistant Director of Housing that the appointment subcommittee had selected her.

Mrs Powell reported to her new place of employment on 1.12.86. But at the same time, one of the other candidates submitted a grievance concerning his unsuccessful application. The council took the view that the selection procedure might have been in breach of their equal opportunity code of practice and on 5.12.86 Mrs Powell was informed that it was not possible to appoint her. At the end of January 1987, it was decided to readvertise the post.

Mrs Powell contended that she had been appointed to the post and that she had continued to carry out its functions from the beginning of December. This was disputed by the council. On 29.1.87, the council wrote to her stating that she had been told that her appointment had not been confirmed and that she should return to her previous position. Mrs Powell's solicitors wrote that this was a repudiatory breach of contract which Mrs Powell did not accept.

A writ was issued and in February the council gave an undertaking that for the next month they would not treat Mrs Powell other than as the Principal Benefits Officer (Policy and Training). The effect of this was that Mrs Powell was to do the work of the post for which she applied.

When the undertaking expired, an interlocutory injunction was sought to restrain the council from advertising the post and requiring them to treat Mrs Powell as if she were properly employed by them in the post. The council opposed the injunction, contending that she had never been effectively appointed and that the injunction should not be granted because the councils did not have the full confidence in Mrs Powell, both as to her competence to do the job and so as to make them willing to have her in the job, as would be required before such an injunction could be made.

The Court of Appeal held: The plaintiff was entitled to an interlocutory injunction requiring the council to treat her as if she was properly employed by them as Principal Benefits Officer (Policy and Training) and to stop the council from advertising or otherwise filling the post until it was determined at the trial of the action whether she had been validly and effectively appointed to the office in question. Although it is a general rule that there cannot be specific performance of a contract of service, part of the basis of which is that mutual confidence is a necessary condition for the contract's satisfactory working, the present case was exceptional. On the evidence before the court, it would not be accepted that the employers did not have such full confidence in the plaintiff as is required before such an injunction may be made.

The court will not by injunction require an employer to let a servant continue in his employment, when the employer has sought to terminate that employment and to prevent the servant carrying out his work under the contract, unless it is clear on the evidence that it is otherwise just to take such a requirement of confidence on the part of the employer in the servant's ability and other necessary attributes for it to be reasonable to make the order. It is unlikely that a plaintiff will be able to satisfy the court that, despite strenuous opposition by her employers to her continuing in the job, nevertheless there subsists the necessary confidence to justify the making of an injunction. Sufficiency of confidence must be judged by reference to the circumstances of the case, including the nature of the work, the people with whom the work must be done and the likely effect on the employer and the employer's operations if the employer is required by injunction to suffer the plaintiff to continue in the work.

The issue of confidence in the present case had two aspects: the plaintiff's competence to do the job and the absence of friction at the workplace. As it was not disputed that the plaintiff had done the job satisfactorily and without complaint for over four months, there was no rational ground for the employers to lack confidence in her competence to do the job pending trial. Nor was there any basis for supposing that there was any defect in the relationship between her and any other person with whom she worked or with whom she might be expected to have to work.

The court would exercise its discretion to grant an injunction in the terms sought. Damages would not be adequate compensation for the plaintiff if she were to succeed at the trial in respect of what she would suffer if the employers were free to exclude her from the post and proceed to fill it after advertisement. Although she could be compensated for loss of earnings, she would have lost the satisfaction of doing a more demanding and rewarding job and would be uncompensated for this distress and embarrassment in having to resume her former job meanwhile. As there was no evidence that the plaintiff was not able to discharge the post satisfactorily, the damage suffered by the employers until the trial by being prevented from treating the plaintiff as never having been appointed to the post would be of no real significance.

The Court of Appeal in this judgment emphasised the fact that as trust and confidence existed between the parties then the injunction should be granted. It may well be argued that the result of this decision is in effect to allow specific performance of the contract, albeit through the back door. The reasoning in *Powell* v *London Borough of Brent* was adopted in:

Hughes v London Borough of Southwark
[1988] IRLR 55

The plaintiffs were social workers employed by the defendants. Each had a post at the Maudsley Hospital, working in multi-disciplinary teams.

As a result of a shortage of funds, the Council was unable adequately to staff all of its community areas. In particular, there was a special difficulty in providing social workers to cope with the workload in Area 7. The Council proposed to set up two teams of Maudsley Hospital social workers to go to Area 7 for three days a week for a temporary period. The plaintiffs were instructed to join those teams. They complained that the Council was unreasonably requiring them to do work which was not part of their contractual duty and sought an interlocutory injunction to prevent the Council from requiring compliance with the instruction.

The High Court held: The defendants were in breach of contract in instructing the plaintiff social workers to cease their normal work at Maudsley Hospital on certain days and carry out other work on those days. The plaintiffs were entitled to an interlocutory injunction restraining the defendants from enforcing the instruction.

It was clear from the decision in *Powell* v *The London Borough of Brent* that the court had the power, if appropriate, to grant an interlocutory injunction in relation to a contract of service. The most important criterion for such an order is whether there is mutual confidence. In the present case, there was no question of the employers not having confidence in the plaintiffs. It was clear that they had great confidence in them. It would be wrong to consider that simply because there is a dispute between employer and employee mutual confidence has gone. If that were so, there could never be a situation in which an injunction could be granted because there will always be a dispute before an application for such an injunction will be made.

In the present case, the reasonableness of the instructions was not confined to the impact on the individual plaintiffs personally in regard to his or her own situation. It also had to take into account the work which the social worker was normally doing, the impact of the instruction on that work and the patients who were at the receiving end of it, and the impact the plaintiffs would make where they were going to be moved. Looking at the whole of the circumstances, it was arguable that the instruction was not reasonable.

If the instruction was implemented, the plaintiffs would suffer loss of job satisfaction and distress at being taken away from what they regard as important work which at common law could not be compensated by damages.

The balance of convenience was in favour of granting an interlocutory injunction. Moving the plaintiffs might only be at best a temporary palliative to a problem needing a permanent solution and would create a crisis at the Maudsley Hospital. The defendants had failed to consult with the hospital or take sufficient steps in investigation properly to inform themselves as to the balance of work priorities. Although it is for managers to manage, that principle was flawed in the present case by their failure to inform themselves of the relevant considerations before deciding on priorities.

Therefore, the requirement that the status quo should prevail would require the court to say that the plaintiffs should remain doing the work they had done.

The decision, again, shows the importance of the duty of trust and confidence. The Court is using it to limit the abilities of the employer and to ensure that employees are treated in an appropriate manner. Further the injunction is in effect ensuring that the existing contract is enforced.

Self check questions
1. Can a contract of employment be subject to an order of specific performance?
2. What is the relationship between the implied term of mutual trust and confidence and an injunction?

Answers

1.   Section 236 of the Trade Union and Labour Relations (Consolidation) Act 1992 states that an order for specific performance cannot be granted to compel the performance of an employment contract.

2.   If an employer is acting in breach of contract and mutual trust and confidence still exists between the employer and employee then the courts may grant an injunction in order to maintain the *status quo*, in other words prevent the employer from acting in breach: *Powell* v *London Borough of Brent* (1987) and *Hughes* (1988).

Problem

Pat is a clerical assistant employed by X Ltd. She has worked at X Ltd for ten years. Pat has received a written statement of her main terms and conditions which refers to a collective agreement made between her trade union and X Ltd. Pat's work has traditionally involved the administration of the pay roll of X Ltd which has been undertaken manually, that is to say without any computerised system.

Advise Pat in the following situations:

(a)   X Ltd seek to alter the way in which Pat undertakes her work by introducing a computerised payroll system. X Ltd offer training but Pat is unwilling to operate modern technology. Pat boycotts the introduction of the new technology but continues to work using the old methods. X Ltd refuse to pay her any wages.

(b)   The Collective Agreement between X Ltd and Pat's trade union guarantees five days continuous holiday at Christmas. X Ltd seek to unilaterally vary this arrangement by reallocating three of the days' holiday to Easter.

(c)   X Ltd order Pat to take on extra work over and above her normal contractual duties. Pat feels that this will affect her existing work.

Advise Pat as to any common law remedies which may be available.

Suggested answer (point form)

(a)   Implied term of duty to obey lawful orders: *Cresswell* v *Board of Inland Revenue*. Implied term of being ready and willing to work and need of entire performance: *Wiluszynski* v *LBC of Tower Hamlets*.

(b)   Relationship between written statement of main terms and collective agreements: *Robertson* v *British Gas Corporation*.

(c)   Implied term of mutual trust and confidence and relationship with injunction: *Powell* v *LB of Brent* and *Hughes* v *LB of Southwark*.

20 UNFAIR DISMISSAL AND REDUNDANCY

1 Introduction

In this chapter we shall examine the protection available to an employee who has had his contract of employment terminated. We have mentioned above the common law and equitable remedies available and in this chapter the statutory concepts of unfair dismissal and redundancy will be discussed. In practical terms the statutory protections are the ones most often used.

An employee, in order to qualify for protection must have been continuously employed for two or more years. The rules for computing the period of continuous employment are contained in sch. 13 of the EPCA, 1978. The rules are complex but can be summarised as follows:

(a) if an employee works more than 16 hours per week then two years' continuous employment is required for protection;

(b) if an employee works between 8-16 hours per week then five years' continuous employment is required for protection;

(c) if an employee works less than 8 hours per week there is no protection.

The provisions, above, relating to part-time workers (that is those working less than 16 hours per week) were held to be incompatible with the following European legislation: art. 119 of the Treaty of Rome, the 'Equal Pay' Directive (75/117/EEC) and the 'Equal Treatment' Directive (76/207/EEC). This was the effect of the decision in:

R v Secretary of State for Employment, ex pa. te Equal Opportunities Commission
[1994] IRLR 176

The EOC, together with Patricia Day, a part-time cleaner who had been employed for 11 hours a week by the Hertfordshire Area Health Authority before she was made redundant, sought judicial review of the Secretary of State's refusal to accept that the UK is in breach of its obligations under EC law on grounds that the effect of the qualifying thresholds governing the right not to be unfairly dismissed, the right to unfair dismissal compensation and the right to statutory redundancy pay is that the conditions of employment of part-time workers are less favourable than those of full-time workers.

It was accepted that some 87% of part-time workers in the UK are women. However, the Secretary of State contended that if and in so far as the relevant provisions have the effect of indirectly discriminating against some, they are objectively justified.

The House of Lords held: No objective justification for the hours per week qualifying thresholds in the Employment Protection (Consolidation) Act had been established by the Secretary of State.

In the present case, the purpose of the qualifying thresholds was to bring about an increase in the availability of part-time work. It could not be said that this was not a necessary aim. However, the threshold provisions had not been shown, by reference to objective factors, to be suitable and requisite for achieving that aim.

The purpose of the thresholds was said to be to reduce the costs to employers of employing part-time workers. The same result, however, would follow from paying part-time workers a lower basic rate than full-time workers. Legislation which permitted a differential of that kind would constitute a gross breach of the principle of equal pay and could not possibly be regarded as a suitable means of achieving an increase in part-time employment. Similar considerations applied to legislation reducing the indirect cost of employing part-time labour, since no distinction in principle can properly be made between direct and indirect labour costs.

Nor, on the evidence before the Divisional Court, had the threshold provisions been proved actually to result in greater availability of part-time work than would be the case without them, so as to prove that the threshold provisions were requisite to achieve the stated aim. The evidence for the Secretary of State consisted principally of the views of the Department, but did not contain anything capable of being regarded as factual evidence demonstrating the correctness of these views.

A declaration would be made that the provisions of the Employment Protection (Consolidation) Act whereby employees who work for fewer than 16 hours per week are subject to different conditions in respect of qualification for redundancy pay from those which apply to employees who work for 16 hours per week or more are incompatible with art. 119 and EEC Equal Pay Directive 75/11, and that the different conditions in respect of the right to compensation for unfair dismissal are incompatible with EEC Equal Treatment Directive 76/207.

The decision relates to the qualification period for redundancy payments. Its effect is to extend these rights to any employee who has been employed for more than two years, irrespective of the number of hours worked. The above principle is also thought to extend to the qualification period for unfair dismissal claims made by former employees of the State. At the time of writing, legislation is awaited to clarify the situation.

It should be noted that the right not to be discriminated against on grounds of race and sex and the right to be a member of a trade union exist from the start of the employment relationship. No continuous employment is required for these rights.

2 Unfair dismissal

Section 54(1) of EPCA, 1978, states: 'In every employment to which this section applies every employee shall have the right not to be unfairly dismissed.' Certain categories of employees are excluded, for example police officers, but the principle is of general application.

2.1 Dismissal

A pre-requisite of an action for unfair dismissal to succeed is that the employee must first establish that he was dismissed within the meaning of s. 55 EPCA, 1978. Section 55(2) provides:

An employee shall be treated as dismissed by his employer if, but only if,

(a) the contract under which he is employed by the employer is terminated by the employer, whether it is so terminated by notice or without notice,

(b) where under that contract he is employed for a fixed term, that term expires without being renewed under the same contract, or

(c) the employee terminates that contract, with or without notice, in circumstances such that he is entitled to terminate it without notice by reason of the employer's conduct.

Criteria (a) and (b) are self-explanatory. The majority of discussion has centred around s. 55(2)(c), the principle of constructive dismissal. The essence of constructive dismissal is that an employee terminates the employment relationship because of the conduct of the employer. The question is what type of conduct entitles the employee to take this action?

Western Excavating Ltd v *Sharp*
[1978] IRLR 27

When Mr Sharp was suspended from work without pay for five days as a disciplinary measure mitigating an initial decision to dismiss him for misconduct, his financial plight forced him to ask the company if he could be given his accrued holiday pay or, alternatively a loan, to make up his social security payments to his normal weekly pay. When the company refused to provide Mr Sharp with assistance, he resigned in order to get his holiday money. He subsequently claimed that he had been constructively dismissed.

The Court of Appeal held: The majority of the industrial tribunal had erred in law in finding that the respondent employee was entitled to resign and claim constructive dismissal by reason of the employer's unreasonable conduct, notwithstanding that the employer had not repudiated the contract of employment or broken a fundamental term of it.

> *Whether an employee is 'entitled' to terminate his contract of employment 'without notice by reason of the employer's conduct' and claim constructive dismissal within the meaning of para. 5(2)(c) of sch. 1 to the Trade Union and Labour Relations Act must be determined in accordance with the law of contract. The words 'entitled' and 'without notice' in para. 5(2)(c) are the language of contract connoting that, as a result of the employer's conduct, the employee has a right to treat himself as discharged from any further performance of the contract.*

(NB para. 5(2)(c) of sch. 1 to TULRA is now contained in s. 55(2)(c) of EPCA 1978.)

In the present case, there had been no suggestion that the employers had been in breach of contract in refusing to give the employee an advance on his accrued holiday pay to cover a period when as a result of misconduct he had been suspended without pay. The Industrial Tribunal's decision that the respondent employee had been constructively dismissed and was entitled to unfair dismissal compensation was perverse and would be set aside.

LORD DENNING MR: An employee is entitled to treat himself as constructively dismissed if the employer is guilty of conduct which is a significant breach going to the root of the contract of employment; or which shows that the employer no longer intends to be bound by one or more of the essential terms of the contract. The employee in those circumstances is entitled to leave without notice or to give notice, but the conduct in either case must be sufficiently serious to entitle him to leave at once. Moreover, the employee must make up his mind soon after the conduct of which he complains. If he continues for any length of time without leaving, he will be regarded as having elected to affirm the contract and will lose his right to treat himself as discharged.

The principle from *Western Excavating* v *Sharp* is that an employee is only able to argue constructive dismissal where the employer has breached the contract in such a way as to justify the employee in treating himself as discharged from further performance. The effect of the 'contractual' test for constructive dismissal has meant that the courts and tribunals have looked to the implied term of trust and confidence (see *Courtaulds* v *Andrew* (above)), when deciding whether or not there has been a breach of contract.

Self check questions
1. Does every employee have the right not to be unfairly dismissed?
2. What does an employee have to show in order to successfully argue constructive dismissal?

Answers
1. Section 54(1) EPCA, 1978, gives the right to every employee not to be unfairly dismissed. However, like any general principle of law, there are exceptions: in particular certain categories of employees, for example a police officer, and an employee who does not have the requisite continuity of service.

2.   An employee must show, given the decision in *Western Excavating* v *Sharp* that the employer has by its conduct breached the contract of employment.

2.2   Reasons for dismissal

There are five categories of reasons which, if one is established by the employer, may make the dismissal fair. Once the employer has established a reason for the dismissal then it has to be shown that the employer acted reasonably in making the decision to dismiss. Therefore, the determination as to the fairness of the dismissal is a two-fold test.

The reasons for dismissal are contained in s. 57(2) EPCA, 1978, and can be summarised as follows:

(a)   Capability of qualifications.
(b)   Conduct.
(c)   Redundancy.
(d)   Illegality of continued employment.
(e)   Some other substantial reason.

It is for the employer to show the reason for dismissal fell into one of the heads in s. 57(2). We shall discuss redundancy below, but an example of the operation of s. 57(2) is provided by:

Whitbread & Co. plc v *Thomas*
[1988] ICR 135

The employees were part-time assistants in one of the off-licences owned by the employers. From 1977 onwards the employers suffered serious stock losses at that off-licence and despite intensive investigations they were unable to find the cause. For periods in 1982 and 1984, they transferred the employees to other branches in the same area whereupon the losses ceased but, when the employees returned to the original shop the losses started again. After the employers had given warnings in accordance with their disciplinary code to employees, they dismissed them in April, 1985 for failing to control stock losses. The employees complained that they had been unfairly dismissed. The industrial tribunal accepted that it had been impossible for the employers to identify the cause of the stock losses or the persons responsible but the industrial tribunal upheld the complaints of unfair dismissal on the ground that the reason for the dismissals related to the employees' conduct, within the meaning of s. 57(2)(b) of the Employment Protection (Consolidation) Act 1978, rather than to any dishonesty and, in those circumstances, the employers had acted unreasonably under s. 57(3) of the Act in dismissing several employees without having regard to which employee was responsible. The employers appealed.

Held: Allowing the appeal, that where an employer could not identify the individual or individuals responsible for an act or acts of commission or omission, an employer was entitled to dismiss a group of employees on grounds that would justify dismissing an identified individual provided that the employer had carried out a proper investigation and could show that the acts had been committed by one or more of the group and each member of that group had been individually capable of having committed the acts complained of. Since the employers' action in dismissing the employees after a proper investigation and after giving warnings to the employees, was a reasonable response to the continuing stock losses, the industrial tribunal had erred in law in finding that the dismissals were unfair.

The case also illustrates the importance of investigation as it emphasises the onus is on the employer to show the reason for dismissal.

2.3   Reasonableness of the decision to dismiss
Once the employer has established the reason for dismissal (within s. 57(2) EPCA, 1978, only) the industrial tribunal must then ask whether s. 57(3) EPCA has been satisfied. Section 57(3) states:

> ... in the circumstances (including the size and administrative resources of the employer's undertaking) the employer acted reasonably or unreasonably in treating it as a sufficient reason for dismissing the employee; and that shall be determined in accordance with equity and substantial merits of the case.

In order to satisfy s. 57(3) the industrial tribunal must decide whether the employer asked reasonably both in terms of the substantive decision to dismiss and the procedure which led up to the dismissal.

When making the decision as to whether an employer acted reasonably, the industrial tribunal is required to have regard to the provisions of the Advisory Conciliation and Arbitration Service (ACAS) Code of Practice, 'Disciplinary Practice and Procedures in Employment'. The essence of the Code of Practice is that a disciplinary procedure ought to contain certain essential elements, for example a system of warnings ought to be used in order to allow employees to improve their conduct. Further employees should be consulted regarding any potential redundancy situation (see further below). The importance of procedures in determining the reasonableness question is shown by the decision of the House of Lords in *Polkey* v *A. E. Dayton Services Ltd* (1988).

Polkey v *A. E. Dayton Services Ltd*
[1988] AC 344

The employee was one of four van drivers employed since 1978 by a company dealing with components for the motor industry. In 1982, the employers decided to replace the four van drivers with two van salesmen and a representative. Only one of the van drivers was considered suitable for transfer to the new duties and it was then decided that the other three van drivers, including the employee, would have to be made redundant. Without prior warning, the employee was called into the branch manager's office and informed that he had been made redundant. He was handed a redundancy letter setting out the payments due to him and sent home. On his complaint that he had been unfairly dismissed because he had been made redundant without any consultation, the industrial tribunal held that the employers had been in breach of their obligation to consult the employee under the provision of the code of practice. They went on, however, to consider whether, if there had been consultation, the result would have been any different and concluded that the result would have been the same and dismissed the employee's complaint. The employee appealed, contending that the industrial tribunal had applied the wrong test in inquiring whether the employee would have been made redundant if he had been consulted. The appeal tribunal dismissed the appeal, and the Court of Appeal dismissed an appeal by the employee. The employee appealed to the House of Lords.

Held: The appeal was allowed. The question that the industrial tribunal had to consider under s. 57(3) of the Employment Protection (Consolidation) Act 1978 was whether the employer had been reasonable or unreasonable in deciding that his reason for dismissing his employee was a sufficient reason and not whether the employee would nevertheless have been dismissed even if there had been prior consultation or warning within the code of practice. Whether the employer could reasonably have concluded that consultation or warning would be useless so that his failure to consult or warn would not necessarily render dismissal unfair was a matter for the industrial tribunal to consider in the light of the circumstances known to the employer at the time when he took his decision to dismiss; and that, accordingly, the matter should be remitted to a differently constituted industrial tribunal for consideration of the correct question.

The decision emphasises the importance of procedures and employers must show the tribunal that they have been followed to the letter.

Self check questions
1.   What questions have to be answered in assessing whether or not a dismissal was fair?
2.   What is the importance of disciplinary procedures in the context of reasonableness?

Answers
1.   The employer must show that the reason for dismissal fell into one of the five categories as outlined in s. 57(2) EPCA; failure to do so renders the dismissal unfair. Secondly, the industrial tribunal must then ask itself whether or not the employee acted reasonably in all the circumstances of the case.
2.   The decision in *Polkey* v *A. E. Dayton Services Ltd* (1988) means that the employer must follow the appropriate disciplinary procedures in order to have acted reasonably. Failure to follow the appropriate procedures may render the dismissal unfair.

2.4   Remedies
A brief mention must be made of the remedies available in an unfair dismissal case. Section 69 EPCA, 1979 allows the complaint to be either reinstated or re-engaged. Reinstatement means that the employer must treat the employee in all respects as if he had not been dismissed; the effect of reinstatement is that the employee gets his actual job together with all the benefits associated with it. Interestingly a reinstatement order in effect specifically enforces the contract of employment.

The above may be compared with an order of re-engagement which means that the employer must take the employee into comparable employment; that is to say not the job from which he was dismissed. It should be noted that neither order is automatic as s. 69(5) EPCA states that in exercising its discretion the industrial tribunal must look at, for example, whether or not it is practicable for the employer to take the employee back. In practical terms the above two orders are rarely used as most complainants do not want their jobs back once they have been dismissed.

The most common form of remedy awarded for unfair dismissal is that of compensation. Compensation has two elements to it: the basic award and the compensatory award. The basic award is assessed in the same way as a redundancy payment (see below) and depends on the age of the employee, his average weekly earnings and length of service. The maximum basic award is, at the time of writing, £6,150.

The compensatory award is 'such amount as the tribunal considers just and equitable in all the circumstances having regard to the loss sustained by the complainant in consequence of the dismissal in so far as the loss is attributable to action taken by the employer' (s. 74(1) EPCA, 1978).

The compensatory award will take into account such factors as expenses incurred as a result of dismissal and estimated future loss of earnings. The maximum compensatory award at the time of writing is £11,000.

Problem

Peter and Janet are lorry drivers employed by Preston Road Hauliers Ltd. since 1980. Helen is the supervisor to whom both Peter and Janet are answerable.

Peter is suspected of stealing goods from the company. Theft is deemed to be gross misconduct under the disciplinary procedure and rules of the company. Despite numerous investigations nothing has been proved. Peter has his lorry stolen with an expensive load on board. He is instantly dismissed without any investigation having been held.

Janet and Helen have a serious personality conflict. Helen insists on questioning Janet's abilities in front of other members of staff and makes references to alleged backhanders received by Janet for 'services rendered' to another supervisor. On one such occasion Janet walks out.

Advise Peter and Janet as to any claim for unfair dismissal available to them.

Suggested answer

1. Both have continuity of employment.

2. (a) Preston Road Hauliers must prove the reason for dismissal: s. 57(2) EPCA, 1978 and *Whitbread* v *Thomas*.

    (b) Have the employers adopted the proper procedures in order to satisfy reasonableness under s. 57(3)? (See decision in *Polkey* v *A. E. Dayton Services Ltd.*)

3. Does Janet have a claim for constructive dismissal? Must be able to show a breach of contract: *Western Excavating* v *Sharp*. Is there a breach of the implied term of trust and confidence: *Courtaulds* v *Andrew*?

3 Redundancy

3.1 Introduction

The purposes of redundancy payments schemes are to compensate employees for loss of job security and to encourage employees to accept redundancy without damaging industrial relations. As we have already seen, redundancy is a reason for dismissal in order to render a dismissal fair (s. 57(2) EPCA). However, once the employer has shown that the dismissal is for reason of redundancy it is then for the employee to show that it was unfair.

EPCA 1978, s. 59

Where the reason or principal reason for the dismissal of an employee was that he was redundant, but it was shown that the circumstances constituting the redundancy applied equally to one or more of the other employees in the same undertaking who held positions similar to that held by him and who have not been dismissed by the employer, and either:

(a) that the reason (or, if more than one, the principal reason) for which he was selected for dismissal was an inadmissible reason; or

(b) that he was selected for dismissal in contravention of a customary arrangement or agreed procedure relating to redundancy and there were no special reasons justifying a departure from that arrangement or procedure in his case,

then for the purpose of this part, the dismissal shall be regarded as unfair.

Section 59 therefore seeks to ensure that all employees are treated equally and that the agreed procedures are followed. Further, s. 57(3) EPCA, 1978 (above) means that the decision to dismiss must be reasonable. Again the importance of procedures (see *Polkey* v *A. E. Dayton*) must be emphasised. We shall for the purposes of discussion below assume that dismissal was fair and the question is whether or not the redundancy provisions are satisfied.

3.2 Dismissal

The same prerequisite as with unfair dismissal (s. 55(2) EPCA) applies; that is there must be a dismissal (s. 83(2) EPCA). We have already discussed some aspects of dismissal, for example constructive dismissal, and the same principles are applicable here.

The main problem in the context of dismissal as a prerequisite for redundancy is whether or not it is a dismissal or merely a variation of contract. The employer may well have the ability to vary the terms of the contract without a breach of contract resulting. Again the contract of employment is central to our discussions. An example of the principle is provided by:

Johnson v Nottinghamshire Combined Police Authority
[1974] ICR 170

The applicants, two women clerks who had for over 20 years worked a five-day week from 9.30 a.m. to 5 p.m. or 5.30 p.m. at a police station, were dismissed when they declined for domestic reasons to change to an alternating shift system, 8 a.m. to 3 p.m. and 1 p.m. to 8 p.m. and a six-day week, introduced by the police authority to achieve greater efficiency in police work. They were replaced by two women clerks doing the same work and working the same number of hours but on the shift system. They claimed redundancy payments on the ground that their dismissals were wholly or mainly attributable to redundancy in that the change in the hours of work was sufficient to affect a change in the kind of work which they had been employed to do. The industrial tribunal dismissed their claims. The applicants appealed to the Court of Appeal.

Held: The appeal was dismissed. The change in the hours of working, without any change in the tasks to be performed or in the total number of hours worked, did not effect a change in the particular kind of work for which the applicants had been required such as to make redundancy the reason for their dismissal. A fortiori where the employers had discharged the burden on them of showing that the hours were altered in order to bring about greater efficiency and not in order to reduce their work force.

Self check questions
1. What is the relationship between redundancy and unfair dismissal?
2. What is the difference between dismissal and variation of a contract?

Answers
1. Redundancy is a reason for dismissal, which if shown, will render a dismissal fair (s. 57(2) EPCA). However, s. 59 requires that the appropriate procedures are followed and s. 57(3) subjects the decision to dismiss to the concept of reasonableness. Failure to satisfy either of these sections will render the dismissal unfair.
2. A dismissal is a prerequisite to a claim for redundancy. A variation of a contract is not a breach and therefore does not amount to dismissal: *Johnson v Nottinghamshire Combined Police Authority.*

3.3 Definition of redundancy
Once a dismissal has been established, a presumption by virtue of s. 91(2) EPCA arises that the reason for dismissal was redundancy. It should be noted that for the purposes of unfair dismissal this presumption does not apply and it is for the employer to show that the dismissal was on grounds of redundancy. The definition of redundancy is contained in:

EPCA, s. 81(2)

For the purposes of this Act an employee who is dismissed shall be taken to be dismissed by reason of redundancy if the dismissal is attributable wholly or mainly to:

(a)   the fact that his employer has ceased, or intends to cease, to carry on the business for the purposes of which the employee was employed by him, or has ceased, or intends to cease, to carry on that business in the place where the employee was so employed, or,

(b)   the fact that the requirements of that business for employees to carry out work of a particular kind, or for employees to carry out work of a particular kind in the place where he was so employed, have ceased or diminished or are expected to cease or diminish.

For purposes of this subsection, the business of the employers together with the business or businesses of his associated employers shall be treated as one unless either of the conditions specified in this subsection would be satisfied without so treating those businesses.

The subsection has been subject to much judicial discussion and a good example is provided by:

North Riding Garages Ltd v Butterwick
[1967] 2 QB 56

The respondent had been employed at a garage for 30 years, becoming workshop manager in charge of the repairs workshop and giving satisfactory service, when in April, 1965, the business was taken over by the appellants. The appellants introduced new methods to which the respondent could not easily adapt himself and he had work put upon him, such as costs estimates. Although he did his best he was not as efficient as he should have been. There was increased emphasis on the sales side of the business, with which the respondent had not been directly concerned, but the appellants were not deliberately running down the repairs side. On January 15, 1966, the respondent was dismissed with due notice, and a new workshop manager engaged. The respondent claimed to be entitled to a redundancy payment. The industrial tribunal considered that the presumption of redundancy was not rebutted, and that there was a reorganisation of the system of the business as a whole, whereby the appellants' requirement for a workshop manager of the old type had ceased; accordingly, the tribunal determined that the appellants should make a redundancy payment to the respondent. The employers appealed.

Held: The appeal was allowed. A claim for redundancy payment was conditional upon a change in the requirements of the business, and if the requirement for employees to carry out a particular kind of work increased or remained constant an employee engaged in such work who was dismissed for personal deficiencies which prevented him from giving satisfaction was not dismissed on account of 'redundancy': for the purposes of the Act an employee remaining in the same kind of work was expected to adapt to new methods and higher standards of efficiency, unless the nature of the work he was required to do was thereby altered so that no requirement remained for employees to do work of the particular kind which was superseded; that the respondent had been dismissed, not because the volume of repair work had diminished but because he could not do his job in accordance with the new methods and standards required by the appellants, and it was irrelevant that the duties of the new manager were not identical with those formerly undertaken by the respondent, for regard should be had to the overall requirements of the business and not to the allocation of duties between individuals, and accordingly, since the tribunal had applied the wrong test, the case would be remitted to them to continue the hearing.

Again the emphasis is being placed on the ability of the employee to be able to adapt to changes in the method of working.

3.4 Alternative offers

An employee who has been dismissed by reason of redundancy will lose his right to a payment if he unreasonably refuses an offer from his employer to renew the contract on the same terms or if he unreasonably refuses an offer from his employer to re-engage him on different terms if that offer is deemed to be of 'suitable employment' (s. 82(3) EPCA).

The key question is what is meant by 'suitable employment'. This is clearly shown by:

Taylor v Kent County Council
[1969] 2 QB 560

The appellant was aged 53, and for ten years had been headmaster of a boys' school when the respondent county education authority decided that the school should be amalgamated with a girls' school. The boys' school as such, ceased to exist and the appellant's appointment was terminated. He was not chosen as headmaster of the new school but was offered, in writing, a post, at the same salary that he had received as headmaster, in a mobile pool of teachers, which he refused. That offer required the appellant to serve in schools in the county as required for short periods, generally one or two terms but not normally longer than a year, and to undertake duties assigned to him by the headmaster of the school to which he was sent. The appellant's application for a redundancy payment was refused by industrial tribunal who found that he had been dismissed by reason of redundancy but that he had unreasonably refused an offer of suitable employment. He appealed.

On the question whether or not the offer of employment in the mobile pool of teachers was an offer of 'suitable employment', in relation to the appellant, which he had unreasonably refused it was held, allowing the appeal: That 'suitable employment' meant employment substantially equivalent to, but not the same as, that which had ceased and did not mean employment of an entirely different nature at the same salary; accordingly, the tribunal had misdirected themselves in that the appellant's age, qualifications and experience negatived the suitability of the offer, even at the same salary as before, requiring him to go for short periods to any place in the county and undertake any duties assigned to him by the headmaster.

The factors taken into account by the court clearly include the status of the person and the type of work previously undertaken.

3.5 Payments

The amount of redundancy payment, assuming the right of payment is established, is calculated by reference to three factors (sch. 4 of EPCA):

(a)   age of claimant;
(b)   length of continuous employment of claimant;
(c)   the weekly pay of the claimant.

Age (inclusive)	Amount (weeks' pay for each year of employment)
18–21	½
22–41	1
42–65	1½

The maximum length of continuous employment which can be used is 20 years. At the time of writing the maximum weekly earnings which count towards the calculation are £205 — i.e., any sum over this amount does not count. (NB the same principles above apply to the calculation of the basic award for unfair dismissal.) The overall maximum is £6,150 at the time of writing.

Problem
Y Ltd employed John and Samantha as technicians. Both have worked for Y Ltd for 15 years and get paid £200 per week each. John is aged 42 and Samantha is aged 30.

Y Ltd introduce new technology and provide the appropriate training. However, John is unable to adapt to the new methods of working and leaves claiming that he has been made redundant.

Y Ltd then suffer a dramatic downturn in their business and have no alternative but to close the factory at which Samantha works. She is offered alternative employment at another factory some 50 miles away but the pay is the same as she is receiving at the moment.

Advise John and Samantha.

Suggested answer (main points)
1.   Continuity of employment sufficient?
2.   Age, rate of pay and length of service relevant if a redundancy payment has to be calculated.
3.   A prerequisite for a redundancy payment is that there must be a dismissal (s. 83(2) EPCA). Has John been dismissed? If so, is there a redundancy situation: s. 81(2) EPCA and *North Riding Garages* v *Butterwick*.
4.   Samantha may well have been made redundant (s. 83(2)). Has there been an offer of suitable alternative employment (s. 83(2) and *Taylor* v *Kent CC*)? Further, assuming the selection for redundancy was according to the appropriate procedures (s. 59 EPCA), how is her redundancy payment to be calculated?

21 COMPANY LAW

1 Introduction

Three main types of business media exists in the UK:

(a) Registered companies.
(b) Partnerships.
(c) Sole traders.

It is very important to be able to identify the different types of business organisation and understand the differences between them as far as the law is concerned.

One thing that is clear — just because an organisation has the word 'company' in its name does not mean that it is automatically a registered company. Partnerships, for example, often employ the word 'Company' in their title, but in law this means nothing.

We will examine the nature of each type of business medium starting with companies.

2 Types of companies

2.1 Public corporations
Fast becoming extinct — these are the nationalised industries. They are not the same as companies quoted on the Stock Exchange (the registered company). They have a number of differences:

(a) They are created and governed by their own Act of Parliament e.g., British Airways was governed by the British Airways Board Act 1977 before privatisation. They do not register under the Companies Act 1985 like registered companies.

(b) They have no shareholders or board of directors. The nearest things they possess which are similar are the tax-payers (shareholders) and the relevant government minister (directors).

(c) They are not subject to the control of the owners (shareholders) unlike registered companies.

(d) They are not subject to the winding-up procedures unlike registered companies.

2.2 Chartered companies
The Crown has a power to create a company by Royal Charter. Early trading companies were established in this way e.g., East India Company. Royal Charters are not used today to create trading companies but are confined to professional organisations and universities e.g., Chartered Accountants.

2.3 Registered companies
These are companies created as a result of registration under the Companies Act 1985. It is this route that is chosen by the majority of trading companies in the UK today. Consequently this is the type of company which needs to be examined in detail.

2.3.1 Classification of registered companies
Registered companies may be classified in two ways:

(a) By reference to the method by which their liability is limited; or
(b) By reference to whether or not they are private or public.

1. By reference to the method by which liability is limited
Companies may have limited or unlimited liability:

(a) Liability limited by shares — It is the shareholders whose liability is limited despite the fact that it is the company that is referred to as having limited liability. The liability of shareholders is limited to the amount unpaid on their shares. So if A buys a share with a nominal value of £1 and pays 50p for it his liability is limited to 50p in the event of the company being wound up and insolvent.

Activity
Think about the government-backed share issues, particularly electricity. How much did the shareholder pay on allotment and how much was he further liable for in future payments?

(b) Liability limited by guarantee — Here members of the company guarantee that in the event of the company being wound up they will contribute up to a certain amount. Their liability is limited to that amount. They used to be able to issue shares but from 1980 new guarantee companies are not permitted to issue shares. Most companies limited by guarantee are charitable or non-profit making organisations.   -

(c)   Unlimited liability — Members of a registered unlimited company have personal liability for the debts of the company and because of this there are very few unlimited liability companies in existence. The only reasons that people form this type of company is to acquire a separate legal personality (see below) and perpetual succession.

2.   *By reference to whether they are public or private companies*

(a)   Public companies — The Companies Act 1985 defines a public company as a company limited by shares or guarantee and;

(i)   the memorandum states that the company is a public limited company;
(ii)   the company has at least two members;
(iii)   the name of the company ends in plc;
(iv)   the company has an authorised (nominal) share capital of not less than £50,000.

(b)   Private companies — The Act does not define a private company and therefore any company which does not fulfil the above criteria is automatically deemed to be a private company.

Activity
Pay attention to the way in which cheques are made out when making a purchase at Marks and Spencer as opposed to C & A. Why does this difference exist?

3   Separate corporate personality

When a company is registered it becomes in law a separate legal entity and acquires a legal personality distinct and separate from the human members who control and administer the company. This principle is fundamental to company law and was established in the case of:

Salomon v A. Salomon & Co. Ltd
[1897] AC 22, HL

Aaron Salomon, a trader, sold his business as a leather merchant and wholesale boot manufacturer to a limited company with a nominal capital of 40,000 shares of £1 each. The only shareholders in the company were the vendor, his wife, a daughter and four sons, who subscribed for one £1 share each. In part-payment of the purchase-money debentures were issued to the vendor; 20,000 shares were also issued to him and paid for out of the purchase-money. The vendor was appointed managing director.

When a year later the company was wound up, it was found that if the amount realised from the assets of the company were to be, in the first place, applied in payment of the debentures, there would be no funds left for payment of the ordinary creditors.

The liquidator, alleging that the company was a mere alias or agent of the vendor, claimed that the vendor was liable to indemnify the company against the claims of the ordinary creditors, and that no payment should be made on the debentures held by him until the ordinary creditors had been paid in full.

The trial court (Vaughan Williams J) gave judgment against Salomon, and this was confirmed by the Court of Appeal. The House of Lords reversed it.

LORD HALSBURY LC: ... It seems to me impossible to dispute that once the company is legally incorporated it must be treated like any other independent person with its rights and liabilities appropriate to itself, and that the motives of those who took part in the promotion of the company are absolutely irrelevant in discussing what those rights and liabilities are.

I will for the sake of argument assume the proposition that the Court of Appeal lays down — that the formation of the company was a mere scheme to enable Aaron Salomon to carry on business in the name of the company. I am wholly unable to follow the proposition that this was contrary to the true intent and meaning of the Companies Act. I can only find the true intent and meaning of the Act from the Act itself; and the Act appears to me to give a company a legal existence with, as I have said, rights and liabilities of its own, whatever may have been the ideas or schemes of those who brought it into existence.

I observe that the learned judge (Vaughan Williams J) held that the business was Mr Salomon's business, and no one else's, and that he chose to employ as agent a limited company; and he proceeded to argue that he was employing that limited company as agent; and that he was bound to indemnify that agent (the company). I confess it seems to me that the very learned judge becomes involved by this argument in a very singular contradiction. Either the limited company was a legal entity or it was not. If it was, the business belonged to it and not to Mr Salomon. If it was not, there was no person and nothing to be an agent at all, and it is impossible to say at the same time that there is a company and there is not. ...

LORD MACNAGHTEN: The company had a brief career, it fell upon evil days. Shortly after it was started there seems to have come a period of great depression in the boot and shoe trade. There were strikes of workmen too, and in view of that danger contracts with public bodies, which were the principal source of Mr Salomon's profit, were split up and divided between different firms. The attempts made to push the business on behalf of the new company crammed its warehouses with unsaleable stock. Mr Salomon seems to have done what he could, both he and his wife lent the company money, and then he got his debentures cancelled and re-issued to a Mr Broderip, who advanced him £5,000, which he immediately handed over to the company on loan. The temporary relief only hastened ruin. Mr Broderip's interest was not paid when it became due. He took proceedings at once and got a receiver appointed. Then, of course, came liquidation and a forced sale of the company's assets. They realised enough to pay Mr Broderip, but not enough to pay the debentures in full, and the unsecured creditors were consequently left out in the cold.

In this state of things the liquidator met Mr Broderip's claim by a counterclaim, to which he made Mr Salomon a defendant. He disputed the validity of the debentures on the ground of fraud. On the same ground he claimed rescission of the agreement for the transfer of the business, cancellation of the debentures, and repayment by Mr Salomon of the balance of the purchase-money. In the alternative, he claimed payment of £20,000 on Mr Salomon's shares, alleging that nothing had been paid on them.

This merely means that there is a predominant partner possessing an overwhelming influence and entitled practically to the whole of the profits, there is nothing in that I can see contrary to the true intention of the Act of 1862 or against public policy, or detrimental to the interests of creditors. If the shares are fully paid up, it cannot matter whether they are in the hands of one or many. If the shares are not fully paid, it is as easy to gauge the solvency of an individual as to estimate the financial ability of the crowd.

The principle in this case has been described as the 'veil of incorporation' which separates the company from its members and gives rise to the following consequences:

(a) The company can sue and be sued in its own name.

(b) The company can make contracts on its own behalf and the members cannot claim the benefit nor be subject to the burdens of such contracts (NB the doctrine of privity in contract).

(c) The company can own property in its own right and the member shares no direct interest in the property of the company but only in the shares of the company. Because the members do not own the property of the company, only shares in the company they cannot pledge or insure such property.

(d) The company has perpetual succession in that the death of a member has no effect on the company or its property. A company must be formally wound up (i.e., dissolved) even if all shareholders are already dead before it too can die.

(e) While the company is operational its debts are not the responsibility of members. However, if the company is wound up and the company was an *unlimited* company the members are personally liable for the debts of the company. Because of this the majority of companies are limited.

The principle of separate legal entity was applied and followed in both *Macaura v Northern Assurance Co. Ltd* (1925) where it was held that the largest shareholders had no insurable interest in the property of the company and that only the company could claim on an insurance policy for damage to company property; and *Lee v Lee's Air Farming Ltd* (1961). Here Lee, the managing director owning all but one of the shares in the company, was employed by the company as a pilot on salary. He was killed when flying for the company, and his wife claimed compensation from the company under the New Zealand Compensation Act 1922. It was contended that as Lee was the company he could not employ himself, and, therefore, compensation could not be claimed under the Act. It was held that the company was a legal person separate from its members, and Mrs Lee could claim compensation as her husband had been employed by the company.

Self check questions
If you owned shares in a limited company would you be able to:

1.	Claim on an insurance policy on the company's property?	YES/NO
2.	Be employed by the company?	YES/NO
3.	Sue the company?	YES/NO

Answers
1. No — As illustrated in *Macaura* v *Northern Assurance Co.*, a shareholder has no insurable interest in the company.
2. Yes — because the company is a legal entity separate from its members and it has to employ people to run its affairs.
3. Yes — for the same reason given in the answer to question 2.

4   Lifting the corporate veil

Although the corporate veil principle is regarded as fundamental to company law, there are instances where it has been lifted or ignored in favour of the economic realities of the situation. This occurs where the courts are prepared to take judicial notice of the identities of the owners or controllers of companies with a view to fixing them with some legal liability.

Exceptions to the rule of separate legal personality have been established by statute and common law. There is no underlying principle to the occasions or reasons the courts give for lifting the corporate veil and the law is by no means clear in this area. All that can be said with any degree of certainty is that a number of examples of occasions where the veil has been lifted in the past do exist and could occur again in the future.

4.1   Statutory exceptions

(a)   *Intent to defraud creditors* — If in the course of the winding up of a company it appears that any business of the company has been carried on with intent to defraud creditors of the company or creditors of any other person or for any fraudulent purpose, the court, on the application of the official receiver, or the liquidator or any creditor or contributory of the company, may, if it thinks proper so to do, declare that any persons who were knowingly parties to the carrying on of the business in the manner aforesaid shall be personally responsible, without any limitation of liability, for all or any of the debts or other liabilities of the company as the court may direct.

On the hearing of any application under this subsection the official receiver or the liquidator, as the case may be, may himself give evidence or call witnesses (Insolvency Act 1986, ss. 213 and 214).

(b)   *Omission of the company name* — If an officer of a company or any person on its behalf signs a cheque, bill of exchange, letter of credit or the like, and the company's name is not mentioned that person shall be personally liable for the amount involved unless it is duly paid by the company (Companies Act 1985, s. 349(4)).

4.2   Common law exceptions

These exceptions show the use of a number of different legal principles as justification for the lifting of the corporate veil.

(a)   *Agency.* In *Smith, Stone & Knight Ltd* v *Birmingham Corporation* (1939) the court ignored the corporate entity of a subsidiary company and *held* that it was not trading on its own behalf but was in fact an agent for the parent company.

(b)   *Nationality.* The courts will often need to determine the true nationality of a company in order to apply statutory provisions as in *Re FG (Films) Ltd* (1953).

(c)   *Fraud.* If the concept of separate corporate entity is being used for fraudulent purposes the courts will ignore it. In *Jones* v *Lipman* (1962) the defendant, in order to avoid an order of specific performance to sell land to Jones, created a company to which he sold the land. The court, ignoring the separate corporate entity of the company, considered it to be a sham to 'avoid the eye of equity', and granted the order of specific performance against the company.

(d)   *Groups.* Many companies trading in the UK are just one of many forming a large multinational group. Company law provides no special rules or regime to regulate groups of companies and this often causes problems — see below for example:

DHN Food Distributors Ltd v *Tower Hamlets LBC*
[1976] 1 WLR 852, CA

A group of three companies had separate interests in property subject to compulsory purchase. If the companies were treated as separate entities the total compensation would be less than if the property were regarded as owned by the group as a whole ignoring their separate legal personalities. The court was willing to pierce the corporate veil and award the group the higher assessment of compensation.

LORD DENNING MR: This case might be called the 'Three in one'. Three companies in one. Alternatively, 'One in three'. One group of three companies. For the moment I will speak of it as 'the firm' . . .

Now comes the point. It is about compensation. Compensation under the statute is to be made for the value of the land and also compensation for disturbance of the business, see s. 5(2) and (6) of the Land Compensation Act 1961.

If the firm and its property had all been in one ownership, it would have been entitled to compensation under those two heads; first, the value of the land, which has been assessed in excess of £360,000. Second, compensation for disturbance in having its business closed down. The figure has not yet been assessed. But the firm and its property were not in one ownership. It was owned by three companies. The business was owned by the parent company, DHN Food Distributors Ltd. The land was owned at the time of acquisition by a subsidiary, called Bronze Investments Ltd. The vehicles were owned by another subsidiary, DHN Food Transports Ltd. The parent company DHN held all the shares both in the Bronze company and in the Transport company. The directors were the same in all three companies. As the result of the business having to be closed down, all the three companies are in liquidation.

The question is: what is the effect of the firm being in truth the three companies? . . .

Mr Dorby, for DHN, took three points before us; first, that they had an equitable interest in the land; second and alternatively, that they had an irrevocable licence; third, that we should lift the corporate veil and treat DHN as the owners. And that, in one or other of these three capacities, they were entitled to compensation for disturbance. . . .

Third, lifting the corporate veil. A further very interesting point was raised by Mr Dorby on company law. We all know that in many respects a group of companies are treated together for the purpose of general accounts, balance sheet, and profit and loss account. They are treated as one concern. Professor Gower in *Modern Company Law*, 3rd ed. (1969) p. 216 says: "there is evidence of a general tendency to ignore the separate legal entities of various companies within a group, and to look instead at the economic entity of the whole group"

This is especially the case when a parent company owns all the shares of the subsidiaries — so much so that it can control every movement of the subsidiaries. These subsidiaries are bound hand and foot to the parent company and must do just what the parent company says. A striking instance is the decision of the House of Lords in *Harold Holdsworth & Co. (Wakefield) Ltd v Caddies*. So here. This group is virtually the same as a partnership in which all the three companies are partners. They should not be treated separately so as to be defeated on a technical point. They should not be deprived of the compensation which should justly be payable for disturbance. The three companies should, for present purposes, be treated as one, and the parent company DHN should be treated as that one. So DHN are entitled to claim compensation accordingly. It was not necessary for them to go through a conveyancing device to get it.

I realise that the President of the Lands Tribunal, in view of the previous cases, felt it necessary to decide as he did. But now that the matter has been fully discussed in this court, we must decide differently from him. These companies as a group are entitled to compensation. Not only for the value of the land, but also compensation for disturbance. I would allow the appeal accordingly.

GOFF LJ: . . . [I]n my judgment, this is a case in which one is entitled to look at the realities of the situation and to pierce the corporate veil. I wish to safeguard myself by saying that so far as this ground is concerned, I am relying on the facts of this particular case. I would not at this juncture accept that in every case where one has a group of companies one is entitled to pierce the veil, but in this case the two subsidiaries were both wholly owned; further, they had no separate business operations whatsoever; thirdly, in my judgment, the nature of the question involved is highly relevant, namely, whether the owners of this business have been disturbed in the possession and enjoyment of it.

They could not have been criticised, still less prevented, if they had chosen to do so. Yet if the decision of the Lands Tribunal be right, it made all the difference that they had not. Thus no abuse is precluded by disregarding the bonds which bundled DHN and Bronze together in a close and, so far as Bronze was concerned, indissoluble relationship.

Why then should this relationship be ignored in a situation in which to do so does not prevent abuse but would on the contrary result in what appears to be a denial of justice? If the strict legal differentiation between the two entities of parent and subsidiary must, even on the special facts of this case, be observed, the common factors in their identities must at the lowest demonstrate that the occupation of DHN would and could never be determined without the consent of DHN itself. If it was a licence at will, it was at the will of the licensee, DHN, that the licence subsisted. Accordingly, it could have gone on for an indeterminate time; that is to say, so long as the relationship of parent and subsidiary continued, which means for practical purposes for as long as DHN wished to remain in the property for the purposes of its business.

The President of the Lands Tribunal took a strict legalistic view of the respective positions of the companies concerned. It appears to me that it was too strict in its application to the facts of this case, which are as I have said, of a very special character, for it ignored the realities of the respective roles which the companies filled. I would allow the appeal.

Compare this decision with the decision and approach taken by the court in:

Woolfson v Strathclyde RC
(1978) 38 P & CR 521, HL

Shop premises including street numbers 53/61 (odd) were occupied by a company, C Ltd, and used by it for the purpose of its business. Nos. 57 and 59/61 were owned by the first appellant, W. Nos. 53/55 were owned by the second appellants, S. Ltd, the shares in which were at all material times held as to two-thirds by W and one-third by his wife. The issued share capital of C Ltd was 1,000 shares, of which 999 were held by W and one by his wife. W was sole director of C Ltd and managed the business, being paid a salary taxed under Schedule E. His wife also worked for C Ltd. C Ltd was shown in the valuation roll as occupier of the premises, but its occupation was not regulated by lease or other formal arrangement. From 1952 to 1963, when Schedule A taxation was abolished, payments by way of rent for nos. 59/61 were credited to W in C Ltd's books. No rent was ever paid or credited in respect of no. 57. From 1962 to 1968. C Ltd paid rent to S Ltd in respect of nos. 53/55. Various financial arrangements were entered into between W and C Ltd. In 1966, a compulsory purchase order was made in respect of the premises by the predecessors of the respondent highway authority, the date of entry being January 19, 1968. The appellants jointly claimed a sum of £80,000 as compensation for the value of the heritage under s. 12(2) of the Land Compensation (Scotland) Act 1963 and a further sum of £95,469 in respect of disturbance under s. 12(6). They argued that this was a case for piercing the corporate veil.

Held: That in the present case there was no grounds on which it was proper to pierce the veil.

LORD KEITH OF KINKEL: ... I can see no grounds whatever, upon the facts found in the special case, for treating the company structure as a mere facade, nor do I consider that *DHN Food Distributors Ltd v Tower Hamlets London Borough Council* is, on a proper analysis, of assistance to the appellants' argument.... It was held by the Court of Appeal (Lord Denning MR, Goff and Shaw LJJ) that the group was entitled to compensation. However, I feel that the facts here are sufficiently distinguishable on the grounds that the companies are not in common ownership.

Activity
Can you find any real differences?

It could be said that the judges appear to be very confused when trying to deal with groups of companies. For example, note the differences in the approach of the judges in the *DHN* case to the issue of piercing the corporate veil.

Problem
Critically analyse the extent to which the courts are prepared to pierce the veil of incorporation.

Suggested answer — an answer plan
Use the following answer plan to construct your own answer.

1. *Preparing the answer*

   (a)   What does the examiner require in this answer? — critical analysis.
   (b)   Subject-matter of the answer — extent to which the corporate veil will be pierced by judges
   (c)   Main thrust of answer — Is piercing the corporate veil basically a good idea? Is the way in which it is approached by the judges sound? Does it leave the law clear, certain and easy to apply?

2. *Main content of the answer*

   (a)   Definition of separate corporate personality, corporate veil. Use cases — *Salomon* v *Salomon*; *Macaura* v *Northern Assurance*; *Lee* v *Lee's Air Farming*.

(b) *Brief* mention of statutory instances where corporate veil lifted. Examples of good practice — clear, certain, easy to apply? Is this what the judiciary ought to be aspiring to?

(c) Examples of instances where judiciary lifts corporate veil. Use cases — *Re FG (Films) Ltd*; *Jones* v *Lipman*. Can you justify these decisions? Is there any underlying theme/principle upon which they are based? Could you predict with certainty when the corporate veil would be pierced? How much confusion exists among the judiciary in this area?

Use and compare the decision in: *DHN* v *Tower Hamlets*; *Smith, Stone & Knight* v *Birmingham Corporation*; *Woolfson* v *Strathclyde RC*. Pay particular attention to the different reasons given by judges for their decisions. Given that groups of companies in particular are here to stay, is the current state of the law satisfactory?

3. Conclusion

To what extent are judges prepared to pierce the corporate veil? Is this done in a consistent, satisfactory manner? Can we improve on the situation — go back to statutory rules on piercing — introduction of more statutory rules?

22 COMPANIES AND CONTRACTS

1 Corporate capacity

Prior to 1990 the law which regulated a company's capacity to contract was very restrictive. When a company is formed it has to submit a number of documents to the Registrar of Companies. Two of the most important documents are the Memorandum and Articles of Association. These form the company's constitution.

The Memorandum governs the company's dealings with the world at large. One of the important clauses in the Memorandum is Clause 3 which sets out the company's objects i.e., the purposes for which the company has been formed, and prior to 1990 a company could only make contracts which fell within the scope of its stated objects. Any activity which the company engaged in which fell outside its objects was deemed to be *ultra vires* (beyond its powers) and void. Thus its capacity to contract was limited. This meant that anyone who had entered into a contract with a company which proved to be *ultra vires* could generally not enforce it. As you can imagine this often caused great inconvenience to business people who thought they had a binding agreement with a company when in fact they did not. To alleviate some of the difficulties caused by the limits the law placed on a company's contractual capacity a review and reform of the law took place.

Following the passing of the Companies Act 1989, the law which limited a company's capacity to contract was greatly relaxed. Section 110 of the 1989 Act inserts a new s. 3A into the Companies Act 1985 which now permits a company to file an objects clause simply stating that the company is to carry on the business as a general commercial company. Where a company adopts this form of words the following will result:

(a) the object of the company is to carry on any trade or business whatsoever, and

(b) the company has power to do all such things as are incidental or conducive to the carrying out of any trade or business by it.

Thus capacity is unlimited if the new form of words is used. However, companies who do not choose this form of words but continue to use the old style objects clause which may contain limitations on its capacity to contract have been helped by other amendments to the law which are contained in the 1989 Companies Act.

Section 108 of the Companies Act 1989 amends s. 35(1) of the Companies Act 1985 and cures any lack of capacity a company may experience by virtue of any provision contained in its memorandum. The effect of s. 35(1) of the Companies Act 1985 as amended by s. 108 of the Companies Act 1989 is to give anyone dealing with the company (the outsider) a prima facie (on the face of it) right to enforce the contract with it. However, there are some limitations on this right to enforce:

(a) A shareholder who discovers that the company is about to enter into a contract which is outside its capacity to make may obtain an injunction under s. 35(2) of the Companies Act 1985 to prevent the company entering the contract.

However, once the contract has been agreed an injunction is not available. An injunction is an order of the court which may require a person either to do something or to refrain from doing something (see Chapter 3 for a more detailed discussion).

(b) A second limitation is concerned not with the company's capacity but with the capacity of the agent (usually a director or managing director) acting on the company's behalf. It is possible to be faced with a situation where even though the company has capacity to enter the contract in question the director or officer of the company purporting to act on its behalf has not had the company's authority delegated to him. In these circumstances the contract will be voidable at the company's option (this means that the company has the right to escape from the contract if it chooses on the ground that it did not authorise it).

In this situation what we are really concerned with is the capacity of the company's officers rather than the capacity of the company itself. The rules governing the capacity of the company's officers are set out below.

Self check questions
1. What is the status of an *ultra vires* contract at common law?
2. What is the effect of s. 35(1) of the Companies Act 1985 on an *ultra vires* contract?
3. What effect will an injunction obtained by a shareholder have?

Answers
1. An *ultra vires* contract is void, i.e., it has never come into existence.
2. The section gives anyone dealing with the company a right to enforce the contract against the company. –

3. An injunction will prevent an otherwise *ultra vires* contract being entered into.

2 Capacity of the company's officers

In addition to ensuring that a company has capacity to enter a particular contract it is also necessary to ensure that the officer of the company acting on its behalf has the proper authority and therefore capacity to contract. Because companies are artificial legal persons, they must contract through human agents. These will normally be either the board of directors or managing director. For a contract to be valid both the company itself and its human agent must have capacity. Note that individual directors have no authority to bind their company — they must act collectively as a board. It is the decision of the board that can bind the company. However, the board may delegate some or all of its powers to a nominee who is known as the managing director. The managing director may then act as an individual within the express authority delegated to him by the board.

We have dealt with the law regulating a company's capacity above and we now turn to the rules which regulate the human agent's capacity. The Company's Articles of Association regulate its internal affairs and govern the procedures for the appointment of its directors and managing director and allow for corporate capacity to contract to be delegated to them. Thus a properly appointed and authorised board of directors will have capacity to contract on behalf of their company. Problems will of course arise where a director or managing director is either not validly appointed to office or is not properly authorised to act. In either case the result is that the contract may be unenforceable by the outsider against the company. To afford outsiders protection in these circumstances a number of rules have been developed by statute and the courts.

Defects in capacity fall into two main categories:

(a) lack of appointment to office; and
(b) lack of authority to contract.

One or more rules discussed below may assist the outsider in either case.

2.1 Lack of appointment to office
In this situation the problem may be as a result of a technical defect in the procedure used to make the attempted appointment. Here the outsider may rely on:

(a) the Companies Act 1985, s. 285, or
(b) The rule in *Turquand*'s case.

In cases where there has been no attempt to appoint the person to office the outsider may rely on the following rules: -

(a) The rule in *Turquand*'s case; or
(b) The agency rule.

2.2   *Lack of authority to contract*

In this situation the director or other officer is validly appointed to the office concerned but exceeds the authority given by virtue of that office in his attempt to enter the contract. Here the outsider may rely on:

(a) the Companies Act 1985, s. 35A, or
(b) The rule in *Turquand*'s case, or
(c) The agency rule.

It is now necessary to discuss these rules in detail.

3   Companies Act 1985, section 285

This section simply states that: 'The acts of a director or manager are valid notwithstanding any defect that may afterwards be discovered in his appointment or qualification'. This section requires no further explanation.

4   The indoor management rule

This rule allows an outsider to assume, in the absence of facts putting him on inquiry, that there has been due compliance with all matters of internal management and procedure. The rationale for the rule is the fact that the internal documents and minutes of a company (e.g., board minutes) are not public documents. Consequently, an outsider has no right of access to the information which would prove whether procedures have been duly complied with or not. Because he cannot discover this information, *Turquand*'s rule says he is entitled to assume all is well and the procedures laid down by the company's articles have been observed. The rule is illustrated in the two cases set out below:

Royal British Bank v *Turquand*
(1856) 6 E & B 327

Turquand was sued, as the official manager of a coal mining and railway company incorporated under the Act of 1844, on a bond for £2,000 which had been given by the company to the plaintiff bank to secure its drawings on current account. The bond was given under the seal of the company and signed by the two directors and the secretary, but the company alleged that under the terms of its registered deed of settlement the directors had power to borrow only such sums as had been authorised by a general resolution of the company, and in this case no sufficiently specific resolution had been passed. The Court of Exchequer Chamber, affirming the judgment of the Court of Queen's Bench, held that even so the company was bound by the bond.

JERVIS CJ: ... We may now take for granted that the dealings with these companies are not like dealings with other partnerships, and that the parties dealing with them are bound to read the statute and the deed of settlement. But they are not bound to do more. And the party here, on reading the deed of settlement, would find, not a prohibition from borrowing, but a permission to do so on certain conditions. Finding that the authority might be made complete by a resolution, he would have a right to infer the fact of a resolution authorising that which on the face of the document appeared to be legitimately done.

Mahony v East Holyford Mining Co.
(1875) LR 7 HL 869

The liquidator of the respondent company sued Mahony as public officer of the National Bank, Dublin, alleging that the bank had paid moneys from the company's account without due authorisation. The bank had acted upon a letter signed by one Wall as secretary of the company, enclosing a copy of a 'resolution' of the board of directors. This 'resolution' named three directors, and instructed the bank to pay cheques signed by any two of them and countersigned by the secretary. Specimen signatures were attached. This instruction was entirely in accordance with the company's memorandum and articles, and would have been in order, except that there had never been any proper appointment of directors or a secretary by the company, the roles having been simply assumed by those who had formed the company. The House of Lords held that the company was bound by cheques which the bank had honoured in accordance with the instruction contained in the letter.

LORD HATHERLEY: ... when there are persons conducting the affairs of the company in a manner which appears to be perfectly consonant with the articles of association, then those so dealing with them, externally, are not to be affected by any irregularities which may take place in the internal management of the company. They are entitled to presume that that of which only they can have knowledge, namely, the external acts, are rightly done, when those external acts purport to be performed in the mode in which they ought to be performed. For instance, when a cheque is signed by three directors, they are entitled to assume that those directors are persons properly appointed for the purpose of performing that function, and have properly performed the function for which they have been appointed....

Then the bankers get a notice from a person who calls himself the secretary, and who says he gives them a resolution under the authority of which, and according to the form there stated, the cheques are to be drawn.... the bankers acted entirely in good faith upon the representations contained in that letter.... The bankers were furnished with the names of three so called 'directors', who sent their signatures in order that the bankers might have an opportunity of verifying the signatures upon any cheques that might be drawn. If the bankers went there [the company's office] and found the secretary sitting there, as the evidence tells us he did all day long from ten till six, and performing the duties of a secretary, and if they found some of these other gentlemen sitting there appearing to be performing the duties of directors, and if they saw those four other gentlemen who might have appointed them as directors sitting there also, witnessing them performing the duties of directors, I must ask what more could be required on the part of those who were dealing with the company, and who had obtained all the external information they could upon the subject. If we are not now to hold that the bankers are to be protected in honouring the drafts of these three persons, who, they were informed, were authorised to draw cheques, I do not know how any person, dealing with a company, can be safe against being bound to inquire into all the minute transactions which may have taken place indoors. . . .

3.1 Exceptions to the indoor management rule

The outsider cannot rely on the indoor management rule in all circumstances. Several exceptions have been developed by the courts:

(a) The presumption of regularity does not apply where the defect in authority would be apparent from an inspection of the company's registered documents.

Irvine v *Union Bank of Australia*
(1877) 2 App Cas 366, PC

The bank sought to enforce a security given to it by the Oriental Rice Co. Ltd over a rice mill situated in Rangoon. The directors of the company had exceeded the limit of an amount equal to half the paid-up capital imposed on their power to borrow by the articles of association, but the bank argued that the company in general meeting might by a special vote have enlarged the directors' powers and that the bank was entitled to assume that this had been done. The contention was rejected; if any such vote had been passed, the fact would have been apparent from the company's registered documents, i.e., a new article would have been lodged with the Registrar of Companies.

SIR BARNES PEACOCK: delivered the opinion of the Privy Council: . . . The case of *Royal British Bank* v *Turquand* was decided with reference to a company registered under [the Act of 1844], and Chief Justice Jervis remarked that the lender finding that the authority might have been made complete by a resolution would have had a right to infer the fact of a resolution authorising that which on the face of the document appeared to be legitimately done. In the present case, however, the bank would have found that, by the articles of association, the directors were expressly restricted from borrowing beyond a certain amount, and they must have known that if the general powers vested in the directors by art. 50 had been extended or enlarged by [a special resolution] a copy of that resolution ought, in regular course, to have been forwarded to the Registrar of Joint Stock Companies, in pursuance of s. 53 of the Companies Act [1862, now the Companies Act 1985, s. 380], and would have been found amongst his records.

Their Lordships are of opinion that the learned Recorder was correct in holding that this case is different from that of *Royal British Bank* v *Turquand*. . . .

(b)   The presumption of regularity cannot be relied on by 'insiders' i.e., persons who by virtue of their position in the company are in a position to know whether or not the internal regulations have been observed.

Howard v *Patent Ivory Manufacturing Co.*
(1888) 38 ChD 156

KAY J: . . . But then a very much more serious question has been raised, and that is this. These debentures were issued by the directors, and it is said that the power of the directors to issue debentures is limited, and the limit is very plain when you look at article 95, which is as follows. The directors are empowered 'to borrow from time to time on behalf of the company such sums of money, not exceeding in the whole at any one time £1,000, as the directors think necessary or advisable, also to raise such further moneys as may be authorised from time to time by resolution of any general meeting of shareholders summoned for the purpose'. So that when the directors have borrowed up to £1,000, and there are existing loans unpaid to that amount, the borrowing power of the directors is exhausted, and no more can be borrowed without the authority of a general meeting of shareholders. Then the next clause is, 'To secure the repayment of any moneys so borrowed, together with the interest, by debentures'. Therefore the directors could only issue valid debentures for moneys borrowed by themselves, without the assent of a general meeting, to the extent of the borrowing power. Beyond that, in order to authorise themselves to borrow and to issue debentures, there must be the assent of the general meeting.
   Now in this case, unfortunately for the holders of these debentures, they are all directors, and therefore the well-known authorities which make it unnecessary to see whether the internal regulations of a company have been observed or not do not apply; because, of course, the directors must be taken to know that the internal requirements of the company had not been observed in the case of these debentures. Accordingly, I am very sorry to say that I cannot treat these debentures as valid to the extent of more than £1,000. How that sum is to be allotted between the different parties I do not know. I have heard nothing on this point. I must treat the issue of the debentures as being invalid within the knowledge of the directors beyond the amount of £1,000. There must be a declaration that the first ten only of the thirty-five debentures, taking them according to their numbers, are valid.

(c)   Neither can the presumption of regularity be relied upon if the contract is a forgery and therefore of no legal effect.

Ruben v *Great Fingall Consolidated*
[1906] AC 439, HL

The question was whether the company was estopped by a share certificate to which the company's seal had been affixed without authority and the forged signatures of two directors added.

LORD LOREBURN LC: ... I cannot see upon what principle your Lordships can hold that the defendants are liable in this action. The forged certificate is a pure nullity. It is quite true that persons dealing with limited liability companies are not bound to inquire into their indoor management, and will not be affected by irregularities of which they had no notice. But this doctrine, which is well established, applies only to irregularities that otherwise might affect a genuine transaction. It cannot apply to a forgery. ...

5 The relationship of agency and the indoor management rule

Where the issue in question is whether a single person has, or is deemed to have, authority to represent the company as its representative or agent, the questions of indoor management may become complicated or confused with other questions from the ordinary law of agency. For example:

(a)   If a person has been appointed to the office of secretary or managing director and acts as such, but there was some technical defect in the procedure by which he was appointed, the indoor management rule will apply so as to protect an outsider dealing with him.

(b)   On the other hand, when a person has been appointed as the company's agent either specifically, to act in a particular transaction, or generally, e.g., to manage a branch office, the questions whether he has exceeded the authority conferred upon him and, if so, whether the company as principal is nevertheless bound *vis-à-vis* a third party, are matters which ought to be determined by the ordinary rules of agency.

(c)   A more complex problem arises when a person holding some office in the company (commonly a director) purports to act on behalf of the company in a matter which is not within the scope of such an officer's usual activities, but would be within the normal functions of another office to which he might have been appointed — e.g., a managing director, or a delegate of the board under such an article as 84 of Table A. Such a person may, depending on the evidence, be regarded as either (1) a delegate under 84 or a managing director defectively appointed, (2) a person held out by the company as a managing director although never appointed as such, or (3) an officer of limited powers who has, without authority, simply exceeded those powers. On the first view, the matter is one governed by the indoor management rule, on the second, by the rules of agency, and in either case the third party with whom he deals will be protected. On the third view, the company will not be bound whichever set of rules is applied. It is perhaps not surprising that the cases sometimes fail to keep the *Turquand* and the agency principles distinct.

Many cases seem to have been argued and decided primarily on the basis of the rule in *Turquand's* case but ought to be reconsidered in the light of *Freeman & Lockyer* v *Buckhurst Park Properties Ltd* (1964).

5.1 Agent's authority

An agent (A) is someone who has 'power' or authority to alter the legal relationships of his principal (P) *vis-à-vis* third parties (T). Once a contract is entered into between P and T, the agent normally drops out of the arrangement.

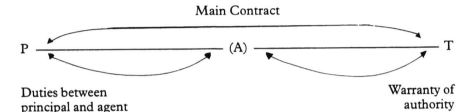

The principal is bound by a contract which an agent purports to make on his behalf if:

   (a)   the agent has *real* or *express* authority;
   (b)   the agent has *usual* or *implied* authority;
   (c)   the agent has *apparent* or *ostensible* authority, or authority by *holding out* which estops the principal from denying the authority of the agent.

The agency rules can be used to regulate the activities of company directors. The company is the principal (P), the director is the agent (A) and the outsider is the third party (T).

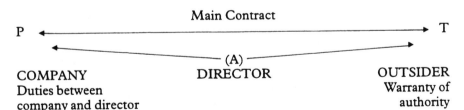

A company's managing director or other delegate may bind the company with an outside party if he possesses one of the three types of authority described above. So, for example, a managing director will possess:

   (a)   real or express authority where he has received actual authority from the company;
   (b)   usual or implied authority by virtue of the nature of his position in the company and the company's business;

(c)   apparent or ostensible authority where he has no authority as described in (a) or (b) above, but either the company holds him out, or he holds himself out with the company's knowledge and consent, as having authority to undertake a particular transaction. In these circumstances the company will be estopped from denying his authority and will be bound. The lack of authority may arise from either:

(i)   defect in the managing director's appointment i.e., procedural defect or complete failure to appoint; or

(ii)   valid appointment but lack of authority to undertake the particular transaction.

The exact circumstances in which apparent or ostensible authority will arise are now set out in:

Freeman & Lockyer v Buckhurst Park Properties (Mangal) Ltd
[1964] 2 QB 480

The defendant company was formed to buy and resell a large estate by Kapoor, a property developer, and Hoon, who contributed half of the capital but played no active part in the company's business. Kapoor, Hoon and a nominee of each were appointed the four directors of the company, and under the articles all four were needed to constitute a quorum. Hoon spent much time abroad, leaving all the day-to-day management of the company's affairs to be conducted by Kapoor. After an initial plan for the immediate resale of the land had fallen through, Kapoor decided to develop the estate, and engaged the plaintiffs, Freeman & Lockyer, a firm of architects and surveyors, to apply for planning permission. The company later refused to pay the plaintiffs' fees on the ground that Kapoor had had no authority to engage them. The county court judge held that the company was bound. The Court of Appeal affirmed his decision.

DIPLOCK LJ: The county court judge made the following findings of fact: (1) that the plaintiffs intended to contract with Kapoor as agent for the company, and not on his own account; (2) that the board of the company intended that Kapoor should do what he could to obtain the best possible price for the estate; (3) that Kapoor, although never appointed as managing director, had throughout been acting as such in employing agents and taking other steps to find a purchaser; (4) that Kapoor was so acting was well known to the board....

The county court judge did not hold (although he might have done) that actual authority had been conferred upon Kapoor by the board to employ agents. He proceeded on the basis of apparent authority, that is, that the defendant company had so acted as to be estopped from denying Kapoor's authority. This rendered it unnecessary for the judge to inquire whether actual authority to employ agents had been conferred upon Kapoor by the board to whom the management of the company's business was confided by the articles of association.

I accept that such actual authority could have been conferred by the board without a formal resolution recorded in the minutes, although this would have rendered them liable to a default fine under s. 145(4) of the Companies Act 1948. But to confer actual authority would have required not merely the silent acquiescence of the individual members of the board, but the communication by words or conduct of their respective consents to one another and to Kapoor. [His Lordship discussed the evidence and continued:] I myself do not feel that there is adequate material to justify the court in reaching the conclusion of fact (which the county court judge refrained from making) that actual authority to employ agents had been conferred by the board on Kapoor.

This makes it necessary to inquire into the state of the law as to the ostensible authority of officers and servants to enter into contracts on behalf of corporations. It is a topic on which there are confusing and, it may be, conflicting judgments of the Court of Appeal which are elaborately analysed and discussed by Slade J in *Rama Corporation Ltd v Proved Tin & General Investments Ltd*. . . . We are concerned in the present case with the authority of an agent to create contractual rights and liabilities between his principal and a third party whom I will call 'the contractor'. This branch of the law has developed pragmatically rather than logically owing to the early history of the action of *assumpsit* and the consequent absence of a general *jus quaesitum tertii* in English law. But it is possible (and for the determination of this appeal I think it is desirable) to restate it upon a rational basis.

It is necessary at the outset to distinguish between an 'actual' authority of an agent on the one hand and an 'apparent' or 'ostensible' authority on the other. Actual authority and apparent authority are quite independent of one another. Generally they coexist and coincide, but either may exist without the other and their respective scopes may be different. As I shall endeavour to show, it is upon the apparent authority of the agent that the contractor normally relies in the ordinary course of business when entering into contracts.

An 'actual' authority is a legal relationship between principal and agent created by a consensual agreement to which they alone are parties. Its scope is to be ascertained by applying ordinary principles of construction of contracts, including any proper implications from the express words used, the usages of the trade, or the course of business between the parties. To this agreement the contractor is a stranger; he may be totally ignorant of the existence of any authority on the part of the agent. Nevertheless, if the agent does enter into a contract pursuant to the 'actual' authority, it does create contractual rights and liabilities between the principal and the contractor. It may be that this rule relating to 'undisclosed principals', which is peculiar to English law, can be rationalised as avoiding circuity of action, for the principal could in equity compel the agent to lend his name in an action to enforce the contract against the contractor, and would at common law be liable to indemnify the agent in respect of the performance of the obligations assumed by the agent under the contract.

An 'apparent' or 'ostensible' authority, on the other hand, is a legal relationship between the principal and the contractor created by a representation, made by the principal to the contractor, intended to be and in fact acted upon by the contractor, that the agent has authority to enter on behalf of the principal into a contract of a kind within the scope of the 'apparent' authority, so as to render the principal liable to perform any obligations imposed upon him by such contract. To the relationship so created the agent is a stranger. He need not be (although he generally is) aware of the existence of the representation but he must not purport to make the agreement as principal himself. The representation, when acted upon by the contractor by entering into a contract with the agent, operates as an estoppel, preventing the principal from asserting that he is not bound by the contract. It is irrelevant whether the agent had actual authority to enter into the contract.

In ordinary business dealings the contractor at the time of entering into the contract can in the nature of things hardly ever rely on the 'actual' authority of the agent. His information as to the authority must be derived either from the principal or from the agent or from both, for they alone know what the agent's actual authority is. All that the contractor can know is what they tell him, which may or may not be true. In the ultimate analysis he relies either upon the representation of the principal, that is, apparent authority, or upon the representation of the agent, that is, warranty of authority.

The representation which creates 'apparent' authority may take a variety of forms of which the commonest is representation by conduct, that is, by permitting the agent to act in some way in the conduct of the principal's business with other persons. By so doing the principal represents to anyone who becomes aware that the agent is so acting that the agent has authority to enter on behalf of the principal into contracts with other persons of the kind which an agent so acting in the conduct of his principal's business has usually 'actual' authority to enter into. . . .

The commonest form of representation by a principal creating an 'apparent' authority of an agent is by conduct, namely, by permitting the agent to act in the management or conduct of the principal's business. Thus, if in the case of a company the board of directors who have 'actual' authority under the memorandum and articles of association to manage the company's business permit the agent to act in the management or conduct of the company's business, they thereby represent to all persons dealing with such agent that he has authority to enter on behalf of the corporation into contracts of a kind which an agent authorised to do acts of the kind which he is in fact permitted to do usually enters into in the ordinary course of such business. The making of such a representation is itself an act of management of the company's business. Prima facie it falls within the 'actual' authority of the board of directors, and unless the memorandum or articles of the company either make such a contract *ultra vires* the company or prohibit the delegation of such authority to the agent, the company is estopped from denying to anyone who has entered into a contract with the agent in reliance upon such 'apparent' authority that the agent had authority to contract on behalf of the company.

If the foregoing analysis of the relevant law is correct, it can be summarised by stating four conditions which must be fulfilled to entitle a contractor to enforce against a company a contract entered into on behalf of the company by an agent who had no actual authority to do so. It must be shown:

(a)   that a representation that the agent had authority to enter on behalf of the company into a contract of the kind sought to be enforced was made to the contractor;

(b)   that such representation was made by a person or persons who had 'actual' authority to manage the business of the company either generally or in respect of those matters to which the contract relates;

(c)   that he (the contractor) was induced by such representation to enter into the contract, that is, that he in fact relied upon it; and

(d)   that under its memorandum or articles of association the company was not deprived of the capacity either to enter into a contract of the kind sought to be enforced or to delegate authority to enter into a contract of that kind to the agent.

Thus a managing director or other delegate of the board although not properly appointed to office or authorised to transact a particular piece of business may acquire apparent or ostensible authority to act on behalf of the company and bind the company in contract if the four conditions set out in the above case are satisfied.

The application of agency rules to those situations traditionally governed by *Turquand*'s case is becoming increasingly common. This is due to the fact that the agency rules are wider in their scope and not hedged around with the kind of exceptions that have beset *Turquand*'s rule, thus making them easier to apply.

6   Companies Act 1985, section 35A

Section 35A helps a third party who has contracted with an officer of a company acting in excess of his or her authority provided the third party can satisfy the criteria set out in the section. These are as follows:

(a)   The third party was an outsider (i.e., an unconnected person dealing with the company).

(b)   The third party was acting in good faith. The Act states that a person shall be deemed to be acting in good faith unless the contrary is proved. The Act goes on to state that a person will not be deemed to be acting in bad faith only by virtue of the fact that he knows that the compay lacks capacity. To be in bad faith it seems that the outsider must know of the lack of capacity and be guilty of some fraud.

(c)   The third party was dealing with the company. Section 35A(2) states that an outsider will be dealing with the company if he is a party to any transaction or other act to which the company is a party.

(d)   The third party was dealing with the directors or others authorised by the board. The term 'others authorised by the board' will include any person to whom the board of directors delegates authority (e.g., a managing director).

(e)   The limitation was one imposed by the company's constitution.

Provided the third party can satisfy the above criteria he will be able to enforce the contract against the company. It is fair to suggest that in the majority of commercial transactions these criteria will be satisfied. Thus this section has the potential to provide a wide protection for third parties dealing with directors and other officers who act outside the scope of their authority.

Self check questions
1.   What is the difference between the ability of a director to bind the company and a managing director to do the same?
2.   What is the effect of the rule in *Royal British Bank* v *Turquand* on invalid contracts?
3.   Explain the three types of authority that an agent may possess.
4.   In which circumstances will an agency by estoppel or holding out arise?

Answers
1.   An individual director has no authority to bind the company in contract. Directors must act collectively as a board. However, the board may delegate some or all of its authority to an individual known as a managing director who can bind the company in contract within the scope of the authority duly delegated.
2.   The rule in *Royal British Bank* v *Turquand* allows outsiders to assume that the company has duly complied with its internal regulations. Thus any contract that is invalid because of some internal irregularity is validated by the rule.
3.   An agent may possess:

   (a)   Real or express authority — this is authority that the agent has actually been given by his principal.
   (b)   Usual or implied authority — this is authority that the agent has by virtue of his office.
   (c)   Apparent or ostensible authority — this is authority that the agent has by virtue of a holding out by the principal. The scope of the authority is limited by reference to the nature of the holding out.

4.   An agency by estoppel or holding out will arise where the criteria set out in *Freeman & Lockyer* v *Buckhurst Park Properties Ltd* are satisfied. They are:

   (a)   that a representation that the agent had authority to enter on behalf of the company into a contract of the kind sought to be enforced was made to the contractor;
   (b)   that such representation was made by a person or persons who had 'actual' authority to manage the business of the company either generally or in respect of those matters to which the contract relates;
   (c)   that he (the contractor) was induced by such representation to enter into the contract, that is, that he in fact relied upon it; and
   (d)   that under its memorandum and articles of association the company was not deprived of the capacity either to enter into a contract of the kind sought to be enforced or to delegate authority to enter into a contract of that kind to the agent.

Problem
Baggins Ltd is a company whose memorandum states that it will 'carry on business as a general commercial company'. The company operates a chain of fast food restaurants. Bill and Bo are the company's directors. However, for the last year Bill has not played an active part in the management of the business due to ill-health. Bo has assumed the office of managing director although he has never been formally appointed to that office. The company's articles restrict the power of the directors to borrow up to £50,000. Any additional amounts must first be authorised by the company's shareholders.

In June 1990 Bo enters into the following agreements on behalf of the company:

(a) a loan of £75,000 from Lend a Lot Bank to re-equip the restaurant kitchens; and
(b) the purchase of 200 kilos of mince beef for the manufacture of beefburgers from BSE Ltd.

In July 1990 three of the company's restaurants are burnt down by anti-vivisectionists. They are not insured and the company goes into liquidation. The loan has not been repaid and BSE Ltd are still awaiting payment for the mince beef. The liquidator argues that neither contract is binding on it as Bo has never been appointed managing director.

Advise Lend a Lot Bank and BSE Ltd.

Suggested answer
1. In all questions on capacity you must first distinguish between issues relating to corporate capacity and whether a particular director has had corporate capacity properly delegated to him and is properly appointed to office. It is only when both aspects can be answered in the affirmative that a valid binding contract will result.

2. *Corporate capacity* Work through the following points:

(a) Does the company's memorandum use the new form of words to describe the company's objects? If yes then the *company* will have unlimited contractual capacity.
(b) If the objects clause is in the old style, spelling out individual activities that the company may indulge in, then the company's capacity will be limited to those activities stated in the clause.
(c) In this question the company uses the new style clause — consequently we can assume that no problems are caused by corporate capacity.

3. *Directors' capacity* Even though the *company* has unlimited contractual capacity this does not automatically ensure that its directors will have. Consider the following:

(a) Is the director, or managing director, properly appointed to office? If no —

(b)   Can the outsider rely on s. 285 CA 1985, the rule in *Royal British Bank v Turquand*, or the agency rule in *Freeman & Lockyer v Buckhurst Park Properties*? If none of these can be relied on the contract cannot be enforced. If they can the defective appointment is cured and the contract is enforceable.

(c)   Are there any restrictions on the director's/managing director's authority to transact? If yes, have the directors acted in accordance with or contrary to the restrictions? If they have acted in accordance with the restrictions, there should be no difficulties. If they have acted contrary to the restrictions you will need to consider whether the outsider can enforce the contract using either s. 35A CA 1985 (as amended CA 1989), the rule in *Turquand's* case or the agency rules as explained in *Freeman & Lockyer v Buckhurst Park Properties*.

4. Conclusion

Status of the contract — In any question dealing with the validity of contracts, your conclusion should deal with the status of the contract by pulling together the main threads of your answer.

(a)   *Defective appointment of Bo* — This will not be cured by s. 285 CA 1985 as there has never been any attempt to appoint Bo to office. However, the problem could be cured by using either the rule in *Turquand's* case or the agency rules in *Freeman & Lockyer v Buckhurst Park Properties*.

(b)   *The contracts with Lend a Lot Bank and BSE Ltd* — Given that the defective appointment can probably be cured using the rules described above, the contract with BSE Ltd should at present be enforceable as it is a contract within the company's capacity made by its managing director. The loan from the bank is clearly beyond the power of even a properly appointed managing director. However, the bank have no means of discovering whether or not the company has complied with its own articles in this instance by obtaining the permission of the shareholders before agreeing the loan.

Consequently, the bank can rely on the rule in *Turquand's* case which allows it to assume that the company has complied with its internal procedures. Therefore, the loan agreement will be enforceable against Baggins Ltd.

23   PARTNERSHIP LAW

1   Introduction

Unlike companies, partnerships can be established with the minimum of formalities. Essentially, so long as a partnership satisfies the definition in s. 1 of the Partnership Act 1890, it will in the eyes of the law be treated as such. This will be the case even though there is no written agreement between the parties. A partnership can be created by conduct, orally, or by writing.

2   Nature and definition of partnership

Section 1 of the Partnership Act (PA) 1890 defines partnership as 'the relationship which subsists between persons carrying on a business with a view to profit'. The relationship arises from contract express or implied.

Whether or not partnership exists is a mixed question of law and fact i.e., written evidence (deed of partnership), or conduct. The definition in s. 1 requires the 'carrying on of a business' — so a contract providing for the commencement of business at a future date does not on its own constitute the relationship even though preparatory steps have been taken.

Keith Spicer Ltd v *Mansell*
[1970] 1 All ER 462

The defendant and B agreed to go into business together and to form a limited company to carry on business in the defendant's restaurant. Before the incorporation of the company, B ordered books from the plaintiffs which he intended for the use of the company; without the word 'Limited'. In an action against the defendant for the price of the goods, which was just under £150, the plaintiffs alleged that the defendant and B were in partnership (having failed to prove that B was the agent of the defendant), that B had ordered the goods for the partnership and that the defendant was liable for the price. The county court judge held that there was no partnership, and the plaintiffs appealed.

HARMAN LJ: ... To what then do the primary facts come? To this, that the defendant and Mr Bishop, having lost their employment elsewhere, decided to go into business together. They decided to run in agreement and to form a limited company which was going to carry on business in the defendant's restaurant. Eventually there was such a company incorporated. They came to the conclusion that they would do certain things preparatory to the formation of the company so that the company could carry on business at once when it was formed, and one of the things that they did, or that Mr Bishop did, was to order these goods. He intended them to be used not by the defendant and himself as partners but by the company when it was formed. I have no doubt that a good deal of loose thinking went on, but we know that everything was done with a view to the company carrying on business. It was all, I think, preparatory to that event, and the question is whether that involves in itself a partnership.

That model piece of legislation the Partnership Act 1890, s. 1(1), provides: 'Partnership is the relation which subsists between persons carrying on a business in common with a view of profit'.

Now were Mr Bishop and the defendant carrying on a business? I do not think there is any evidence of that. There is evidence of the buying of these goods by Mr Bishop. There is evidence of the opening of a banking account and the banker saying 'You cannot put the word "Limited" after the name because the company is not formed, but you can use the same title without "Limited"', but what happened about that banking account is left in shadow, the bank being in liquidation; and I do not think that there is enough in the act of going to the bank and opening an account in the name without the word 'limited' to show that they were then as such carrying on business in partnership. They were preparing to carry on business as a company as soon as they could. I think that the learned county court judge was justified in saying that they never intended to be partners and that therefore they were not partners because they never carried on business as such.

EDMUND DAVIES and WIDGERY LJJ concurred, EDMUND DAVIES LJ commenting that: The burden of establishing the existence of a partnership was, of course, on the plaintiffs. ...

Not every transaction between two people preparatory to the formation of a company is sufficient to constitute them partners. There was the most exiguous evidence called on the plaintiffs' behalf, and such evidence as was called is quite ambivalent.

But note, partners who have commenced business in pursuance of an agreement to form a partnership will be partners pending the signing of a partnership deed i.e., partners by intention and conduct. Also note, the term 'business' is a wide term which signifies anything which is an occupation of duty as opposed to recreation or pleasure. Likewise, taking a share of profits was at one time taken as being the main test of whether a person was a partner or not — until *Cox* v *Hickman* (1860) held that an arrangement whereby a trader assigned his property to trustees representing creditors of his business so that the creditors might be paid off out of the profits, did not raise a partnership between the debtor and the creditors. Profit sharing was regarded as cogent but not conclusive evidence of partnership. Lord Cranworth noted:

> ... the real ground for liability is, that the trade has been carried on by persons acting on his behalf. It is not correct to say that his right to share in the profits makes him liable to the debts of the trade. The correct mode of stating the proposition is to say ... that the trade has been carried on on his behalf, i.e., that he stood in the relation or principal towards the persons acting ostensibly as traders.

Cox v *Hickman* received statutory approval in s. 2(3) PA 1890, which states: the receipt by a person of a share of the profits of a business is prima facie evidence that he is a partner in the business, but the receipt of such a share, or a payment contingent on or varying with the profits of a business, does not of itself make him a partner in the business.

The following are examples of situations provided for by s. 2(3) PA 1890.

(a)   *Cox* v *Hickman* is an example of para. (a) of s. 2(3) PA 1890.

(b)   *Walker* v *Hirsch* (1884) is an example of para. (b) of s. 2(3) PA 1890. P previously a clerk in the firm, agreed to advance £1,500 to the firm in return for a salary of £180 and $^1/_5$th of profits.

Held: He remained a servant and as such could not move for winding up of the firm.

(c)   Para. (c) of s. 2(3) PA 1890 permits a widow or child annuitant of a deceased partner to receive an annuity out of profits without ranking as a partner purely by reason of the receipt of such annuity.

(d)   Para. (d) of s. 2(3) PA 1890 deals with the person advancing money by way of loan and receiving a share of profits or interest at a rate which varies with profits.

(e)   Para. (e) of s. 2(3) PA 1890 provides that the seller of goodwill who receives in return an annuity of part of the profits is not, by reason only of such receipt, a partner in the business.

3   Types of partners

3.1   General partners

The Limited Partnerships Act 1907 differentiates between general and limited partners.

A general partner is an ordinary active partner with right to participate in the management of the business. He also has unlimited liability for the debts of the partnership. This means that if the partnership is unable to pay its debts as they fall due, its creditors may call upon the partners' to satisfy the debt to the extent of the partners' personal fortune.

3.2 Sleeping or limited partner

A distinction is drawn between active and sleeping partners. A sleeping or limited partner puts in capital and takes a share of the profits, but does not participate in the management of the partnership and enjoys limited liability. This means that his liability will be limited to the amount of capital he agrees to contribute to the partnership. In the event of the partnership being unable to pay its debts as they fall due its creditors cannot call upon the sleeping or limited partner to satisfy the debt. However, a partnership cannot be entirely made up of limited partners. There must be at least one general partner with unlimited liability who can be called upon to satisfy the debts of the partnership to the extent of his personal fortune.

4 Maximum number of partners

Section 717 Companies Act 1985 applies to trading partnerships only. It states that the maximum number of partners allowed is 20. Certain professional partnerships may exceed 20 e.g., solicitors, accountants, stock brokers, etc.

5 Choice of name

Choice of name is governed by the Business Names Act 1985. If partners carry on a business under their own name — e.g., Bloggs and Jones — then no special requirements apply. If another name is used e.g., in the case of a partnership running a public house 'The Rose and Crown' the requirements of s. 4 must be met. These are:

(a) The name of each partner must be contained on all business letters, written orders for goods or services to be supplied, invoices, receipts that are issued in the course of the business and the written demands for payment.

(b) The address within the UK at which any document relating to the business can be served must also be displayed on all the above documents.

(c) A notice containing the names and addresses as described above must be displayed at the place of business — s. 4 Business Names Act 1985.

6 Relations of partners with persons dealing with them

Agency constitutes the central feature of partnership. Lord Cranworth in *Cox v Hickman* explained: 'The liability of one partner for the acts of his co-partner is in truth the liability of a principal for the acts of his agent'. In agency law we must draw distinction between apparent and actual authority. Let us re-cap on the points made in Chapter 21 — regarding an agent's authority.

Apparent authority is the authority an agent appears to hold. Actual authority is the authority an agent actually holds. Section 5 PA 1890 explains the power of partner to bind the firm — every partner is an agent of the firm, and his other partners, for the purpose of the business of the partnership, and the acts of every partner who does not act for carrying on in the usual way business of the kind carried on by the firm of which he is a member, bind the firm and his partners, unless the partner so acting has in fact no authority to act for the firm in the particular matter, and the person with whom he is dealing either knows that he has no authority or does not know or believe him to be a partner.

Section 5 shows that a partner's apparent authority is confined to acts connected with the business of the kind carried by the firm and performed in the usual way. Whether or not a particular act falls within the scope of the partnership business is essentially a question of fact. Read the judgment of Mocatta J, below.

Mercantile Credit Co. Ltd v *Garrod*
[1962] 3 All ER 1103

MOCATTA J: ... There is no doubt that Mr Garrod and Mr Parkin had been carrying on a business in partnership from some time in November 1959, down to and including some little time after May 19, 1960. The business was carried on, so far as name goes, in the name of Hamilton Garages, or Hamilton Garage in the singular. . . .

[A detailed description of the firm's premises is then made by Mocatta J.]

The plaintiffs claim the return of £700 as money had and received, or as money paid for a total failure of consideration because, as is admitted, the transaction under which the plaintiffs in fact paid out £700 was a fraudulent one. The transaction was the familiar one these days of a hire-purchase finance company purchasing a car from a motor dealer and entering into a hire-purchase agreement with the customer of the dealer. . . .

(T)he suppliers, shown as Hamilton Garage and signed as 'A. I. Parkin, per pro Hamilton Garage', offered to sell to the plaintiffs goods as described in the above agreement; that is to say, the Mercedes Benz for £1,900 less the initial payment of £1,200, that is to say £700. Under that agreement, a cheque dated May 19, 1960, for £700 was drawn by the plaintiffs, made payable to Hamilton Garages, and was paid into the bank account of the partnership or, at any rate, into the bank account containing the name and trade name which I have already read. It is common ground that this hire-purchase agreement and payment to the £700 under it by the plaintiffs were really obtained by fraud and I need not go into detail. It is sufficient to say that Mr Cox never got the Mercedes Benz car, and apparently never paid the initial payment of £1,200 and that Mr Parkin subsequently pleaded guilty to a charge of obtaining money by false pretences in relation to this transaction.

The defence really is that the defendant, who certainly knew nothing whatever of the fraudulent nature of this transaction, had never authorised Mr Parkin to indulge in the buying or selling of cars as part of the partnership business. Not only had he not authorised this, but the argument goes further and is to the effect that it was definitely excluded from the field of business activities to be carried on by this partnership in which Mr Parkin was the active partner and the defendant, the sleeping partner. It is further argued on behalf of the defendant that what I have to look at and determine in this

matter is the partnership deed, in so far as that regulated the position as
between the partners, and what the business was that was in fact carried on
as distinct from any ostensible or apparent authority that Mr Parkin may
have had *vis-à-vis* the outside world in general and the plaintiffs in particular.
It seems to me that the first thing which I have to determine as a matter of
law before examining the facts, is whether it is sufficient to have regard to the
ostensible authority of Mr Parkin or not. Mr Parkin, as I have said, was the
active partner, and it was with him that Mr Bone, the local manager of the
plaintiffs, had most of his dealings and certainly all his detailed discussions of
business transactions, including this particular one. . . .

Mr Bone, on behalf of the plaintiffs, thought that he was dealing with the
partnership trading under the name of Hamilton Garage.

When I have to consider whether the defendant was bound by what Mr
Parkin did in relation to this hire-purchase agreement for this Mercedes
Benz, have I to look at the partnership deed between the two partners in so
far as that regulated their relationship, or have I to look at that and also the
details of the business that had been carried on by them since they started the
partnership in November 1959? Or have I to look, as a matter of law, at the
position as it appeared to Mr Bone acting on behalf of the plaintiffs? Counsel
for the plaintiffs says that the latter is the right legal approach, and he relies
on s. 5 of the Partnership Act 1890. . . .

[Mocatta J then recites s. 5.]

It is not contended here, and could not possibly be, that Mr Bone thought
otherwise than that Mr Parkin had authority, and it is admitted that Mr
Parkin was a partner and that Mr Bone knew he was a partner. Accordingly,
counsel for the plaintiffs says that the question in this case is whether the act
of Mr Parkin in tendering into the sale to the plaintiffs of this Mercedes Benz
on behalf of the Hamilton Garages partnership, as part and parcel of a
hire-purchase transaction, was doing an act for carrying on in the usual way
business of a kind carried on by the firm of which he was a member. If it was
such an act, counsel for the plaintiffs submits that the section makes it clear
and enacts that his act binds the firm and his partner, to wit, the defendant.
Counsel for the plaintiffs relies on a passage in *Linley on Partnership* in
interpretation of s. 5, if such interpretation be necessary. The passage reads:
'It will be observed that what is done in carrying on the partnership business
in the usual way in which businesses of a like kind are carried on, is made the
test of authority where no actual authority or ratification can be proved.'

If it is somewhat of an impertinence for me to say so, I am of the view that
that is clearly the right interpretation of this section. If that is so, as in
my judgment it is, it follows that I must have regard to deciding this matter
to what was apparent to the outside world in general and Mr Bone in
particular, and to the facts relevant to businesses of a like kind to that of
the business of this partnership so far as it appeared to the outside world and
Mr Bone. . . .

What I have to ask myself is whether anybody dealing with that
partnership, who had not been told of any express limitation on the authority
of the partnership with whom he was actively dealing, would be put on

inquiry as to the authority of that active partner when such partner sought, in the firm's name, to sell a car to him. The place was as I have described it. The name of the partnership was as I have described. No doubt business was carried out on these premises of repairing motor cars. Whether or not it be the case, as Mr Bone suggested, that there were from time to time one or more cars on the premises not requiring repairs and available for sale — that being a matter which was strongly contested on behalf of the defendant — it seems to me that, if I am allowed to use any knowledge of the world at all, the answer to the question that I have posed must be that a reasonable man dealing with the firm in the circumstances which I have outlined would not be put on such inquiry. It may well be that such a reasonable man might think that the security behind such a sale was dubious, in that the establishment seemed to be a bit primitive and a small one, but that is quite a different matter.

Note that the test is an objective one. The partnership will also be liable where it has ratified the unauthorised act of a partner but the ratification is only valid where the agent professedly acted as a partner. To decide whether a partner was apparent authority, it is important to know what kind of authority partners are usually deemed to have.

6.1 Powers normally held by all partners

(a) *To sell goods or personal chattels of the firm.* In *Dore* v *Wilkinson* (1817) a firm was held bound when a partner without authority sold the partnership books to a person who wanted the names of its customers.

(b) *To purchase on account of the firm goods necessary for or usually employed in the business.* In *Bond* v *Gibson* (1808) A and B were in partnership as harness-makers and B bought bits to be made into bridles on the firm's account. B later pawned them and kept the money. It was *held*: Firm liable to pay the person from whom B bought his bits.

(c) *To receive payments and debts due to the firm and give valid receipts.*

(d) *To employ employees for business.*

(e) *To engage a solicitor to defend the firm.*

In addition trading partners can:

(a) Draw, issue, accept, transfer and endorse bills of exchange, either by signing the firm's name or the partner's own name — 'for and on behalf of the firm'.

(b) To borrow money on the credit of the firm, regardless of any limitations of authority agreed between the partners, unless such limitation is known to the outsider.

(c) To secure a loan by pledging personal property of the firm or by depositing title deeds.

Partners cannot:

(a) Bind the firm by deed unless they have the agreement of all other partners.
(b) Compromise a debt.
(c) Submit a dispute to arbitration.
(d) Give a guarantee for another debt.

6.2 Contractual ability of partnerships
Unlike companies, partnerships are not subject to restrictions on contractual capacity. Partnership business can be altered allowing the firm to move into new areas of business provided all the partners agree. Thus, it is a more flexible medium for trade than a company in this respect.

7   Liability of the firm and the partners

Partnership Act 1890 — s. 6

An act of instrument relating to the business of the firm and done or executed in the firms name, or in any other manner showing an intention to bind the firm, by any person thereto authorised, whether a partner or not, is binding on the firm and all the partners.

Partnership Act 1890 — s. 7

Where one partner pledges the credit of the firm for a purpose apparently not connected with the firm's ordinary course of business, the firm is not bound, unless he is in fact specially authorised by the other partners; but this section does not affect any personal liability incurred by an individual partner.

Section 7 therefore sets certain limitations on s. 5. For example, in *Bignold* v *Waterhouse* (1813) a special favour granted to a consignor of goods by one partner in a firm of coach proprietors operating between London and Norwich resulted in personal profit to one partner. It was *held* that where a customer of a trading firm negotiates with one of the partners for a special advantage in the conduct of their business with him for a consideration which is good as between himself and the partner, but of no value to the firm, the firm is not bound by this agreement, and incurs no obligation in respect of any business done in pursuance of it.

7.1 Liabilities of incoming and outgoing partners
The general rule states that partners are only liable in respect of partnership liabilities incurred whilst they are a member of the firm. Thus they are prima facie not liable for things done before they enter or after they leave the firm. Section 17 PA 1890 lays down three rules:

Partnership Act 1890 — s. 17

(a)   *New partners* A person who is admitted as a partner into an existing firm does not thereby become liable to the creditors of the firm for anything done before he became a partner.

(b)   *Retiring partners* A partner who retires from the firm does not thereby create to be liable for partnership debts or obligations incurred before his retirement.

(c)   *Retiring partners* A retiring partner may be discharged from any existing liabilities by an agreement to that effect between himself and the members of the firm as newly constituted, and the creditors, and this agreement may be either express or informed as a fact from the course of dealing between the creditors and the firm as newly constituted.

This latter process is known as novation. Creditors do not have to accept or participate in a novation (see below). The retiring partner should get an indemnity from the new firm so that if he is sued he can be reimbursed by the firm.

Two questions need to be satisfied before novation takes place:

(a)   Has the new firm assumed liability?

(b)   Has the creditor agreed to accept the new firm as his debtor and to discharge the old firm from its liability?

7.2   Liability of retiring partners

Any person who deals with the firm is entitled to regard all apparent members as such until he has notice otherwise or until one dies. Consequently it is important for a partner who retires to ensure that adequate notice of his retirement is provided. The position is now governed by the Partnership Act.

Section 36(1) PA 1890 states that to avoid liability a partner must: (i) ensure individual notices are sent to all customers who dealt with the firm while he was a member; (ii) advertise the fact of his leaving the firm in the *London Gazette*. This operates as a notice to all who have *not* dealt with the firm before. Section 6(2) PA 1890 states that a notice in the *London Gazette* operates even in respect of those persons who have not read it, i.e., constructive notice will apply. In respect of those who had no previous dealings with the firm and did not know X was a partner, there is no need to advertise in the *Gazette* and obviously it is impossible to send notices — *Tower Cabinet Co. Ltd v Ingram* (1949).

Under s. 36(3) the estate of a deceased or bankrupt partner is not liable for debts incurred after death or bankruptcy as the case may be even if no advertisement or notice of any kind has been given. In addition it should be noted that a retiring partner can restrain his former partners from using his name after his retirement e.g., on letter heads or otherwise, in such a way that would expose him to litigation.

Provisions of s. 36 do not apply to a sleeping partner except as regards those who happen to know that he is a partner. Those who are in on the secret should be informed of the retirement.

7.3   Liability of partners for the debts of the firm

All general partners are personally liable. There is no limited liability. Each general partner is liable to the extent of his personal fortune. So in the event of the partnership not being able to meet its liabilities its creditors may look to the general partners to meet any outstanding amounts. However, limited or sleeping partners do enjoy limited liability. Their liability is limited to the amount of capital contributed to the partnership, but they have no right to manage the partnership.

8   The relationship between partners *inter se*

Two principles need to be recognised in connection with the internal partnership relationships:

(a)   Partners are free to make their own rules, so far as is consistent with the nature of the partnership, and within the considerable area which the law leaves to the partners themselves.

Partners are advised to set out their intentions in a Partnership Agreement or Deed of Partnership, this will supersede the 1890 Act. The Act will only be referred to where the agreement is ambiguous, or where no agreement exists. An agreement should cover matters such as:

(i)   profit sharing;
(ii)   capital contributions;
(iii)   holidays;
(iv)   duties in managing business;
(v)   liability to contribute to debts of the firm.

(b)   The principle of *'uberrimae fidei'* which requires the utmost good faith between partners. This means that the partners must at all times demonstrate honesty, trust and good faith in their dealings with each other.

8.1   Rules as to interests and duties of partners subject to special agreement

Section 24 1890 Act is a miniature code of rules which governs the internal partnership relationships to the extent that the parties have not excluded or varied such rules by their own agreement.

Partnership Act 1890 — s. 24

The interests of partners in the partnership property and their rights and duties in relation to the partnership shall be determined, subject to any agreement express or implied between the partners, by the following rules:

(1)   All the partners are entitled to share equally in the capital and profits of the business, and must contribute equally towards the losses whether of capital or otherwise sustained by the firm.

Sharing equally in profit and capital may be rebutted by evidence to the contrary i.e., the proportions in which capital was originally contributed.

(2)   The firm must indemnify every partner in respect of payments made and personal liabilities incurred by him—

(a)   in the ordinary and proper conduct of the business of the firm; or,
(b)   in or about anything necessarily done for the preservation of the business or property of the firm.

(3)   A partner making, for the purpose of the partnership, any actual payment or advance beyond the amount of capital which he has agreed to subscribe, is entitled to interest at the rate of five per cent per annum from the date of the payment or advance.

(4)   A partner is not entitled, before the ascertainment of profits, to interest on the capital subscribed by him.

(5)   Every partner may take part in the management of the partnership business. [NB there can be an agreement to exclude one of the partners e.g., in the case of a dormant or sleeping partner.]

(6)   No partner shall be entitled to remuneration for acting in the partnership business.

(7)   No person may be introduced as a partner without the consent of all the partners.

(8)   Any difference arising as to ordinary matters connected with the partnership business may be decided by a majority of the partners, but no change may be made in the nature of the partnership business without the consent of all existing partners.

8.2   Partnership accounts

Section 28 PA 1890 states that: 'Partners are bound to render true accounts and full information of all things affecting the partnership to any partner or his legal representatives'.

8.3   Sale of partnership share

A partner with superior knowledge of the affairs of the firm, such as a managing partner who superintends the finances and accounts of the firm, must put a partner whose share in the firm he proposed to acquire in full possession of all material facts and circumstances. Unless the parties stand on equal footing, a failure to make full and frank disclosures of material facts entitles the 'innocent' party to avoid the sale or other transaction although the right of avoidance is lost if such party elects to waive the failure to disclose or, when put on inquiry by certain facts, decides to pursue the matter no further.

8.4   The partner as fiduciary

During currency of partnership, partners are fiduciaries in respect of their dealings with co-partners. Three aspects of this duty were discussed in *Dean* v *McDowell* (1878):

(a)   A partner is not permitted to receive an exclusive advantage for himself by reason of the use of partnership property or information. For example, *Gardner* v *McCutcheon* (1843). Here one of two part-owners of a ship who were trading with it for their common benefit used it for private trading and was *held* accountable for profits so made.

(b)   He must not derive any exclusive advantage by engaging in transactions in rivalry with the firm. For example, *Sommerville* v *Mackay* (1810) where the partnership was founded to supply goods to a firm in Russia and one partner supplied similar goods to this firm himself. It was held that he had to account for the profits.

(c)   He is not allowed in transacting the partnership affairs to carry on for his own benefit any separate trade or business which, were it not for his connection with the partnership, he could not have been in a position to carry on. For example, *Russell* v *Austwick* (1826) where a partner who had obtained a contract from the mint to carry silver by a route other than the route on which he and another had already received a contract to carry bullion for the mint was *held* accountable for the profits of the contract awarded to him personally.

The above aspects of the fiduciary duty have received statutory approval and are now contained in ss. 29-30 PA 1890.

8.5   *Accountability for private profits*
A partner must account for any private profit made by virtue of his being a partner.

8.6   *Competing business*
A partner is not allowed to carry on a competing business unless he has the permission of all the other partners which should only be given after full disclosure of all the material facts.

8.7   *Dissolution of the partnership*
A partnership may be dissolved with or without the aid of the court. Section 32 of the 1890 Act governs situations where it may be dissolved without the aid of the court. Section 35 governs situations where it may be dissolved with the aid of the court.

9   Some comparisons between companies and partnerships

The table below illustrates the major differences between partnerships and limited companies.

Partnership	*Limited company*
1. *Advantages*	*Disadvantages*
(a) Fewer formation formalities and expenses than limited company.	(a) Has registration expenses and capital duty to pay and considerable formality.

(b) Fewer running formalities.

(b) Has very formal and complex rules about its day to day running, particularly regarding corporate finance.

(c) Has confidential accounts.

(c) Has to file accounts at the Companies Registry where they are available for public inspection.

(d) Has no limitations placed on contractual capacity.

(d) Limitations may exist on corporate capacity in a company's memorandum and articles of association.

Partnership
1. *Disadvantges*

Limited company
2. *Advantages*

(a) No corporate personality.
(b) Partners are personally liable.
(c) Unless specifically agreed, partnership ends on the death of a partner and no provision for new members.
(d) Partners have to hold property in their names.
(e) Members who are not managers are still liable as though they were.
(f) Share in business not transferable except by agreement.
(g) Generally, not more than 20 partners may be in a firm.

(h) Borrowing harder — no floating charges possible.

(a) Corporate personality.
(b) Limited liability.
(c) Membership can change because of perpetual succession possible.

(d) Company can hold property in own name.
(e) Members and managers need not be the same.
(f) Shares are freely transferable.

(g) Minimum limitation on number of members only. No maximum limit.
(h) Can find borrowing more easy.

Activity
Look up ss. 32 and 35 PA 1890 and identify the circumstances in which a partnership may be dissolved without and with the aid of the court.

Self check questions
1. What is the definition of a partnership?
2. Explain the differences between a general and a 'sleeping' or 'limited' partner.
3. In what circumstances may one partner bind the others in contract?
4. What should a retiring partner do to ensure he incurs no further liability for the debts of the partnership after retirement?
5. Explain the principle of '*uberrimae fidei*'.

Answers
1. A partnership is defined as the 'relationship which subsists between persons carrying on a business with a view to profit'.

2. A general partner does not enjoy limited liability but is entitled to manage the partnership.

A sleeping or limited partnership enjoys limited liability (i.e., liability is limited to the amount of the partner's contributed capital), but has no right to manage the partnership.

3. A partner is an agent for his co-partners and as such may bind them in contract so long as the contract falls within the scope of the partnership business.

4. To ensure he incurs no liability after retirement a retiring partner should do the following:

(i) notify all the customers of the partnership in writing that he has retired; and

(ii) insert an advertisement in the *London Gazette* to notify the world at large of his retirement.

5. The principle of '*uberrimae fidei*' (the utmost good faith) requires partners at all times to demonstrate honesty, trust and good faith in their dealings with each other.

Problem

Bryan, Gary and Terry, retired international footballers, agree to form a partnership to provide football coaching sessions to young footballers. They consult their solicitor, who arranges for a deed of partnership to be drafted. In the meantime Bryan, Gary and Terry sign a lease to rent an office to conduct the business from, and buy 100 footballs from Kick Ltd. Following a dispute over who should direct the coaching sessions, Terry refuses to sign the deed of partnership and leaves. Bryan and Gary sign the deed and commence trading.

One of the clauses in the deed prevents a partner from incurring liability in the name of the partnership for more than £5,000. Gary purchases a training pitch from Synthetic Surfaces Ltd for £7,500. Due to injuries to Bryan's heel and Gary's toe the partners have failed to fulfil their coaching commitments and the business is facing serious financial difficulties. Kick Ltd is owed £700 for the footballs and Synthetic Surfaces Ltd £7,500 for the training pitch.

Bryan refuses to pay Synthetic Surfaces Ltd claiming Gary had no authority to contract.

Advise Kick Ltd and Synthetic Surfaces Ltd.

Suggested answer

The following points should form the basis of any answer to the above problem:

1. Does a partnership exist?

Your starting place in any answer is to establish whether or not a partnership exists.

In this particular answer you will need to consider whether:

(a) Bryan, Gary and Terry formed a partnership; and whether

(b) Bryan and Gary formed a partnership following Terry's departure.

Point (a) is important in relation to the contract with Kick Ltd. Were the footballers partners prior to the drafting of the deed?

Using the definition contained in s. 1 PA 1890 you will need to decide whether the parties fulfil the criteria set out in the definition.

The aspect of the definition that is particularly important is 'carrying on a business'. There was clearly an intention to carry on a business with a view to profit as evidenced by the fact that a solicitor was instructed to draft the partnership deed. However, were the parties carrying on a business as partners by conduct prior to Terry's departure? You will need to examine the case of *Keith Spicer Ltd* v *Mansell* (1970) to determine this.

Having applied the principle in this case you will be in a position to advise Kick Ltd as to whom they may sue.

Point (b) is important in relation to the contract of Synthetic Surfaces Ltd. Following the signing of the partnership deed Bryan and Gary are clearly partners.

2. The effect of restrictions on a partner's authority

Following the signing of the deed Bryan and Gary become partners and therefore agents of each other. The effect of restrictions on a partner's authority in these circumstances is limited to bind those outsiders who have *actual knowledge* of the restriction. Use the case *Mercantile Credit Co. Ltd* v *Garrod* (1962) to illustrate this point.

Having applied the principle in this case you will be in a position to advise Synthetic Surfaces Ltd.

INDEX

Index